WORLD WAR II
FACT BOOK

Peter Darman

BROWN REFERENCE GROUP

ISBN: 978-1-933-83489-4

The Brown Reference Group Ltd
First Floor, 9-17 St. Albans Place
London N1 ONX
www.brownreference.com

Editor: Alan Marshall
Designer: Colin Woodman
Production Director: Alastair Gourlay

Printed and bound in Thailand

Picture credits
Robert Hunt Library: front cover

Front cover photograph: (from left to right) Winston Churchill,
Franklin D. Roosevelt, and Joseph Stalin
at the Yalta Conference in February 1945.

CONTENTS

ABOUT THIS BOOK

The *World War II Fact Book* presents a wealth of information about mankind's most destructive conflict in the form of hundreds of questions and answers, revealing quotations, and fascinating "did-you-know?" boxes. Question topics cover strategy, tactics, battles, uniforms, weapons, espionage, equipment, and the individuals who led armies and nations between 1939 and 1945, such as Hitler, Roosevelt, Stalin, Patton, and Eisenhower. This book is a whole new way to learn about World War II—or to test what you already know about the conflict.

ROAD
TO
WAR

In the 1920s and 1930s, economic depressions in Europe created the conditions in which extremist politics could flourish. The people of Germany elected Adolf Hitler and the Nazi Party. While, in the Far East, Imperial Japan's territorial ambitions brought it into conflict with the United States.

Q What effect did the 1919 Treaty of Versailles have on Germany?

A At the end of World War I Germany was in dire straits: her population was near starvation and devoid of hope, and her army and navy were in disarray. The Treaty of Versailles of June 1919 added to Germany's woes as it removed her overseas possessions, implemented the occupation of part of the Rhineland (to ensure she complied with provisions of the treaty), and imposed huge reparations for the damage inflicted on France and other countries.

Q Was Germany in a position to pay reparations?

A No. Germany was almost bankrupt, which meant it was extremely unlikely that she would be able to pay—even less so when the world slump of 1921 added to her woes.

> **THE GODDESS OF THE ETERNAL TRIBUNAL OF HISTORY WILL TEAR APART THE SENTENCE OF THE COURT**
> ADOLF HITLER AT HIS TRIAL
> FOLLOWING THE MUNICH PUTSCH

Q Why did France occupy the Ruhr in 1923?

A In 1922 Germany defaulted on reparations payments for the second year running. In retaliation, France, showing amazing short-sighted-ness, occupied the Ruhr Valley, the center of German industry. This not only reduced the already slim chances of Germany paying any reparations, but also increased hostility between the two countries. The stoppage of the Ruhr industry had a calamitous effect on the mark, which plummeted in value. Overnight savings were wiped out, leaving millions penniless and destitute; their careers, hopes, and finances totally destroyed.

DID YOU KNOW

AT THE AGE OF NINE ADOLF HITLER BECAME A CHOIRBOY IN THE
CATHOLIC CHURCH AT LAMBACH, AND CLAIMED IN LATER YEARS THAT HIS
GREAT VOCAL POWER HAD DEVELOPED WHILE SINGING HYMNS. HE WAS AN
AVERAGE, LAZY, AND REBELLIOUS STUDENT, WITH A TALENT FOR DRAWING.
THIS TALENT DECIDED HIM ON A CAREER IN ART. HIS ORATORICAL
REHEARSALS WERE NOT OVERLOOKED, THOUGH. AUGUST KUBIZEK, HIS
CLOSE BOYHOOD FRIEND, RECALLED YOUNG ADOLF PRACTISING
ELOCUTION IN AN OPEN FIELD. FROM HIS SCHOOL DAYS HITLER WAS A
FANATICAL GERMAN NATIONALIST WITH A RANCOROUS HATRED OF OTHERS,
MOSTLY SLAVIC RACES WHICH MADE UP THE AUSTRO-HUNGARIAN EMPIRE.

Q **What were *Freikorps*?**

A The *Freikorps* were groups of right-wing ex-soldiers that sprang up
all over Germany following the end of World War I. Essentially,
gangs of brutalized men whose allegiance was to their commanders only,
the *Freikorps* fought for the elimination of all "traitors to the Fatherland."

Q **What was the NSDAP?**

A *National Sozialistische Deutsche Arbeiter Partei* (National Socialist
German Workers' Party—NSDAP), the Nazi Party led by Adolf
Hitler.

Q **Why was the city of Danzig a potential flashpoint between
Germany and Poland in the interwar years?**

A Danzig was in theory a "free city" administered by the League of
Nations organization, but in reality the Nazis had gained control of
the city in 1934 and did largely what they liked. Hitler ranted that it and
the strip of land that divided Germany and East Prussia should be
returned to the Reich.

Q What was the "Polish Corridor"?

A Recreated after World War I, Poland had been given access to the sea via a corridor of land which reached the Baltic at Danzig. It had been formerly German territory, and Hitler was determined it would be again. Hitler ranted that Danzig and the strip of land that divided Germany and East Prussia should be returned to the Reich. Few people in the West knew or cared what the "Polish Corridor" was, but in March 1939 Britain and France took the fateful step of pledging themselves to the defense of Poland, which neither of them was in a military position to do.

Q What river flowed into the sea at Danzig?

A The Vistula.

> ## TODAY WE ARE 600 STRONG, BUT IN SIX YEARS' TIME THERE WILL BE 600,000 OF US
> JOSEF GOEBBELS, SPEAKING TO NAZIS IN BERLIN, 1927

Q On which side did Japan fight in World War I?

A Japan had fought on the side of the Allies against Germany's Pacific colonies during the war, and after 1918 was rewarded with territorial acquisitions throughout the Pacific.

Q Why was Japan aggrieved after World War I?

A Although Japan had gained some Pacific colonies, she was forced to relinquish Chinese regions conquered during the 1904–05 Russo-Japanese War. Worse, insult was added to injury in 1922 when the Washington Naval Treaty limited the size of the Japanese Navy to below that of the U.S. and British fleets.

DID YOU KNOW

In Japan before World War II almost every vital domestic and industrial product, including food, rubber, and most metals, had to be imported, and the United States supplied around 60 percent of Japanese oil. The dependence on the outside world rubbed salt into the Japanese wound, and many felt that Japan had been relegated to a second-class nation within a geographical area in which it should have been dominant. The Japanese were particularly aggrieved by the fact that what they felt was their natural sphere of influence from which they could obtain the raw materials to run a modern economy was largely occupied by colonial powers: the British in Malaya, the French in Indochina, the U.S. in the Philippines, and above all the Dutch in the oil-rich region of the Dutch East Indies—what is now Indonesia.

Q Why did Japan invade China in 1931?

A First, China was the one big area where there was no colonial power on the Asian mainland. Second, Manchuria, a northern province semi-independent of China, occupied in 1931, was rich in mineral resources.

Q Who were the Brownshirts?

A Their proper title was *Sturmabteilung* (Storm Detachment), or SA. They were tough, unemployed ex-soldiers who frequented Munich beer halls such as the Torbräukeller near the Isar Gate. They were recruited by Ernst Röhm to protect Nazi speakers at public meetings. The Brownshirts, as they became known, were party uniformed supporters who wore brown shirts (hence their nickname) and who acted as bodyguards. They were to grow in number during the 1920s and early 1930s, acting under Röhm's orders rather than Hitler's.

Q In Germany, who were the "November Criminals"?

A A term used by the Nazis and others on the right in the interwar years for those individuals who had signed the Treaty of Versailles, plus the communists, Jews, profiteers, and social democrats who had betrayed the army during World War I—the "stab-in-the-back" theory—and who still worked for Germany's downfall. These ideas were very popular with ex-soldiers, serving soldiers and the vast reservoir of anti-Semitism and antidemocratic resentment that existed in Germany during the interwar period.

Q What was the Reichswehr?

A The 100,000-man German Army of the Weimar Republic.

❝MANKIND HAS GROWN STRONG THROUGH STRUGGLES AND WILL ONLY PERISH THROUGH PEACE❞
ADOLF HITLER, *MEIN KAMPF*

Q Why did Japanese expansion and tales of her atrocities infuriate many in the West in the 1930s?

A The United States was particularly aggrieved by Japan's actions. It had long-standing missionary and trade connections with China, and close associations with the Nationalist leader Chiang Kai-shek. China was also militarily important to the U.S. and European powers, as "extraterritoriality" agreements permitted the Western nations to establish sovereign commercial settlements on Chinese territory with the accompanying ability to station military units.

DID YOU KNOW

APPEASEMENT HAS, SINCE THE END OF WORLD WAR II, BEEN EQUATED WITH COWARDICE AND IS HELD IN CONTEMPT. IN THE 1930S, HOWEVER, APPEASEMENT AS PRACTISED BY BRITISH PRIME MINISTER NEVILLE CHAMBERLAIN AND FRENCH LEADERS SUCH AS EDOUARD DALADIER ENCAPSULATED REASONABLE STEPS THAT MIGHT BE TAKEN TO PREVENT HITLER TAKING THE LAW INTO HIS OWN HANDS. IT WAS ALSO THE MANIFESTATION OF A VERY REAL DESIRE TO AVOID ANOTHER GENERAL EUROPEAN WAR. APPEASEMENT HAD ITS ROOTS IN THE GROWING FEELING IN THE EARLY 1930S IN BRITAIN AND FRANCE THAT THE TERMS OF THE VERSAILLES TREATY HAD BEEN HARSH ON GERMANY. SEEN IN THIS LIGHT, HITLER'S DEMANDS FOR A REARMED GERMANY AND THE RESTORATION OF "GERMAN" TERRITORIES APPEARED REASONABLE. THUS, BY ASSENTING TO THESE ESSENTIALLY "JUST" DEMANDS, CHAMBERLAIN BELIEVED HE COULD LAY THE FOUNDATIONS FOR A LASTING EUROPEAN PEACE. UNFORTUNATELY, APPEASEMENT RELIED ON THE GOODWILL OF BOTH PARTIES TO BE A SUCCESS. THUS, AFTER THE MUNICH CONFERENCE IN SEPTEMBER 1938, CHAMBERLAIN AND DALADIER AGREED TO HITLER'S DEMANDS FOR THE INCORPORATION INTO THE THIRD REICH OF THE GERMAN-SPEAKING CZECH SUDETENLAND. FOR HIS PART, HITLER HAD EXPECTED A CONFRONTATION OVER THE ISSUE, AND BRITAIN AND FRANCE'S FAILURE TO STAND UP TO HIM ENCOURAGED MORE BRINKMANSHIP. HE OCCUPIED THE REST OF CZECHOSLOVAKIA IN MARCH 1939, SIGNALING DE FACTO THE END OF APPEASEMENT AS A WORKABLE POLICY.

11

Q **Who became the Japanese prime minister in 1940?**

A Prince Konoye.

Q **Who were his minister of war and foreign minister?**

A Hideki Tojo and Yosuke Matsuoka, respectively.

Q The book originally titled *Four and a Half years of Struggle against Lies, Stupidity, and Cowardice* was later called what?

A *Mein Kampf—My Struggle*, the autobiography written by Adolf Hitler while in prison in the 1920s.

Q *Deutschland Erwache* (Germany Awake) was a popular Nazi phrase. What was its origin?

A Hitler borrowed the phrase from one of Richard Wagner's works.

Q Who was the Nazi Party's head of propaganda?

A Josef Goebbels.

> ## IT IS THE LAST TERRITORIAL CLAIM
> # WHICH I HAVE TO MAKE
> # IN EUROPE
> ADOLF HITLER, ON THE SUDETENLAND AND CZECHOSLOVAKIA

Q What was *Lebensraum*?

A *Lebensraum* was an integral part of Nazi ideology, which linked the twin concepts of space and race. Hitler believed that Germany needed more farmland to support itself—the need to be self-sufficient. Given the Nazi theory of race, it was only natural that she should take lands from the "inferior" Slav peoples of Poland and the Soviet Union.

Q What was *Weltanschauung*?

A World View, i.e. the Nazi view of the world and its peoples, such as seeing the Aryan-Nordic race as the founder and maintainer of civilization, whereas the Jews were destroyers.

DID YOU KNOW

A FORECASTER IN 1928 WOULD HAVE PREDICTED NOTHING BUT DOOM AND GLOOM FOR THE NSDAP. IN FACT, THE NAZI PARTY WAS IN STEEP DECLINE; IT WAS GOING TO "HELL ON A HANDCART." IT SUFFERED A SIGNIFICANT HUMILIATION IN THE POLLS THAT YEAR. THE POLITICAL SITUATION WAS DIRE, THERE WAS LITTLE TO CELEBRATE, AND HENCE THERE WAS NO PARTY DAY IN 1928 (AT TIMES THE NAZIS GAVE THE APPEARANCE OF BEING SULKY CHILDREN). THE WEIMAR REPUBLIC, WHICH HITLER HAD SO BITTERLY CRITICIZED, WAS DEFEATING THE NAZIS RESOUNDINGLY IN ONE POLITICAL SKIRMISH AFTER ANOTHER. HITLER HAD RAVED ABOUT THE OCCUPATION OF THE RUHR, WHICH HAD BEEN OCCUPIED BY THE FRENCH AND BELGIANS IN JANUARY 1923 FOLLOWING GERMAN FAILURE TO MAKE TIMELY REPARATIONS PAYMENTS; WHEN THE FRENCH WITHDREW, THE WEIMAR GOVERNMENT REAPED THE REWARD. HITLER RANTED ABOUT INFLATION; AGAIN, THE WEIMAR GOVERNMENT STABILIZED THE SITUATION. HITLER'S PROTESTATIONS ON LAW AND ORDER WERE OVERLOOKED; WHEN IT WAS TEMPORARILY RESTORED AGAIN THE WEIMAR GOVERNMENT RECEIVED THE APPLAUSE. POLITICALLY, THE NAZIS WERE FADING FAST. THE WORLD ECONOMIC DEPRESSION OF 1929, HOWEVER, WOULD SEE THEM BECOME A FORCE AGAIN IN GERMAN POLITICS, AS HITLER BLAMED JEWS AND COMMUNISTS FOR GERMANY'S ECONOMIC TROUBLES.

13

Q What was the Night of the Long Knives?

A The liquidation of Ernst Röhm and the SA leadership by the SS in June 1934.

Q Why did German troops occupy the Rhineland in March 1936?

A The Treaty of Versailles had turned the Rhineland into an unoccupied buffer zone between Germany and France. Hitler had been burning to send troops marching back into the Rhineland, both in order to assert that it was an indivisible part of his new Germany and to show his contempt for the Treaty of Versailles.

Q What was the *Anschluss*?

A The Union between Nazi Germany and Austria in March 1938.

Q Why did Hitler wish to invade Czechoslovakia in 1938?

A After his success in absorbing Austria into Germany in March 1938, Adolf Hitler looked covetously at Czechoslovakia, where about three million people in the Sudeten area were of German origin. It became known in May 1938 that Hitler and his generals were drawing up a plan for the occupation of Czechoslovakia.

> ## A QUARREL IN A FARAWAY COUNTRY BETWEEN PEOPLE OF WHOM WE KNOW NOTHING
> NEVILLE CHAMBERLAIN, ON THE CZECH CRISIS, 1938

Q What was the Munich Agreement?

A A four-power conference in September 1938 to settle the dispute between Germany and Czechoslovakia over the Sudetenland.

Q What was the result of the Munich Agreement?

A The German Army was to complete the occupation of the Sudetenland by October 10, 1938, and an international commission would decide the future of other disputed areas. Czechoslovakia was informed by Britain and France that it could either resist Germany alone or submit to the prescribed annexations. The Czechs capitulated.

1939

War broke out when Germany invaded Poland at the beginning of September. The German Blitzkrieg defeated the Poles in three weeks, which stunned the British and French general staffs. No fighting took place in the West, though conflict did erupt between Finland and the USSR.

Q Which German battleship was launched in February 1939?

A The *Bismarck*. The launching ceremony on February 14 was attended by thousands of people, military personalities, government officials, and yard workers. Adolf Hitler delivered the prelaunch speech and the hull was then christened by Frau Dorothea von Loewenfeld, granddaughter of the German chancellor Otto von Bismarck, after whom the ship was named. Moments afterwards, at 13:30 hours, *Bismarck*'s hull slipped into the water.

Q Which firm built this ship?

A Blohm & Voss. The keel was laid down on July 1, 1936, at the Blohm & Voss shipyard facilities in Hamburg.

" THE AIM WILL BE
TO DESTROY POLISH MILITARY STRENGTH
ADOLF HITLER, APRIL 1939 "

Q Which German battleship was launched in April 1939?

A The *Tirpitz*.

Q Which treaty did Adolf Hitler repudiate in April 1939?

A The Anglo-German Naval Treaty, signed in June 1935. This allowed Germany to have one-third of the tonnage of the Royal Navy's surface fleet (the largest in the world at this time) and an equal tonnage of submarines.

DID YOU KNOW

ADOLF HITLER (1889–1945), THE FOUNDER OF NAZI GERMANY, WAS BORN IN AUSTRIA. HIS EXPERIENCES AS A FAILED ARTIST IN VIENNA AND DECORATED SOLDIER IN WORLD WAR I HELPED SHAPE HIS EXTREMIST POLITICAL AMBITIONS, WHICH LED TO THE NAZI PARTY'S FOUNDATION. HE EXPLOITED WEIMAR GERMANY'S POLITICAL TURBULENCE AND SOCIAL UNREST TO MANEUVER HIMSELF INTO POWER IN 1933. VIOLENCE AND INTIMIDATION SECURED HIS POSITION AS DICTATOR. HIS NAZISM FUSED NATIONALISM WITH RACISM AND FORMED POWERFUL EXPANSIONIST AMBITIONS. HITLER ARTICULATED THE DREAM OF CREATING AN EMPIRE BY DESTROYING GERMANY'S SUPPOSED RACIAL AND IDEOLOGICAL ENEMIES. HITLER'S DESIRE TO REALIZE HIS TERRITORIAL AMBITIONS PLUNGED EUROPE INTO DIPLOMATIC CHAOS AND, ULTIMATELY, WAR.

Q **Which two territories were occupied by Germany in March 1939?**

A Bohemia and Moravia were occupied as "Protectorates," and as a result Czechoslovakia disappeared from the map of Europe.

Q **What was the Anti-Comintern Pact?**

A An agreement concluded first between Germany and Japan and then between Italy, Germany, and Japan before the war. Ostensibly it was directed against the Communist International (Comintern) but, by implication, specifically against the Bolshevik Soviet Union. The treaties were sought by Adolf Hitler, who at the time was publicly inveighing against Bolshevism and who was interested in Japan's successes in the opening war against China. The Japanese were angered by a Soviet-Chinese nonaggression treaty of August 1936 and by the subsequent sale of Soviet military aircraft and munitions to China. For propaganda purposes, Hitler and Benito Mussolini. Italy's dictator, were able to present themselves as defenders of Western values against the threat of Soviet communism.

THIS MEANS THE
END OF GERMANY
WILHELM CANARIS, ON THE GERMAN ATTACK ON POLAND

Q Who was head of the German SS organization?

A Heinrich Himmler.

Q What was *Blitzkrieg*?

A Lightning War. A term used by the Nazis to describe a military strategy that aimed to inflict a total defeat upon an enemy through a "lightning" offensive. This was achieved by speed, firepower, and mobility. General Heinz Guderian's book *Achtung! Panzer!* (1933) articulated the strategy that aimed to avoid the protracted, costly, and indecisive trench warfare of 1914–1918.

Q What did *Blitzkrieg* rely on for success?

A Tanks, mobile artillery, and aircraft. In the first *Blitzkrieg* against Poland in 1939, German attacks always avoided strong resistance in order to sustain the momentum of an assault, which concentrated upon rear areas to break lines of supply and communication. Once this was achieved, less-mobile forces could annihilate isolated pockets of resistance. The *Blitzkrieg* doctrine not only required new technology, it also needed commanders with the tactical vision and flexibility to fully exploit opportunities and overcome obstacles in order to sustain an attack's momentum.

Q **What was Gestapo short for?**

A *Geheime Staats Polizei*—Secret State Police. The Gestapo became the political police of Nazi Germany. The Gestapo ruthlessly eliminated opposition to the Nazis within Germany and its occupied territories, and in the war was responsible for the roundup of Jews throughout Europe for deportation to extermination camps.

Q **Were there any checks on the Gestapo?**

A No. The Gestapo operated without restraints. It had the authority of "preventative arrest," and its actions were not subject to judicial appeal. Thousands of leftists, intellectuals, Jews, trade unionists, political clergy, and homosexuals simply disappeared into concentration camps after being arrested by the Gestapo.

DID YOU KNOW

IT IS A LITTLE-KNOWN FACT THAT JOSEF GOEBBELS, GERMAN MINISTER OF PROPAGANDA, WAS OPPOSED TO A EUROPEAN WAR. HE REALIZED THAT GERMANY WOULD BE TAKING UNNECESSARY RISKS AND THAT HER POSITION OF POWER WOULD BE WEAKENED. DESPITE THE VICTORIES OF 1940 GOEBBELS SAID: "WE MUST NOT FOOL OURSELVES. IT WILL BE A LONG AND DIFFICULT WAR. ITS OUTCOME WILL NOT DEPEND ON BOISTEROUS VICTORY PARTIES BUT ON A DETERMINATION TO DO ONE'S DAILY DUTY." HE WAS PROBABLY THE ONLY NAZI LEADER TO CORRECTLY JUDGE THE LENGTH AND GRAVITY OF THE WAR. AS THE WAR TURNED AGAINST GERMANY, GOEBBELS SAW HIMSELF AS A GENERAL, HIS MINISTRY AS A GENERAL STAFF, AND THE PROPAGANDA WAR AS IMPORTANT AS THAT AT THE FRONT. IN BERLIN IN MAY 1945, IN THE BUNKER WITH HITLER, GOEBBELS AND HIS WIFE MAGDA COMMITTED SUICIDE. HE SHOT HIMSELF WHILE SHE TOOK POISON, THEN AN SS ORDERLY GAVE THEM THE COUP DE GRÂCE TO ENSURE THAT THE COUPLE WERE INDEED DEAD.

Q What were the Nuremberg Laws?

A Introduced in 1935, the Reich Citizen's Law, and Law for the Protection of German Blood and German Honor, were known thereafter as the Nuremberg laws. The laws defined two degrees of humanity: the *Reichbürger*, the Citizen of Pure German Blood, and the *Staatsangehörige*, the subject of the state, i.e. Jews. Intermarriage between the two groups was strictly forbidden. The lot of Jews living in Germany was getting progressively worse, and many were leaving the country. Some 250 decrees followed these laws, which excluded Jews from economic life.

Q In Nazi Germany what was a *Gauleiter*?

A A senior Nazi Party administrative figure in a *Gau* (District). In 1938 there were 32 Nazi Party districts; by 1942 there were 40.

DID YOU KNOW

THE *SS VERFÜGUNGSTRUPPE* (MILITARIZED SS) WAS ORIGINALLY AN ARMED FORCE AT HITLER'S PERSONAL DISPOSAL AND NOT A PART OF THE ARMED FORCES OR OF THE POLICE FORCES ALREADY IN EXISTENCE. THEREFORE, IT WAS ABLE TO BE LEGITIMATELY TRAINED BY THE *REICHSFÜHRER-SS* IN NAZI THEORIES OF RACE AND ALSO TO BE MANNED BY VOLUNTEERS WHO HAD COMPLETED THEIR COMMITMENT IN THE *REICHSARBEITSDIENST*, THE REICH LABOUR SERVICE. IN TIME OF WAR, ELEMENTS OF THE *TOTENKOPFVERBÄNDE* (DEATH'S HEAD UNITS) WOULD REINFORCE THE *SS-VERFÜGUNGSTRUPPE*. IF MOBILIZED, IT WOULD BE USED FIRSTLY BY THE COMMANDER-IN-CHIEF OF THE ARMY UNDER THE JURISDICTION OF THE ARMY, MAKING IT SUBJECT ONLY TO MILITARY LAW AND ORDER, BUT STILL REMAINING A BRANCH OF THE NAZI PARTY AND OWING ITS ALLEGIANCE ULTIMATELY TO THAT ORGANIZATION. SECONDLY, IN THE EVENT OF AN EMERGENCY WITHIN GERMANY, THE *SS-VERFÜGUNGSTRUPPE* WOULD BE UNDER HITLER'S CONTROL THROUGH HIMMLER.

" HOW CAN A COUNTRY GO TO WAR WITH A POPULATION SO DEAD AGAINST IT?

WILLIAM SHIRER, U.S. JOURNALIST IN GERMANY

Q **What was the *Reichstag*?**

A The home of the German parliament in Berlin. After it was burnt down in February 1933, the parliament met in Berlin's Kroll Opera House.

Q **Why was the German Army suspicious of the armed SS?**

A The army had always been suspicious of the SS. As the supposed sole arms bearers of the state, it regarded the creation of armed units within the SS as a betrayal by Hitler. It had been hypothesized that Hitler was playing a double game and allowing the expansion of the *SS-Verfügungstruppe* as a counter to any possible coup by the army. In the early stages of his regime this was extremely unlikely, and Hitler bent over backwards in his efforts to appease the army.

Q **What was the Aryan race?**

A A term first used by the linguistic scholar Friedrich Max Müller to describe a group of people who migrated into Europe in ancient history; as used by the Nazis, it applied to the "Nordic" peoples of Europe, who formed the so-called "Aryan race."

Q What was the treaty signed between Germany and the Soviet Union in August 1939?

A The Russo-German Nonaggression Treaty.

Q What was at the heart of the treaty?

A Neither party would attack the other and mutual spheres of influence were agreed regarding the Baltic states and Poland.

Q Why was the treaty so important to Hitler?

A It meant Germany could attack and defeat Poland quickly, thus avoiding a two-front war if Britain and France came to Poland's aid.

> **❝ I KNOW I SUDDENLY REALIZED THAT BOTH MY HUSBAND AND BROTHER WOULD BE IN DANGER ❞**
> HEIDI BRENDLER, GERMAN HOUSEWIFE, SEPTEMBER 1939

Q Why was the treaty disastrous for Poland?

A Notwithstanding the many assurances she received, speedy assistance from the West was most improbable. Powerful enemies (Nazi Germany and the Soviet Union), who had just become reconciled to each other and were hungry to devour her, now hounded her on both sides.

Q Who was the British ambassador in Berlin in August 1939?

A Sir Neville Henderson.

DID YOU KNOW

HITLER'S FIRST DIPLOMATIC OVERTURES TO MOSCOW IN AUGUST 1939 WERE NOT SUCCESSFUL. THE SOVIETS WERE STALLING FOR TIME AS THEY WERE ALREADY NEGOTIATING WITH GREAT BRITAIN AND FRANCE. HITLER, DESPERATE TO CONCLUDE AN AGREEMENT, DECIDED TO INTERVENE PERSONALLY AND ON AUGUST 20 SENT A TELEGRAM TO STALIN ASKING HIM TO RECEIVE HIS FOREIGN MINISTER IMMEDIATELY. ON THE EVENING OF AUGUST 21, HITLER WAS HANDED A TELEGRAM FROM STALIN. THE FÜHRER WAS OVERCOME WITH UNCONTROLLABLE EXCITEMENT. "TO THE CHANCELLOR OF THE GERMAN REICH, A. HITLER. I THANK YOU FOR YOUR LETTER. I HOPE THAT THE GERMAN-SOVIET NONAGGRESSION PACT WILL BRING ABOUT AN IMPORTANT IMPROVEMENT IN THE POLITICAL RELATIONS BETWEEN OUR COUNTRIES. THE PEOPLE OF OUR COUNTRIES NEED TO LIVE IN PEACE WITH EACH OTHER. THE SOVIET GOVERNMENT HAVE INSTRUCTED ME TO INFORM YOU THAT THEY AGREE TO RECEIVING YOUR HERR VON RIBBENTROP ON AUGUST 23 IN MOSCOW."

23

Q Did Hitler believe Britain and France would go to war over Poland?

A No. He believed there would be a Western renunciation of military intervention similar to those that had taken place in 1936, 1938, and again in the spring of 1939.

Q Name the date when Nazi Germany attacked Poland.

A September 1, 1939.

Q What was the Gleiwitz incident?

A A feigned attack on a German radio station on the Polish border by the SS on August 30, which left dead concentration camp inmates dressed in Polish uniforms at the site.

Q What was the German attack plan against Poland?

A Plan White, directed by General Walther von Brauchitsch, aimed to paralyze Poland's 24 divisions by swift encirclement to cut their lines of supply and communication. Poland's ill-prepared forces, lacking both air power and armor, were largely placed well forward on the border to meet the invaders. They were quickly overrun as reinforcements often arrived too late to halt German offensives.

Q Did Nazi Germany declare war on Britain and France?

A No. On September 2 ultimatums were delivered by Britain and France to Germany demanding her immediate withdrawal from Poland. The next day Britain and France declared war on Nazi Germany after their ultimatums expired.

> ## YOU'VE GOT YOUR WAR!
> # IT'S ALL YOUR DOING
> HERMANN GÖRING TO JOACHIM VON RIBBENTROP

Q Which other countries declared war on Nazi Germany in September 1939?

A Australia, New Zealand, South Africa, and Canada.

Q Who was the prime minister of South Africa in 1939?

A Jan Christian Smuts.

Q Which was the first German army to reach Warsaw?

A The Tenth Army under General Walter von Reichenau, which reached the outskirts of the city on September 8.

Q Which British aircraft carrier was sunk on September 17, 1939?

A HMS *Courageous* was sunk by *U-29*, commanded by *Kapitänleutnant* Otto Schuhart. The aircraft carrier *Ark Royal* managed to escape a similar attack just three days beforehand. The Royal Navy acted quickly and withdrew its carriers to preserve these valuable vessels.

DID YOU KNOW

IN 1939 BEGAN THE SUBJUGATION OF NONGERMAN-SPEAKING NATIONALI-
TIES TO THE TOTALITARIAN NAZI POLICE STATE. WHEN GERMANY STARTED
WORLD WAR II, IT CAME AS THE LOGICAL OUTCOME OF HITLER'S PLANS.
THUS, HIS FIRST YEARS WERE SPENT IN PREPARING THE GERMANS FOR THE
APPROACHING STRUGGLE FOR WORLD CONTROL AND IN FORGING THE
INSTRUMENT THAT WOULD ENABLE GERMANY TO ESTABLISH HER MILITARY
AND INDUSTRIAL SUPERIORITY AND THEREBY FULFIL HER AMBITIONS. WITH
MOUNTING DIPLOMATIC AND MILITARY SUCCESSES, THE AIMS GREW IN
QUICK SUCCESSION. THE FIRST AIM WAS TO UNITE ALL PEOPLE OF GERMAN
DESCENT WITHIN THEIR HISTORIC HOMELAND ON THE BASIS OF "SELF-
DETERMINATION." THE NEXT STEP FORESAW THE CREATION OF A
GROSSWIRTSCHAFTSRAUM (LARGE ECONOMIC UNIFIED SPACE) OR A
LEBENSRAUM (LIVING SPACE) THROUGH THE MILITARY CONQUEST OF
POLAND AND OTHER SLAVIC NATIONS TO THE EAST. THEREBY THE
GERMANS WOULD ACQUIRE SUFFICIENT SOIL TO BECOME ECONOMICALLY
SELF-SUFFICIENT AND MILITARILY IMPREGNABLE. THERE, THE GERMAN
MASTER RACE (*HERRENVOLK*) WOULD RULE OVER A HIERARCHY OF
SUBORDINATE PEOPLES AND ORGANIZE AND EXPLOIT THEM WITH
RUTHLESSNESS AND EFFICIENCY.

Q Did the Soviet Union invade Poland in 1939?

A Yes. In accordance with a secret clause in the 1939 Nazi–Soviet Pact, the Red Army invaded Poland on September 17. Little resistance was encountered on Poland's eastern border as the Polish Army was already fighting in the west.

Q Did Britain and France declare war on the Soviet Union?

A Surprisingly, no. Both London and Paris made no threats as the Soviets occupied eastern Poland.

Q Who was the commander of the British Expeditionary Force that landed in France in September 1939?

A General Lord Gort. Some 160,000 men and 24,000 vehicles arrived throughout the course of September.

Q What was the most effective and largest Polish offensive of the 1939 campaign?

A A counterattack by 10 divisions, under General Tadeuz Kutrzeba, over the Bzura River against Germany's Eighth Army. It achieved only a limited success, however.

" THE POLES FOUGHT HARD,
EVEN THOUGH WE HAD GREAT SUPERIORITY IN ARMS "
PAUL STRESEMAN, GERMAN SOLDIER IN POLAND

Q Who assassinated Romanian Prime Minister Armand Calinescu in September 1939?

A A fascist Romanian group, the Iron Guard.

Q Estimate German and Polish losses in the 1939 campaign.

A Germany lost 10,572 troops and the Soviet Union had 734 troops killed in the campaign. Around 50,000 Poles were killed and 750,000 captured.

Q What was the dividing line between the German and Soviet occupation zones in Poland?

A The River Bug.

Q What three Baltic states were forced to sign "mutual assistance" agreements with the Soviet Union in 1939?

A Lithuania, Latvia, and Estonia.

Q What was the Winter War?

A The war between Finland and the USSR that began in 1940. Finland, refusing to concede to the Soviet Union's territorial demands, mobilized her armed forces in October. On November 30 a Soviet force of over 600,000 men, supported by air and naval power, attacked Finland.

> **"** POLISH TROOPS OF THE REGULAR ARMY
> # HAVE BEEN ON OUR TERRITORY
> # DURING THE NIGHT **"**
> ADOLF HITLER, SEPTEMBER 1, 1939

Q Who led Finland's armed forces in 1939?

A Field Marshal Karl von Mannerheim.

Q What was the Mannerheim Line?

A A 1914–1918 system of fortifications on the Karelian Isthmus which ran through rugged terrain and dense forest.

DID YOU KNOW

WHEN WORLD WAR II BROKE OUT, NORWAY, TOGETHER WITH SWEDEN, DENMARK, AND FINLAND, ANNOUNCED HER NEUTRALITY. IN SEPTEMBER 1939, GERMANY ASSURED NORWAY THAT SHE WOULD RESPECT HER TERRITORIAL INTEGRITY, BUT WARNED HER THAT THE THIRD REICH WOULD NOT TOLERATE AN INFRINGEMENT OF THAT NEUTRALITY BY A THIRD POWER. GERMANY AT THIS TIME WAS SINCERE ABOUT RESPECTING NORWEGIAN NEUTRALITY, BUT ADMIRAL RAEDER KEPT REMINDING HITLER THAT NAVAL BASES IN NORWAY WOULD BE VERY USEFUL IN CARRYING THE WAR TO GREAT BRITAIN. IN ADDITION, RAEDER REMINDED THE FÜHRER THAT A BRITISH OCCUPATION OF NORWAY WOULD BE DISASTROUS FOR GERMANY, BECAUSE SWEDEN WOULD THEN COME ENTIRELY UNDER BRITISH INFLUENCE. THIS WOULD INTERFERE WITH IRON-ORE SUPPLIES AND OPERATIONS IN THE BALTIC. IN ADDITION, ALLIED AID THAT WAS BEING SENT TO THE FINNS MIGHT LEAD TO AN OCCUPATION OF NORWEGIAN PORTS. HITLER THUS BEGAN TO CONSIDER AN INVASION OF NORWAY.

29

Q **What was the German ship involved in the Battle of the River Plate?**

A The pocket battleship *Admiral Graf Spee*.

Q **Who was her captain?**

A Captain Hans Langsdorff.

Q **What was the result of the battle?**

A After engaging the British cruisers HMS *Exeter*, *Ajax*, and *Achilles* on December 13, the *Admiral Graf Spee* made for Montevideo, Uruguay, for repairs. On December 17, Langsdorff, believing that a superior force awaited him outside the port, scuttled his ship.

Q How was the British battleship HMS *Royal Oak* sunk?

A The *Royal Oak* was sunk, with 786 lives lost, after *U-47* passed through antisubmarine defenses at Scapa Flow, where the Home Fleet was anchored. Defenses were improved at the main fleet base after this dramatic attack.

Q What happened at the Battle of Suomussali in December 1939?

A The Soviet 163rd Division approached Suomussali village in eastern Finland. Halted by freezing conditions, its troops were targeted by the Finnish 9th Division, which severed its supply lines. The Soviet 44th Division, sent as a relief force, was blocked by Finnish attacks and both forces were forced to capitulate. Total Soviet losses in this defeat were 27,500 men.

" I CANNOT FORECAST TO YOU THE ACTION OF RUSSIA. IT IS A RIDDLE WRAPPED IN A MYSTERY INSIDE AN ENIGMA "
WINSTON CHURCHILL

Q Where was the location of the attempt on Hitler's life in November 1939?

A The Bürgerbräukeller in Munich. A bomb exploded shortly after Hitler left the hall on the 16th anniversary of the Munich *Putsch*.

Q What was the German OKW?

A *Oberkommando der Wehrmacht* (OKW), High Command of the Armed Forces.

1940

Repeating its success in Poland, the Wehrmacht defeated Allied armies in Scandinavia, France, and the Low Countries. Italy launched an abortive offensive in North Africa, while the Royal Air Force won the Battle of Britain and thus saved the country from a Nazi invasion.

Q Why did a plane crash in Belgium in January 1940 lead Hitler to say: "It's things like this that can lose us the war"?

A On January 10, a German military plane crash-landed near the Belgian town of Mechelen-sur-Meuse. The aircraft, on a flight from Münster to Cologne, became lost in thick cloud. After it came down, one of the passengers jumped out and raced for a clump of bushes, where he set fire to papers he had taken from his briefcase. Belgian soldiers closed in and retrieved the partly burnt papers. The man was Major Helmut Reinberger, a Luftwaffe staff officer, and the papers were operational plans, complete with maps, for a German airborne attack on the West, to begin on January 14 with saturation bombing attacks on French airfields.

" IN THREE WEEKS ENGLAND WILL HAVE HER NECK WRUNG LIKE A CHICKEN'S

GENERAL WEYGAND, APRIL 1940 **"**

Q Why did Hitler order an unlimited U-boat war in February 1940?

A To stop essential supplies of food and war materials reaching Great Britain from the United States.

Q What did this order allow U-boat captains to do?

A Torpedo without warning any ship that was under British control. The policy was already in effect, as was made evident by the sinking of Danish, Dutch, Norwegian, and Swedish ships in the days that preceded the order. Danish newspapers protested loudly at the sinking of one of their ships, the *5177*, by a U-boat.

DID YOU KNOW

THE *DEUTSCHE ARBEITSFRONT* (DAF)—GERMAN LABOR FRONT—WAS
THE ORGANIZATION OF ALL GERMAN PROFESSIONAL AND MANUAL
WORKERS. IT INCLUDED, IN PARTICULAR, THE MEMBERS OF THE FORMER
LABOR UNIONS, OF THE UNIONS OF EMPLOYEES, AND OF THE FORMER
ASSOCIATIONS OF EMPLOYERS, WHICH WERE UNITED IN THE LABOR FRONT
ON A FOOTING OF COMPLETE EQUALITY. THE AIM OF THE LABOR FRONT
WAS THE FORMATION OF A REAL NATIONAL COMMUNITY OF ALL GERMANS.
THE LABOR FRONT HAD THE DUTY OF ADJUSTING THE LEGITIMATE
INTEREST OF ALL PARTIES IN A MANNER CONFORMING WITH NATIONAL
SOCIALIST PRINCIPLES. ATTACHED TO THE LABOR FRONT WAS THE
"STRENGTH THROUGH JOY" LEISURE ORGANIZATION. THE LABOR FRONT
HAD THE FURTHER DUTY OF LOOKING AFTER THE "PROFESSIONAL
EDUCATION" OF ITS ADHERENTS.

Q Who took over as commander of Soviet forces in the war against Finland in early 1940?

33

A Semyon Timoshenko.

Q Which treaty ended the Winter War?

A The Treaty of Moscow between Finland and the Soviet Union in March 1940. Battered but not defeated, Finland retained its independence but had to surrender the Karelian Isthmus and Hangö (10 percent of Finnish territory). Campaign losses were: 200,000 Soviets and 25,000 Finns.

Q Who resigned as France's prime minister in March 1940?

A Edouard Daladier.

Q What was the *Altmark* incident?

A In February 1940 the British destroyer *Cossack* violated Norway's neutrality to rescue 299 British merchant seamen aboard the German transport *Altmark*.

Q What was Berlin's response to this incident?

A Germany accelerated its invasion preparations, believing that Britain was planning more military actions in Norway.

DID YOU KNOW

HEINRICH HIMMLER WAS APPOINTED DEPUTY SS LEADER AND THEN NATIONAL LEADER IN JANUARY 1929 WHEN HE COMMANDED APPROXIMATELY 1,000 MEN, WHEN THE SS WAS STILL PART OF THE SA. HE GRADUALLY ASSERTED THE SEPARATION OF THE SS FROM THE SA. HIMMLER BECAME *POLIZEIPRÄSIDENT* OF MUNICH AFTER HITLER BECAME CHANCELLOR IN JANUARY 1933. THIS MODEST POST ENABLED HIM GRADUALLY TO GAIN CONTROL OF THE GERMAN POLICE NETWORK EXCEPT IN PRUSSIA, WHERE GÖRING WAS MINISTER OF THE INTERIOR. BUT HE FINALLY ACHIEVED COMPLETE CONTROL IN 1936. HIMMLER DEVOTED HIS LIFE TO THE EXPANSION OF THE SS, GIVING IT MANY FACETS. THESE INCLUDED THE SS-FINANCED RESEARCH ORGANIZATION, THE *AHNENERBE*. FROM THE SECURITY POINT OF VIEW HE TOOK OVER THE GESTAPO AND MADE IT A EUROPE-WIDE ORGANIZATION. HE CONTROLLED THE CONCENTRATION CAMP SYSTEM, AND IN 1943 BECAME MINISTER OF THE INTERIOR AS WELL. HIMMLER WAS APPOINTED CHIEF OF THE HOME ARMY IN 1944, AND A WEEK BEFORE HITLER'S SUICIDE HE MADE AN EFFORT TO NEGOTIATE THE SURRENDER OF GERMANY. HITLER, HAVING HEARD OF HIMMLER'S TREACHERY, DISMISSED HIM FROM ALL POSTS. CAPTURED BY THE BRITISH IN MAY 1945, HIMMLER BIT ON A CYANIDE PHIAL AND WAS DEAD WITHIN SECONDS.

Q Why was Norway of interest to both Germany and the Western Allies?

A Swedish iron ore supplies passed through the ice-free port of Narvik in Norway to Germany.

❝ I HAVE TOLD YOU ONCE AND I WILL TELL YOU AGAIN—YOU BOYS WILL
NOT BE SENT INTO ANY FOREIGN WARS
FRANKLIN D. ROOSEVELT, CAMPAIGN SPEECH, 1940 **❞**

Q What happened to the British destroyer HMS *Glowworm* in April 1940?

A She intercepted part of the German invasion fleet bound for Norway. *Glowworm* was sunk after ramming the heavy cruiser *Admiral Hipper*.

35

Q Why did the Allies want to mine Norwegian waters?

A To force Nazi ships carrying Swedish iron ore into the open seas and expose them to naval attack.

Q What was the German OKH?

A *Oberkommando des Heeres*—Army High Command.

Q What was the codename of the German invasion of Denmark and Norway?

A *Fall Weserübung* or Operation Weser Exercise.

Q What was notable about the German invasion of Denmark in April 1940?

A It was the first example in any war of a successful airborne operation.

Q Was the German invasion of Denmark costly in terms of casualties?

A No. Two German aircraft were shot down and a few armoured cars damaged. Thirteen Danish soldiers were killed and another 23 wounded. It was nothing more than a skirmish.

> " FRANCE HAS LOST THE BATTLE
> # BUT SHE HAS NOT LOST
> # THE WAR
> CHARLES DE GAULLE, 1940 "

Q Name at least two German ships sunk during the invasion of Norway.

A German naval losses were heavy, with three cruisers, *Karlsruhe*, *Königsberg*, and *Blücher*, being sunk and a battleship damaged.

Q What was the British naval operation codenamed Wilfred?

A The laying of mines off the Norwegian coast in April 1940.

DID YOU KNOW

THE GERMAN NORWEGIAN INVASION FORCE INCLUDED SIX GROUPS. THE NORTHERNMOST FORCE—GROUP 1—CONSISTED OF THE 139TH REGIMENT OF THE ÉLITE 3RD MOUNTAIN DIVISION, EMBARKED IN 10 DESTROYERS WITH ONLY MINIMAL SUPPLIES AND EQUIPMENT. IN COMMAND WAS MAJOR-GENERAL EDUARD DIETL, A FOX-FACED AUSTRIAN IN WHOM HITLER PLACED CONSIDERABLE CONFIDENCE. DIETL'S MISSION WAS RISKY AT BEST: TO SEIZE AND HOLD NARVIK UNTIL RELIEVED BY FRIENDLY FORCES ADVANCING FROM SOUTHERN NORWAY. THIS LINK-UP WOULD DEPEND ON THE SUCCESS OF GROUP 2, CONSISTING OF THE 3RD MOUNTAIN DIVISION'S OTHER REGIMENT, THE 138TH, WHICH HAD TO SEIZE AND HOLD TRONDHEIM. FARTHER SOUTH, GROUP 3 CONSISTED OF TWO BATTALIONS OF THE 69TH INFANTRY DIVISION, WITH BERGEN AS THEIR OBJECTIVE. A COMPANY OF THE LUFTWAFFE'S 1ST PARACHUTE REGIMENT, MEANWHILE, WOULD SEIZE THE VITAL SOLA AIRFIELD NEAR STAVANGER. GROUPS 4 AND 6, WHOSE MISSION WAS TO SECURE THE PORTS OF KRISTIANSAND, ARENDAL, AND EGERSUND ON NORWAY'S SOUTH COAST, CONSISTED OF SEVERAL SMALL DETACHMENTS OF THE 163RD INFANTRY DIVISION. FINALLY, THE HIGH COMMAND ALLOCATED TO GROUP 5 THE MOST IMPORTANT OBJECTIVE: THE CAPTURE OF OSLO, THE NORWEGIAN CAPITAL. THE ASSAULT WAVE WOULD CONSIST OF TWO BATTALIONS OF THE 163RD INFANTRY DIVISION ABOARD THE POCKET BATTLESHIP *LÜTZOW*, THE HEAVY CRUISER *BLÜCHER*, A LIGHT CRUISER, AND VARIOUS SMALLER CRAFT. THE GERMANS ALSO ASSIGNED TWO PARACHUTE COMPANIES TO SEIZE FORNEBU AIRPORT SLIGHTLY WEST OF THE CITY. FOLLOW-ON WAVES WOULD THEN REINFORCE OSLO AND ADVANCE NORTH AND WEST TO LINK UP WITH THE OTHER GROUPS. IN A SUBSIDIARY OPERATION, *WESER* EXERCISE SOUTH, TWO GERMAN INFANTRY DIVISIONS AND A MOTORIZED RIFLE BRIGADE WOULD SIMULTANEOUSLY OCCUPY DENMARK.

37

Q **Who was the Norwegian commander-in-chief in April 1940?**

A Major General Carl Otto Ruge.

Q Why did the geography of Norway both aid the attacker and defender?

A Norway is an elongated, rugged country, whose major population centers are located on its coastline. This ruggedness favors the defense, but only if it is speedily and properly organized. Conversely, as the Norwegians discovered to their cost, the same feature lays the defense open to defeat in detail because of the scarcity of communications between the separated and exposed centers of population. This disadvantage is compounded if, as happened in April 1940, an attacker achieves surprise.

Q What were Norwegian tactics after the Germans had invaded?

A Based on the assumption that Anglo-French forces would arrive soon, they concentrated on delaying the German advance north of Oslo.

DID YOU KNOW

A TYPICAL GERMAN MOUNTAIN DIVISION COMPRISED A HEADQUARTERS, TWO RIFLE OR GEBIRGSJÄGER REGIMENTS, AN ARTILLERY REGIMENT, AND SUPPORT UNITS, INCLUDING A BATTALION OF SIGNALERS, RECONNAISSANCE TROOPS, ANTITANK GUNNERS, AND ENGINEERS—AROUND 13,000 MEN IN ALL. AS THE TROOPS WERE TRAINED FOR COMBAT IN INHOSPITABLE TERRAIN, THERE WAS A HIGH PROPORTION OF MULES AND HORSES, AND SUPPORT WEAPONS WERE LIGHTER THAN NORMAL FOR EASY BREAKDOWN INTO MAN-PORTABLE LOADS. THE MEDIUM ARTILLERY BATTALION, FOR EXAMPLE, HAD 105MM GUNS IN PLACE OF 150MM PIECES. THE GERMANS FOUND THAT A PERSONAL LOAD OF 40 LB (18.1 KG) WAS THE MAXIMUM THAT COULD BE CARRIED—HEAVIER LOADS IMPAIRED INDIVIDUAL SPEED AND MOBILITY.

Q Did the Germans use tanks in Norway in 1940?

A Yes. The first detachment of German light tanks in Norway went into action on April 16 and proved devastating against the Norwegians, who possessed no antitank guns.

" YOU ASK: "WHAT IS OUR AIM?"
I CAN ANSWER IN ONE WORD: "VICTORY!"
WINSTON CHURCHILL, HOUSE OF COMMONS,
MAY 13 ,1940 **"**

Q Why was air power decisive against the Allied navies during the Norwegian Campaign?

A German air power largely nullified Anglo-French naval superiority. The occupation of Denmark had proved an unqualified success, and with Danish as well as Norwegian bases the Luftwaffe was able to dominate southern and central Norway. Consequently, on April 9 German bombers successfully engaged the British Home Fleet west of Bergen, inflicting little physical damage but scoring an important psychological victory by demonstrating the threat to warships operating near the coast. Henceforth, the British Admiralty exercised great caution and risked only submarines to interdict German shipping en route to Oslo, with little success.

Q Why did the conquest of Norway cause long-term problems for Nazi Germany?

A Norwegian bases would prove useful against the Soviet Union beginning in 1941, but Norway became a drain on German resources as Hitler continually reinforced the garrison against a British invasion that never materialized. In addition, the failure to capture the Norwegian government on April 9 contributed to German problems in the long term, as the government-in-exile established in London fostered patriotic resistance and subversion.

39

Q Who replaced Neville Chamberlain as British prime minister in May 1940?

A Chamberlain was severely criticized over the Norwegian campaign during a House of Commons debate. He resigned after a significant fall in government support in a vote of confidence and the opposition Labour Party's refusal to serve under him in a coalition government. Winston Churchill replaced him and immediately formed a coalition government.

Q Who became Soviet commissar for defence in May 1940?

A General Semyon Timoshenko, who replaced Marshal Kliment Voroshilov.

Q What was the German plan codenamed Case Yellow?

A The attack on Belgium, Holland, and France.

" WE WOULD RATHER SEE LONDON LAID IN
RUINS THAN IT SHOULD BE
TAMELY ENSLAVED
WINSTON CHURCHILL, JULY 14, 1940 **"**

Q What was the original German plan in Case Yellow?

A The German Army would outflank the French forces deployed along the fortified Maginot Line by a sweep into neutral Belgium and Holland. In truth, this plan remained an unimaginative one with little to recommend it. After a successful push into central Belgium, for example, the planners intended simply to leave it to the field commanders on the spot to recognize a tactical opportunity that they could exploit.

DID YOU KNOW

AT THE BEGINNING OF MAY 1940 IN THE WEST, IN TERMS OF NUMBERS OF DIVISIONS, BOTH SIDES WERE EVENLY MATCHED. THE FRENCH DEPLOYED NEARLY 50 DIVISIONS HELD IN OR IMMEDIATELY BEHIND THE MAGINOT LINE ALONG THE FRANCO-GERMAN BORDER. TO KEEP THESE FRENCH DIVISIONS FIXED IN THE SOUTH LONG INTO THE CAMPAIGN, THE GERMANS UNDERTOOK A DECEPTION SCHEME THAT FEIGNED AN INTENDED ATTACK BY ARMY GROUP C AGAINST THE LINE. IN A CLEVER *RUSE DE GUERRE*, THE GERMANS LEAKED FALSE INFORMATION THROUGH DOUBLE AGENTS THAT SUGGESTED THAT THE GERMANS WOULD LAUNCH AN OUTFLANKING ATTACK ON THE MAGINOT LINE BY VIOLATING THE NEUTRALITY OF NORTHWESTERN SWITZERLAND. AGAIN, THIS CONSTITUTED A CLEVER DECEPTION: BY APPEARING TO THREATEN THE OBVIOUS ACHILLES' HEEL OF THIS SUPPOSEDLY IMPREGNABLE DEFENSIVE BARRIER, THE GERMANS CLEVERLY TAPPED INTO THE SENSITIVITIES OF A MILITARY COMMAND THAT HAD NEARLY BANKRUPTED THE FRENCH ECONOMY CONSTRUCTING THE LINE IN THE FIRST PLACE.

41

Q Who was the French commander-in-chief in May 1940?

A General Maurice Gamelin.

Q What was the French plan called the Breda Variant?

A In response to a German attack in the West, French forces were to advance 102 miles (164 km) to reach the town of Breda in southern Holland to reinforce the Dutch Army. To achieve this new mission, Gamelin increased the forces committed to the maneuver from 20 to 32 divisions, largely by stripping the French strategic reserve of its mobile divisions and allocating them to General Giraud's Seventh Army in its coastal dash to Breda.

Q What was the codename of the final German plan for the attack in the West?

A *Sichelschnitt* (Cut of the Scythe).

Q Who devised it?

A Major General Erich von Manstein.

Q What did Cut of the Scythe entail?

A A swift surprise advance by concentrated mechanized formations through the Ardennes.

> **" HAD THE BRITISH HELD ON FOR ANOTHER TWO HOURS I WOULD HAVE WITHDRAWN**
> EDUARD DIETL, GERMAN COMMANDER AT NARVIK **"**

Q Why was Cut of the Scythe risky?

A The terrain of the Ardennes was very restrictive for large mechanized forces. The narrow, winding roads with steep banks on each side, the heavily forested and hilly ground, and the numerous fast-flowing rivers severely hampered movement. To move seven panzer divisions with 1,900 tanks, 41,000 motor vehicles, and 175,000 men through these communication routes—often only on a single vehicle frontage—would involve march columns that were 100 miles (160 km) long!

DID YOU KNOW

THE FINAL GERMAN PLAN FOR THE ATTACK IN THE WEST IN MAY 1940 ADVOCATED A CONCENTRATED MECHANIZED STRIKE THROUGH THE WEAK FRENCH CENTER, WHICH DISPOSED JUST 14 DIVISIONS FOR ITS DEFENSE. IF THE FRENCH SENT LARGE FORCES INTO BELGIUM AND HOLLAND TO IMPLEMENT THE BREDA VARIANT, AS GERMAN INTELLIGENCE BELIEVED THEY WOULD, THIS REDEPLOYMENT WOULD AID THE MANSTEIN PLAN BY SUCKING BRITISH AND FRENCH FORCES TO THE NORTH AWAY FROM THE CENTER. TO BE ABLE TO INFILTRATE THE WEAK FRENCH CENTER, THE GERMANS NEEDED TO ENCOURAGE THE EXISTING FRENCH MALDEPLOY-MENT. HENCE, THEY PLANNED TO LAUNCH A POWERFUL SECONDARY EFFORT INTO NORTHERN BELGIUM AND SOUTHERN HOLLAND. THE GERMAN ARMY HIGH COMMAND ASSUMED THAT THE FRENCH WOULD REGARD THIS AS THE MAIN GERMAN EFFORT. THE GERMANS THEREFORE EXPECTED THAT SUBSTANTIAL FRENCH AND BRITISH FORCES WOULD BE DRAWN AWAY FROM THE CENTER BY THIS DECEPTION ATTACK IN THE NORTH. ONCE THESE FORCES HAD REDEPLOYED NORTH, THIS POWERFUL GERMAN SECONDARY ATTACK COULD FIX THESE FORCES THERE IN A CONTACT BATTLE, WHILE THE MAIN GERMAN OFFENSIVE LANCED THROUGH THEIR REAR.

43

Q Did the Germans have more tanks than the Allies in May 1940?

A No. The attacking German forces fielded some 2,574 tanks out of their total arsenal of 3,380 machines, many of the uncommitted vehicles being the scarcely combat-worthy Panzer I light tank. The Allies had a total of 4,296 armored vehicles in the northeastern theater. The idea that the Germans had an overwhelming superiority in tanks is a myth: they just used their vehicles more imaginatively than did the British and French.

Q What was "Fortress Holland"?

A The Dutch main defensive position in the west of Holland.

Q Following the German attack on May 10, 32 divisions of General Billotte's First French Army Group, plus the British Expeditionary Force (BEF), crossed into Belgium and moved to their designated positions around Breda and thence south along the River Dyle in Belgium down to Sedan. The Luftwaffe did not impede these movements. Why?

A The Luftwaffe did not undertake major efforts to hinder this movement since it actually played into German hands by removing powerful enemy forces from the decisive central sector of the front.

Q Where did the Germans pierce the Allied line in the Ardennes?

A At Sedan.

Q Who commanded the German forces at Sedan?

A General Heinz Guderian.

DID YOU KNOW

DESPITE THE ADVERSE TERRAIN, THE GERMANS NEEDED TO ADVANCE SWIFTLY THROUGH THE ARDENNES IN MAY 1940, OTHERWISE THE FRENCH WOULD BE ABLE TO REDEPLOY FORCES TO BLOCK ANY GERMAN EGRESS ON TO THE PLAINS BEYOND. TO ENSURE MOMENTUM, THE GERMANS UTILIZED EFFECTIVE ALL-ARMS COOPERATION. A KEY COMPONENT OF THIS WAS THE PRACTICE OF UTILIZING MISSION ANALYSIS (*AUFTRAGSTAKTIK*). THIS FLEXIBLE ETHOS GAVE CONSIDERABLE LEEWAY TO SUBORDINATE COMMANDERS AND OBVIATED THE NEED TO PAUSE DURING OPERATIONS TO AWAIT FURTHER ORDERS FROM ABOVE. ON SEVERAL OCCASIONS THE COMMAND VEHICLE USED BY DIVISIONAL COMMANDERS WAS THE LEAD VEHICLE IN THEIR DIVISION—ALLOWING THEM TO MAKE RAPID AND WELL-INFORMED TACTICAL DECISIONS.

Q What units did he command?

A XIX Panzer Corps, comprising the 1st, 2nd, and 10th Panzer Divisions as well as the élite motorized *Grossdeutschland* Regiment.

> **I WONDERED WHAT HE WAS LIKE, THIS MAN I WOULD KILL. WOULD HE DIE WITH THE FÜHRER'S NAME ON HIS LIPS?**
> RICHARD HILLARY, RAF PILOT, BATTLE OF BRITAIN

Q Why did the German breakthrough at Sedan in May 1940 spell disaster for the Allies?

A It threatened to turn the southern flank of the still-cohesive British, French, and Belgian forces deployed on the Dyle River and in the Gembloux Gap down to the Meuse at Dinant.

45

Q What was the "Panzer Corridor"?

A The advance of the German panzer divisions from the River Meuse in the Ardennes to the English Channel in May 1940, which isolated Allied armies to the north from the forces in the south.

Q What was the "Miracle of Dunkirk"?

A Between May 27, and June 4, 1940, British, French, and Belgian forces resolutely defended the shrinking defensive perimeter they held around Dunkirk to permit the evacuation of a large part of these isolated forces. In this nine-day period, some 861 small boats transported 226,000 British and 112,000 French and Belgian soldiers to safety.

Q Why did the French put so much faith in the Maginot Line?

A World War I had devastated northeastern France, and from this the French military concluded that in the next major war the defensive firepower of artillery and the machine gun would dominate the tactical battlefield. Consequently, France based her interwar military strategy on a defensive posture, an orientation encapsulated by the construction of the Maginot Line during 1930–1935. This orientation also reflected French reaction to the huge casualties they had suffered during World War I, which had significantly reduced the country's adult male population.

Q Why wasn't the Maginot Line extended from Luxembourg along the Franco-Belgian border to the North Sea?

A French strategy prior to 1936 planned to send forces into central Belgium to help the latter resist any German onslaught. The construction of the world's most powerful defensive barrier along the Franco-Belgian border would hardly have sent the right message to the Belgian government. The fact that the construction of the existing 225 miles (362 km) of the Maginot Line had already virtually bankrupted France also influenced this decision not to extend the line to the coast.

Q Which supposedly impregnable Belgian fort dominated the German route of advance into central Belgium.

A Eben Emael.

" THE BATTLEFIELD WAS STREWN WITH
**BROKEN AND ABANDONED
EQUIPMENT**
CYRIL JOLY, BRITISH TANK COMMANDER IN
NORTH AFRICA, 1940 **"**

Q How did the Germans intend to capture the fort?

A German planners had concluded that this powerful Belgian fortress remained vulnerable due to its lack of antiaircraft defenses. Consequently, they formulated a daring plan to land by surprise a glider-borne force on to the roof of the fort—the first time such a tactic had ever been attempted. Once on the roof, the German troops would use a novel lightweight weapon—hollow-charged rounds—to blast through the thick concrete walls of the fort.

Q Were these tactics successful?

A Yes. The German paratroopers, using explosive charges, had soon neutralized the fort's guns and forced the surrender of the garrison.

DID YOU KNOW

GERMANY'S SENSATIONAL SEIZURE OF FRANCE AND THE LOW COUNTRIES WAS THE PINNACLE OF BLITZKRIEG STRATEGY AND SECURED ADOLF HITLER'S MASTERY OF WESTERN EUROPE. THE INVASION THAT BEGAN ON MAY 10 FIRST STRUCK THE LOW COUNTRIES, WHICH HAD RELIED UPON THEIR NEUTRALITY TO SAVE THEM, AND WERE IN NO CONDITION TO RESIST THE WEHRMACHT. AS BRITISH AND FRENCH FORCES RUSHED INTO BELGIUM IN RESPONSE TO GERMANY'S DIVERSIONARY ATTACK, THE NAZIS LAUNCHED THEIR MAIN ASSAULT BY ADVANCING THROUGH THE ARDENNES FOREST. THE ALLIES HAD DISMISSED THIS AREA AS BEING UNSUITABLE FOR ANY TANK ADVANCES, WHICH ALLOWED THE GERMAN UNITS TO MOVE STRAIGHT THROUGH AGAINST MINIMAL OPPOSITION. THIS GATEWAY INTO FRANCE ENABLED THE FAST-MOVING ARMORED COLUMNS TO ADVANCE INTO THE ALLIED REAR AND DISABLE COMMUNICATIONS. AS THE PANZERS RACED WESTWARD TO THE SEA, THE ALLIED ARMIES IN THE NORTH WERE EFFECTIVELY ISOLATED FROM POTENTIAL REINFORCEMENTS IN THE SOUTH. THE ALLIES WERE UNABLE TO MATCH GERMANY'S EFFECTIVE EXPLOITATION OF ARMOR AND AIRPOWER OR DEVELOP A CREDIBLE STRATEGY TO COUNTERATTACK THE INVADERS.

DID YOU KNOW

PRIME MINISTER PAUL REYNAUD FAILED TO MOTIVATE HIS GOVERNMENT TO CONTINUE FIGHTING IN JUNE 1940 AND RELEASED FRANCE FROM ITS AGREEMENT WITH BRITAIN NOT TO MAKE ANY SEPARATE PEACE. FRANCE REJECTED A BRITISH IDEA TO CREATE A UNION BETWEEN THE COUNTRIES. REYNAUD, AFTER LOSING THE SUPPORT OF HIS CABINET, RESIGNED; AND MARSHAL HENRI-PHILIPPE PÉTAIN REPLACED HIM (16TH). PÉTAIN REQUESTED GERMANY'S ARMISTICE TERMS (17TH), AND THE SIGNING CEREMONY WAS HELD AT COMPIÈGNE (22D), SITE OF THE WORLD WAR I ARMISTICE AGREEMENT. UNDER THE TERMS, GERMANY OCCUPIED TWO-THIRDS OF METROPOLITAN FRANCE, INCLUDING THE ENTIRE CHANNEL AND ATLANTIC COASTLINES. THE SOUTH HAD A NOMINAL FRENCH ADMINISTRATION AND KEPT ITS COLONIES. AFTER ITALY'S ARMISTICE WITH FRANCE (24TH) A CEASEFIRE OCCURRED ON ALL FRONTS. FRENCH LOSSES SINCE MAY 10 WERE 84,000–92,000 MEN; BRITISH LOSSES 3,475; AND GERMAN LOSSES 27,074.

Q In German military thinking, what was the concept of the integral battle of annihilation (*Vernichtungsschlacht*)?

A This military strategy was based, in part, on the Prussian/German High Command's interpretation—or, rather, distortion—of Clausewitz's ideas on the climactic, decisive, individual battle, an event that was prominent during the Napoleonic period. This military strategy centered on the intent to defeat an opponent swiftly through one single, continuous offensive action.

Q Who replaced the French premier, Paul Reynaud, in June 1940?

A Marshal Henri-Philippe Pétain.

Q What was the role of the Luftwaffe during the campaign in France in 1940?

A As the ground forces commenced their attacks on the border defenses, massed formations of German bombers and fighter-bombers began attacking enemy air bases. These attacks proved particularly successful in Belgium and Holland, where dozens of aircraft were caught on the ground and destroyed. These aerial operations represented a classic attritional counter-air campaign designed to achieve local air superiority over the theater. Once this had been accomplished, the Germans could then employ their air power to facilitate the ground advance through undertaking the missions of aerial reconnaissance, battlefield air interdiction (BAI), and close air support (CAS).

> ## FOR SEVERAL DAYS AFTER THE OCCUPATION THE GERMAN ARMY IGNORED
> # THE POPULATION OF PARIS
> DEMAREE BESS, AMERICAN IN PARIS, JUNE 1940

Q What was Operation Dynamo?

A The evacuation of Allied troops from Dunkirk.

Q What was Operation Red?

A The codename for the German conquest of France in June 1940.

Q Where was the Weygand Line?

A The French Weygand Line stretched along the Somme and Aisne Rivers and aimed to protect Paris and the interior.

Q Why was Paris declared an "open city" by the French in June 1940?

A To save it from destruction at the hands of the Germans (all French forces had withdrawn to the south of the capital).

Q Was any British territory under German control in the war?

A Yes. The Channel Islands, which were invaded in June 1940.

Q What was the Special Operations Executive?

A A British organization to give support secretly to resistance groups across Nazi-occupied Europe.

Q What was Führer Directive No. 16?

A Preparation for the German invasion of Britain.

" THE ENGINE EXPLODED AND THE MACHINE LURCHED VIOLENTLY FOR A SECOND

ROGER HALL, RAF PILOT, BATTLE OF BRITAIN, 1940 "

Q Upon what did it rely for success?

A Control of the sea for transporting the invasion force and the destruction of Britain's fighter capability to ensure a safe crossing for the army.

DID YOU KNOW

THE BATTLE OF BRITAIN WAS GERMANY'S ATTEMPT TO ACHIEVE AIR
SUPERIORITY OVER THE SKIES OF SOUTHERN ENGLAND. WITH THIS
ACHIEVED, SHE COULD THEN CONTROL THE ENGLISH CHANNEL FOR THE
CROSSING OF THE INVASION FORCE,WHICH WAS BEING PREPARED ON THE
CONTINENT. GERMANY'S AIR FORCE COMMANDER, HERMANN GOERING,
ASSEMBLED 2,800 AIRCRAFT AGAINST BRITAIN'S 700 FIGHTERS.
WIDESPREAD GERMAN ATTACKS ON PORTS, SHIPPING, AND AIRFIELDS
LURED BRITISH FIGHTERS INTO ACTION AND INFLICTED HEAVY LOSSES.
BRITAIN'S FATE RESTED UPON THE BRAVERY, DETERMINATION, AND SKILL OF
ITS FIGHTER PILOTS. THESE MEN WERE DRAWN FROM THE BRITISH EMPIRE,
NORTH AMERICA, CZECHOSLOVAKIA, POLAND, AND OTHER ALLIED
NATIONS. THE PERFORMANCE OF THE HURRICANE AND SPITFIRE FIGHTERS
THEY FLEW ALSO PLAYED A KEY ROLE.

Q Why was the French surrender of 1940 signed in a railway carriage?

A The French surrender was signed at Compiègne, in the same railway carriage where the Germans surrendered in November 1918. It was a deliberate insult to the French.

Q What was the German Operation Otto of August 1940?

A Hitler secretly ordered his staff to prepare a plan for the invasion of the Soviet Union, to be codenamed "Otto."

Q What happened at the Battle of Punta Stilo in July 1940?

A The British Mediterranean Fleet tried to separate the Italian Fleet from its Taranto base. An Italian battleship and cruiser were damaged, and Italian aircraft hit a British cruiser. The Australian cruiser HMAS *Sydney* and four destroyers engaged two Italian light cruisers. The Italians lost a cruiser and the *Sydney* was damaged.

Q Why did the Royal Navy attack French ships in Algerian ports in July 1940?

A Britain, fearing that France's navy would be seized by Germany, sent two battleships, a battlecruiser, and a carrier (Force H) to neutralize French vessels at Oran and Mers-el-Kebir, Algeria.

Q What was the result of the attack?

A After negotiations failed, the British sank one battleship and damaged two more. In Britain, two French battleships, nine destroyers, and other craft were acquired with minimal force. French naval forces in Alexandria, Egypt, were disarmed without a struggle.

> **❝** ALONG THE PROMENADE, IN PARTIES
> OF 50, THE REMNANTS OF ALL THE
> ## LAST REGIMENTS WERE
> ## WEARILY TRUDGING ALONG **❞**
> CAPTAIN RICHARD AUSTIN, DUNKIRK, MAY 1940

Q What was the Burma Road?

A A road linking Burma with China. When it was built, Burma was a British colony.

Q Why did the British close the Burma Road in July 1940?

A British Prime Minister Winston Churchill agreed to close the Burma Road to disrupt supplies to the Chinese in order to avoid a confrontation with the Japanese. The onset of the monsoon season meant that supply lines were disrupted anyway.

Q In the first phase of the Battle of Britain, what were the targets of German aircraft?

A In July 1940 Hermann Goering, the Nazi air force chief, ordered attacks on shipping and ports in the English Channel. The movement of Allied vessels in the Channel was soon restricted as a result of British naval and aircraft losses.

Q In July 1940 America restricted the export of oil and metal products outside the Americas. Who was this directed at?

A This measure was particularly directed towards Japan, which was heavily dependent upon imports of these resources.

Q What was the consequence of America's action?

A As a consequence, Japanese strategic planning devoted greater attention to the resources of the Dutch East Indies and Malaysia to relieve their raw material shortages.

53

DID YOU KNOW

WINSTON SPENCER CHURCHILL (1874–1965), SOLDIER, JOURNALIST, AND STATESMAN, HAD HELD MINISTERIAL OFFICES BUT WAS RELEGATED TO THE MARGINS OF POLITICAL LIFE IN BRITAIN DURING THE 1930S FOR HIS ANTI-APPEASEMENT STANCE. HE WAS PROPELLED INTO POWER, HOWEVER, AS PRIME MINISTER IN 1940 AS THE NAZIS APPEARED CLOSE TO TOTAL VICTORY. CHURCHILL REVERSED THE FORTUNES OF THE NATION BY DISMISSING ANY SIGN OF DEFEATISM. THE BOLD BUT OFTEN IMPATIENT PRIME MINISTER CONSTANTLY URGED HIS MILITARY COMMANDERS TO TAKE OFFENSIVE ACTION. CHURCHILL FORGED A COALITION OF ALLIED NATIONS, BUT IT WAS THE SOLID SUPPORT HE SECURED FROM THE UNITED STATES THAT WAS CRITICAL TO BRITAIN'S SURVIVAL.

Q What factors aided the British in the Battle of Britain?

A A centralized command-and-control structure and radar network enabled fighters to be effectively concentrated to meet enemy attacks. The RAF also benefitted from longer flying time as it operated over its own territory. In addition, crews that baled out were able to resume fighting, unlike their opponents who parachuted into captivity.

Q In the Battle of Britain, what was "Eagle Day"?

A A four-day German air offensive designed to destroy Britain's Fighter Command with raids on military airfields and industrial targets.

Q Who led the RAF in the Battle of Britain?

A Air Chief Marshal Sir Hugh Dowding.

Q What change in German strategy in September 1940 resulted in the RAF winning the Battle of Britain?

A Germany's gravest strategical error was the decision, from September 7 onward, to concentrate on bombing British cities, despite eroding the capability of Fighter Command by widespread and incessant raids across southern England. This change in strategy enabled the RAF to concentrate its fighters and inflict heavier losses on the Luftwaffe.

“ THE HOUSE ABOUT 30 YARDS FROM OURS
STRUCK BY A BOMB.
COMPLETELY RUINED
VIRGINIA WOOLF, LONDON, SEPTEMBER 1940 **”**

DID YOU KNOW

HITLER DID NOT WANT A CONFLICT ON HIS SOUTHERN FLANK IN THE BALKANS, AND HAD RESTRAINED HIS AXIS PARTNER MUSSOLINI ON SEVERAL OCCASIONS DURING THE SPRING AND SUMMER OF 1940 FROM INITIATING PLANS FOR AN ITALIAN INVASION OF YUGOSLAVIA AND GREECE. MUSSOLINI RELUCTANTLY ACCEPTED HITLER'S WISHES AS HE WAS DEPENDENT ON GERMANY FOR RAW MATERIALS NEEDED FOR ARMAMENTS.

Q Which World War II leader said: "One death is a tragedy, one million is a statistic"?

A Joseph Stalin.

Q Who was Chief of the Army General Staff in the German Army in 1940?

A General Franz Halder.

Q Which three countries did the Soviet Union occupy in June 1940?

A Lithuania, Latvia, and Estonia.

Q What was a T-34?

A A Russian medium tank.

Q What were the design features that made the T-34 such a good tank?

A One of the most innovative designs was its sloped armor, which not only saved weight compared with rolled plate, but was also more difficult for antitank rounds to penetrate. In addition, its Christie-type suspension, combined with a diesel powerplant, gave it an excellent power-to-weight ratio and good cross-country mobility.

Q Why did the Winter War encourage Hitler to attack the Soviet Union?

A The performance of the Red Army did little to lessen the disdain with which Hitler and the Nazis viewed the Soviet regime. Indeed, the fact that a small "Nordic" country had withstood the onslaught of a nation of 180 million Slavs further convinced Hitler of the overall superiority of the Aryan race. How much worse would the Red Army fare against the mighty Wehrmacht?

DID YOU KNOW

THE DICTATOR OF THE SOVIET UNION WAS NOT RADICALLY DIFFERENT FROM ADOLF HITLER. BOTH MEN SHARED A DISLIKE OF LIBERALISM AND WEAKNESS, AND BOTH SAW TREASON AND INCOMPETENCE EVERYWHERE. UNLIKE HITLER, STALIN HAD NOT SEEN WAR SERVICE (HE WAS FOUND TO BE UNFIT FOR MILITARY SERVICE BY THE RUSSIAN AUTHORITIES). THIS PUT HIM AT A DISADVANTAGE WHEN IT CAME TO CONFERENCES WITH SENIOR RED ARMY COMMANDERS DURING THE WAR, DUE TO HIS LACK OF PRACTICAL MILITARY KNOWLEDGE. HOWEVER, HE WAS QUITE HAPPY TO GIVE A CERTAIN LATITUDE TO HIS GENERALS, SECURE IN THE KNOWLEDGE THAT HIS SECRET POLICE MAINTAINED AN IRON GRIP OVER THE SOVIET PEOPLE AND THAT HE COULD ALWAYS HAVE INCOMPETENT OFFICERS EXECUTED OR SENT TO THE GULAG IF THEY FAILED IN THEIR DUTY TO MOTHER RUSSIA.

Q Which two Romanian provinces did the Soviet Union seize in June 1940?

A Bessarabia and Northern Bukovino.

Q What was the name of Hitler's retreat in the Bavarian Alps?

A The Berghof.

> ## THE ICY WATER WAS ALREADY TAKING A GRIP ON ME AND I LOOKED AROUND
> # FOR SOMETHING TO FLOAT ON
> RONALD HEALISS, ON THE TORPEDOED
> HMS *GLORIOUS*, JUNE 1940

Q What was the Iron Guard?

A A Romanian fascist movement.

Q Which Romanian leader was nicknamed "Red Dog"?

A Romanian dictator Ion Antonescu. He was nicknamed "Red Dog" because of his hair color.

Q Who said "If Russia is laid low, then Britain's last hope is wiped out, and Germany will be master of Europe and the Balkans."?

A Adolf Hitler in July 1940.

Q Who commanded Italian forces in Libya in 1940?

A Marshal Rodolfo Graziani.

Q How many Italian troops invaded Egypt in September 1940?

A 250,000.

Q Who was the British commander who opposed them?

A General Sir Richard O'Connor.

"FIRE A BOW TORPEDO AT A LARGE FREIGHTER OF ABOUT 6000 TONS AT A RANGE OF 750 METERS"
CAPTAIN OTTO KRETSCHMER, *U-99*, OCTOBER 1940

Q What was the British Selective Service Bill of September 1940?

A It authorized the conscription of men aged 21–35.

Q Why did the Germans suspend Operation Sealion?

A In September 1940 Adolf Hitler decided to suspend Operation Sealion after Germany's failure to achieve aerial supremacy over southern England.

DID YOU KNOW

THE PANZER IV BECAME THE BACKBONE OF THE GERMAN PANZER ARM ON THE EASTERN FRONT. CONTINUALLY UPGRADED IN TERMS OF ARMAMENT AND ARMOR THROUGHOUT THE WAR, THE PANZER IV SOLDIERED ON UNTIL THE SURRENDER OF GERMANY IN 1945, BY WHICH TIME 8,600 OF ALL VARIANTS HAD BEEN BUILT. ORIGINALLY ARMED WITH THE SHORT-BARRELLED 75MM GUN, EXPERIENCE IN RUSSIA REVEALED THIS WEAPON TO BE TOTALLY INADEQUATE AGAINST SOVIET T-34 AND KV-1 TANKS. THE PANZER IV HAD ORIGINALLY BEEN DESIGNED TO DESTROY "SOFT" TARGETS SUCH AS INFANTRY, SOFT-SKINNED VEHICLES, AND ANTITANK EMPLACE-MENTS, WHILE THE PANZER IIIS WERE FOR TANK-VERSUS-TANK COMBAT. THEREFORE, THE LONG-BARRELLED 75MM L/43 OR L/48 GUNS WERE INSTALLED IN PANZER IVS TO ENABLE THEM TO KNOCK OUT SOVIET TANKS. THE PANZER IV WAS NOT AN IDEAL DESIGN, HAVING RELATIVELY THIN, NON-SLOPING ARMOR THAT PRODUCED MANY SHOT TRAPS AND A HIGH, BOX SHAPE. HOWEVER, IT WAS A PLATFORM WHERE THE GUNS AND ARMOR COULD BE CONTINUALLY UPGRADED.

59

Q In naval warfare, what was a "Wolf Pack"?

A In this tactic, some 15–20 U-boats were deployed across the approaches to Britain. When a U-boat found a convoy, it tracked the vessels and awaited the gathering of the entire "Wolf Pack" for a combined attack. Germany launched its first successful "Wolf Pack" operation in the Atlantic in September 1940, sinking 12 ships.

Q What was Operation Felix?

A The codename of a German plan to capture Gibraltar.

Q Which senior Nazi served in the same regiment as Hitler in World War I?

A Rudolf Hess.

Q Which position did this individual hold in the Third Reich?

A Deputy Leader.

Q What does *panzerkampfwagen* mean in English?

A Armored fighting vehicle.

"THEY HAVE BLOWN THE BRIDGE UP. HE MUST BE ADVANCING AGAIN

SERGEANT PEXTON, BRITISH SOLDIER IN FRANCE, MAY 1940"

Q What was the Waffen-SS?

A The military wing of the SS.

Q Does Wehrmacht mean German Army?

A No. Wehrmacht means armed forces, which included the army.

DID YOU KNOW

THE 9MM MP38 WAS THE STANDARD GERMAN SUBMACHINE GUN OF
WORLD WAR II. AS ITS DESIGNATION SUGGESTS, IT WAS FIRST ISSUED IN
1938. TWO YEARS LATER, IT WAS REPLACED BY THE MP40, WHICH WAS
IDENTICAL EXCEPT IT UTILIZED LESS EXPENSIVE STAMPED METAL FOR
CERTAIN PARTS, WHICH WAS MORE COST EFFECTIVE FOR A MASS-PRODUCED
WEAPON. IT WAS A VERY SUCCESSFUL FIREARM, AND EVEN ALLIED FORCES
PREFERRED IT OVER THEIR OWN SUBMACHINE GUNS AND SCAVENGED
MP40S WHENEVER POSSIBLE. IT HAD A 32-ROUND MAGAZINE AND A
CYCLIC RATE OF FIRE OF 500 ROUNDS PER MINUTE. BETWEEN 1939 AND
1945 THE GERMAN ARMY RECEIVED 689,403 MP38/40 SUBMACHINE
GUNS, MOST OF WHICH WENT TO FRONTLINE UNITS, ESPECIALLY
PANZERGRENADIER FORMATIONS.

Q Which German ships sank the aircraft carrier HMS *Glorious* in June 1940?

A *Scharnhorst* and *Gneisenau*.

Q What type of warship was the *Prinz Eugen*?

A A heavy cruiser.

Q Who was the leader who replaced Neville Chamberlain as leader of the British Conservative Party in October 1940?

A Winston Churchill.

Q List the main roles of the Luftwaffe during a German ground
offensive.

A First, to destroy the enemy's air force (preferably on the ground).
Second, to provide close air support for ground units, which
included interdicting enemy supplies and communications to bring about
his paralysis.

Q Which leader said in 1940: "I make decisions; I need men who
obey."?

A Adolf Hitler.

" ROUSED OUT OF IT AT 6AM AND
PUT ON THE ROAD. I'M JUST
BEGINNING TO REALIZE
THAT I'M A PRISONER
SERGEANT PEXTON, FRANCE, MAY 1940 "

Q After the defeat of France Hitler created 12 field marshals.
Name at least five of them.

A Brauchitsch, Keitel, Rundstedt, Bock, Leeb, List, Kluge, Witzleben,
Reichenau, Milch, Kesselring, and Sperrle.

Q How many were from the air force?

A Three: Milch, Kesselring, and Sperrle.

DID YOU KNOW

THE GREATEST RED ARMY GENERAL OF WORLD WAR II AND ONE OF THE MOST FAMOUS COMMANDERS OF THE CONFLICT, GEORGI ZHUKOV, WAS BORN IN 1896 INTO AN IMPOVERISHED PEASANT FAMILY NEAR MOSCOW. HE WAS GOING TO BE A CRAFTSMAN, BUT THE OUTBREAK OF WORLD WAR I CHANGED HIS LIFE FOREVER. DRAFTED IN 1915, BY 1918 HE WAS SERVING IN THE RED ARMY CAVALRY AND A YEAR LATER JOINED THE COMMUNIST PARTY. WHAT MARKED OUT THE YOUNG MAN WAS HIS THIRST FOR KNOWLEDGE. DURING THE NEXT 20 YEARS HE DEVOURED MASSES OF WRITTEN WORKS ON THE MILITARY ART. BY 1938 HE WAS IN COMMAND OF THE ÉLITE 4TH CAVALRY DIVISION. HOWEVER, IT WAS WHEN IN COMMAND OF TANKS THAT HE GAINED HIS FIRST VICTORY, OVER THE JAPANESE IN MONGOLIA AT KHALKHIN GOL IN AUGUST 1939. BY MAY 1940 HE WAS A GENERAL AND IN CHARGE OF THE KIEV MILITARY DISTRICT. WHEN THE GERMANS INVADED THE SOVIET UNION IN JUNE 1941 ZHUKOV ADVOCATED ABANDONING KIEV, AN IDEA THAT PROMPTED AN OUTBURST FROM STALIN. ZHUKOV OFFERED TO RESIGN BUT STALIN, PROBABLY RECOGNIZING HIS GENERAL WAS RIGHT, REFUSED THE OFFER. KIEV FELL ANYWAY AND ZHUKOV WAS GIVEN COMMAND OF THE RESERVE FORCES SITUATED TO THE EAST OF MOSCOW. WHEN THE GERMAN MOSCOW OFFENSIVE STALLED AT THE END OF NOVEMBER 1941, ZHUKOV LAUNCHED A COUNTEROFFENSIVE ALONG THE WHOLE FRONT, WHICH NOT ONLY SAVED MOSCOW BUT ALSO GAVE THE GERMANS THEIR FIRST STRATEGIC DEFEAT. IN AUGUST 1942 ZHUKOV BECAME DEPUTY SUPREME COMMANDER-IN-CHIEF OF THE RED ARMY, SECOND ONLY TO STALIN. BY NOW HIS STAR WAS IN THE ASCENDANT. HE MASTERMINDED THE OPERATION THAT DESTROYED THE GERMAN SIXTH ARMY AT STALINGRAD AND THEN PLANNED AND EXECUTED THE RED ARMY DEFENSE AT KURSK. AFTER THE BATTLE HE WENT ON TO LIBERATE THE UKRAINE AND RETAKE KIEV. HIS GREATEST OPERATION WAS PROBABLY BAGRATION IN JUNE 1944, WHICH DESTROYED THE GERMAN ARMY GROUP CENTER. THOUGH STALIN WAS JEALOUS OF ZHUKOV'S POPULARITY AND MILITARY VICTORIES, HE AGREED TO HIM HAVING THE HONOR OF TAKING BERLIN IN 1945, WHICH HE DID—ALBEIT WITH TERRIBLE LOSSES AND WITH THE HELP OF KONEV. ZHUKOV DIED IN 1974.

Q Where were the Ploesti oilfields?

A Romania.

Q Japan signed the Tripartite Pact in September 1940. Why?

A The pact pledged that each country would wage war on any state that declared war on an Axis state. Japan was keen to deter intervention by the United States in the Far East and thus signed the pact.

Q Who commanded Italian troops during the invasion of Greece in October 1940?

A General Sadasiano Visconti-Prasca.

DID YOU KNOW

THE FAMOUS GERMAN 88MM FLAK 18 PROVED ITSELF TO BE NOT ONLY AN EXCELLENT ANTIAIRCRAFT WEAPON BUT ALSO AN IDEAL TANK-KILLER DUE TO ITS HIGH MUZZLE VELOCITY AND EFFICIENT HEAVY PROJECTILE. BY MID-1943 IT HAD BUILT UP AN IMPRESSIVE REPUTATION. IN FRANCE IN 1940 IT HAD TRIUMPHED AGAINST THE HEAVILY ARMORED FRENCH CHAR B1-BIS HEAVY TANKS AND BRITISH MK II MATILDA INFANTRY TANKS. IN NORTH AFRICA IT WAS A FEARED TANK-KILLER THAT COULD KNOCK OUT ANY ALLIED TANK AT RANGES WELL OVER 3,280 FT (1,000 M). AND IN RUSSIA IT WAS THE ONLY GUN CAPABLE OF DEALING WITH SOVIET T-34/76 MEDIUM TANKS AND KV-1 HEAVY TANKS. IT HAD A MUZZLE VELOCITY OF 820 METRES PER SECOND AND A RANGE OF 9.25 MILES (14.8 KM). THE 88MM ANTIAIRCRAFT GUNS WERE USUALLY DEPLOYED IN THE HEAVY FLAK BATTERIES. THEY COULD PRISE OPEN ANY ALLIED TANK LIKE A TIN OPENER, AND WERE FEARED BY ENEMY TANK CREWS.

> ## SUDDENLY THERE WAS A BLOODY FLASH
> ## ON MY PORT WING
> # AND I FELT A BLOW ON
> # MY LEFT ARM
>
> D.H. WISSLER, RAF PILOT, OCTOBER 1940

Q Who commanded Greek forces?

A General Alexander Papagos.

Q Why did the Italians attack Greece?

A Italy hoped to rival Germany's conquests of 1940.

65

Q What factors impeded the Italian advance in Greece in October 1940?

A The mountainous terrain and absence of maps for commanders hampered the invasion. In addition, the winter weather limited Italian air support and led to thousands of deaths from hypothermia. Finally, Greek resistance was stiffer than expected.

Q Who was elected president of the United States in November 1940?

A Franklin D. Roosevelt, for an unprecedented third time.

Q When did British forces occupy the Greek island of Crete?

A The end of October 1940.

Q What happened at the Battle of Taranto in November 1940?

A British torpedo aircraft from the carrier HMS *Illustrious* attacked Italian ships at Taranto.

Q What was the result of the battle?

A Three Italian ships were sunk and two others damaged.

Q The assault against Taranto was the blueprint for which Axis aerial assault in 1941?

A The Japanese attack against Pearl Harbor.

> **IN THE MORNING, I WOULD WALK ALONG CLARKEHOUSE ROAD LOOKING FOR SHRAPNEL**
> GEORGE MACBETH, A BOY IN SHEFFIELD, ENGLAND, AUTUMN 1940

Q Which British general, outnumbered three to one, won a famous victory over the Italians in North Africa in December 1940?

A Major General Richard O'Connor.

Q What was the name of the force he commanded?

A The Western Desert Force.

1941

This year the Germans launched Operation Barbarossa, the invasion of the Soviet Union. In North Africa Rommel turned the tide against the British, while in the Pacific Japan mounted a surprise attack on the U.S. fleet at Pearl Harbor. And, in the Atlantic, German U-boats preyed on Allied merchant ships.

Q Who commanded British forces in the Sudan in early 1941?

A General William Platt.

Q What was the name of the German force formed to fight in North Africa in January 1940?

A The *Deutsches Afrika Korps* (or DAK)—the German Africa Corps.

Q Who commanded it?

A General Erwin Rommel.

" DEAREST LU, WE'VE BEEN ATTACKING
SINCE THE 31ST WITH
DAZZLING SUCCESS
ROMMEL TO HIS WIFE, NORTH AFRICA, APRIL 1941 "

Q What was the DAK composed of in early 1941?

A Initially, just two German divisions: the 5th Light (which later became the 21st Panzer) and the 15th Panzer, formed the core of the Africa Corps.

Q When he arrived in North Africa, was Rommel under German or Italian command?

A He was technically under Italian command, though he did have the right to refer to Berlin if he was unhappy concerning the way his command was being handled.

DID YOU KNOW

WHEN ROMMEL ARRIVED IN LIBYA IN FEBRUARY 1941, ITALIAN FORCES HAD BEEN PUSHED BACK TO EL AGHEILA. THE INITIAL GERMAN FORCE, WHICH COMPRISED JUST THE 5TH LIGHT DIVISION, BENEFITED FROM A REDIRECTION OF MANY OF THE BRITISH COMMONWEALTH FORCES DEPLOYED IN EASTERN LIBYA AWAY FROM THAT THEATER TO DEFEND MAINLAND GREECE. THIS REDEPLOYMENT LEFT JUST INEXPERIENCED COMMONWEALTH TROOPS, PARTLY EQUIPPED WITH CAPTURED ITALIAN WEAPONS, TO DEFEND THE BRITISH FRONT IN LIBYA. ROMMEL, EVER THE AUDACIOUS ARMORED COMMANDER, IGNORED THE ADVICE OF HIS SUPERIORS AND SEIZED THE OPPORTUNITY PRESENTED BY THIS MOMENTARY BRITISH WEAKNESS BY INITIATING AN IMMEDIATE OFFENSIVE.

Q In February 1941 the U.S. Navy was divided into three fleets. What were they?

A Atlantic, Asiatic, and Pacific.

Q Who became chief of the Soviet general staff and deputy commissar for defense in February 1941?

A Georgi Zhukov.

Q Why did Hitler wish to see a stable Balkans that was either neutral or, preferably, pro-German?

A Hitler desired these conditions to ensure that events in the Balkans did not disrupt Germany's preparations for Barbarossa, the planned invasion of the Soviet Union, slated to begin in late spring 1941.

" MECHILI LANDING GROUND WAS
LITTERED WITH
DESTROYED PLANES
HEINZ WERNER, AFRICA CORPS, APRIL 1941 "

Q Why did the Italian invasion of Greece threaten Germany's preparations for the invasion of the USSR?

A Hitler feared that Greece would secure a military alliance with Great Britain against the Italians, an agreement that the British could then fashion into an antiGerman front to threaten the southern flank of the German concentration areas for Barbarossa. Even worse, from Greek air bases British long-range bombers could attack the Ploesti oilfields in Romania, from where the Wehrmacht obtained most of its fuel.

Q How did Hitler intend to resolve this issue?

A Hitler decided to initiate decisive military action during the spring of 1941 to settle permanently the Balkan imbroglio before Barbarossa commenced. This action comprised nothing less than an intended German conquest of Greece, staged from Bulgarian soil.

Q Who raided the Lofoten Islands in March 1941?

A An Anglo–Norwegian commando raid and naval assault on the Lofoten Islands, off Norway, destroyed fish-oil plants used in explosives production, captured 215 Germans, rescued 300 Norwegians, and sank 10 ships.

Q What was the U.S. Lend-Lease Bill of March 1941?

A President Franklin D. Roosevelt signed the Lend-Lease Bill that allowed Britain to obtain supplies without having immediately to pay for them in cash.

Q What was the Japanese "Greater East Asia Co-Prosperity Sphere"?

A An East Asia free of colonial influence and united under Japanese hegemony. Japan hoped that the Co-Prosperity Sphere would lead many colonial Asian countries to work, violently or otherwise, toward their independence from British, Dutch, and U.S. influence.

Q What was the position of Yugoslavia in early 1941?

A In early 1941, Hitler began the necessary diplomatic moves to bring Romania and Bulgaria into the Axis pact, a situation that placed the Yugoslav government, certainly not a staunch enemy of Berlin, in a difficult position. During February and March, German forces moved first on to Romanian and then Bulgarian soil. Bowing to the political wind, the Yugoslavs reluctantly discussed with Germany plans for a joint invasion of Greece, thereby intending to avoid a German violation of Yugoslav sovereignty as a stepping-stone for its attack on Greece.

Q Why did Germany invade Yugoslavia in April 1941?

A A pro-British regime had seized power in Yugoslavia on 27 March.

DID YOU KNOW

FOLLOWING THE FALL OF FRANCE IN JUNE 1940, U.S. PRESIDENT FRANKLIN D. ROOSEVELT PURSUED A POLICY OF SUPPLYING BRITAIN WITH THE SUPPLIES IT REQUIRED TO CARRY ON THE FIGHT AGAINST NAZI GERMANY. AS DEPENDENCE ON THESE IMPORTS INCREASED, IN DECEMBER 1940 THE BRITISH PRIME MINISTER, WINSTON CHURCHILL, PROPOSED AN ARRANGEMENT WHEREBY THE ALLIED NATIONS COULD OBTAIN ESSENTIAL U.S. GOODS AND EQUIPMENT BUT WOULD REPAY THE UNITED STATES AFTER THE WAR.

Q Who was the British commander at the Battle of Cape Matapan in March 1941?

A Admiral Sir Andrew Cunningham.

Q What was the result of the battle?

A British torpedo-bombers damaged the Italian battleship *Vittorio Veneto* and crippled the cruiser *Pola*. Three British battleships then engaged two cruisers sent to cover the *Pola*. The Battle of Cape Matapan claimed five Italian ships and 3,000 men killed. The British lost only one aircraft in the action.

Q What was the strategic situation of Yugoslavia in early April 1941?

A In strategic terms the defensive power of the Yugoslav Army was fundamentally compromised by the fact that it faced hostile Axis powers—Italy (including Albania), the Austrian parts of the Reich, Romania, Hungary, and Bulgaria—on three sides.

Q What was the strategic situation of Greece in early April 1941?

A Though the Greek Army enjoyed a strong geostrategic position, the inconclusive war with Hitler's Italian allies had already tied down some two-thirds of the Greek Army in the northwestern part of the country, leaving a small force to resist the German invasion.

> ❝ SUDDENLY, THE U-BOAT SPOTTED US
> **AND IN A CLOUD OF SPRAY**
> **HE CRASH-DIVED** ❞
> CAPTAIN DONALD MACINTYRE, ROYAL NAVY,
> MARCH 1941

DID YOU KNOW

ERWIN ROMMEL (1891–1944) WAS A DECORATED WORLD WAR I OFFICER WHO COMMANDED HITLER'S BODYGUARD AND WAS RESPONSIBLE FOR THE FÜHRER'S PERSONAL SAFETY DURING THE POLISH CAMPAIGN. HE THEN TOOK COMMAND OF THE 7TH PANZER DIVISION FOR THE 1940 INVASION OF FRANCE. HIS SPEEDY ADVANCE ACROSS THE MEUSE RIVER AND DRIVE TO THE ENGLISH CHANNEL EARNED HIM A REPUTATION AS A DARING TANK COMMANDER. FOLLOWING THE FAILED ITALIAN CAMPAIGN IN NORTH AFRICA, HE WAS SENT THERE TO LEAD THE AFRIKA KORPS IN 1941. ROMMEL BECAME A MASTER OF DESERT WARFARE TACTICS WITH HIS ABILITY TO EXPLOIT OPPORTUNITIES, EMPLOY UNORTHODOX METHODS, AND DEPLOY HIS ARMORED FORCES TO MAXIMUM EFFECT. AFTER RECAPTURING TOBRUK IN 1942, HE PUSHED THE ALLIES BACK TO EL ALAMEIN IN EGYPT. THE "DESERT FOX" WAS PROMOTED TO FIELD MARSHAL, HAVING LED THE AFRIKA KORPS TO A STRING OF VICTORIES.

Q Turkey and the Soviet Union were allies of Yugoslavia in April 1941. True or false?

A True. But when Germany attacked Yugoslavia neither wished to get involved in a conflict against Europe's premier military machine, and so avoided criticizing the German invasion. Stalin, in particular, wished to avoid worsening his already delicate relations with Hitler, in the hope that the Führer would not invade the Soviet Union while Britain remained undefeated.

Q Which German general accepted the Greek capitulation in April 1941?

A Colonel-General Alfred Jodl, chief of staff of OKW.

Q What was Operation Demon?

A The British evacuation from Greece in April 1941.

Q How did the SS *Leibstandarte* Division cross the Corinth Canal in April 1941?

A In requisitioned fishing boats.

Q Why did the Germans decide to invade Crete in May 1941?

A The Allied possession of Crete posed a major threat to Axis operations. From there, British aircraft could interdict the naval convoys crossing the Mediterranean to resupply Rommel's forces in North Africa and could still undertake long-range missions to attack the Ploesti oilfields in Romania.

> " THE WAR AGAINST RUSSIA WILL BE SUCH
> THAT IT CANNOT BE CONDUCTED
> # IN A CHIVALROUS
> ## FASHION "
> ADOLF HITLER, MARCH 1941

Q What was the codename of the German invasion of Crete?

A Operation Mercury.

Q What happened at the Battle of Keren, Eritrea, in March 1941?

A Italian troops were forced to retreat toward the capital, Asmara. The Italians lost 3,000 men compared to British fatalities of 536. Asmara fell five days later.

DID YOU KNOW

DURING THE NORTH AFRICAN CAMPAIGN, BOTH THE GERMANS AND BRITISH DENIGRATED THE FIGHTING CAPABILITIES OF ITALIAN TROOPS. AFTER THE WAR, THE ANGLO-GERMAN ACCOUNTS OF THE CAMPAIGN DEVELOPED THE IDEA OF THE ITALIANS AS A "NONMARTIAL" RACE, IN A CARICATURE BASED ON THE ALLEGED "LATIN" TEMPERAMENT. THE ITALIANS SUPPLIED THE BULK OF THE AXIS TROOPS FIGHTING IN NORTH AFRICA, AND TOO OFTEN THE GERMAN ARMY UNFAIRLY RIDICULED ITALIAN MILITARY EFFECTIVENESS EITHER DUE TO ITS OWN ARROGANCE OR TO CONCEAL ITS OWN MISTAKES AND FAILURES. IN REALITY, A SIGNIFICANT NUMBER OF ITALIAN UNITS FOUGHT SKILLFULLY IN NORTH AFRICA, AND MANY "GERMAN" VICTORIES WERE THE RESULT OF ITALIAN SKILL-AT-ARMS AND A COMBINED AXIS EFFORT. THE BRITISH CREATED SOMETHING OF A MYTH AROUND ROMMEL, SINCE THEY PREFERRED TO JUSTIFY THEIR DEFEATS WITH THE PRESENCE IN THE ENEMY CAMP OF AN EXCEPTIONAL GENERAL, RATHER THAN RECOGNIZE THE SUPERIOR QUALITIES OF THE COMBATANTS, WHETHER ITALIAN OR GERMAN. THAT CERTAIN ITALIAN FORMATIONS FOUGHT AS EFFECTIVELY AS THEY DID REMAINED AN IMPRESSIVE FEAT CONSIDERING THAT ON THE HOME FRONT ITALY'S POPULATION HAD LITTLE STOMACH FOR THE WAR.

75

Q Why did the United States occupy Greenland in April 1941?

A To prevent the Danish colony falling into German hands.

Q Who was the commander of the Crete garrison in May 1941?

A Major General Bernard Freyberg.

> ## " TOWERING COLUMNS OF WATER SPURTING INTO THE AIR
>
> THE FIRST SALVO FROM HOOD FELL JUST ASTERN—ONE COULD SEE THE GREAT
>
> Esmond Knight, on board
> HMS *Prince of Wales*,
> May 1941 "

Q What was the size of the Allied garrison on Crete?

A 42,000 troops, including 11,000 Greek soldiers.

Q What were the problems facing the garrison on the eve of the German assault?

A First, many of the British, Commonwealth, and Greek forces that had withdrawn from the mainland had managed to transport only a fraction of their equipment with them. Second, the RAF had taken heavy casualties on the mainland and was able to offer only minimal air cover to the ground forces.

Q How did the Germans plan to conquer Crete?

A Some 16,000 élite airborne troops—both paratroopers and gliderborne soldiers—of the 7th Parachute Division would land on Crete's three main airfields at Maleme, Retimo, and Heraklion, as well as near the capital, Canea. Once these forces had captured these landing strips, German aircraft would transport some 3,000 reinforcements from the 5th Mountain Division to these locations. Simultaneously, maritime convoys would carry a further 7,000 mountain soldiers to Crete for amphibious assault operations.

Q Who was the commander of Germany's paratroopers in 1941?

A General Kurt Student.

Q What was the main gun on the Panzer III Ausf G?

A The 50mm KwK L/42 gun.

Q What was the decisive moment in the battle for Crete in May 1941?

A On May 23 Freyberg ordered his forces at Maleme to withdraw to Canea. The Germans immediately followed up the enemy withdrawal, and prepared themselves for an attack that would break through the British defenses at Canea and enable them to race east to rescue their encircled comrades at Retimo and Heraklion.

77

DID YOU KNOW

DURING GERMANY'S EARLY BLITZKRIEG CAMPAIGNS, PARTICULARLY THAT IN FRANCE DURING MAY–JUNE 1940, THE GERMAN ARMY HAD EXTENSIVELY USED AIR ASSAULTS BY PARACHUTE AND GLIDERBORNE TROOPS TO SUSTAIN THE TEMPO AND MOMENTUM OF THE ADVANCING GROUND TROOPS. THE CATASTROPHIC LOSSES THAT THE GERMAN AIRBORNE FORCES SUFFERED DURING THEIR MAY 1941 AIR ASSAULT ON CRETE, HOWEVER, CONVINCED HITLER THAT SUCH OPERATIONS WERE NOW TOO COSTLY TO REMAIN STRATEGICALLY JUSTIFIED. AT A MEDAL CEREMONY IN MID-JULY 1941, HITLER INFORMED GENERAL STUDENT, COMMANDER OF GERMAN AIRBORNE TROOPS, THAT THE EXPERIENCE OF CRETE HAD LED HIM TO CONCLUDE THAT THE DAY OF THE LARGE-SCALE AIR ASSAULT WAS OVER.

Q Why did Rudolf Hess fly to Britain in May 1941?

A Hess believed a diplomatic coup was possible if he could have an audience with George VI, whom he believed he could persuade to dismiss Churchill. Peace could then be implemented between the two countries and they could act in concert against a common enemy: the Soviet Union.

Q What name did Hess give on landing in Britain by parachute?

A On landing he gave his name as Captain Horn and asked to be escorted to the Duke of Hamilton, whom he had met at the 1936 Berlin Olympic Games.

DID YOU KNOW

AS WITH OTHER BLITZKRIEG CAMPAIGNS, THE USE OF THE LUFTWAFFE WAS CRUCIAL TO GERMAN SUCCESS IN THE BALKANS. IN YUGOSLAVIA ACTUAL OPERATIONS WERE CARRIED OUT BY VIII AIR CORPS UNDER LIEUTENANT GENERAL WOLFRAM VON RICHTHOFEN. THE WEHRMACHT INAUGURATED ITS ATTACK ON YUGOSLAVIA, AT HITLER'S PERSONAL INSISTENCE, WITH OPERATION RETRIBUTION, A TERROR BOMBING ATTACK ON BELGRADE, THE YUGOSLAV CAPITAL. DESPITE THE YUGOSLAV DECLARATION OF APRIL 4 THAT BELGRADE WAS AN "OPEN CITY" FREE OF MILITARY UNITS, SOME 500 GERMAN AIRCRAFT POUNDED THE CITY DURING APRIL 6–7. THESE AERIAL ATTACKS DEVASTATED LARGE PARTS OF THE CITY AND KILLED PERHAPS AS MANY AS 6,000 CIVILIANS. IN ADDITION TO THE PROPAGANDA BENEFITS OBTAINED FROM THIS DEMONSTRATION OF GERMAN AERIAL POWER, THE OPERATION ALSO ACHIEVED THE USEFUL TACTICAL MISSION OF SMASHING THE YUGOSLAV COMMAND AND CONTROL FACILITIES LOCATED IN THE CITY.

Q Did Hess meet George VI?

A No. He was immediately arrested.

Q Which ship sank the British battlecruiser HMS *Hood* in May 1941?

A The German battleship *Bismarck*.

"

IF WE SEE THAT GERMANY IS WINNING THE WAR WE OUGHT TO HELP RUSSIA

HARRY S. TRUMAN, JULY 24, 1941

"

79

Q What was the Soviet-Japanese Neutrality Pact of April 1941?

A The pact stated that each party would "respect the territorial integrity and inviolability of the other party; and should one of the Contracting Parties become the object of hostilities on the part of one or several third powers, the other Contracting Party will observe neutrality throughout the duration of the conflict." The pact would initially last for five years.

Q How did the signatories to the pact benefit?

A The pact freed up Red Army divisions facing the Japanese in the East for deployment elsewhere and allowed Japan to concentrate on its ambitions in China and Southeast Asia.

Q What was Operation Brevity?

A A British offensive in North Africa in May 1941. The British attacked the Axis positions at Sollum, the Halfaya Pass, and Capuzzo.

Q Was it a success?

A No. After a successful initial British advance some 15 miles (24 km) west, Rommel counterattacked and recaptured all the ground his forces had just relinquished.

Q Who led the pro-Axis coup in Iraq in April 1941?

A Rashid Ali.

Q What was the codename of the German attack on the Soviet Union in June 1941?

A Operation Barbarossa.

Q Who was Barbarossa?

A A medieval German emperor who had fought the Slavs.

" GIVE US THE TOOLS, AND WE WILL
FINISH THE JOB
WINSTON CHURCHILL TO PRESIDENT ROOSEVELT,
FEBRUARY 9, 1941 **"**

DID YOU KNOW

THE OBJECTIVES OF OPERATION BARBAROSSA REMAINED A CONFUSED MIXTURE OF CONTRADICTORY AIMS. THE PLAN INCLUDED ECONOMIC OBJECTS SUCH AS THE AGRICULTURE OF THE UKRAINE, THE INDUSTRY OF THE DON BASIN, AND THE OIL OF THE CAUCASUS; IT TARGETED THE POPULATION CENTERS THAT DOUBLED AS KEY COMMUNICATIONS NODES, SUCH AS MOSCOW, KIEV, AND KHARKOV; AND IT ALSO AIMED FOR MARITIME CENTERS SUCH AS LENINGRAD, ROSTOV, AND SEVASTOPOL, WHOSE CAPTURE WOULD PROTECT THE FLANKS OF THE AXIS ADVANCE. THE PURSUIT OF SO MANY DIFFERENT TARGETS LEFT THE AXIS INVASION FORCES WITHOUT A CLEAR, OVERRIDING OBJECTIVE TOWARD WHICH THEIR MAIN EFFORT COULD BE DIRECTED.

Q In Barbarossa, who commanded Army Group North?

A Field Marshal Ritter Wilhelm von Leeb.

Q In Barbarossa, who commanded Army Group Center?

A Field Marshal Fedor von Bock.

Q In Barbarossa, who commanded Army Group South?

A Field Marshal Gerd von Rundstedt.

Q What was Army Group North's Barbarossa mission?

A To capture Leningrad, link up with Finnish forces pushing south from Karelia, and then push on to capture Archangel on the White Sea.

Q **What was Army Group Center's Barbarossa mission?**

A To advance through Belorussia along the direct route via Smolensk to Moscow, and thence through Gorky and Kazan to the Ural Mountains.

Q **What was Army Group South's Barbarossa mission?**

A To advance through the Ukraine—via Kiev and Kharkov—to Rostov on the Sea of Azov, and thence thrust southeast into the oil-rich Caucasus and east through Kazakhstan to the southern Urals around Orsk.

Q **Führer Directive 21 (Case Barbarossa) set out the strategic objective of Barbarossa. What was this?**

A The destruction of the bulk of the Red Army located in the western areas of the Soviet Union. The Germans sought to destroy the Red Army in the 250 mile (400 km) border region up to the Dnieper and Dvina rivers. Once the German Army had achieved this task, it was to push on toward the Ural mountains.

Q **Who was the commander of the German Second Panzer Group during Operation Barbarossa?**

A Colonel General Heinz Guderian.

Q What was Hitler's Commissar Order of June 1941?

A Hitler's Directive for the Treatment of Political Commissars stated that Red Army commissars would be immediately shot when captured.

Q What was the Soviet equivalent of a German army group?

A A front.

Q What was the Lucy Spy Ring?

A A Soviet espionage group, part of the so-called Red Orchestra spy group. It contained senior German figures.

DID YOU KNOW

IN DECEMBER 1940, A SERIES OF OKH WAR GAMES AND INDEPENDENT STUDIES REGARDING A GERMAN WAR IN THE EAST, CONDUCTED UNDER THE DIRECTION OF HEAD QUARTERMASTER OF THE GENERAL STAFF, MAJOR GENERAL FRIEDRICH PAULUS, CONCLUDED THAT GERMAN FORCES WERE "BARELY SUFFICIENT FOR THE PURPOSE" ASSIGNED TO THEM. IN ADDITION, THE WEHRMACHT WOULD HAVE NO RESERVES LEFT BY THE TIME IT REACHED MOSCOW, FORCING THE ARMY TO UNDERTAKE AN ATTACK AGAINST THE CITY WITH NO REINFORCEMENTS. AND THE VOLGA–ARCHANGEL LINE WAS A TARGET THAT WAS BEYOND THE REACH OF THE WEHRMACHT. MORE WORRYINGLY, THE STUDIES REVEALED THAT IN A CAMPAIGN AREA THE SIZE OF THE WESTERN USSR, THE PANZER COLUMNS AND SLOWER-MOVING INFANTRY WOULD QUICKLY BECOME SEPARATED, LEAVING THE FLANKS OF THE PANZER FORCES DANGEROUSLY EXPOSED.

Q What important piece of intelligence did the Lucy Spy Ring send to Moscow in mid-June 1941?

A That the German attack on the USSR would begin on June 22.

Q Who was the president of Turkey in 1941?

A President Inönü.

Q What was Turkey's position in 1941?

A Despite German pressure on Turkey to side with the Axis powers, President Inönü was of the opinion that the Axis powers could not win the war. And despite pressure, Turkey did not allow Axis troops, ships, or aircraft to pass through or over Turkey and its territorial waters.

Q What was the strength of a Soviet mechanized corps in June 1941?

A 36,000 men and 1,031 tanks.

DID YOU KNOW

THERE IS LITTLE DOUBT THAT THE GERMAN CAMPAIGN IN THE BALKANS IN THE SPRING OF 1941 HAD A DETRIMENTAL EFFECT ON THE OUTCOME OF BARBAROSSA. THE DECISION TO INVADE YUGOSLAVIA AND GREECE WAS MADE ON MARCH 27, POSTPONING THE START OF BARBAROSSA FROM MID-MAY. ON APRIL 7, OKH DELAYED BARBAROSSA AGAIN, BY FOUR WEEKS, THUS PUTTING THE START DATE IN MID-JUNE. ONLY ON JUNE 17 DID HITLER SET THE START DATE FOR THE INVASION OF THE SOVIET UNION FOR JUNE 22.

**❝ DON'T LET'S BE BEASTLY TO THE GERMANS,
DO LET'S BE BEASTLY TO
THE HUNS ❞**
NOËL COWARD SONG, 1941

Q **What was the Soviet Stavka?**

A *Shtab vierhovnogo komandovani*—Headquarters of the Main Command.

Q **What prompted Finland to declare war on the Soviet Union in June 1941?**

A On June 25, a force of 500 Soviet bombers attacked cities and airfields in Finland. Finnish Prime Minister Rangell announced that, as a result, Finland was at war with the USSR.

Q **Who became commander of the Soviet Northwest Front at the end of June 1941?**

A General Petr Sobennikov.

Q **At the end of June how were the German Second and Third Panzer Groups reorganized?**

A They were brought under the overall command of Field Marshal Günther von Kluge's Fourth Army, which was renamed the Fourth Panzer Army.

Q What was a Pak 38?

A A German 50mm antitank gun.

Q What was a Soviet *glavkom*?

A A theater command. Several were established in July 1941 to coordinate front defenses more effectively. *Glavkom* Northwest was headed by Marshal Voroshilov (Northern and Northwest Fronts and Baltic and Northern Fleets), Marshal Timoshenko commanded *Glavkom* West (Western Front and Pinsk Flotilla), and *Glavkom* Southwest was under Marshal Budenny (Southwestern and Southern Fronts and the Black Sea Fleet).

" BELIEVE! OBEY! FIGHT! "
ITALIAN WAR SLOGAN

Q Who replaced General Sir Archibald Wavell as the Middle East commander of British forces in July 1941?

A General Sir Claude Auchinleck.

Q Why was he replaced?

A Wavell's Middle East Command had achieved considerable success against numerically superior Italian forces despite supply shortages. Further commitments in Greece, Iraq, and Syria then overstretched his forces. Nevertheless, Churchill wanted a decisive offensive in the desert, and his failure to achieve this led to his transfer.

DID YOU KNOW

Q **What does *Einsatzgruppen* mean?**

A Special Action Groups.

Q **What was their task?**

A To follow immediately behind the German armies as they advanced into the USSR, and round up Jews, gypsies, political commissars, and anyone else who was perceived by the Nazis as being a real or potential threat to the "New Order" being established in the East. All persons thus taken were to be executed immediately.

Q **What was their composition?**

A Each one contained a mixture of Waffen-SS, Gestapo, Kripo (Criminal Police), SD (Security Police), and regular uniformed police personnel.

Q **Who commanded Einsatzgruppe A?**

A SS-Brigadeführer Franz Stahlecker.

Q Who commanded *Einsatzgruppe* B?

A SS-Gruppenführer Arthur Nebe.

Q Who commanded *Einsatzgruppe* C?

A SS-Oberführer Dr Otto Rasch.

Q Who commanded *Einsatzgruppe* D?

A SS-Gruppenführer Otto Ohlendorf.

❝ I RECEIVED MY FIRST WAR DECORATION,
NAMELY, THE TANK ASSAULT
MEDAL. I WEAR
IT PROUDLY
❞
SERGEANT KARL FUCHS, GERMAN SOLDIER,
EASTERN FRONT, JUNE 1941

Q Why did U.S. troops move into Iceland in July 1941?

A To protect shipping from German U-boat attacks.

Q To which position did Stalin appoint himself on July 21, 1941?

A Defense Commissar.

Q Why was the Fourth Panzer Army disbanded at the end of July 1941?

A The Fourth Panzer Army was disbanded, with the Fourth Army becoming an infantry force once again. Guderian's Second Panzer Group was thus removed from under Kluge's command and placed directly under the control of Army Group Center. This was due to disagreements between Guderian and Kluge regarding strategy and objectives, which were having an adverse effect on operations.

Q Which was the most successful U-boat of the war?

A *U-48*. During her career she sank 51 merchant vessels and one warship. She was scuttled on May 3, 1945.

Q Which Vichy French commander surrendered Syria to the Allies in July 1941?

A General Henri Dentz.

89

DID YOU KNOW

IN MARCH 1941, THE U.S. CONGRESS PASSED THE LEND-LEASE ACT AND GAVE ROOSEVELT WIDE-RANGING POWERS TO SUPPLY GOODS AND SERVICES TO "ANY COUNTRY WHOSE DEFENSE THE PRESIDENT DEEMS VITAL TO THE DEFENSE OF THE UNITED STATES." ALMOST $13 BILLION HAD BEEN ALLOCATED TO THE LEND-LEASE ARRANGEMENT BY NOVEMBER 1941. ALTHOUGH BRITAIN NOW HAD THE OPPORTUNITY TO INCREASE THE AMOUNT OF U.S. IMPORTS, HER OWN WAR PRODUCTION HAD BEEN INCREASING DURING THIS PERIOD. FOOD AND OIL FROM THE UNITED STATES, HOWEVER, WAS STILL CRUCIAL TO HER SURVIVAL.

Q Who headed the Czech government-in-exile?

A Edouard Benes.

Q With which state did this government sign a mutual assistance agreement in July 1941?

A The Soviet Union.

Q What was the British Operation Substance of July 1941?

A The British transportation of supplies from Gibraltar to Malta.

Q Name the two Soviet pockets destroyed on the Eastern Front in early August 1941.

A The Smolensk and Uman Pockets.

DID YOU KNOW

IN AUGUST 1939, HITLER AND STALIN HAD SIGNED A NONAGGRESSION TREATY, THE MOLOTOV-RIBBENTROP PACT. THE PACT DID NOT, HOWEVER, ALTER THE UNDERLYING TENSION THAT EXISTED BETWEEN THE TWO COUNTRIES. RATHER, THE TREATY WAS SIMPLY A TEMPORARY PIECE OF CYNICAL EXPEDIENCY BY BOTH LEADERS. IN THE PACT THE TWO AGREED JOINTLY TO INVADE AND THEN DIVIDE POLAND, WHILE STALIN ALSO GUARANTEED TO SEND LARGE GRAIN EXPORTS TO GERMANY UNTIL MID-JUNE 1941—NOTE THAT DATE! THUS, HITLER OBTAINED A FREE HAND FROM A QUIESCENT STALIN TO DEAL WITH THE WEST IN 1940 WITHOUT FEAR OF THE TRADITIONAL GERMAN STRATEGIC SPECTER OF A TWO-FRONT WAR. THE PERIOD ALSO GAVE STALIN TIME TO PREPARE FOR A WAR HE WAS CERTAIN WOULD COME.

“ THE HEAT WAS TREMENDOUS, THOUGH
INTERSPERSED WITH SUDDEN
SHOWERS
GENERAL BLUMENTRITT, GERMAN ARMY,
RUSSIA, JULY 1941 **”**

Q **What was the Russian Katyusha multiple rocket launcher better known as?**

A Stalin's Organ.

Q **Why did Britain and the Soviet Union invade Iran in August 1941?**

A Because of the British and American need to transport war materials across Iran to the Soviet Union, which would have violated Iranian neutrality.

Q **Was the invasion justified?**

A Yes. The occupation of Iran was vital to the Allied cause. Britain, the USSR, and the United States together would ship more than 5 million tons (5.08 million tonnes) of munitions and other war materiel across Iran to the USSR between 1941 and 1945.

Q **At which port did the first convoy of aid from Britain to the Soviet Union land?**

A Archangel.

91

Q What was the German Operation Beowulf of September 1941?

A An amphibious assault against the Estonian islands on the Eastern Front, which were defended by 23,600 troops and 140 artillery pieces of the Soviet Eighth Army.

Q Who took command of Vichy French forces in North Africa in August 1941?

A Admiral Jean Darlan.

Q What was the base of the Soviet Baltic Fleet?

A Leningrad.

"CARELESS TALK COSTS LIVES"
BRITISH POSTER, 1941

Q What was the codename for the German assault on Moscow?

A Operation Typhoon.

Q How did the Germans intend to capture Moscow?

A The Ninth Army and Third Panzer Group would drive to the north of the city, and the Second Panzer Group and Second Army would attack from the south. In this way Moscow would be enveloped by a double pincer movement, with the panzer formations forming the outer pincers.

DID YOU KNOW

TIMING HAD A CRITICAL INFLUENCE ON THE OUTCOME OF THE MOSCOW
ATTACK, CODENAMED TYPHOON, BUT THERE WERE OTHER FACTORS THAT
INFLUENCED ITS COURSE. FIRST, ALTHOUGH ARMY GROUP NORTH HAD
SUCCEEDED IN ENCIRCLING LENINGRAD IN EARLY SEPTEMBER, THE FACT
THAT THE CITY WAS STILL IN SOVIET HANDS MEANT THAT ARMY GROUP
NORTH COULD NOT CONTRIBUTE TO OPERATION TYPHOON BY MOUNTING
A FLANKING ATTACK AGAINST THE SOVIET CAPITAL FROM THE NORTHWEST.
IN ADDITION, HITLER'S INSISTENCE THAT ARMY GROUP SOUTH SHOULD
DIRECT ITS COMBAT STRENGTH TOWARD THE CONQUEST OF THE DONETS
BASIN, ROSTOV, AND THE CRIMEA MEANT IT COULD NOT PARTICIPATE
DIRECTLY IN TYPHOON. NEVERTHELESS, BOTH HITLER AND OKH
BELIEVED THAT ARMY GROUP CENTER, SUITABLY REINFORCED, COULD
DEFEAT RED ARMY FORCES IN FRONT OF MOSCOW AND CAPTURE THE CITY
BEFORE THE END OF THE YEAR.

Q How many Soviet troops were captured in the Kiev Pocket in September 1941?

A 665,000.

Q What happened at Babi Yar in September 1941?

A A German SS unit, *Sonderkommando* 4a, working in conjunction with Ukrainian auxiliary police, began the mass murder of Kiev's Jews at Babi Yar ravine. In two days of shooting, 33,771 Jews were murdered. Tens of thousands of others would be slaughtered at Babi Yar over the next months.

Q Which Luftwaffe ace sank the Soviet battleship *Marat* in September 1941?

A Hans-Ulrich Rudel.

Q **What was the Atlantic Charter?**

A Formulated in August 1941 by Winston Churchill and Franklin D. Roosevelt, it was an ideology that asserted liberal policies that articulated their intentions not to acquire any territories or change national borders without the support of the populations concerned. People were also to be granted self-determination regarding how they were governed, and equal access was to be given to economic resources.

Q **Jews in Germany were forced to wear what symbol from September 1, 1941?**

A A yellow Star of David.

Q **Which post was Reinhard Heydrich appointed to in September 1941?**

A Protector of Bohemia and Moravia.

Q **What ancient curse did Heydrich violate when he assumed his new position?**

A Heydrich was shown the crown jewels of Czechoslovakia by President Hacha, who told him of an intriguing legend that surrounded them. It was said that any person not the true heir who put the crown on his head was sure to die. It is said that Heydrich laughed and placed the crown on his head.

Q Which German auxiliary cruiser fought the Australian cruiser HMAS *Sydney* in November 1941?

A The *Kormoran.*

Q What happened in this encounter?

A The cruiser was deceived by the disguised German raider's pretence of being an innocent Dutch freighter and came too close. The concealed guns quickly inflicted serious damage and a torpedo hit damaged the *Sydney* seriously. The cruiser replied effectively with her guns, but both ships caught fire and were heavily damaged. The *Sydney* drifted away and was never seen again, and the *Kormoran* sank.

DID YOU KNOW

HITLER'S DIRECTIVE 33 OF JULY 19, 1941, SHIFTED THE GERMAN MAIN EFFORT SOUTH AWAY FROM MOSCOW TOWARD THE UKRAINE. HERE, AFTER MID-AUGUST, THE GERMANS PLANNED TO ENACT ANOTHER GREAT DOUBLE ENVELOPMENT THROUGH THE COOPERATION OF KLEIST'S FIRST PANZER GROUP FROM ARMY GROUP SOUTH WITH GUDERIAN'S SECOND PANZER GROUP FROM ARMY GROUP CENTER. BACK IN MID-JULY, KLEIST'S ARMOR HAD COMMENCED ITS PREPARATORY OPERATIONS WITH A THRUST SOUTHEAST TOWARD THE RIVER DNIEPER TO TURN THE SOUTHERN FLANK OF A MASS OF IMMOBILE ENEMY INFANTRY WEST OF KIEV. ELEMENTS OF KLEIST'S FORMATION ALSO THRUST SOUTH TO LINK UP ON AUGUST 3 WITH THE SEVENTEENTH ARMY TO CREATE AN ANCILLARY ENCIRCLEMENT OF 200,000 SOVIET INFANTRYMEN AT UMAN. MEANWHILE, KLEIST'S FORCES CONTINUED TO THRUST RAPIDLY EAST UNTIL, ON AUGUST 12, THEY CAPTURED KREMENCHUG ON THE DNIEPER RIVER, 110 MILES (177 KM) BEHIND THE MAIN NORTH-SOUTH SOVIET DEFENSIVE LINE BETWEEN GOMEL AND KIEV. IF KLEIST'S PANZERS COULD PUSH NORTH TO MEET THE INTENDED THRUST SOUTH BY GUDERIAN'S ARMOR, THE ENSUING ENCIRCLEMENT WOULD ENGULF FIVE SOVIET ARMIES. THEY COULD AND DID, AND THE TRAP CLOSED ON 665,000 RED ARMY SOLDIERS IN THE KIEV POCKET.

Q Was the German Army that invaded the Soviet Union in 1941 fully motorized?

A No. Contrary to popular belief, the 1941 German Army was not a motorized force. Outside its small number of elite mechanized divisions, the bulk of the army comprised infantry divisions equipped with horse-drawn vehicles; some 625,000 German Army horses invaded the Soviet Union in 1941.

Q Why did the Germans have problems using the Russian rail network in 1941?

A The Germans planned to use Soviet railroads to resupply their troops, but as these were on a wider gauge than the European lines, engineers had to regauge every mile of track before German locomotives could operate along them.

Q What was a *Vernichtungskrieg*?

A A war of racial annihilation, as waged by Nazi Germany against Bolshevik Russia.

DID YOU KNOW

ON JUNE 23–24, 1941, THE SECOND AND THIRD DAYS OF OPERATION BARBAROSSA, ELEMENTS OF BOTH HOEPNER'S FOURTH PANZER GROUP IN LITHUANIA AND KLEIST'S FIRST PANZER GROUP NEAR THE BUG RIVER EXPERIENCED THEIR FIRST ENCOUNTER WITH THE NEW SOVIET KV-1 HEAVY TANK. TO THE GERMAN TROOPS' DISMAY, AT RANGES AS LOW AS 2700 FT (820 M), EVEN THE ROUNDS FIRED BY THE 50MM KWK L/42 GUN MOUNTED IN THEIR MOST MODERN PANZER III TANKS SIMPLY BOUNCED OFF THE FRONT OF THESE SOVIET HEAVY TANKS.

" A NEW ORDER FOR EUROPE "

THE SLOGAN TAKEN FROM
THE REPORT OF A MEETING BETWEEN
HITLER AND MUSSOLINI, AUGUST 1941

Q **What were panzergrenadiers?**

A German motorized infantry.

Q **During the first 48 hours of Operation Barbarossa the Luftwaffe destroyed enemy aircraft at a rate of one every 80 seconds. True or false?**

A True. During the first 48 hours of Barbarossa the Luftwaffe committed its 2,150 available first-line aircraft to a concentrated counter-air campaign to secure aerial superiority over the theater. Aided by total surprise, massed German aerial formations attacked the rows of enemy planes sitting on the runways of the western Soviet Union. In these first 48 hours alone, the Luftwaffe succeeded in destroying 2,200 Soviet aircraft.

Q **Why did Stalin lift the ban on religion throughout the USSR in October 1941?**

A To boost civilian morale.

Q **Why did the Finns refuse to attack Leningrad in 1941?**

A Following the Winter War of 1939–1940, Finland was eager to get back the territory she had lost to the USSR. When Operation Barbarossa was launched, the Finns were quick to point out that they were participating only to retake Finnish territory lost in 1940.

Q Which leader stated in November 1941: "The German invaders are straining their last forces. There is no doubt that Germany cannot keep up such an effort for any long time"?

A Joseph Stalin in Red Square, Moscow, on the anniversary of the October Revolution.

Q Which general was placed in command of U.S. forces in the Far East in July 1941?

A Douglas MacArthur.

Q Which firm manufactured the German Bf 109 fighter?

A Messerschmitt.

Q What was the Royal Air Force's first monoplane fighter?

A The Hawker Hurricane.

" IT WAS A STRANGE FEELING TO
BE DROPPED SUDDENLY INTO AN
ALIEN LAND WITH ORDERS
TO CONQUER IT
BARON VON DER HEYDTE, GERMAN PARATROOPER,
CRETE, MAY 1941 "

DID YOU KNOW

THE INVASION OF THE USSR BY NAZI GERMANY WAS A DISASTER FOR THE SOVIET ECONOMY. BY THE END OF 1941, FOR EXAMPLE, THE USSR HAD LOST THE GRAIN LANDS OF BELORUSSIA AND THE UKRAINE; ONE-THIRD OF ITS RAIL NETWORK; THREE-QUARTERS OF ITS IRON ORE, COAL, AND STEEL SUPPLY; AND 40 PERCENT OF ITS ELECTRICITY GENERATING CAPACITY. THIS CATASTROPHE WOULD HAVE BEEN MUCH WORSE HAD IT NOT BEEN FOR THE EVACUATION OF HUNDREDS OF FACTORIES AND TENS OF THOUSANDS OF WORKERS EAST TO THE URALS, TO THE VOLGA REGION, TO KAZAKHSTAN, AND TO EASTERN SIBERIA. THE SCALE OF THE MOVEMENT WAS ASTOUNDING: BETWEEN JULY AND DECEMBER 1941, 1,523 ENTERPRISES, THE MAJORITY STEEL, IRON, AND ENGINEERING PLANTS, WERE TRANSPORTED EAST.

Q What type of aircraft was the British Handley Page Hampden?

A A medium bomber.

Q How many crew did it have?

A Four.

Q What was its nickname?

A The "Flying Suitcase."

Q Which German battlecruiser was torpedoed by British aircraft at Brest in April 1941?

A *Gneisenau.*

Q What type of warship was the German *Emden*?

A Light cruiser.

DID YOU KNOW

TIMING HAD A CRITICAL INFLUENCE ON THE OUTCOME OF THE MOSCOW ATTACK, CODENAMED TYPHOON, BUT THERE WERE OTHER FACTORS THAT INFLUENCED ITS COURSE. FIRST, ALTHOUGH ARMY GROUP NORTH HAD SUCCEEDED IN ENCIRCLING LENINGRAD IN EARLY SEPTEMBER, THE FACT THAT THE CITY WAS STILL IN SOVIET HANDS MEANT THAT ARMY GROUP NORTH COULD NOT CONTRIBUTE TO OPERATION TYPHOON BY MOUNTING A FLANKING ATTACK AGAINST THE SOVIET CAPITAL FROM THE NORTHWEST. IN ADDITION, HITLER'S INSISTENCE THAT ARMY GROUP SOUTH SHOULD DIRECT ITS COMBAT STRENGTH TOWARD THE CONQUEST OF THE DONETS BASIN, ROSTOV, AND THE CRIMEA MEANT IT COULD NOT PARTICIPATE DIRECTLY IN TYPHOON. NEVERTHELESS, BOTH HITLER AND OKH BELIEVED THAT ARMY GROUP CENTER, SUITABLY REINFORCED, COULD DEFEAT RED ARMY FORCES IN FRONT OF MOSCOW AND CAPTURE THE CITY BEFORE THE END OF THE YEAR. THUS, ON SEPTEMBER 15, OKH ORDERED THE FOURTH PANZER GROUP TO WITHDRAW HALF ITS ARMOR AND TRANSFER IT TO ARMY GROUP CENTER. THIS TRANSFER BEGAN TWO DAYS LATER. UNFORTUNATELY FOR ARMY GROUP CENTER, THE LATE CONCLUSION OF THE BATTLE OF KIEV AND THE TIME-CONSUMING REGROUPING OF REINFORCEMENTS FROM THE NORTH AND SOUTH MEANT THAT PREPARATIONS FOR TYPHOON WERE CONCLUDED ONLY BY THE END OF SEPTEMBER. IN ADDITION, THE PANZER DIVISIONS INVOLVED WERE ONLY 40–50 PERCENT OF THEIR ORIGINAL COMBAT STRENGTH.

> ## THE MESSERSCHMITTS COME IN CLOSE FOR THE KILL. AT THIS
> # RANGE THEIR CAMOUFLAGE LOOKS DIRTY
> "JOHNNIE" JOHNSON, RAF FIGHTER PILOT, AUGUST 1941

Q Which German pocket battleship was damaged by British aircraft off Norway in June 1941?

A The *Lützow*.

Q Which British aircraft carrier supported the British offensive against the Italians in Somaliland in 1941?

A HMS *Hermes*.

Q Which British warship was made famous in the film *In Which We Serve*?

A HMS *Kelly*.

Q What calibre was the German Light Field Howitzer 18 (le FH 18)?

A 105mm.

Q What was a *Nebelwerfer*?

A A German multiple rocket launcher.

Q On the Eastern Front, the Sinyavino Offensive took place near which city?

A Leningrad.

Q What was the title of the 1st SS Panzer Division?

A The *Leibstandarte* Division.

Q Who commanded this division in 1941?

A Josef "Sepp" Dietrich.

> **AFTER THREE DAYS OF HEAVY FIGHTING WE ARE FINALLY GRANTED A WELL-DESERVED REST**
> SERGEANT KARL FUCHS, 25TH PANZER REGIMENT, RUSSIA, JUNE 25, 1941

Q What was the name of the area of the Ukraine controlled by the Romanians between the Rivers Bug and Dniester?

A Transnistria.

Q Which city, the capital of the Crimea, was captured by the Germans in early November 1941?

A Simferopol.

DID YOU KNOW

The question of how much the United States knew about the Japanese attack on Pearl Harbor has excited conspiracy theorists and historians alike ever since that fateful day. The more fanciful theories suggest that the U.S. knew an attack was imminent, but allowed it to happen so that the U.S. could enter the war on the Allies' side. They point to the fact that U.S. carriers were not in the harbor when the attack took place, and that the wealth of intelligence pointing to a Japanese attack leading up to December 1941 was impossible to miss. Whilst it was certainly unfortunate that the intelligence collected did not raise the alarm earlier, and the coincidence that the carriers were absent is almost unbelievable, simple intelligence failure seems to be the most likely cause of the surprise.

Q When the Japanese sent their forces into the south of Indochina in July 1941, how did the Western powers retaliate?

A Japanese assets in the U.S. were seized, and the U.S. placed a ferocious trade embargo on Japan, which reduced her oil supplies by 90 percent. The British and the Dutch also imposed their own economic sanctions, and in total Japan's foreign trade was cut by 75 percent.

Q Did the Allied response push the Japanese toward war?

A Yes. The oil embargo meant that the Japanese fleet would be confined to port by the spring of 1942.

Q Who commanded the Imperial Japanese Navy in 1941?

A Admiral Isoroku Yamamoto.

Q What was the size of the Japanese Army in 1941?

A 1.8 million men.

Q How many aircraft did the Japanese Air Force have on the eve of Pearl Harbor?

A 2,000.

> **"** NOTHING IN THE LANDSCAPE TO REST
> OR DISTRACT THE EYE; NOTHING
> ## TO HEAR BUT ROARING
> ## TRUCK ENGINES
> PRIVATE CRIMP, 7TH ARMOURED DIVISION, LIBYA,
> OCTOBER 1941 **"**

Q What was the U.S. Two Ocean Naval Expansion Act?

A A massive naval building program which would set a ratio of Japanese to U.S. ships of 3:10 by 1944.

Q Which panzer group was nearing the Soviet city of Rostov in early November 1941?

A The First Panzer Group.

Q Which panzer corps captured the Soviet city of Tikhvin on November 9, 1941?

A XXXIX Panzer Corps.

Q Who was the leader of fascist Italy?

A Benito Mussolini.

Q Which country first introduced a series of radar stations on her home soil?

A Britain, in 1938, in response to the threat of German bomber raids.

Q Which Soviet front defended Moscow against the German Operation Typhoon?

A The Western Front.

DID YOU KNOW

AIRCRAFT RADAR, INTRODUCED IN 1941, INITIALLY ENABLED NIGHTFIGHTERS TO LOCATE TARGETS AND EVENTUALLY AIDED BOMBER NAVIGATION. U-BOATS THAT SURFACED IN DARKNESS FOR SAFETY COULD ALSO BE DETECTED BY AIRCRAFT, WHICH THEN ILLUMINATED THE SUBMARINES WITH LIGHTS BEFORE ATTACKING THEM. GROUND-BASED RADAR ALSO HELPED BOMBER CREWS HIT TARGETS BY PRECISELY TRACKING AND RELAYING INFORMATION TO THE AIRCRAFT. IN THE WAR AT SEA, RADAR WAS USED TO DETECT ENEMY AIRCRAFT AND ALSO DIRECTED GUNFIRE, WHICH COULD BE EFFECTIVELY EMPLOYED EVEN IN COMPLETE DARKNESS WITH THE NEW TECHNOLOGY. RADAR THEREFORE BECAME A KEY TECHNOLOGY IN LAND, SEA, AND AIR OPERATIONS DURING THE WAR.

Q Name one of the three Soviet fronts that took part in the Soviet counteroffensive that began on December 5, 1941?

A The Kalinin Front, Western Front, and Southwestern Front.

Q Name the two German panzer groups that took the full fury of Zhukov's offensive.

A The Second and Third Panzer Groups. The Third Panzer Group was forced to conduct a fighting retreat to Klin. The Tenth Army ploughed into the southern flank of the Second Panzer Group, forcing Guderian to order a withdrawal to the Don, Shat, and Upa Rivers.

DID YOU KNOW

BENITO MUSSOLINI, JOURNALIST, SOLDIER, AND POLITICIAN, EXPLOITED THE INSTABILITY OF INTERWAR ITALY TO BECOME THE DICTATOR OF A FASCIST STATE. AFTER RISING TO POWER IN 1922, HE SUPPRESSED OPPOSITION AND PROMISED THE NATION THAT A NEW ROMAN EMPIRE WOULD ARISE. MUSSOLINI PRESENTED HIMSELF AS A TOUGH ALTERNATIVE TO PREVIOUS LIBERAL STATESMEN AND A PATRIOTIC ENEMY OF COMMUNISM. FASCIST PROPAGANDA HID HIS REGIME'S ECONOMIC INSTABILITY, AND THE CONQUEST OF ETHIOPIA (1935–36) AND ALBANIA (1939) ATTEMPTED TO DIVERT PUBLIC ATTENTION AWAY FROM DOMESTIC PROBLEMS. MUSSOLINI ESTABLISHED CLOSE RELATIONS WITH ADOLF HITLER, BUT INSISTED THAT ITALY WOULD NOT BE READY TO ENTER INTO WAR UNTIL 1942. AFTER THE FALL OF FRANCE IN JUNE 1940, HOWEVER, HE WAS KEEN TO CAPITALIZE ON GERMANY'S CONQUESTS AND DECLARED WAR ON THE ALLIES. MILITARY BLUNDERS IN FRANCE, NORTH AFRICA, AND GREECE LEFT ITALY DEPENDENT ON GERMANY MILITARY ASSISTANCE. MUSSOLINI, PHYSICALLY AND MENTALLY WEAKENED, FACED GROWING PUBLIC APATHY AND POLITICAL THREATS AS HIS COUNTRY FALTERED.

Q Who was Chief of the German Army General Staff in December 1941?

A Field Marshal Walter von Brauchitsch.

Q What happened to him at the end of 1941?

A He suffered a heart attack and tendered his resignation, an offer not immediately accepted by Hitler.

> ## FOUR OF MY TANKS WERE BLAZING INFERNOS; THREE OTHERS JUST SAT THERE, SAD AND ABANDONED
> CAPTAIN ROBERT CRISP, 3RD ROYAL TANK REGIMENT, SIDI REZEGH, NOVEMBER 28, 1941

107

Q The Soviet December 1941 counteroffensive prompted Hitler to issue which directive?

A Führer Directive Number 39.

Q What were its main points?

A (a) To hold areas which are of great operational or economic importance to the enemy.
(b) To enable forces in the East to rest and recuperate as much as possible.
(c) Thus to establish conditions suitable for the resumption of large-scale offensive operations in 1942.

Q Which city, recaptured by the Red Army on December 9, 1941, allowed supplies to be sent into Leningrad?

A Tikhvin.

Q Which dam did the Germans blow up on December 11, 1941, in an effort to slow the Red Army's advance?

A The Istra Dam.

Q What cargo was the old cattle boat the *Struma* carrying when it sailed from Romania in December 1941?

A A total of 769 Jews who had spent their savings to avoid Nazi persecution.

Q What was the ship's destination?

A Istanbul.

Q Did it get there?

A Yes, but the Jews were not allowed off the boat (the British refused to allow them passage to Palestine). The boat was towed out to sea by the Turks, where it was sunk by a Soviet submarine.

Q How many citizens of Leningrad starved to death on Christmas Day 1941?

A 3,700.

Q What was the daily death rate in the city at this time?

A 1,500. Very few due to German bombs or shells; most to starvation and hypothermia.

Q Why did Hitler dismiss Heinz Guderian at the end of December 1941?

A For his retreats and insubordination.

Q Who replaced him as commander of the Second Panzer Group?

A General Rudolf Schmidt.

IN THE LONG RUN
NATIONAL SOCIALISM AND RELIGION WILL
NO LONGER BE ABLE
TO EXIST TOGETHER
ADOLF HITLER, JULY 1941

Q Estimate the total number of Luftwaffe aircraft lost on the Eastern Front in 1941?

A 2,100.

Q How many tanks did the Soviets lose on the Eastern Front in 1941?

A 20,000.

Q What were Soviet losses in combat aircraft in 1941?

A 10,000.

> ❝ I WAS WORKING ON THE USS SHAW. IT
> WAS ON A FLOATING DRY DOCK,
> IT WAS IN FLAMES ❞
> JOHN GARCIA, PEARL HARBOR, DECEMBER 7, 1941

Q What was the Soviet scorched earth policy?

A First used in 1941 on the Eastern Front, in the words of Stalin: "In case of a forced retreat ... all rolling stock must be evacuated, the enemy must not be left a single engine, a single railway car, not a single pound of grain or gallon of fuel. The collective farmers must drive off all their cattle and turn over their grain to the safe keeping of the state authorities for transportation to the rear. All valuable property, including non-ferrous metals, grain, and fuel that cannot be withdrawn, must be destroyed without fail. In areas occupied by the enemy, guerrilla units must set fire to forests, stores, and transports."

DID YOU KNOW

THE SOVIET KV-1 HEAVY TANK SHARED MANY COMPONENTS WITH THE T-34 TANK, SUCH AS THE ENGINE AND 76.2MM MAIN GUN. ALTHOUGH UNRELIABLE (IN 1941 MANY OF THE 639 KV-1S BROKE DOWN ON THE WAY TO THE BATTLEFIELD), IT WAS CONTINUALLY UPGRADED THROUGHOUT THE WAR. DESIGN "FEATURES" INCLUDED TRANSMISSION GEARS THAT WERE SO DIFFICULT TO SHIFT THAT DRIVERS WERE ISSUED WITH A HAMMER TO KNOCK THEM INTO PLACE!

Q **What were *Feldgendarmerie*?**

A German field police.

Q **What does *Festung* mean?**

A It is German for fortress.

Q **What is Flak short for?**

A *Fliegerabwehrkanone*—a German term meaning antiaircraft gun.

Q **In the German armed forces, what were *Freiwilligen* units?**

A Used mainly by the Waffen-SS to denote units composed of foreign volunteers.

Q What is an artillery airburst?

A The bursting of a high-explosive shell in the air above the target.

Q What happens in a gun's chamber?

A The cartridge explodes and is thus fired from the barrel.

Q What is an artillery piece's cradle?

A The part of the gun that supports the barrel and recoil system.

> **I REPEAT THAT THE UNITED STATES
> CAN ACCEPT NO RESULT SAVE
> VICTORY, FINAL AND
> COMPLETE**
> PRESIDENT ROOSEVELT, RADIO BROADCAST,
> DECEMBER 9, 1941

Q In artillery parlance, what is direct fire?

A Artillery fire in which there is a direct line of sight between gun and target.

Q Define the term howitzer.

A A gun that uses variable charges and fires at an angle up to and above 45 degrees to enable it to drop shells behind obstacles.

Q What is a muzzle brake?

A An attachment to the muzzle of a gun which deflects propellant gases sideways or slightly to the rear.

Q What is its function?

A It reduces the rearward thrust of recoil and thus permits the firing of heavy charges without the need for a heavy carriage.

Q Define field artillery.

A Artillery that is part of an infantry or armored division, and which provides the division's fire support.

DID YOU KNOW

THERE WERE CRUCIAL PIECES OF EVIDENCE IN THE MONTHS PRIOR TO THE JAPANESE ATTACK ON PEARL HARBOR. U.S. INTELLIGENCE OFFICIALS NOTED THAT THE JAPANESE CARRIERS HAD DISAPPEARED FROM THEIR USUAL MOORINGS. SIMILARLY, IN NOVEMBER 1940, LOW-FREQUENCY SIGNALS, THE KIND USED BY JAPAN'S CARRIERS, WERE DETECTED NORTHWEST OF HAWAII BUT NOT INVESTIGATED. DUTCH INTELLIGENCE INTERCEPTED AN ENCRYPTED MESSAGE SENT TO THE JAPANESE AMBASSADOR IN BANGKOK SUGGESTING AN ATTACK ON THE PHILIPPINES AND HAWAII, AND THE DUTCH INFORMED THE U.S., BUT THE WARNING WAS DISMISSED (THE U.S. WAS ALSO AWARE THAT THE JAPANESE WERE TELLING THEIR DIPLOMATIC OFFICIALS TO DESTROY CODE BOOKS AND TO PREPARE FOR WAR). SADLY FOR SERVICEMEN WHO LOST THEIR LIVES AT PEARL HARBOR, THESE WARNINGS WERE MISSED OR MISREAD.

Q What is the difference between armor-piercing shell and armor-piercing shot?

A The shell is hollow and carries a charge of explosive, while shot is solid steel.

Q What is homogeneous armor?

A Armor that is of a similar density and hardness all the way through.

Q What is face-hardened armor?

A Armor that has had carbon absorbed into the face of the plate, making it extremely hard.

114

DID YOU KNOW

AS THE RELATIVELY FEW AXIS MECHANIZED FORMATIONS PUSHED FORWARD DURING OPERATION BARBAROSSA, THE BULK OF THE INVADING FORCE, SOME 126 INFANTRY DIVISIONS—WITH 625,000 HORSES—WOULD MARCH FORWARD TRYING DESPERATELY NOT TO FALL TOO FAR BEHIND THE PANZER SPEARHEADS. IN ADDITION TO OCCUPYING GROUND AND MOPPING UP, THESE INFANTRY FORMATIONS WOULD HELP THE FOUR PANZER GROUPS TO REDUCE THE SOVIET POCKETS. TOGETHER THESE ACTIONS WERE CONCEIVED AS PARTS OF A SINGLE, CONTINUOUS, OFFENSIVE EFFORT THAT WOULD WIN THE WAR IN A MATTER OF MONTHS. THE KEY QUESTION REMAINED, HOWEVER, AS TO WHETHER THE GERMAN ARMY COULD MAINTAIN ITS ADVANCE IN A COUNTRY OF THIS SIZE AGAINST AN ENEMY AS POWERFUL AS THE SOVIETS IF THE LATTER'S COHESION DID NOT SWIFTLY COLLAPSE. THE FIRST FEW WEEKS INDICATED THAT IT COULD.

Q In British artillery nomenclature, what does QF mean?

A Quick firing.

Q What does the abbreviation APDS mean?

A Armor-Piercing Discarding Sabot.

> **WE FLEW THROUGH AND OVER THICK
> CLOUDS WHICH WERE
> AT 2000 METERS**
> TAISA MITSUO, JAPANESE PILOT AT PEARL HARBOR

115

Q What was a *Kettenkrad*?

A A German tracked motorcycle.

Q What is an artillery limber?

A A wheeled carriage that can be attached to the trail end of a gun to support it for transport.

Q What is a mortar?

A In specific terms, any gun that fires only at elevation angles greater than 45 degrees. However, in reality, the term is confined to infantry mortars.

DID YOU KNOW

A KEY REASON FOR THE GERMAN INABILITY TO REPLACE THE LOSSES SUFFERED DURING BARBAROSSA WAS HITLER'S SPRING 1941 DECISION TO SCALE BACK SIGNIFICANTLY ARMAMENTS PRODUCTION FOR THE GROUND FORCES, ESPECIALLY LIGHT HOWITZERS AND MORTARS. DURING THE WINTER OF 1941–42, THE BADLY WEAKENED GERMAN ARMY IN THE EAST FOUND ITSELF—DESPITE ALL THE VAST TACTICAL SUCCESSES IT HAD ACHIEVED—FACING A MORE POWERFUL ENEMY THAN EVER BEFORE THAT WAS RUTHLESSLY DETERMINED TO DRIVE THE BRUTAL AXIS FORCES OFF SOVIET SOIL. IN ADDITION, HITLER WAS MAKING EXORBITANT DEMANDS ON THE ALREADY SHAKEN TROOPS, AS GUDERIAN NOTED: "WE HAD SUFFERED A GRIEVOUS DEFEAT IN THE FAILURE TO REACH THE CAPITAL, WHICH WAS TO BE SERIOUSLY AGGRAVATED DURING THE NEXT FEW WEEKS THANKS TO THE RIGIDITY OF OUR SUPREME COMMANDER [HITLER]: DESPITE ALL OUR REPORTS, THESE MEN FAR AWAY IN EAST PRUSSIA COULD FORM NO TRUE CONCEPT OF THE REAL CONDITIONS OF THE WINTER WAR IN WHICH THEIR SOLDIERS WERE ENGAGED."

Q Name two of the the six Japanese aircraft carriers that were involved in the attack on Pearl Harbor.

A *Akagi, Kagi, Hiryu, Soryu, Zuizaku,* and *Shokaku.*

Q Who commanded the Japanese carrier strike force at Pearl Harbor?

A Vice Admiral Chuichi Nagumo.

Q How many Japanese air strikes were launched against Pearl Harbor?

A Two.

Q Why was the Japanese attack against Pearl Harbor a strategic failure?

A The strike at Pearl Harbor failed to destroy any U.S. aircraft carriers, which were out at sea. Many of the damaged ships were repaired quickly. Furthermore, Nagumo called off a third strike aimed at destroying Pearl Harbor's oil and shore facilities. Such a raid could have rendered Pearl Harbor inoperable. Instead, it continued to function.

Q Why was Singapore so vital to the Allies in late 1941?

A It was the Allies' main port for control of the Malacca Strait between Malaya and the Dutch East Indies.

Q Which Japanese army launched the Burma offensive in December 1941?

A The Fifteenth Army.

Q Who commanded the army?

A Lieutenant General Shojiro Iida.

117

" ON NOVEMBER 13 WE AWOKE AND
SHIVERED. AN ICY BLAST FROM THE NORTH
KNIFED ACROSS THE SNOW
Heinrich Haape, German Army, Russia,
winter of 1941–42 "

Q Which two British battleships were sunk by the Japanese in the South China Sea in December 1941?

A HMS *Prince of Wales* and HMS *Repulse*.

Q What was at Victory Point in Burma?

A An important Allied air base. It fell to the Japanese on December 16, 1941.

Q Who was the Thai prime minister in 1941?

A Field Marshal Pibul Songgram.

“ PRINCE OF WALES LOOKED MAGNIFICENT.
WHITE-TIPPED WAVES RIPPLED OVER
HER PLUNGING BOWS
O.D. GALLAGHER, WAR CORRESPONDENT **”**

Q Why was the conquest of the Dutch East Indies in December 1941 of such importance to the Japanese?

A Conquest of the Dutch East Indies gave the Japanese vital natural resources, including oil and rubber. It consolidated their control of southwest Pacific seas, and enabled them to dominate or even invade Australia.

Q Who replaced Admiral Husband Kimmel as commander of the U.S .Pacific Fleet in December 1941?

A Rear Admiral Chester Nimitz.

DID YOU KNOW

THE JAPANESE ASSAULT ON PEARL HARBOR WAS PLANNED BY ADMIRAL ISOROKU YAMAMOTO (COMMANDER-IN-CHIEF, IMPERIAL JAPANESE NAVY) AND COMMANDED BY VICE ADMIRAL CHUICHI NAGUMO. IT WAS DELIVERED BY A STRIKE FORCE OF SIX AIRCRAFT CARRIERS, TOGETHER CONTAINING AROUND 450 AIRCRAFT, WITH A DEFENSIVE/LOGISTICAL ACCOMPANIMENT OF TWO BATTLESHIPS, TWO CRUISERS, SEVERAL DESTROYERS, AND EIGHT SUPPORT VESSELS. THIS LARGE BODY OF SHIPPING MANAGED TO SAIL COMPLETELY UNDETECTED FROM THE KURILE ISLANDS NORTH OF JAPAN TO ATTACK POSITIONS ONLY 275 MILES (443 KM) NORTH OF HAWAII.

Q Who was the governor of Hong Kong in 1941?

A Sir Mark Young.

Q What was the Mitsubishi A6M fighter better known as?

A The Zero.

Q What was its armament?

A Two 20mm cannon and two 7.7mm machine guns.

Q Whose words are these: "Yesterday, December 7, 1941—a date that will live in infamy—the United States of America was suddenly and deliberately attacked by naval and air forces of the Empire of Japan."

A U.S. President Franklin Delano Roosevelt.

Q In the Pacific theater, where was the port of Davao?

A On Mindanao in the southern Philippines.

Q Why was its fall to the Japanese in December 1941 a major blow to the Allies?

A It was used as a staging post for subsequent Japanese invasions of the Dutch East Indies, and it opened another front in the Japanese offensive against the Philippines, which until this point has been concentrated in the north against Luzon.

> **"** AS THE P-40S DIVED TO ATTACK,
> EVERYBODY WENT A
> ## LITTLE CRAZY
> ## WITH EXCITEMENT
> CLAIRE CHENNAULT, "FLYING TIGERS",
> CHINA, DECEMBER 1941 **"**

Q Who was the prime minister of Australia in 1941?

A John Curtin.

Q Why did U.S. troops on Luzon withdraw to the Bataan Peninsula in December 1941?

A To avoid the Japanese encirclement of Manila.

1942

In North Africa and on the Eastern Front Axis offensives were initially successful, but were halted and then defeated by a series of Allied and Soviet counterattacks. In the Pacific, meanwhile, the Japanese juggernaut was at first successful. But then the U.S. Navy won a decisive victory at Midway in June.

Q What was the name of General Rommel's halftrack in North Africa?

A "Griffin."

Q What was signed at the Arcadia Conference in January 1942?

A Allied countries signed the United Nations Declaration pledging to follow the Atlantic Charter principles.

Q What does *Sturmgeschütz* mean?

A It is the German word for assault gun.

> " NEVER BEFORE HAVE WE HAD SO LITTLE
> # TIME IN WHICH TO DO
> ## SO MUCH
> PRESIDENT ROOSEVELT, FEBRUARY 1942 "

Q The SS was a Nazi organization. But what do the letters SS mean?

A *Schutzstaffel*: literally Protection Force or Defense Squad.

Q What was the ABDACOM?

A The American, British, Dutch, and Australian (ABDA) Command.

DID YOU KNOW

THE JAPANESE SURPRISE ATTACK ON THE AMERICAN FLEET AT PEARL HARBOR WAS DESIGNED TO CRIPPLE THE AMERICAN PACIFIC FLEET TO SUCH AN EXTENT THAT THE GREATER EAST ASIA CO-PROSPERITY SPHERE, JAPAN'S INNOCENT-SOUNDING NAME FOR HER TERRITORIAL ACQUISITIONS, WOULD BE BEYOND THE RANGE OF U.S. FORCES AFTER THE AMERICAN CARRIERS HAD BEEN DESTROYED. THOUGH THE CARRIERS WERE NEVER FOUND AND DESTROYED, JAPANESE STRATEGY FOR 1942 WAS BUILT UPON THIS SAME PRECEPT: PROTECTION. THE JAPANESE HIGH COMMAND IN TOKYO DECIDED THAT THE GREATER EAST ASIA CO-PROSPERITY SPHERE HAD TO BE PROTECTED BY A DEFENSIVE LINE EXTENDING SOUTH AND NORTH OF THE MARSHALL ISLANDS. THIS MEANT THAT CERTAIN ISLANDS THAT LAY WITHIN THIS PERIMETER HAD TO BE TAKEN AND FORTIFIED. THIS INCLUDED THE PHILIPPINES, WHERE THE U.S. HAD 130,000 MEN STATIONED, THE KEY STRATEGIC ISLAND OF CORREGIDOR, NEW GUINEA, THE SOLOMON ISLANDS, AND THE GILBERT ISLANDS.

123

Q Who was the commander of ABDACOM?

A The British General Sir Archibald Wavell.

Q Who was made commander-in-chief of Allied forces in China in January 1942?

A The Chinese Nationalist leader Chiang Kai-shek.

Q Was the Japanese Type 95 tank a light, medium, or heavy tank?

A Light tank.

"HOSPITAL SHELLED AND DIVE-BOMBED FROM 2 P.M. TILL DUSK—GHASTLY EXPERIENCE"

DOCTOR FISHER, MEDICAL OFFICER, SINGAPORE, FEBRUARY 1942

Q Who was the prime minister of Burma in early 1942?

A U Saw.

Q Why was he arrested by the British in January 1942?

A He was planning Burmese independence.

Q Why did the government of Thailand declare war on Britain and the USA in January 1942?

A It believed Japan would win the war.

Q What threat did the Japanese prime minister, General Hideki Tojo, issue to Australia in January 1942?

A "If you continue your resistance, we Japanese will show you no mercy."

Q Which U.S. aircraft carrier was damaged by a Japanese suicide aircraft attack in February 1942?

A USS *Enterprise*.

Q Why did Colonel General Ernst Udet, head of Luftwaffe aircraft production and development, commit suicide in January 1942?

A Over his failure to provide adequate replacements and new improved aircraft models.

Q What was Operation Drum Beat in January 1942?

A The first coordinated attack carried out by five U-boats initially against U.S. shipping along the East Coast of the United States.

Q How many ships were sunk by German U-boats during the first month of Drum Beat?

A 20.

DID YOU KNOW

THE INFANTRY UNITS OF THE RED ARMY WERE IN A CONSTANT STATE OF FLUX DURING THE FIRST TWO YEARS OF THE WAR ON THE EASTERN FRONT. HUGE LOSSES REQUIRED CONSTANT REORGANIZATION TO KEEP THE UNITS IN SOME SORT OF FIGHTING ORDER. THE REASONS FOR THESE MASSIVE LOSSES ARE NOT HARD TO FIND: DURING 1941–42, UNITS WERE QUICKLY FORMED AND OFTEN THROWN INTO BATTLE WITH LITTLE OR NO TRAINING. STALIN'S PURGES IN THE 1930s MEANT THAT THOUSANDS OF INEXPERIENCED OFFICERS WERE PROMOTED BEYOND THEIR LEVEL OF COMPETENCE. THIS RESULTED IN POOR LEADERSHIP ON THE BATTLEFIELD. TO COMPOUND PROBLEMS, EACH RIFLE DIVISION HAD AN INADEQUATE NUMBER OF RADIOS, WHICH MADE COORDINATING ARTILLERY SUPPORT ALL BUT IMPOSSIBLE (GERMAN COMMENTATORS DURING BARBAROSSA NOTED THE ALMOST TOTAL ABSENCE OF ARTILLERY SUPPORT FOR ATTACKING RED ARMY INFANTRY UNITS).

Q What was the "Channel Dash" in February 1942?

A Protected by Luftwaffe fighters and smaller naval units, the German battleships *Scharnhorst* and *Gneisenau* and the cruiser *Prinz Eugen* made a dash from Brest up the English Channel to reach ports in Germany. Taken by complete surprise, the British Royal Navy and Royal Air Force were unable to stop the operation, losing a considerable number of planes and naval vessels in the attempt.

Q Which German city was devastated by an RAF bomber raid on March 28, 1942?

A Lübeck on the Baltic.

Q What did Hitler and Mussolini discuss at Berchtesgaden in April 1942?

A Future Axis strategy in North Africa and the Mediterranean, the main objectives being the reduction of Malta and the seizure of the Suez Canal.

Q Why did the commander of the German Army Group North, Field Marshal von Leeb, resign in January 1942?

A Red Army units were threatening to cut off 100,000 troops around Demyansk. Leeb requested permission to retreat. Hitler refused, whereupon Leeb resigned.

> THE TANKS MADE A LAST ATTACK ON
> THE ROADBLOCK, BUT IT WAS
> ## DEFENDED BY SEVERAL
> ## ANTITANK GUNS
> GENERAL SLIM, BURMA, APRIL 1942

DID YOU KNOW

HITLER'S AIM IN THE EAST WAS VERY CLEAR: ACQUIRING *LEBENSRAUM* IN THE EAST UP TO THE URAL MOUNTAINS. THESE LANDS WERE OCCUPIED BY GROUPS THAT HITLER AND NAZISM DESPISED: BOLSHEVIKS, SLAVS, AND JEWS. UNDER THE NEW ORDER, THESE PEOPLES WOULD EITHER BECOME SLAVES UNDER GERMAN OVERLORDS OR WOULD BE EXTERMINATED. HITLER WAS TO STATE IN 1942: "IF WE DO NOT COMPLETE THE CONQUEST OF THE EAST UTTERLY AND IRREVOCABLY, EACH SUCCESSIVE GENERATION WILL HAVE WAR ON ITS HANDS." FOR HIM THE WAR IN RUSSIA WAS A RACIAL CONFLICT, IN WHICH THE RACIALLY SUPERIOR GERMAN ARYAN RACE WAS LOCKED IN A STRUGGLE WITH THE "SUB-HUMAN" SLAVS. THIS MADE RETREAT IN THE FACE OF "INFERIOR" PEOPLES UNIMAGINABLE, FOR THE FÜHRER COULD NOT CONCEIVE OF THE RACIALLY INFERIOR SLAVS BEING ABLE TO DEFEAT A SUPERIOR RACE. AS HE STATED ON THE EVE OF KURSK: "GERMANY NEEDS THE CONQUERED TERRITORIES OR SHE WILL NOT EXIST FOR LONG. SHE WILL WIN HEGEMONY OVER THE REST OF EUROPE. WHERE WE ARE—WE STAY."

127

Q Who replaced Leeb as Army Group North's commander?

A Georg von Küchler.

Q On the Eastern Front, what was the Demyansk Pocket?

A In February 1942, the jaws snapped shut on 90,000 German troops around Demyansk as the Soviet First Shock and Eleventh Armies linked up on the Lovat River, northern Russia. Inside the German pocket were the 12th, 30th, 123rd, and 290th Infantry Divisions, plus the 3rd SS *Totenkopf* Division.

Q How did the Germans intend to supply those troops trapped in the Demyansk Pocket?

A The units had to rely on the Luftwaffe for supplies of food and ammunition.

Q What was the PTRD?

A A Red Army 14.5mm antitank rifle.

Q What was the main armament of the Panzer III Ausf G?

A A 50mm gun.

DID YOU KNOW

THE FAILURE OF OPERATION TYPHOON HERALDED A CRISIS FOR THE GERMAN ARMY ON THE EASTERN FRONT AT THE END OF 1941. UNDERSTRENGTH AND EXHAUSTED DIVISIONS LACKED THE MANPOWER WITH WHICH TO DEFEND EVERY MILE OF THE FRONT, ESPECIALLY IN THE FACE OF THE RED ARMY COUNTEROFFENSIVE THAT BEGAN IN EARLY DECEMBER. TO COMPOUND THE PROBLEM, PREWAR TRAINING HAD LARGELY SHUNNED ANYTHING TO DO WITH DEFENSIVE OPERATIONS IN WINTER CONDITIONS. INDIVIDUAL COMMANDERS AND UNITS THEREFORE HAD TO LEARN FAST IF THEY WERE TO AVOID BEING ANNIHILATED BY THE MORE NUMERICAL AND OFTEN BETTER EQUIPPED ENEMY. IN RESPONSE, THE GERMANS ADOPTED SO-CALLED HEDGEHOG TACTICS TO BEAT OFF RED ARMY ATTACKS AND PRESERVE THEIR LINES.

REMEMBER PEARL HARBOR!
U.S. SLOGAN

Q What was the standard main armament of all British cruiser and infantry tanks up to 1942?

A The two-pounder gun.

Q What caliber was the BESA machine gun?

A 7.92mm.

Q Was the Panzer 38(t) a German tank?

A No. It was originally built by the Czechs. It was taken into German service when the Third Reich absorbed Czechoslovakia before the war.

Q Which German medium bomber was nicknamed "The Flying Pencil"?

A The Dornier Do 17.

Q Why did it have this name?

A It had a slender rear fuselage.

Q What was a *Bergepanzer*?

A A German armored recovery vehicle.

Q Who chaired the Wannsee Conference in Berlin in January 1942?

A The deputy chief of the SS, Reinhard Heydrich.

Q What was the purpose of the conference?

A To decide the fate of the Jews in German-occupied territory.

" WHEN I THINK ABOUT IT I REALIZE
THAT I'M EXTRAORDINARILY HUMANE
HITLER DISCUSSING THE JEWS, APRIL 1942 **"**

Q What was the decision of the conference?

A Heydrich received permission to begin deporting all Jews in German-controlled areas to Eastern Europe to face forced labor or extermination (the killing of Jews in Eastern Europe was already commonplace).

Q Why did the Nazis use poison gas to exterminate people?

A Execution by shooting was inefficient and a strain for the troops engaged. Using poison gas was more efficient.

DID YOU KNOW

THE SECRET WANNSEE CONFERENCE IN BERLIN OFFICIALLY LAUNCHED THE NAZI PROGRAM TO EXTERMINATE THE JEWISH PEOPLE, WHO WERE REGARDED AS THE RACIAL ENEMY OF THE "ARYAN" GERMANS. THE PREVIOUS PERSECUTION AND KILLING OF JEWS IN NAZI-OCCUPIED EUROPE WAS TRANSFORMED INTO A HIGHLY EFFICIENT OPERATION. EUROPEAN JEWS WERE SYSTEMATICALLY HERDED INTO CONCENTRATION CAMPS IN EASTERN EUROPE WHERE THEY WERE WORKED LIKE SLAVES. MILLIONS DIED FROM MALTREATMENT, EXHAUSTION, DISEASE, AND STARVATION. IN EXTER-MINATION CAMPS, POISON GAS CHAMBERS WERE USED TO KILL THOUSANDS OF PEOPLE. MANY OTHER PEOPLE DEEMED "UNDESIRABLE" BY THE NAZIS, INCLUDING GYPSIES, POLITICAL OPPONENTS, AND THE MENTALLY AND PHYSICALLY HANDICAPPED, ALSO SHARED THE SAME FATE AS THE JEWS.

Q Which Axis garrison in Libya fell to British troops on January 17, 1942?

A Halfaya.

Q Who became Norwegian prime minister in February 1942?

A Vidkun Quisling.

Q What position did Lieutenant General Joseph Stilwell assume in February 1942?

A Commander-in-chief of the U.S. forces in the China-Burma-India theater, and chief of staff to Chiang Kai-shek. The fact that he spoke Chinese and had an understanding of Chinese culture made him especially suitable for this position.

> A TSAR ONCE REMARKED THAT TWO
> OF HIS BEST GENERALS IN
> # HIS ARMY WERE
> ## JANUARY AND FEBRUARY
> Bryan Perrett, *A History of Blitzkrieg*

Q The Italian torpedo boat *Circe* sank which British submarine off Taranto on February 13, 1942?

A HMS *Tempest*.

Q How many Axis air raids were launched against the island of Malta in March 1942?

A 275.

Q What type of weapon was the Beretta Model 1938A?

A A submachine gun.

Q What was the Carro M13/40?

A An Italian medium tank.

Q What was the Semovente da 75/18?

A An Italian assault gun.

Q How many engines did the Italian Savoia Marchetti SM.81 bomber have?

A Three.

Q What caliber was the Cannone Da 75/18 Modello 37 field gun?

A 75mm.

DID YOU KNOW

THE GERMANS NEVER RECOVERED FROM THE HORRENDOUS LOSSES OF THE 1941 CAMPAIGN IN RUSSIA. BY APRIL 1942 THE ARMY HAD LOST ONE-THIRD OF THE TROOPS, 40 PERCENT OF THE ANTITANK GUNS, HALF THE HORSES, AND 79 PERCENT OF THE ARMOR THAT HAD BEGUN THE CAMPAIGN. MASSIVE VEHICLE LOSSES HAD SIGNIFICANTLY REDUCED MOBILITY, WHILE MUNITIONS STOCKS HAD FALLEN TO ONE-THIRD OF JUNE 1941 LEVELS. NEW PRODUCTION AND REPLACEMENTS COULD NOT OFFSET LOSSES; AND, AS A RESULT, INFANTRY, OFFICER, AND EQUIPMENT STRENGTHS PLUMMETED. MOREOVER, LIMITATIONS IMPOSED BY TERRAIN AND WEATHER, BY SHORTAGES IN TROOPS, EQUIPMENT, AND SUPPLIES, AS WELL AS BY HITLER'S HOLD-FAST ORDERS, PREVENTED THE GERMANS DURING THE WINTER OF 1941–42 FROM CONDUCTING THE ELASTIC DEFENSE IN DEPTH PROSCRIBED BY ESTABLISHED DOCTRINE. INSTEAD, THE ADAPTABLE GERMANS SWIFTLY ADOPTED EXPEDIENT, IMPROVISED DEFENSIVE TECHNIQUES DICTATED BY THE CIRCUMSTANCES THAT FACED THEM. THE RED ARMY LAUNCHED HEAVY, IF UNSOPHISTICATED, ILL-COORDINATED, AND DISPERSED, FRONTAL ASSAULTS ALL ALONG THE CENTRAL SECTOR OF THE FRONT TO DRIVE THE GERMANS BACK FROM MOSCOW AND GAIN SOME OPERATIONAL ROOM FOR MANEUVER. THIS COUNTEROFFENSIVE EMBROILED THE DEPLETED AND EXHAUSTED PANZER DIVISIONS THAT HAD SPEARHEADED THE GERMAN ADVANCE ON THE SOVIET CAPITAL IN HEAVY DEFENSIVE FIGHTING, FOR WHICH THEY WERE ILL-SUITED.

Q What was the Persian Corridor?

A When the Germans invaded Russia, the United States set up a mission to provide Lend-Lease aid to the Soviets. One of the supply routes was through the Middle East, called the Persian Corridor.

Q Which American organization coordinated operations along the Persian Corridor?

A The U.S. Military Iranian Mission.

Q Where was its headquarters?

A Baghdad, Iraq.

DID YOU KNOW

GERMAN MILITARY OPERATIONS IN THE EAST REMAINED DOMINATED BY THE NOTION, BASED ON A DISTORTED INTERPRETATION OF CLAUSEWITZ'S MILITARY THOUGHT, THAT WAR OVERWHELMINGLY CONSTITUTED A CLASH OF MORAL FORCES. WHILE THIS CONCEPT DID—AND STILL DOES—SHED CONSIDERABLE LIGHT ON MILITARY OPERATIONS, DURING WORLD WAR II THE IMPACT OF NAZI IDEOLOGY FURTHER DISTORTED GERMAN UNDER-STANDING OF THE CONCEPT. GIVEN THE NAZIS' SUPREME BELIEF IN THE SUPERIOR RACIAL WILL OF THE ARYAN GERMANS, MOST GERMAN COMMANDERS BELIEVED THAT THE WILL OF THE "SEMILITERATE" SLAVIC SOVIETS WOULD NOT BE ABLE TO RESIST THE ONSLAUGHT OF THE TECHNO-LOGICALLY ADVANCED WEHRMACHT. CONSEQUENTLY, BARBAROSSA WOULD PROVE A SHORT AND DECISIVE CAMPAIGN. THE APPALLINGLY BRUTAL, 900-DAY GERMAN SIEGE OF LENINGRAD, HOWEVER, PROVED HOW WRONG WAS THE GERMAN APPRECIATION OF THE ENEMY FACING THEM. THE SIEGE DEMONSTRATED HOW MUCH SUFFERING THE SOVIETS COULD ENDURE IN THEIR DESPERATE STRUGGLE TO RESIST THE AXIS ONSLAUGHT.

" I SHALL RETURN

DOUGLAS MACARTHUR, LEAVING THE PHILIPPINES,
MARCH 11, 1942 "

Q **What was the U.S. Air Force's Halverson Detachment?**

A A special group of B-24 bombers that found itself in the Middle East in early June 1942. It was named after its commander, Colonel Harry A. Halverson. It consisted of 23 B-24D Liberator heavy bombers with hand-picked crews.

Q **Who was Chief of Staff of the U.S. Army in 1942?**

A General George C. Marshall.

Q **On the Eastern Front, what was a "flak nest"?**

A A German strongpoint containing multiple antiaircraft guns.

Q **Which Red Army units took part in the Soviet Barvenkovo-Lozavaia Offensive of January 1942?**

A The Southwestern and Southern Fronts.

Q **What was the aim of the offensive?**

A To recapture Kharkov, Krasnograd, and Pavlograd in the Ukraine.

135

Q In January 1942, Hitler ordered the setting up of the *Luftflotte* 2 command on Sicily. What units did it contain?

A *Fliegerkorps* II and X.

Q What was *Luftflotte* 2's mission?

A To command the waters around Malta and in the eastern Mediterranean.

Q Which Allied aircraft carriers were used to fly in Spitfire fighters to the island of Malta in spring 1942?

A The British carriers HMS *Argus* and *Eagle* and the American carrier HMS *Wasp*.

> " CIVIL WAR CONDITIONS ALL OVER AGAIN.
> # CHINESE OUT OF CONTROL.
> ## FIFTH COLUMN BUSY
> JOSEPH STILWELL, BURMA, MAY 4, 1942 "

Q What type of aircraft was the Vickers Wellesley?

A A British general-purpose bomber.

Q What was the size of its crew?

A Two.

DID YOU KNOW

THROUGHOUT THE COMBAT ON THE EASTERN FRONT IN 1942, THE FIGHTING QUALITIES OF THE INDIVIDUAL GERMAN SOLDIER REMAINED HIGH. THIS WAS UNDOUBTEDLY BOLSTERED BY IDEOLOGICAL TRAINING. IN LATE SPRING 1942, FOR EXAMPLE, THE GERMANS STEPPED UP THEIR EFFORTS TO MOTIVATE PSYCHOLOGICALLY THEIR FRONTLINE SOLDIERS IN THE EAST. DURING MAY, UNIVERSITY LECTURERS VISITED THE ELITE *GROSSDEUTSCHLAND* DIVISION—ONLY RECENTLY EXPANDED FROM REGIMENTAL SIZE—AND DELIVERED DISCUSSIONS ON THE EVILS OF COMMUNISM. IN ADDITION, THE DIVISION CREATED A NEW APPOINTMENT, THAT OF EDUCATION OFFICER, WHO COORDINATED ALL THE ACTIVITIES UNDERTAKEN TO BOLSTER THE MORALE AND DETERMINATION OF THE TROOPS. THE OFFICER PROCURED SEVERAL HUNDRED NEW PROPAGANDISTIC BOOKS FOR THE DIVISION'S LIBRARY VAN, AND GAVE SEMINARS THAT STRESSED BOTH THE INHERENT SUPERIORITY OF THE GERMAN ARMY AND THE INEVITABILITY OF ITS ULTIMATE VICTORY TO "STRENGTHEN SOLDIERLY QUALITIES" AND INSTILL "STEADFASTNESS DURING CRISES" WITHIN THE TROOPS.

Q Which British aircraft was nicknamed the "Shagbat"?

A The Supermarine Walrus.

Q What type of aircraft was this?

A A seaplane designed to operate from Royal Navy aircraft carriers.

Q What was the most successful variant of the British Spitfire fighter?

A The Mk XI version. Some 5,665 were built.

DID YOU KNOW

HITLER DID NOT BELIEVE THAT SLAVS AND JEWS DESERVED TO SHARE THE SAME CONTINENT WITH THE GERMAN PEOPLE. THEY WERE EITHER TO BE FORCED TO EMIGRATE, ENSLAVED, OR, ULTIMATELY, EXTERMINATED. FOR THIS REASON, IT WAS IMPOSSIBLE FOR HITLER TO CONTEMPLATE ANY KIND OF NEGOTIATED PEACE WITH STALIN; EITHER THE SOVIET UNION HAD TO BE DESTROYED OR GERMANY WOULD BE DESTROYED TRYING. IN APRIL 1945, AS DEFEAT LOOMED, HE RANTED: "I HAVE ALWAYS BEEN ABSOLUTELY FAIR IN MY DEALINGS WITH THE JEWS. I GAVE THEM ONE FINAL WARNING. I TOLD THEM THAT IF THEY PRECIPITATED ANOTHER WAR THEY WOULD NOT BE SPARED."

Q **What was the Supermarine Seafire?**

A A Spitfire configured for service on aircraft carriers.

Q **What hampered its performance as a carrier-borne aircraft?**

A It had a long nose and narrow-track main landing gear units.

Q **Which British aircraft was nicknamed the "Flying Suitcase"?**

A The Handley Page Hampden.

Q **Which British bomber built by Avro was retired in June 1942?**

A The Avro Manchester.

Q How many engines did it have?

A Two.

Q What was the RAF's most successful heavy bomber in World War II?

A The Avro Lancaster.

Q The German Bf 110 aircraft was a heavy fighter. What did this term mean?

A During the 1930s air strategists believed twin-engine "heavy fighters" to be essential to offensive air operations.

Q The Bf 110 was dubbed *Zerstörer*. What does this mean?

A Destroyer.

Q What was the Organization Todt?

A A paramilitary construction organization of the Nazi Party, auxiliary to the Wehrmacht. Named after its founder, Dr Todt.

> DEFEAT IS BITTER.
> BITTER TO THE COMMON
> SOLDIER, BUT TREBLY
> BITTER TO HIS GENERAL
> WILLIAM SLIM

Q What was the aircraft that provided the Germans with the bulk of their battlefield reconnaissance capability in World War II?

A The Henschel Hs 126.

Q What type of aircraft was the German Henschel Hs 129?

A A close-support, antitank aircraft.

Q What was its main armaments?

A Two 20mm cannon.

> " SEAS ARE RUNNING MUCH ROUGHER AND
> HUGE SWELLS ARE ROLLING US
> ## 40 AND 50 DEGREES
> ## AT A ROLL "
> FRANK CURRY, ROYAL CANADIAN NAVY,
> JANUARY 1942

Q What was Operation Munich on the Eastern Front in March 1942?

A Joined by a Luftwaffe detachment, German troops attacked partisan bases around Yelnya and Dorogobuzh.

Q What was Operation Bamberg launched in the same month?

A Another German anti-partisan mission on the Eastern Front, near Bobruisk.

DID YOU KNOW

THE KATYUSHA MULTIPLE ROCKET LAUNCHER WAS BETTER KNOWN AS "STALIN'S ORGAN," NAMED THUS BY GERMAN TROOPS DUE TO ITS RESEMBLANCE TO A PIPE ORGAN. STALIN'S ORGAN WAS SEEN IN MANY FORMS DURING WORLD WAR II, THE ROCKETS BEING MOUNTED ON VARIOUS TRUCKS (OFTEN AMERICAN LEND-LEASE STUDEBAKER US6 VEHICLES), TANKS, AND EVEN ON FARM TRACTORS. BEFORE THE GERMAN INVASION, THE RED ARMY'S ARTILLERY BRANCH WAS UNIMPRESSED BY THE KATYUSHA BECAUSE IT TOOK UP TO 50 MINUTES TO LOAD AND FIRE THE ROCKETS IN ONE SALVO (A HOWITZER COULD FIRE UP TO 150 ROUNDS IN THE SAME TIME). HOWEVER, THE GREAT ATTRIBUTE OF THE KATYUSHA WAS ITS SIMPLICITY. IT COMPRISED A RACK OF PARALLEL RAILS ON WHICH 16 OR MORE ROCKETS WERE MOUNTED, WITH A FOLDING FRAME TO RAISE THE RAILS TO LAUNCH POSITION.

Q Which general, who later defected to the Nazis, commanded the Soviet Second Shock Army in early 1942?

A General Andrei Vlassov.

Q What happened to Vlassov's army?

A Surrounded in northern Russia by German forces, it was annihilated in June 1942.

Q Who was the commander of the SS *Totenkopf* Division in 1942?

A Theodor Eicke.

Q **What was the subject of Führer Directive No. 41 of April 1942?**

A The forthcoming summer offensive on the Eastern Front.

Q **Was the offensive to be along the whole Eastern Front?**

A No. As Hitler stated: "In pursuit of the original plan for the Eastern campaign, the armies of the central sector will stand fast, those in the north will capture Leningrad and link up with the Finns, while those on the southern flank will break through into the Caucasus."

Q **What was the codename of the German offensive into the Caucasus in 1942?**

A Operation Blue.

DID YOU KNOW

DESIGNED BY GEORGE SHPAGIN, THE RUSSIAN PPSH-41 SUBMACHINE GUN ENTERED SERVICE SHORTLY BEFORE THE GERMAN INVASION OF THE SOVIET UNION IN JUNE 1941. THE PPSH-41 WAS DESIGNED TO BE AS SIMPLE AS POSSIBLE. IT USED A MINIMUM NUMBER OF PARTS, A SIMPLE BLOW-BACK ACTION, AND FIRED FROM THE OPEN BOLT POSITION. IT SOON PROVED ITSELF TO BE EFFECTIVE AS A WEAPON AS WELL AS EASY TO MANUFACTURE, AND BECAME ONE OF THE MOST FAMOUS SMALL ARMS OF WORLD WAR II. FACTORIES AND WORKSHOPS THROUGHOUT THE SOVIET UNION BEGAN TURNING OUT THIS RELIABLE WEAPON, AND MORE THAN FIVE MILLION WERE PRODUCED BY 1945.

"AS DARKNESS APPROACHED, THE FIGHTING INTENSIFIED, THE SHELLING INCREASED "

BRITISH GUNNER, BATTLE OF GAZALA,
JUNE 1942

Q On the Eastern Front, what was Operation Bustard in May 1942?

A The German Eleventh Army launched Operation Bustard to destroy enemy forces in the Kerch Peninsula. For this task it deployed XXXII, VII Romanian, and XXX Corps (LIV Corps covered Sevastopol).

Q What was the function of the Central Staff of the USSR Partisan Movement?

A To direct partisan operations behind German lines.

Q Where was its headquarters?

A In Moscow.

Q Did the Red Army consider Soviet troops who surrendered to the enemy to be traitors?

A Yes. The Red Army field manual stated that a loyal soldier was either fighting or was dead; surrender was considered to be treason. The wartime edition of the official Soviet encyclopedia stated that "the penalty for premeditated surrender into captivity not necessitated by combat conditions is death by shooting."

Q Who was the Allied commander at the Battle of the Java Sea in February 1942?

A Dutch Rear Admiral Karel Doorman.

Q Who was the Japanese commander?

A Vice Admiral Takagi Takeo.

Q What happened at the battle?

" THE DOMINANT FEELING OF THE
BATTLEFIELD IS
LONELINESS
WILLIAM SLIM, ADDRESSING THE 10TH INDIAN DIVISION,
JUNE 1942 "

A Two Allied cruisers and three destroyers were sunk, the British cruiser HMS *Exeter* withdrew owing to battle damage, and Doorman was killed. The Japanese force under the command of Takeo suffered only one damaged destroyer.

Q What was the composition of the Allied force at the Battle of the Java Sea?

A It was a mixed unit of U.S., Dutch, British, and Australian warships.

DID YOU KNOW

THOUGH THE U.S. HAD BELIEVED THAT A WAR AGAINST JAPAN WAS INEVITABLE LONG BEFORE PEARL HARBOR—INDEED, AIR BASES AND OTHER FACILITIES WERE BEING CONSTRUCTED ON WAKE ISLAND AND THE MARSHALL ISLANDS IN THE MONTHS LEADING UP TO WAR—THE JAPANESE SURPRISE ATTACK CAUGHT THE U.S. OFF GUARD. THEREFORE, THE INITIAL U.S. STRATEGY FOR 1942 WAS AT FIRST DISORGANIZED AND LACKING COHERENCE. THE U.S. LACKED THE MANPOWER OR THE EQUIPMENT TO HOLD ON TO WHAT PACIFIC TERRITORY IT HAD, AND HAD LITTLE WAY OF REINFORCING THE PHILIPPINES OR ANY OTHER ISLANDS IN THE FACE OF JAPANESE INVASION. THUS, U.S. STRATEGY WAS TO HOLD ON FOR AS LONG AS POSSIBLE WHILST U.S. STRATEGISTS CAME UP WITH A PLAN. HOWEVER, STRATEGIC THINKING IN 1942 WAS LIMITED BY SEVERAL FACTORS. FIRSTLY, THE SHOCK OF PEARL HARBOR AND THE DESTRUCTION OF VITAL SHIPPING THERE TOOK ITS TOLL. SECONDLY, SUPERIOR JAPANESE PLANNING IN THE LEAD-UP TO 1942 GAVE THEM AN ADVANTAGE OVER THE AMERICANS. LASTLY, THE CONDITION OF U.S. UNPREPAREDNESS COULD BE IMPROVED ONLY OVER A PERIOD OF TIME, NOT OVERNIGHT.

145

Q Name the Japanese commander who led the attack on Singapore in February 1942.

A Lieutenant General Yamashita.

Q Which army did he command?

A The Twenty-Fifth Army.

Q Who was the British commander at Singapore?

A Lieutenant General Percival.

Q What was a decisive factor in the fall of Singapore?

A The defense of Singapore became futile when Japanese forces took control of the island's reservoirs and severed Singapore City's water supply.

"
THE JAPS MADE NO MOVE TO
FEED US. MANY HAD TASTED
NO FOOD IN FOUR DAYS
WILLIAM DYESS, THE "BATAAN DEATH MARCH,"
APRIL 1942
"

Q What was the U.S. Government's Executive Order 9066?

A Executive Order 9066 enabled the war secretary to displace people from military areas; and Japanese-Americans, already alienated following Pearl Harbor, were the primary victims of this policy. Some 11,000 Japanese-Americans were initially moved from the Pacific coast to camps in Arkansas and Texas.

Q How many Japanese-Americans were interned during the war?

A 112,000.

Q Was California attacked by the Japanese in 1942?

A Yes. In February the Japanese submarine *I-17* shelled an oil refinery at Ellwood, California. In total, 17 rounds were fired, inflicting only minor damage to a pier and an oil well derrick.

Q Which Japanese army captured Rangoon in March 1942?

A The Fifteenth Army.

Q Who replaced Douglas MacArthur as commander of Allied forces on Bataan in March 1942?

A Lieutenant General Jonathan Wainwright.

Q What was the Allied codename for the Japanese Nakajima B5 bomber?

A Kate.

DID YOU KNOW

AS C-IN-C OF THE COMBINED FLEET FROM JULY 1939, ISOROKU YAMAMOTO (1884–1943) WAS JAPAN'S GREATEST WARTIME NAVAL STRATEGIST. BORN IN 1884 IN NAGAOKA, HE JOINED THE NAVAL ACADEMY SHORTLY AFTER THE TURN OF THE CENTURY, GAINING COMBAT EXPERIENCE IN THE RUSSO-JAPANESE WAR OF 1904. HE WENT TO THE U.S. IN 1919 TO STUDY ENGLISH, AND ALSO TO LEARN ABOUT U.S. NAVAL AND INDUSTRIAL STRENGTHS. YAMAMOTO RETURNED TO JAPAN IN 1921 AND ROSE QUICKLY THROUGH A SERIES OF INFLUENTIAL POSITIONS. MOST SIGNIFICANTLY, HE BECAME AN EXPERT IN THE NEW ART OF NAVAL AVIATION WARFARE, SOMETHING HE LATER PUT TO DEVASTATING EFFECT AS ARCHITECT OF THE PEARL HARBOR ATTACK. HOWEVER, YAMAMOTO WAS NOT A SUPPORTER OF JAPANESE AGGRESSION, CORRECTLY BELIEVING THAT U.S. INDUSTRIAL POWER WOULD TRIUMPH IN A SUSTAINED CAMPAIGN. BUT ONCE WAR WAS INEVITABLE HE COMMITTED HIMSELF TO JAPANESE VICTORY. PEARL HARBOR ABLY DEMONSTRATED THE FORWARD-THINKING AND TACTICAL CAPABILITIES OF YAMAMOTO, AND IT FULFILED ALL HIS CLAIMS FOR NAVAL AVIATION BEING THE FUTURE OF WAR AT SEA.

Q Which British aircraft carrier was sunk by Japanese aircraft in early April 1942?

A Near Ceylon a Japanese scout plane spotted the carrier HMS *Hermes* and the destroyer HMAS *Vampire*. The subsequent air strike sank HMS *Hermes* in only 10 minutes after 40 bomb hits, and the *Vampire* went down after suffering 13 explosions. This effectively finished the British Pacific Fleet as a significant force in the region.

Q What was the "Bataan Death March"?

A In April 1942, 78,000 U.S. and Filipino troops fell into Japanese hands on Bataan and were made to walk 65 miles (104 km) in the most dreadful conditions to prison camps. Around one in three men died in what became known as the "Bataan Death March."

" WE KNEW NOW THE JAPS WOULD RESPECT NEITHER AGE NOR RANK. THEIR FEROCITY GREW AS WE MARCHED "

WILLIAM DYESS, THE "BATAAN DEATH MARCH," APRIL 1942

Q Who was the leader of the Indian Congress Party?

A Pandit Nehru.

Q What was the Doolittle Raid in April 1942?

A Sixteen U.S. B-25 Mitchell bombers flying from the aircraft carrier USS *Hornet* and led by Colonel James Doolittle achieved a major propaganda victory by bombing the Japanese capital, Tokyo.

DID YOU KNOW

THE USS *ENTERPRISE* WAS ONE OF THE MOST INFLUENTIAL WARSHIPS OF WORLD WAR II. A "YORKTOWN" CLASS AIRCRAFT CARRIER THAT JOINED THE PACIFIC FLEET IN 1938, THE USS *ENTERPRISE* WAS IMMEDIATELY SENT INTO ACTION FOLLOWING THE JAPANESE ATTACK ON PEARL HARBOR. THE SHIP MADE ITS FIRST SUCCESSFUL ENGAGEMENT OF THE WAR ON DECEMBER 11, 1941, WHEN ITS AIRCRAFT SANK THE JAPANESE SUBMARINE *I-170*. THE USS *ENTERPRISE*'S DEFINING ENGAGEMENT CAME IN JUNE 1942 DURING THE BATTLE OF MIDWAY. AIRCRAFT FLYING FROM THE USS *ENTERPRISE*, PARTICULARLY THE DOUGLAS SBD DAUNTLESS DIVE-BOMBER, SANK THE JAPANESE CARRIERS *KAGA* AND *AKAGI*, ASSISTED IN THE SINKING OF THE CARRIER *HIRYU*, AND LATER SANK THE HEAVY CRUISER *MIKUMA*.

Q What was the first major carrier battle of World War II?

A The Battle of the Coral Sea in May 1942.

Q Which American carrier was lost during the battle?

A USS *Lexington*.

Q Which Japanese aircraft carrier was sunk in the battle?

A The *Shoho*.

Q Why was the Battle of the Coral Sea a decisive engagement?

A The battle halted Japanese expansion plans in Papua and the Solomon Islands, and signaled the first major Japanese reverse in the war.

Q What was Australia's first home-produced wartime aircraft?

A The Commonwealth CA-12 Boomerang.

Q When did it make its first flight?

A May 1942.

Q Around which Pacific island did the Japanese plan to destroy the US Pacific Fleet in mid-1942?

A Midway.

> " LOWERED AWAY TO HOUSETOPS
> AND SLID OVER WESTERN OUTSKIRTS
> ## INTO LOW HAZE
> ## AND SMOKE
> COLONEL JAMES DOOLITTLE, RAID ON TOKYO,
> APRIL 1942 "

Q Three new panzer divisions were formed in 1942. Name two of them.

A The 25th, 26th, and 27th Panzer Divisions.

Q What was the main armament of an M4 Sherman tank?

A A 75mm gun.

Q On the Eastern Front, what German armies took part in Operation Blue into the Caucasus in June 1942?

A Sixth Army (330,000 troops and 300 tanks and assault guns); Second Army (95,000 troops); Seventeenth Army (150,000 troops and 180 tanks and assault guns); First Panzer Army (220,000 troops and 480 tanks and assault guns); and Fourth Panzer Army (200,000 troops and 480 tanks).

Q Which non-German formations took part in Operation Blue?

A The Hungarian Second and Italian Eighth Armies.

Q From which country did the Allied convoy PQ-17 sail in July 1942?

A Iceland.

Q How many ships were lost to German attack?

A 24 out of 35.

DID YOU KNOW

IN JUNE 1942 HITLER VISITED MARSHAL MANNERHEIM IN FINLAND TO OFFER CONGRATULATIONS ON THE FINN'S 75TH BIRTHDAY, AND TO STRENGTHEN THE MUTUAL RELATIONSHIPS BETWEEN GERMANY AND FINLAND. THE TWO MEN MET NEAR THE QUIET FINNISH BORDER TOWN OF IMATRA. THE MEETING WAS NOT A SUCCESS: AT ONE POINT HITLER DEMANDED THAT FINNISH JEWS BE DEPORTED; MANNERHEIM ANSWERED, "OVER MY DEAD BODY."

Q Summarize the reorganization of the German Army Group South in July 1942 as it advanced into the Caucasus.

A Army Group South was divided into Army Groups A and B.

Q What was the purpose of this reorganization?

A Army Group B (Second, Fourth Panzer, and Sixth Armies and the Hungarian Second Army) was ordered to destroy Soviet forces between the upper Donets and middle Don and secure a crossing of the Don near Voronezh. The Fourth Panzer and Sixth Armies would then race east to Stalingrad, from whence they would sweep south to support Army Group A in the Caucasus.

DID YOU KNOW

IN JULY 1942, IN THE FACE OF GERMAN ADVANCES IN THE CAUCASUS, STALIN ISSUED ORDER NO. 227. IN THIS HE ALLUDED TO HIS CONCERN ABOUT GERMAN GAINS: "THE TERRITORY OF THE SOVIET UNION IS NOT A WILDERNESS, BUT PEOPLE—WORKERS, PEASANTS, INTELLIGENTSIA, OUR FATHERS AND MOTHERS, WIVES, BROTHERS, CHILDREN. TERRITORY OF USSR THAT HAS BEEN CAPTURED BY THE ENEMY AND WHICH THE ENEMY IS LONGING TO CAPTURE IS BREAD AND OTHER RESOURCES FOR THE ARMY AND THE CIVILIANS, IRON AND FUEL FOR THE INDUSTRIES, FACTORIES AND PLANTS THAT SUPPLY THE MILITARY WITH HARDWARE AND AMMUNITION; THIS IS ALSO RAILROADS. WITH THE LOSS OF UKRAINE, BELORUSSIA, THE BALTICS, DONETS BASIN, AND OTHER AREAS WE HAVE LOST VAST TERRITORIES; THAT MEANS THAT WE HAVE LOST MANY PEOPLE, BREAD, METALS, FACTORIES, AND PLANTS. WE NO LONGER HAVE SUPERIORITY OVER THE ENEMY IN HUMAN RESOURCES AND IN BREAD SUPPLY. CONTINUATION OF RETREAT MEANS THE DESTRUCTION OF OUR MOTHERLAND. THE CONCLUSION IS THAT IT IS TIME TO STOP THE RETREAT. NOT A SINGLE STEP BACK! THIS SHOULD BE OUR SLOGAN FROM NOW ON."

> THE SUN BEATS DOWN—AS USUAL—
> AND WHEN IT GETS HOT ENOUGH—
> ## A COOL SHOWER
> ## COMES ALONG
> SERGEANT KAZAZKOW, U.S. ARMY, SOUTH PACIFIC,
> MARCH 1942

Q In July 1942 SS chief Heinrich Himmler ordered the start of Operation Reinhard. What was this?

A Its objectives were: to kill Polish Jews; to exploit the skilled or manual labor of some Polish Jews before killing them; to secure the personal property of the Jews (clothing, currency, jewellery); and to identify and secure immovable assets such as factories, apartments, and land. The camps used for the extermination were Belzec (opened March 1942), Sobibor (opened May 1942), and Treblinka (opened July 1942).

Q How many people did Operation Reinhard kill?

A In total 1.7 million Jews were killed during Reinhard, plus an unknown number of Poles, gypsies, and Soviet prisoners of war.

Q Who attended the First Moscow Conference in August 1942?

A British Prime Minister Winston Churchill and US Ambassador W. Averell Harriman, representing President Roosevelt.

Q What was the purpose of the conference?

A To discuss a common war strategy. Churchill, with the support of Ambassador Harriman, informed Stalin that it would be impossible for the British and Americans to open a second front in Europe in 1942.

Q Why was the city of Stalingrad an important symbol to both Hitler and Stalin?

A Stalingrad, "the city of Stalin," acted as a magnet for German forces because, for Hitler, it assumed a massive psychological significance—he became obsessed by it. Similarly, for Stalin the city was also an obsession. It had been named after him as a result of his defense of the city during the Russian Civil War. He insisted that it should be held at all costs. On a more practical level, he knew that if the Germans took the city Moscow would be vulnerable to an attack from the south.

Q How many citizens of Stalingrad were killed in the Luftwaffe air raids over two days in August 1942?

A 40,000.

" FROM EARLY MORNING OUR BATTERIES KEPT POURING A **MASSED SHELL-FIRE INTO THE ENEMY TANKS**
PRIVATE WOLFGANG KNOBLICH, GERMAN ARMY, RUSSIA, APRIL 1942 "

Q Who commanded the Japanese First Carrier Striking Force at the Battle of Midway?

A Vice Admiral Chuichi Nagumo.

Q Name at least two carriers that made up the First Carrier Striking Force.

A There were four carriers in total: *Akagi, Kaga, Hiryu,* and *Soryu.*

DID YOU KNOW

THE JAPANESE PLANS FOR THE BATTLE OF MIDWAY CENTERED AROUND THEIR
EFFORTS TO LURE THE U.S. PACIFIC FLEET INTO THE OPEN AND DESTROY IT.
HOWEVER, AS WAS COMMON IN JAPANESE STRATEGIC PLANNING, THE OPERA-
TION WAS OVER COMPLEX, MADE UNJUSTIFIED ASSUMPTIONS ABOUT HOW U.S.
NAVAL FORCES WOULD REACT, AND FAILED TO CONCENTRATE FORCE. INDEED,
EVEN THE CHOICE OF MIDWAY ISLAND WAS FLAWED, AND DEEPLY UNPOPULAR
WITH IMPERIAL JAPANESE NAVY CAPTAINS. A DIVERSIONARY FORCE WOULD BE
SENT TO THE ALEUTIANS TO DRAW OFF PART OF THE U.S. FLEET, WHILST THE
JAPANESE FORCES UNDER ADMIRAL YAMAMOTO WOULD CAPTURE MIDWAY.
THIS WOULD FORCE THE AMERICANS TO TRY TO RETAKE THE ISLAND, WHICH
WOULD GIVE YAMAMOTO THE OPPORTUNITY TO DESTROY NIMITZ'S CARRIERS
WITH HIS CARRIER-BASED AIRCRAFT, AIDED BY LAND-BASED BOMBERS
STATIONED ON THE NEWLY CAPTURED ISLAND. THIS WOULD LEAVE THE WEST
COAST OF AMERICA AT THE MERCY OF THE JAPANESE AND FORCE THE U.S. TO
NEGOTIATE A PEACE, OR SO THE THEORY WENT.

Q **What forces did the American deploy at the Battle of Midway?**

A Task Force 17 commanded by Rear Admiral Fletcher and containing
the carrier USS *Yorktown* (patched up from the Coral Sea action),
and Rear Admiral Spruance's Task Force 16 with the carriers USS *Hornet*
and USS *Enterprise*.

Q **How many aircraft carriers did the Japanese lose at Midway?**

A Four.

Q **How many aircraft carriers did the Americans lose at Midway?**

A One, USS *Yorktown*.

Q The fortress of Bir Hacheim featured in which North African battle?

A The Battle of Gazala in mid-1942.

Q At this battle, what was the "Cauldron"?

A German forces were temporarily encircled by Commonwealth forces during part of the battle. The area in which they were encircled was called the "Cauldron," mainly because it was under artillery fire and German forces had their backs to British minefields.

Q Which major North African port fell to Erwin Rommel in June 1942?

A Tobruk.

Q What was the name of the British Army that fought the Battle of Alam Halfa in autumn 1942?

A The Eighth Army.

Q Who was its commander?

A General Bernard Montgomery.

" OUR ARTILLERY OPENED UP IN ITS FULL FURY BY WAY OF A PRELUDE TO **THE INFANTRY ASSAULT**
GENERAL VON MANSTEIN DIRECTING THE
GERMAN ASSAULT ON SEVASTOPOL, JUNE 1942 **"**

DID YOU KNOW

THE BURMA-THAILAND RAILWAY WAS ONE OF THE GREATEST, AND MOST APPALLING, ENGINEERING FEATS OF WORLD WAR II. IN MID-1942, THE JAPANESE WERE FACED WITH CHRONIC PROBLEMS IN SUPPLYING THEIR FORCES FIGHTING IN BURMA, PARTICULARLY AS SHIPPING ROUTES TO RANGOON WERE INCREASINGLY INTERDICTED BY ALLIED AIRCRAFT, SHIPS, AND SUBMARINES. THE SOLUTION WAS TO BUILD A RAILROAD EXTENSION BETWEEN THANBYUZAYAT IN BURMA AND NONG PLADUK IN THAILAND, WHICH, WHEN LINKED TO EXISTING RAIL ROUTES, WOULD PROVIDE A LOGISTICAL LIFELINE THROUGHOUT BURMA AND GIVE BETTER ACCESS TO SHIPPING SUPPLIES RUNNING UP THROUGH THE GULF OF SIAM.

Q How many Allied prisoners and forced laborers worked on the Burma-Thailand railway?

A 61,000 Allied prisoners and more than 270,000 laborers from Japanese-occupied territories.

Q How many died due to the inhuman working conditions?

A Some 12,000 Allied prisoners and 90,000 other laborers—an average of 425 deaths for every mile of track laid.

Q Why did the island of Guadalcanal become so important to the Japanese after the Battle of Midway?

A After the setback at the Battle of Midway in June 1942, the Japanese concentrated their efforts on defense of their territorial gains—what they euphemistically called the Greater East Asia Co-Prosperity Sphere—basically the areas of Asia that gave Japan the raw materials and resources she needed to fight the war. This strategy of defense included building an airfield on Guadalcanal as a way of using land-based aircraft in support of carrier-borne units against any U.S. attack.

Q Which American four-engined bomber mounted a slender wing above a tall fuselage bay?

A The Consolidated B-24 Liberator.

Q What was the U.S. Navy's first cantilever monoplane flying boat?

A The Consolidated PBY Catalina.

Q Which American warplane sank more Japanese shipping than any other Allied aircraft during the war?

A The Douglas SBD Dauntless dive-bomber.

" A PINT OF SWEAT WILL SAVE A
GALLON OF BLOOD
GEORGE S. PATTON, TO U.S. FORCES
AT CASABLANCA, NOVEMBER 8, 1942 "

Q The Douglas DC-3 transport aircraft is better known in its military form. What was this?

A The C-47 Skytrain, known as the Dakota in British service.

Q General Eisenhower said that the Dakota was one of the four decisive weapons of World War II. What were the other three?

A The Jeep, the Bazooka, and the M4 Sherman tank.

Q Which company developed the SBD Dauntless dive-bomber?

A Northrop.

Q Who was chief designer on the project?

A Ed Heinemann.

DID YOU KNOW

THE .30IN-CALIBER M1 GARAND RIFLE WAS THE FIRST SELF-LOADING RIFLE ISSUED AS A STANDARD FIREARM TO AN ARMY. IT WAS ACTUALLY ACCEPTED INTO MILITARY SERVICE IN 1932, BUT HAD A LONG TECHNICAL GESTATION PERIOD IN WHICH ITS DESIGNER, JOHN C. GARAND, REFINED IT INTO A FIRST-CLASS COMBAT WEAPON. THE M1 WAS A GAS-OPERATED RIFLE FED BY AN INTERNAL MAGAZINE HOLDING EIGHT ROUNDS, REFILLED BY PUSHING AN EIGHT-ROUND CLIP DOWN THROUGH THE OPENED BOLT. IF ANYTHING, THE MAGAZINE SYSTEM PROVED TO BE THE ONLY PRACTICAL FLAW OF THE M1; THE RIFLE COULD BE LOADED ONLY WHEN EMPTY, AND THE MAGAZINE COULD NOT BE TOPPED UP WITH INDIVIDUAL ROUNDS. ALSO, THE EMPTY CLIP WAS EJECTED WITH AN EMPHATIC "PING," SIGNALING TO ENEMY SOLDIERS THAT THE INFANTRYMAN HAD TO RELOAD. HOWEVER, IN OTHER RESPECTS THE M1 WAS A SUPERB WEAPON. IT WAS EXTREMELY RUGGED, AND PROVIDED UTTERLY DEPENDABLE SERVICE TO U.S. SOLDIERS IN ALL THEATERS OF WAR. ITS SEMIAUTOMATIC ACTION ALLOWED UNITS TO GENERATE THE HEAVY FIREPOWER SO ESSENTIAL IN THE JUNGLE COMBAT OF THE PACIFIC WAR, AND ITS .30IN ROUND HAD DECISIVE STOPPING POWER. THE M1 WAS ALSO ACCURATE, THOUGH ONLY IN TRAINED HANDS, EXPLAINING WHY TWO LATER SNIPER VERSIONS—THE M1C AND M1D—NEVER SAW LARGE-SCALE PRODUCTION.

> " ANIMALS FLEE THIS CITY; THE HARDEST
> STORMS CANNOT BEAR IT FOR
> LONG; ONLY MEN ENDURE "
>
> ANONYMOUS GERMAN OFFICER AT STALINGRAD,
> OCTOBER 1942

Q What cargo ships were nicknamed "American ugly ducklings"?

A Liberty ships.

Q Who replaced Rommel as the commander of Panzer Army Africa in September 1942?

A General George Stumme.

Q What happened to this commander during the Battle of El Alamein in October 1942?

A He died of a heart attack.

Q The British attack plan at the Battle of El Alamein was divided into two distinct phases. What was the first phase?

A Codenamed Operation Lightfoot, it involved a diversionary assault in the south by XIII Corps, while farther to the north XXX Corps launched the main British break-in thrust to open up two corridors in the enemy minefields.

Q What was the second phase of the British plan?

A Codenamed Operation Supercharge, the armor of XXX Corps would advance through the corridors in the enemy minefields.

Q What was the size of a Tiger I's crew?

A Five.

Q What task did each crew member perform?

A Commander, gunner, loader, radio operator, and driver.

Q What was distinctive about the Tiger's suspension?

A It was composed of driving sprocket, rear idler, and interleaved road wheels (36 in total).

Q What problems did this present in cold weather?

A Mud, ice, and rocks could jam the track mechanism and immobilize the tank.

DID YOU KNOW

FOLLOWING ENCOUNTERS WITH SOVIET T-34 AND KV-1 TANKS IN 1941, GERMAN TANK DESIGNERS WERE INSTRUCTED TO PRODUCE A HEAVY TANK THAT WOULD RESTORE MASTERY OF THE BATTLEFIELD TO THE GERMANS. THE RESULT WAS THE PANZER VI AUSF E—THE TIGER I—WHICH ENTERED SERVICE IN AUGUST 1942. IT WAS ARMED WITH THE POWERFUL 88MM GUN (ORIGINALLY DEVELOPED FROM THE 88MM FLAK 36 L/56 GUN), WHICH MEANT IT COULD KNOCK OUT ANY ALLIED TANK THEN IN SERVICE. ITS THICK (BUT NOT SHOT-DEFLECTING) ARMOR MADE IT VIRTUALLY INDESTRUCTIBLE (THE U.S. SHERMAN, ARMED WITH A 76MM GUN, AND RUSSIAN T-34/85, ARMED WITH AN 85MM GUN, STOOD A CHANCE ONLY AGAINST A TIGER AT CLOSE RANGE, AND ONLY WITH A SHOT AGAINST ITS SIDE OR REAR).

Q Which Soviet army defended the city of Stalingrad in 1942?

A The Sixty-Second Army.

Q Who was its commander?

A General Vasily Chuikov.

Q What was the German army that tried to capture Stalingrad in 1942?

A The Sixth Army.

DID YOU KNOW

CONVOYS PROVIDED PROTECTIVE ESCORTS FOR MERCHANT VESSELS AGAINST ENEMY SURFACE, SUBMERGED, OR AIR ATTACK. ALLIED CONVOYS, OFTEN CONTAINING MORE THAN 50 VESSELS, SAILED IN COLUMNS AND WEAVED THEIR WAY ACROSS THE SEA-LANES. IN THE ATLANTIC AND ARCTIC, THE BAD WEATHER REDUCED VISIBILITY, FROZE THE CREWS, AND CREATED GREAT WAVES THAT LEFT VESSELS VULNERABLE TO COLLISION. THE MAIN THREAT TO ALLIED CONVOYS WERE THE U-BOATS, WHICH INFLICTED CRITICAL LOSSES UPON SHIPPING. ANTISUBMARINE MEASURES GRADUALLY IMPROVED, HOWEVER, WITH ENHANCED AIR–SEA COORDINATION, NEW TACTICS, AND SCIENTIFIC INNOVATIONS. SHIPBUILDING WAS ALSO INCREASED TO REPLACE LOST VESSELS. THE INTERCEPTION OF GERMAN RADIO TRANSMISSIONS, CENTIMETRIC RADAR, ESCORT CARRIERS, U-BOAT-DETECTION TECHNOLOGY (ASDIC AND SONAR), IMPROVED DEPTH CHARGES, AND LAUNCHERS ALL HELPED PROTECT CONVOYS. GERMANY'S CAMPAIGN TO DESTROY ALLIED CONTROL OF THE ATLANTIC SEA-LANES WAS ESPECIALLY CRITICAL AS BRITAIN CAME TO RELY UPON NORTH AMERICAN AID. IN THE NORTH ATLANTIC ALONE, SOME 2,232 VESSELS WERE SUNK, BUT THE DESTRUCTION OF 785 U-BOATS SECURED ALLIED COMMAND OF THE SEA-LANES.

Q The Soviets planned to encircle Axis units fighting in and around Stalingrad by launching a massive offensive. What was its codename?

A Operation Uranus.

Q When did this operation commence?

A November 19, 1942.

> " I'VE ONLY GOT DISMAL AND DEPRESSING NEWS FOR YOU TODAY. OUR MANY
> **JEWISH FRIENDS ARE BEING TAKEN AWAY** "
> ANNE FRANK, DIARY ENTRY, OCTOBER 9, 1942

163

Q Which South American country declared war on Germany and Italy in August 1942?

A Brazil.

Q The Nazis cleared a Jewish ghetto in which city in September 1942?

A Warsaw. More than 50,000 Jews were killed by poison gas or sent to concentration camps.

Q Which German field marshal was dismissed in September 1942?

A Field Marshal Wilhelm List, commander of Army Group A.

Q Who replaced Franz Halder as chief of the German General Staff in September 1942?

A Kurt Zeitzler.

Q What was the codename for the British and American landings in Morocco and Algeria (French North Africa) in November 1942?

A Operation Torch.

> " THIS IS NOT THE END. IT IS NOT EVEN THE
> BEGINNING OF THE END. BUT
> ## IT IS, PERHAPS, THE END
> ## OF THE BEGINNING "
> WINSTON CHURCHILL, NOVEMBER 10, 1942,
> AFTER EL ALAMEIN

Q Why did the Allies invade French North Africa in 1942?

A To seize French North Africa as a springboard for future operations to clear the whole of North Africa of Axis forces.

Q Who was Vichy commissioner in Africa at the time?

A Admiral Jean François Darlan.

DID YOU KNOW

DURING 1942 EFFORTS WERE MADE TO STRENGTHEN THE GERMAN PANZER DIVISIONS AT THE FRONT. ON AVERAGE, THE PANZER DIVISIONS THAT COMMENCED BLUE FIELDED JUST 126 TANKS EACH—40 PERCENT FEWER THAN IN BARBAROSSA. TO OFFSET THIS, HOWEVER, A TINY PROPORTION OF THESE AFVS—JUST 133 IN FACT—WERE THE LATEST PANZER IV MODEL F2 VEHICLES THAT MOUNTED THE POTENT LONG-BARRELLED 75MM KwK 40 L/48 CANNON AND FEATURED FRONTAL ARMOR INCREASED TO 1.96 IN (50 MM) THICKNESS. THE GUN OF THE F2 DELIVERED A MUZZLE VELOCITY OF 2,430FPS (740MPS) AND COULD PENETRATE 3.5 IN (89 MM) OF WELL-SLOPED ARMOR AT THE TYPICAL COMBAT RANGE OF 3,282 FT (1,000 M), SUFFICIENT TO PUNCH THROUGH EVEN THE FRONTAL ARMOR OF THE T-34. WHAT THE GERMANS DESPERATELY NEEDED, THOUGH, WAS LARGER NUMBERS OF THE PANZER IV MODEL F2 TO NEUTRALIZE THE IMPACT THE T-34 THEN EXERTED ON THE TACTICAL BATTLEFIELD.

Q Which three Japanese aircraft carriers protected a Japanese supply convoy as it attempted a resupply mission to Guadalcanal in August 1942?

A The *Ryujo, Zuizaku,* and *Shokaku.*

Q What was the name of the U.S. force that intercepted the Japanese convoy?

A Task Force 61.

Q What was the result of the subsequent battle on August 24?

A U.S. and Japanese carrier aircraft dealt mutual blows, the U.S. sinking the *Ryujo* and the Japanese damaging, although not critically, the USS *Enterprise.* The carrier forces separated, but the next day U.S. Marine dive-bombers flying from Henderson Field sunk two Japanese transporters (*Jintsu* and *Kinryu Maru*) and the destroyer *Mutsuki.*

Q What was the name of the American airfield on Guadalcanal?

A Henderson Field.

Q Who led the Japanese attack by 20,000 troops against this airfield in late October 1942?

A General Masao Maruyama.

Q Which Japanese naval force moved toward Guadalcanal in support of Maruyama's offensive in late October 1942?

A The Combined Fleet.

DID YOU KNOW

ADMIRAL CHESTER W. NIMITZ WAS ONE OF THE MOST GIFTED NAVAL COMMANDERS OF WORLD WAR II. BORN IN 1885 IN TEXAS, NIMITZ FIRST SET HIS SIGHTS ON A CAREER IN THE U.S. ARMY, BUT OWING TO A LACK OF PLACES AT WEST POINT HE BEGAN ATTENDANCE AT THE NAVAL ACADEMY CLASS IN 1905. NIMITZ'S CROWNING ACHIEVEMENT CAME WHEN HE REPLACED REAR-ADMIRAL KIMMEL AS C-IN-C OF THE U.S. PACIFIC FLEET AFTER THE ATTACK ON PEARL HARBOR, NIMITZ BEING PROMOTED TO FULL ADMIRAL. THROUGHOUT THE PACIFIC CAMPAIGN, NIMITZ DEMONSTRATED AN AGGRESSIVE DEFENSIVE ATTITUDE COMBINED WITH A DEEP PRACTICAL UNDERSTANDING OF NAVAL WARFARE, AND AN AFFABLE PERSONALITY THAT MADE HIM POPULAR AND RESPECTED. NIMITZ PRESIDED OVER THE GREAT NAVAL BATTLES OF THE PACIFIC WAR, AND HAD AN EXCELLENT GRASP OF HOW TO SUPPORT AMPHIBIOUS LAND CAMPAIGNS. IT IS A SIGN OF HIS CAPABILITIES THAT, IN NOVEMBER 1945, HE WAS MADE CHIEF OF NAVAL OPERATIONS ON THE RETIREMENT OF ADMIRAL KING.

RECKLESS COUNTERATTACKS, WITH HUGE LOSSES, GOT NOWHERE. ## IN SHORT, WE WERE SURROUNDED

BENNO ZIESER, GERMAN SOLDIER AT STALINGRAD, DECEMBER 1942

Q **Name the U.S. Navy units sent to intercept this force.**

A U.S. Task Forces 16 and 17, containing the carriers USS *Hornet* and USS *Enterprise*.

Q **What was the name of the resulting battle when the two naval fleets clashed?**

A The Battle of Santa Cruz.

167

Q **What happened at the Battle of Santa Cruz in October 1942?**

A At first light on October 26 both the Americans and Japanese put flights of attack aircraft into the sky. Over the course of a four-hour battle, the Japanese carriers *Zuiho* and *Shokaku* were badly damaged, while the USS *Enterprise* suffered a smashed flight deck and the USS *Hornet* was destroyed by two torpedo and six bomb strikes and had to be abandoned. The Japanese claimed victory in the battle, but lost more than 100 pilots and aircraft, unacceptably high losses that rendered many of the carriers almost inoperable.

Q **In the Pacific theater, where was "Ironbottom Sound"?**

A Between the coast of Guadalcanal and Savo Island. So called because of the many sunken ships lying on the seabed.

> **PRACTICALLY EVERY BUILDING OF THE DISMAL PLACE WAS EITHER FLAT OR LITTLE MORE THAN A HEAP OF RUBBLE**
>
> GENERAL ERWIN ROMMEL, ON ENTERING TOBRUK, JUNE 21, 1942

Q On the Eastern Front, what was the aim of the Soviet Operation Little Saturn in December 1942?

A The destruction of the Italian Eighth Army and isolation of Group Hollidt west of Stalingrad.

Q The Germans mounted a relief operation in December 1942 to rescue Axis forces trapped in the Stalingrad Pocket. What was its codename?

A Operation Winter Storm.

Q Who commanded this relief operation?

A Field Marshal Erich von Manstein.

Q Who was the commander of the trapped German Sixth Army at Stalingrad?

A General Friedrich Paulus.

Q What was the codeword that was to signal the Sixth Army to break out of the Stalingrad Pocket and link up with the German relief force?

A Thunderclap.

1943

Allied victories in Papua New Guinea, the Solomon Islands, and Burma forced the Japanese on to the defensive in the Pacific. Axis forces were cleared from North Africa, allowing the Allies to invade Italy. And on the Eastern Front the Germans suffered two decisive defeats: at Stalingrad and Kursk.

Q The U.S. Fifth Army was formed in North Africa in January 1943. Who was its commander?

A General Mark Clark.

Q Who replaced Admiral Erich Raeder as commander-in-chief of German naval forces in January 1942?

A Admiral Karl Dönitz.

Q Why did Admiral Raeder resign his post?

A Because of German naval blunders made at the Battle of the Barents Sea in December 1942.

> " THE DUTY OF THE MEN AT STALINGRAD
> ## IS TO BE DEAD
> ADOLF HITLER, JANUARY 1943 "

Q Which brother and sister were executed in Munich in February 1943 for the crime of distributing traitorous literature?

A Hans and Sophie Scholl.

Q Which anti-Nazi group did they belong to?

A The White Rose group.

DID YOU KNOW

THE RED ORCHESTRA WAS ESTABLISHED IN 1939 BY LEOPOLD TREPPER, AN AGENT IN THE SOVIET MILITARY INTELLIGENCE SERVICE. IT COLLECTED INTELLIGENCE FROM AGENTS IN NAZI-OCCUPIED EUROPE AND NEUTRAL SWITZERLAND. IT COMPRISED THREE MAIN SECTIONS: THE NETWORK IN FRANCE, BELGIUM, AND HOLLAND; A NETWORK IN BERLIN (WHICH INCLUDED HARRO SCHULZE-BOYSEN, AN INTELLIGENCE OFFICER ASSIGNED TO THE GERMAN AIR MINISTRY, AND ARVID VON HARNACK, WHO WORKED IN THE MINISTRY OF ECONOMICS); AND THE "LUCY SPY RING" THAT OPERATED FROM SWITZERLAND. THE LATTER INCLUDED SOME HIGH-RANKING GERMAN INDIVIDUALS: LIEUTENANT GENERAL FRITZ THEILE, WEHRMACHT COMMUNICATIONS BRANCH; AND RUDOLF VON GERSDORFF, WHO BECAME ARMY GROUP CENTER'S INTELLIGENCE OFFICER ON THE EASTERN FRONT.

Q On the Eastern Front, what was the Soviet Operation Ring of January 1943?

A The codename for the destruction of the German Sixth Army at Stalingrad.

Q On the Eastern Front, what was the Soviet Operation Iskra?

A An offensive designed to push the German Eighteenth Army out of the Schlusselburg-Mga salient and thus reopen a supply line to the besieged city of Leningrad.

Q Georgi Zhukov was promoted to marshal following his Operation Mars. Why was this somewhat surprising?

A Because Mars cost the Red Army nearly 500,000 troops killed, wounded, or captured (German casualties were around 40,000).

Q What was the last German airfield to fall in the Stalingrad Pocket?

A Gumrak, on January 23, 1943.

Q Which German airfield in the Stalingrad Pocket was captured on January 16, 1943?

A Pitomnik.

Q Why did Hitler promote the commander of the Sixth Army at Stalingrad, Friedrich Paulus, to field marshal at the end of January 1943?

A It was a cynical move to prompt the commander at Stalingrad to commit suicide rather than surrender (no German field marshal had yet surrendered to the enemy).

DID YOU KNOW

GERMAN PANZERGRENADIER DIVISIONS WERE INTEGRAL TO BLITZKRIEG WARFARE, WITH MOTORIZED INFANTRY ACCOMPANYING AND SUPPORTING THE FAST-MOVING PANZER DIVISIONS. THE INFANTRY TRAVELED IN HALFTRACK ARMORED PERSONNEL CARRIERS TO AND ON TO THE BATTLE-FIELD. HOWEVER, THERE WERE NEVER ENOUGH HALFTRACKS, SO EACH DIVISION ALSO USED TRUCKS TO TRANSPORT ITS MEN. IN ADDITION, EARLIER MOTORIZED DIVISIONS ALSO HAD LARGE NUMBERS OF MOTOR-CYCLE-MOUNTED TROOPS, ALTHOUGH THEY DISAPPEARED AS THE WAR WENT ON BECAUSE MOTORCYCLES WERE VULNERABLE TO SMALL-ARMS FIRE.

TELL THEM FROM ME THEY ARE
UNLOADING HISTORY
WINSTON CHURCHILL, TELEGRAM TO THE
PORT COMMANDER AT TRIPOLI, FEBRUARY 24, 1943

Q Did Hitler's tactic work?

A No. Paulus surrendered at Stalingrad on January 31, 1943. Hitler was disgusted, stating: "Here is a man who can look on while fifty or sixty thousand are dying and defending themselves with courage to the end—how can he give himself up to the Bolsheviks?"

Q How many troops did the Germans lose when the Sixth Army surrendered at Stalingrad?

A 150,000 dead and another 90,000 taken prisoner, including 24 generals and 2,000 officers (only 6,000 returned home to Germany in the 1950s).

Q How many aircraft did the Luftwaffe lose during the abortive Stalingrad airlift?

A 488 aircraft and 1,000 air crews.

Q Why did Stalin create a communist-led Polish army in February 1943?

A As a counterweight to the Western Allied-sponsored Polish Army that was being formed in Iran. Both units were staffed by Poles who were former prisoners of the Soviets. Because of the lack of Polish cadres left in the USSR, though, many of the commanders and specialists in Stalin's Polish Army would be Russian.

Q In North Africa, where was the Mareth Line?

A On the Libyan-Tunisian border.

Q What was the name of the German army that confronted Anglo-American forces in Tunisia at the end of 1942?

A The Fifth Panzer Army.

Q Who commanded this army?

A Colonel General Hans-Jürgen von Arnim.

Q Where did Axis forces attack American troops in western Tunisia between February 14 and 22, 1943?

A At the Kasserine Pass.

Q What was the result?

A The attack successfully advanced 60 miles (96 km) in the face of collapsing American cohesion.

> ## YOU'LL NEVER GET THE
> # PURPLE HEART HIDING IN A
> ## FOXHOLE! FOLLOW ME!
> LIEUTENANT-COLONEL HENRY P. CROWE,
> JANUARY 13, 1943

DID YOU KNOW

GERMAN PANZERGRENADIER DIVISIONS HAD A TANK ELEMENT, WHICH COULD BE QUITE SIZEABLE. AT THE BATTLE OF KURSK, FOR EXAMPLE, THE ÉLITE *GROSSDEUTSCHLAND* DIVISION HAD 45 PANZER IVs, 46 PANTHERS, 13 TIGER Is, AND 35 ASSAULT GUNS. BY THE MIDDLE OF THE WAR, THE PANZERGRENADIERS THAT TRAVELED IN HALFTRACKS PRECEDED THE PANZERS ON TO THE BATTLEFIELD, TO SEARCH OUT AND DESTROY ENEMY ANTITANK GUN POSITIONS AND ENEMY INFANTRY TANK-DESTRUCTION PARTIES LYING IN WAIT FOR THE PANZERS. ON PAPER EACH DIVISION NUMBERED ON AVERAGE 13,900 TROOPS, DIVIDED BETWEEN TWO MOTORIZED INFANTRY REGIMENTS; ONE ARMORED BATTALION; ONE ARTILLERY REGIMENT (WITH 12 105MM HOWITZERS, 16 150MM HOWITZERS AND 8 SELF-PROPELLED 105MM HOWITZERS); 1 ANTITANK BATTALION (28 75MM ASSAULT GUNS OR TANK DESTROYERS AND 12 TOWED 75MM ANTI-TANK GUNS); AN ARMORED RECONNAISSANCE BATTALION; AN ANTIAIRCRAFT BATTALION; ENGINEER BATTALION; SIGNALS BATTALION; AND VARIOUS SUPPORT SERVICES.

175

Q What was Erwin Rommel's last battle in North Africa?

A At Medinine on March 6–7, 1943.

Q Was it a success?

A No. He attacked Montgomery's forces that faced him on the Mareth Line. He concentrated three panzer divisions with 160 tanks that were supported by some 200 guns and 10,000 infantry. Yet. Montgomery, due to his foreknowledge of the attack (ULTRA intercepts had provided the British commander with vital intelligence), had managed to assemble a force of 400 tanks, 350 artillery pieces, and 470 antitank guns to halt Rommel. The weight of Allied numbers soon defeated Rommel's thrust and inflicted heavy casualties on Axis forces.

DID YOU KNOW

The introduction of Panzer VI Model E Tiger I heavy tanks into the North African theater during December 1942 helped the Axis restabilize the strategic situation following the twin disasters of Operation Torch and Rommel's "Great Retreat" after the Second Battle of El Alamein. The Tiger I heavy tank was a squat and angular 55-ton (56-tonne) vehicle that mounted the lethal 88mm KwK 43 L/56 gun. It possessed impressive levels of protection, with frontal armor some 3.9 in (100 mm) thick, plus 3.1 in (80 mm) plates on its sides and rear. Apart from the earliest vehicles, the Tiger was powered by a 700hp Maybach HL 230 engine that delivered a satisfactory top road speed of 23.5mph (38kph) but only a modest 12.5mph (20kph) off road. Since the Tiger was too large to be transported on the standard German railroad flat-car, the manufacturers, Henschel, developed a novel two-track system for the vehicle. In battle the Tiger utilized wide 28.5 in (725 mm) combat tracks, but when being moved by rail these were replaced with narrower transportation tracks. The Tiger made its operational debut during August 1942 on the Eastern Front, but fought many of its earliest actions in North Africa during early 1943. Though the Tiger both mounted an extremely potent gun and was heavily armored, its combat effectiveness was undermined somewhat by persistent mechanical unreliability and its limited mobility. Nevertheless, when employed in the defensive battles that dominated the German Army's experiences from 1943 onward, the Tiger proved a formidable tank-killer that bolstered German defensive resistance against superior Allied numbers. Unfortunately for the German Army, there always remained too few Tigers available—only 1,354 were built—to restore the steadily deteriorating strategic situation during the second half of the war.

Q How many Axis troops surrendered to the Allies in North Africa in May 1943?

A 275,000.

Q What happened at the Battle of Huon Gulf in early January 1943?

A Waves of U.S. aircraft attacked Japanese supply convoys destined for Papua New Guinea, sinking three Japanese transports and downing eighty Japanese aircraft with few losses.

Q Why was the U.S. capture of Guadalcanal in February 1943 so important to Allied war aims?

“ GUADALCANAL IS NO LONGER MERELY THE NAME OF AN ISLAND. IT IS THE GRAVEYARD OF THE JAPANESE ARMY
Major General Kiyotake Kawaguchi, 1943 **”**

177

A Ejecting the Japanese from Guadalcanal was a crucial land victory for the U.S., giving it a base from which to penetrate Japan's Pacific conquests and providing security for Australia and New Zealand.

Q Who was the British general who conducted guerrilla warfare behind Japanese lines in Burma beginning in February 1943?

A Orde Wingate.

Q What was the formation he commanded?

A The 77th Indian Brigade.

Q Orde Wingate's 77th Indian Brigade, which fought the Japanese in Burma, had another name. What was it?

A The Chindits.

Q Where did this name come from?

A They were named after the stone lions seen guarding Buddhist temples.

Q What was the mission of the 77th Indian Brigade?

A To disrupt Japanese communications and tactical deployments, and pave the way for more opportunities for conventional offensives.

> ## THE VULNERABLE ARTERY IS THE LINE OF COMMUNICATIONS WINDING THROUGH THE JUNGLE
> ORDE WINGATE, BURMA, 1943

Q In the Pacific theater, what was the Allied Elkton Plan?

A Initiated in February 1943, it was the campaign to eject Japanese forces from New Guinea, New Britain, and the Solomon Islands and isolate the Japanese base at Rabaul.

Q What was the Japanese response to the plan?

A In response to Allied victories in Papua and Guadalcanal, the Japanese began pouring reinforcements into New Guinea, including the Eighteenth Army under Lieutenant General Adachi Hatazo and the Fourth Air Army.

DID YOU KNOW

By 1943, it was becoming apparent to a number of Japanese commanders that they were fighting a losing battle. After failing to knock
out the U.S. carriers at Pearl Harbor, the hope for 1942 had rested
on securing a perimeter wide and deep enough to protect its territories. Yamamoto, commander of the Combined Fleet, felt that the
qualitative difference in national strength between Japan and the
U.S. was patently obvious, and that any prolonged war between the
two countries could only end in defeat for Japan. He hoped that
the rapid destruction of the main force of the U.S. fleet and the
strategy of continually seeking decisive engagements would weaken
the morale of both the U.S. Navy and the people, forcing the
government to seek peace at the negotiation table.

Q What was the American Operation Cleanslate of February 1943?

A A force of U.S. assault battalions captured the diminutive Russell Island to the northwest of Guadalcanal.

Q Cleanslate was part of a wider Allied strategy in the Pacific in early 1943. What was this strategy?

A The occupation was the first in a series of U.S. campaigns to reclaim the Solomon Islands, and looked to cut off the Japanese naval and air base at Rabaul, New Britain, in a wider pincer operation called "Operation Cartwheel." Cleanslate was also the first element in General MacArthur and Admiral Nimitz's plan to reconquer the Pacific by working up from the south and east through Japanese-occupied territory in a systematic island-hopping strategy.

Q Who was the commander of the U.S. Fourteenth Army Air Force in China?

A Major General Claire Chennault.

Q Who attended the Casablanca Conference in January 1943?

A Winston Churchill and Franklin D. Roosevelt.

Q The conference highlighted differences between the British and Americans regarding the defeat of Hitler. What was British strategy regarding the defeat of Germany?

A The British wanted to keep fighting in the Mediterranean before the main attack on the Continent via the English Channel. They proposed invasions of Sicily and Italy as a means of drawing German reserves away from France and the Low Countries, which would cause the fall of Mussolini, and establish air bases in Italy, from where German armaments factories and Romanian oil fields could be bombed.

> ❝ THE REMAINDER OF THE TANKS WITHDREW BACK DOWN THE ROAD AND SAT
> ## ON THE HIGH GROUND ❞
> MAJOR C. MIDDLETON, ROYAL ARTILLERY,
> NORTH AFRICA, FEBRUARY 21, 1943

Q What was American strategy for the same aim?

A The Americans believed the British plan would only dissipate resources for the cross-Channel invasion, and tie down forces in a sideshow. They believed the quickest way to defeat Hitler was an invasion of northern France. However, as a cross-Channel invasion was not possible in 1943, they grudgingly accepted that Sicily should be invaded (though Italy was not on the agenda).

Q At the conference, which took priority; the defeat of Germany or Japan?

A The defeat of Nazi Germany.

DID YOU KNOW

THERE WERE TWO FORMS OF ALLIED INTELLIGENCE IN THE PACIFIC THEATER, KNOWN AS ULTRA AND MAGIC. ULTRA REFERRED TO THE DECRYPTION OF MILITARY COMMUNICATIONS, WHEREAS MAGIC RELATED TO DIPLOMATIC SOURCES. BOTH WERE PART OF THE MASSIVE ALLIED CODE-BREAKING EFFORT WHICH HIT A HIGH SPOT WHEN THE BRITISH DECIPHERED GERMAN ENIGMA MACHINE CODES. AS THE WAR PROGRESSED, THE BRITISH AND U.S. INTELLIGENCE COMMUNITIES BEGAN TO COMBINE THEIR EFFORTS TO DECIPHER JAPANESE EQUIVALENTS. ON MAY 17, 1943, THE BRUSA (BRITAIN AND THE UNITED STATES OF AMERICA) AGREEMENT FORMED A WORKING INTELLIGENCE PARTNERSHIP, THE U.S. ARMY OVERSEEING DECRYPTION OF JAPANESE MILITARY CODES AND CIPHERS, WHILE THE BRITISH CONCENTRATED MAINLY ON THE EUROPEAN THEATER. MAGIC CODES—WHICH WERE PRODUCED ON THE FORMIDABLE "PURPLE" CODING MACHINE—WERE ACTUALLY BEING BROKEN BEFORE DECEMBER 1941, GIVING THE U.S. AN INDICATION OF THE OUTBREAK OF WAR, BUT NOT TELLING IT WHERE THE FIRST ATTACK WOULD COME. SUCH WAS TYPICAL OF MAGIC INTELLIGENCE, AND IT PROVED MORE USEFUL AS A GENERAL GUIDE TO FUTURE JAPANESE INTENTIONS THAN AS A SCRIPT TO FUTURE JAPANESE OPERATIONS.

181

Q What was the Japanese Operation I of April 1943?

A A program of bombardment against Allied shipping in the Solomon Islands and New Guinea.

Q Was it a success?

A No. Three Allied transports, one destroyer, and one corvette were sunk, as well as seven Allied aircraft destroyed. The Japanese lost 19 aircraft, and the offensive was a disappointment, indicating Japanese problems in making good the loss of well-trained pilots in recent campaigns.

Q In February 1943 British and U.S. bombers launched Operation Gondola. What was this?

A A series of raids aimed at destroying German U-boats in the Bay of Biscay.

Q Who was appointed Inspector General of Armored Troops in Germany in February 1943?

A General Heinz Guderian.

Q At the beginning of March 1943 the British launched a four-month bombing offensive against which German industrial region?

A The Ruhr.

DID YOU KNOW

IN EARLY 1943, THE AMERICAN GRUMMAN F6F HELLCAT CARRIER-BORNE FIGHTER BEGAN ITS OPERATIONAL DEPLOYMENT TO THE PACIFIC THEATER, HAVING FIRST FLOWN IN PROTOTYPE FORM IN JUNE 1942. THE HELLCAT HAD THE MANEUVERABILITY, POWER, AND ARMAMENT TO TAKE ON AND SURPASS THE BEST OF JAPANESE AIRCRAFT, AND ITS KILL RATE WAS FORMIDABLE—5,156 JAPANESE AIRCRAFT DESTROYED BETWEEN 1943 AND 1945. SOME 480 F6FS OF U.S. TASK FORCE 58 WERE AT THE FRONT-LINE OF THE SLAUGHTER OF MORE THAN 400 JAPANESE AIRCRAFT DURING THE BATTLE OF THE PHILIPPINE SEA; AND, IN TOTAL, F6FS ACCOUNTED FOR THREE-QUARTERS OF ALL JAPANESE AIRCRAFT DOWNED DURING THE WAR. THE F6F WAS PRODUCED IN A NUMBER OF FORMS, INCLUDING THE RADAR-EQUIPPED F6F-3E AND F6F-3N AND THE F6F-5 FIGHTER-BOMBER. TOTAL PRODUCTION OF F6FS WAS 12,275.

" OUR MEN WILL FIGHT LIKE THE DEVIL, BUT
WHEN THE BATTLE'S OVER, IT'S OVER.
THEY TREAT WAR LIKE
A FOOTBALL GAME
BRIGADIER GENERAL THOEDORE ROOSEVELT JR.,
NORTH AFRICA, MARCH 25, 1943 "

Q On March 13, 1943, an attempt was made on Hitler's life. Who made it?

A German Army officers.

Q How did they attempt to kill Hitler?

A By placing a bomb in his aircraft.

183

Q Why did the assassination attempt fail?

A The bomb failed to explode.

Q Name one of the two Allied Atlantic convoys which were badly mauled by German U-boats in March 1943.

A Convoys HX-229 and SC-122. They fought a running battle with 20 U-boats, losing a total of 20 ships.

Q Which Japanese commander was killed by U.S. Lockheed P-38 Lightning fighters on April 18, 1943?

A The Commander-in-Chief of the Combined Fleet and the tactician behind the Pearl Harbor attack, Admiral Isoroku Yamamoto.

> ❝ THE FÜHRER HAS SOLEMNLY PROMISED TO
> GET US OUT OF HERE. THIS HAS
> BEEN READ OUT TO US ❞
> ANONYMOUS GERMAN SOLDIER AT STALINGRAD,
> JANUARY 1943

Q How did Allied aircraft locate Admiral Yamamoto?

A Allied code breakers alerted Allied commanders in advance that Yamamoto was traveling among key bases, allowing them to prepare an ambush and demonstrate the increasingly vital role ULTRA intelligence was playing in the Allied war effort.

Q Who took over command of the Japanese Combined Fleet following the death of Admiral Yamamoto?

A Admiral Mineichi Koga.

Q On the Eastern Front, who commanded the SS Panzer Corps in early 1943?

A SS-Obergruppenführer und General der Waffen-SS Paul Hausser.

Q Why did he incur Hitler's wrath in February 1943?

A He ignored the Führer's orders and ordered a withdrawal from the city of Kharkov, which was being encircled by Soviet forces.

Q What was Hausser's nickname?

A "Papa."

Q Who commanded the German counteroffensive against Red Army forces in the Ukraine beginning on February 19, 1943?

A Field Marshal Erich von Manstein.

Q Manstein had two panzer armies in his order of battle. What were they?

A The First Panzer Army (III, XXX, and XXXX Panzer Corps) and the Fourth Panzer Army (XXXXVIII Panzer and LVII Corps).

Q What other two formations did Hausser have at his disposal?

A Army Detachment Hollidt and the SS Panzer Corps (*Leibstandarte*, *Das Reich*, and *Totenkopf* Divisions).

DID YOU KNOW

NICKNAMED "HITLER'S BUZZ SAW," THE MG42 MACHINE GUN WAS DESIGNED TO REPLACE THE MG34, ALTHOUGH IN REALITY IT NEVER DID. THE MG42 WOULD BE MASS PRODUCED AND MORE RUGGED IN THE FIELD THAN THE HIGH-MAINTENANCE MG34. THE RESULT OF THESE EFFORTS CREATED PERHAPS THE WORLD'S BEST MACHINE GUN, WHICH HAD A UNIQUE DELAYED BLOW-BACK SYSTEM OF FIRING. HERE, AN ADDITIONAL RESTRAINT OR BRAKE IS PLACED ON THE BOLT OR OTHER BREECH CLOSURE IN ORDER TO DELAY OR SLOW DOWN THE OPENING, ALTHOUGH NOT ACTUALLY LOCKING THE BREECH. ROBUST, RELIABLE, AND POSSESSING AN INCREDIBLE RATE OF FIRE, THIS WEAPON WAS THE PRIDE OF THE GERMAN INFANTRY. ITS RATE OF FIRE WAS 1,500 ROUNDS PER MINUTE, OR 25 ROUNDS PER SECOND! THIS MEANT RED ARMY INFANTRY ATTACKS COULD BE BROKEN UP WITH SHORT BURSTS. FIRE RATES AS HIGH AS THIS CAUSED BARRELS TO OVERHEAT, BUT THE DESIGNERS HAD THOUGHT OF THIS AND HAD DEVISED A QUICK-CHANGE FACILITY. THIS MEANT A TRAINED GUNNER COULD CHANGE A BARREL IN LESS THAN SEVEN SECONDS. A TOTAL OF 414,964 MG42s WERE BUILT DURING THE WAR.

Q Who delivered the so-called "total war" speech in Berlin in February 1943?

A Propaganda Minister Goebbels. To thunderous applause he announced the implementation of total war: "Do you want total war? Do you want it, if necessary, more total and more radical than we could even imagine today?" Afterwards Goebbels wrote in his diary: "This hour of idiocy! If I had said to the people, jump out the fourth floor of Columbushaus, they would have done that too."

DID YOU KNOW

FOR ALLIED FORCES IN THE PACIFIC, THE STRATEGIC OUTLOOK FOR 1943 COULD NOT HAVE BEEN MORE DIFFERENT FROM THE PREVIOUS YEAR. COMPARED WITH THE POSITION OF WEAKNESS AFTER PEARL HARBOR, THE PLANNING FOR 1943 WAS AGGRESSIVE, BOLD, AND DETERMINED. OPERATION CARTWHEEL, THE TWO-PRONGED ASSAULT ON THE JAPANESE STRONGHOLD AT RABAUL ON NEW BRITAIN, BEGAN IN EARNEST. THIS CALLED FOR LARGE-SCALE ATTACKS ON NEW GUINEA AND THE SOLOMON ISLANDS. WITHIN THE HIGHEST LEVELS OF THE U.S. COMMAND THERE HAD BEEN DISAGREEMENT ABOUT WHAT KIND OF STRATEGY TO TAKE (TWO INDEPENDENT, COORDINATE COMMANDS, ONE IN THE SOUTHWEST PACIFIC UNDER GENERAL OF THE ARMY DOUGLAS MACARTHUR, AND THE OTHER IN THE CENTRAL, SOUTH, AND NORTH PACIFIC OCEAN AREAS UNDER FLEET ADMIRAL CHESTER W. NIMITZ, WERE CREATED EARLY IN THE WAR). EXCEPT IN THE SOUTH AND SOUTHWEST PACIFIC, EACH CONDUCTED ITS OWN OPERATIONS WITH ITS OWN GROUND, AIR, AND NAVAL FORCES IN WIDELY SEPARATED AREAS. THE ARGUMENT CENTERED ON WHETHER TO MOVE THROUGH THE SOUTHWEST PACIFIC TOWARD THE PHILIPPINES (THE PLAN FAVORED BY GENERAL MACARTHUR) OR TO STRIKE AT FORMOSA THROUGH THE CENTRAL PACIFIC (THE METHOD FAVORED BY ADMIRAL NIMITZ). IT WAS THE ENDORSEMENT OF MACARTHUR'S PLAN THAT SAW OPERATION CARTWHEEL LAUNCHED.

> **TOMORROW MORNING I SHALL SET FOOT ON THE LAST BRIDGE. THAT'S A LITERARY WAY OF DESCRIBING DEATH**
> Anonymous German soldier at Stalingrad, January 1943

Q Which major Ukrainian city was recaptured by German forces in March 1943?

A Kharkov.

Q Which Jewish ghetto did the Germans destroy in mid-March 1943?

A The Krakow Ghetto.

Q Which SS officer supervised the operation?

A SS-Untersturmführer Amon Göth.

Q What was the nickname of the German Close Combat Bar?

A The "Eyeball-to-Eyeball" medal.

Q Following the German recapture of Kharkov in March 1943, the city's Red Square was renamed. What was its new name?

A "Platz der Leibstandarte," in honor of the SS Panzer Corps' exploits in retaking the city.

Q In the Battle of the Atlantic, May 1943 was called "Black May" by the Germans. Why?

A U-boat losses rose dramatically, and Admiral Karl Dönitz admitted defeat in the Battle of the Atlantic by withdrawing U-boats from the troubled waters. Up to May there were 40 U-boats in place each day in the Atlantic, but between February and May 91 U-boats had been lost and such losses could not be sustained. A combination of long-range bombers, radar, and submarine hunter groups had made the Atlantic a hazardous place for U-boats.

Q The Jews of which ghetto mounted an uprising against the Germans in April 1943?

A Warsaw.

> **"** SURRENDER IS FORBIDDEN. SIXTH ARMY
> WILL HOLD THEIR POSITIONS
> ## TO THE LAST MAN AND
> ## THE LAST ROUND
> ADOLF HITLER TO THE SIXTH ARMY AT STALINGRAD,
> JANUARY 24, 1943 **"**

Q In air warfare, what was saturation bombing?

A A technique of mass bombing in which concentrations of bombers mounted a giant raid on a single city, with the object of completely demolishing it.

Q Which head of British Bomber Command favored using saturation bombing against German cities?

A Arthur Harris.

DID YOU KNOW

By 1943 the Japanese in the Pacific had suffered a series of serious setbacks, such as the Battle of Midway in mid-June 1942. They therefore set about devising another way of holding back the American tide. They were determined to hold what they could, and this meant vigorously fighting for and reinforcing New Guinea and the neighboring islands. By using the fortified base at Rabaul, the Japanese hoped to strike at the Americans with air- and sea-based power. Meanwhile, in Burma and on the Indian border, the Japanese went ahead with Operation U-Go, the assault on Imphal, and Operation Ha-Go, a diversionary attack on the Arakan Peninsula. By striking into India, the Japanese planned to take the communication centers of Imphal and Kohima and thus deliver a crippling blow against the British build-up for operations to retake Burma.

Q Estimate the number of Jews captured in the Warsaw ghetto uprising of April–May 1943.

A 56,000, of whom 7,000 were shot.

Q Yakov Stalin, son of the Soviet dictator, died in April 1943. Where and how?

A Lieutenant Yakov Stalin had been a German prisoner since July 1941. He died in Sachsenhausen camp after running into the electric fence surrounding the camp, apparently so overcome by shame at the news of his father's massacre of Polish officers at Katyn.

Q The Germans had wanted to exchange Yakov Stalin for whom?

A The Germans had wanted to exchange him for Field Marshal Paulus, but Stalin would not hear of it.

Q What was Hitler's Operational Order No. 16 dated April 12, 1943?

A The destruction of enemy forces in the Kursk salient on the Eastern Front. Codenamed Operation Citadel; it would begin on May 3, 1943.

Q In April 1943 Radio Berlin announced the discovery of a mass grave of 4,500 Polish officers who had been murdered. Where?

A Katyn Wood.

Q Whom did the Germans blame for this atrocity?

" THE RUSSIANS STAND AT THE DOOR OF OUR BUNKER. WE ARE DESTROYING OUR EQUIPMENT

SIXTH ARMY HQ AT STALINGRAD TO HIGH COMMAND, JANUARY 31, 1943 "

A The Soviet NKVD.

Q What was the Soviet response?

A The Soviet government responded by counter-charging that the Germans had killed the Poles.

Q Who was responsible for the Katyn Wood massacre?

A In November 1989 the Russians admitted responsibility for the Katyn shootings.

Q Which senior U.S. commander in the European theater was killed in early May 1943?

A General Frank Andrews.

Q Who replaced him?

A General Jacob Devers.

DID YOU KNOW

IN DECEMBER 1942, THE FIRST OF THE FINAL PRODUCTION SERIES OF THE GERMAN STUG III—THE AUSF G—ROLLED OFF THE PRODUCTION LINE IN GERMANY. WHEN PRODUCTION CEASED IN MARCH 1945, A TOTAL OF 7,720 HAD BEEN BUILT. THE HULL OF THE AUSF G WAS NOT RADICALLY DIFFERENT FROM PREVIOUS MODELS, THE MAIN CHANGES BEING TO THE SUPERSTRUCTURE. A CUPOLA WITH PERISCOPES WAS ADDED FOR THE COMMANDER, WHILE A SHIELD FOR THE MACHINE GUN WAS INSTALLED IN FRONT OF THE LOADER'S HATCH. THE SUPERSTRUCTURE INCORPORATED SLANTED SIDES, WITH THE ADDITION OF SLANTED PLATES TO PROTECT THE FRONT OF BOTH PANNIERS. DURING THE PRODUCTION RUN OTHER CHANGES WERE INCORPORATED, SUCH AS THE INTRODUCTION OF THE "SOW'S HEAD" (SAUKOPF) GUN MANTLET FOR THE STUK40 L/48 GUN, A COAXIAL MACHINE GUN IN EARLY 1944, A CLOSE-IN DEFENSE WEAPON, AND A REMOTE-CONTROLLED MACHINE GUN TO THE SUPERSTRUCTURE ROOF IN THE SPRING OF 1944. BY MID-1943, THERE WERE 28 INDEPENDENT STUG DETACHMENTS, FOUR DIVISIONAL STUG DETACHMENTS, TWO RADIO-CONTROLLED COMPANIES, AND 12 STUG PLATOONS, ALL READY FOR THE KURSK OFFENSIVE IN JULY. LATER, THE STUGS WERE DISTRIBUTED AMONG PANZER AND ANTITANK UNITS.

Q On May 11, 1943, a U.S. amphibious force landed 11,000 men of the 7th Infantry Division on Attu, beginning the campaign to take which group of islands?

A The Aleutian Islands.

Q Which national leaders attended the Trident Conference in Washington in May 1943?

A British Prime Minister Churchill and U.S. President Roosevelt.

Q What was the main British concern raised at the conference?

A Despite a unified confirmation of the Germany First strategy, including setting a date for the Allied invasion of occupied Western Europe, the British were concerned that the Pacific war was diverting too many resources away from European operations.

Q Who replaced the South West Pacific and Commander-in-Chief India, Sir Archibald Wavell, in June 1943?

A Sir Claude Auchinleck.

" LIKE RAGING WOLVES, VENGEFUL
SOLDIERS FELL ON
THE HELPLESS VICTIMS TO
STEAL PERSONAL BAGGAGE **"**
JOACHIM WIEDER, GERMAN SOLDIER CAPTURED
AT STALINGRAD

DID YOU KNOW

IN THE SPRING OF 1943 ADOLF HITLER STILL BELIEVED HE WOULD ACHIEVE TOTAL VICTORY OVER HIS ENEMIES, DESPITE THE MASSIVE DEFEATS SUFFERED BY THE WEHRMACHT IN THE SOVIET UNION AND NORTH AFRICA DURING THE PREVIOUS SIX MONTHS (SOME 500,000 GERMAN TROOPS HAD BEEN KILLED OR CAPTURED IN DEFEATS AT STALINGRAD AND EL ALAMEIN, AND IN TUNISIA). EVER THE OPTIMIST, THE FÜHRER MAINTAINED A PUBLIC VENEER OF CONFIDENCE THAT THE THIRD REICH WOULD SURVIVE FOR 1,000 YEARS. HITLER WAS CONVINCED THAT HE WOULD PREVAIL BECAUSE HIS OPPONENTS, LED BY AN ALLIANCE OF SLAVS AND JEWS, WERE RACIALLY INFERIOR TO GERMANY'S ARYANS. IT WAS JUST BEYOND HIS IMAGINATION THAT THE RUSSIAN *UNTERMENSCHEN*, OR "SUB-HUMANS," COULD BE CLEVER OR STRONG ENOUGH TO CHALLENGE GERMAN SUPREMACY (SIMILAR TO THE ATTITUDE OF EUROPEAN COLONIALISTS IN THE NINETEENTH CENTURY, WHO BELIEVED THAT AFRICAN AND ASIAN ENEMIES WERE NOT IN ANY WAY EQUAL OPPONENTS).

193

Q Which U.S. bomber began its career in May 1943 as the chief medium bomber of the Eighth Air Force in the European theater?

A The Martin B-26 Marauder.

Q What record did this aircraft set in the European theater?

A The lowest loss rate of any U.S. bomber in Europe.

Q Which U.S. fighter aircraft was nicknamed the "Jug"?

A The Republic P-47 Thunderbolt.

> " AM GOING ON A RAID THIS AFTERNOON
> OR EARLY IN THE MORNING.
> ## THERE IS A POSSIBILITY
> ## I WON'T RETURN "
> SERGEANT CARL GOLDMAN, U.S. AIR FORCE,
> FEBRUARY 1943

Q Which U.S. gull-wing fighter entered service with the U.S. Marines in the Solomons in February 1943?

A The Vought F4U Corsair.

Q What type of aircraft was the Ilyushin Il-2 Shturmovik?

A A close-support aircraft.

Q How many Il-2s were built in World War II?

A 40,000.

Q Which British Dreadnought battleship, launched in 1913, fought at the Battle of Jutland in 1916 but also saw active service in World War II?

A HMS *Warspite*.

Q This ship was severely damaged during the Allied invasion of Italy in 1943. What type of weapon inflicted the damage on her?

A German air-launched glider bombs.

Q What was the codename of the Allied invasion of Sicily in July 1943?

A Operation Husky.

Q How many Axis troops defended Sicily in July 1943?

A 130,000 Italian and 30,000 German troops.

Q Name the two élite German divisions that defended Sicily against the Allies.

A The 15th Panzergrenadier Division and the *Hermann Göring* Panzer Division.

Q Why was the *Hermann Göring* Division stationed in the Mediterranean theater in 1943?

A Named after the flamboyant chief of the Luftwaffe, its presence in Sicily and then Italy had much to do with Göring's political support for Kesselring as the only Luftwaffe officer who commanded a major theater of operations. The prestige of the Luftwaffe was at stake in the Mediterranean, and Göring was keen to ensure his protégé was not short of men and equipment.

195

DID YOU KNOW

THE ITALIAN CAMPAIGN WAS BY FAR THE GERMAN ARMY'S MOST SUCCESSFUL PROLONGED DEFENSIVE EFFORT OF THE WAR. FROM THE FIRST BRITISH AND AMERICAN LANDINGS IN SICILY IN JULY 1943 TO JUST BEFORE THE FINAL SURRENDER IN MAY 1945, THE OUTNUMBERED GERMAN UNITS, LED BY THE REDOUBTABLE FIELD MARSHAL ALBERT KESSELRING, ALWAYS HELD THE LINE AND PREVENTED THE ALLIES ACHIEVING A DECISIVE BREAKTHROUGH.

Q What was the Soviet Comintern?

A Founded in 1919 by Lenin and the Bolsheviks, it was dedicated "by all available means, including armed force, for the overthrow of the international bourgeoisie and for the creation of an international Soviet republic as a transition stage to the complete abolition of the State."

Q Why did Stalin dissolve it in May 1943?

A It was a gesture designed to reassure his Western Allies that the USSR was no longer trying to foment world revolution. The Americans in particular were keen for this organization to be disbanded.

DID YOU KNOW

THE GERMANS AT KURSK WERE FACED WITH DEEP SOVIET DEFENSES AND NO WAY TO GO AROUND THEM. THEY THEREFORE DEVISED A NEW TACTICAL FORMATION TO BREAK THROUGH. THE *PANZERKEIL*, OR ARMORED WEDGE, CAN BE LIKENED TO A TIN OPENER THAT HAD TO RIP OPEN THE SOVIET PAK-FRONTS. THEY WERE LED BY TIGER I HEAVY TANKS AND FERDINAND TANK DESTROYERS, WHICH WERE HEAVILY ARMORED AND LARGELY IMMUNE TO ENEMY ANTITANK ROUNDS THAT HIT THEM HEAD ON. THE LIGHTER PANTHERS, PANZER IVS, AND PANZER IIIS FOLLOWED ON BEHIND, WITH ABOUT 328 FT (100 M) BETWEEN EACH TANK. TO AID THE ADVANCE, THERE WAS CONSTANT RADIO CONTACT BETWEEN EACH *PANZERKEIL* AND LUFTWAFFE GROUND-ATTACK AIRCRAFT AND SUPPORTING GROUND ARTILLERY. DURING THE BATTLE, RED ARMY TANKS AND ANTITANK GUNS HAD TO BE KNOCKED OUT BY THE PANZERS AND LUFTWAFFE AIRCRAFT, WHILE ENEMY TRENCHES AND PILLBOXES HAD TO BE CLEARED BY GERMAN INFANTRY USING SMALL ARMS AND HAND GRENADES. OFTEN, THE *PANZERKEILS* WERE HELD UP BY MINE-FIELDS, THROUGH WHICH A ROUTE HAD TO BE CLEARED BY ENGINEERS. AS A RESULT, THE ADVANCE WAS OFTEN AGONIZINGLY SLOW AND BLOODY, AS EACH METER OF GROUND HAD TO BE FOUGHT OVER. SOON AFTER THE BATTLE STARTED, SOME PANZER DIVISIONS WERE SUFFERING DAILY TANK LOSSES OF 10 PERCENT. THIS RATE OF ATTRITION WAS JUST WHAT THE STAVKA HAD WANTED.

> ## BATTLE IS THE MOST MAGNIFICENT COMPETITION IN WHICH A HUMAN BEING CAN INDULGE
> GEORGE S. PATTON, JULY 1943

Q Why did Hitler decide to postpone Operation Citadel, his offensive at Kursk, on May 4, 1943?

A To allow more Tiger and the new Panther tanks to take part in the offensive.

Q What was his new start date for the offensive?

A June 13.

Q What happened on this new date?

A Nothing. Hitler was still waiting for his Panther tanks.

Q The German attack against the Kursk salient involved two giant pincers, one in the north, the other in the south. What armies made up these pincers?

A In the north was the Ninth Army, under the command of Colonel General Model. In the south was the Fourth Panzer Army, commanded by Colonel General Hermann Hoth; and Army Detachment Kempf, commanded by General Walter Kempf.

Q Name the Waffen-SS corps that fought at Kursk.

A II SS Panzer Corps.

Q Which of the German pincers at Kursk was the strongest?

A The southern pincer, with nearly 350,000 men, 1,269 tanks, and 245 assault guns, excluding reserves. In the north the Germans had 335,000 men, 590 tanks, and 424 assault guns.

Q How many Russian civilians were used to construct the Red Army's defenses in the Kursk salient?

A 300,000.

Q At the Battle of Kursk, where did the decisive clash take place on July 12, 1943?

A At the village of Prokhorovka.

Q Why did Hitler halt Operation Citadel on July 13, 1943?

A He was worried about a possible Allied invasion in the south of Europe (the Allies had landed in Sicily on July 10). Hitler informed the commanders of Army Group Center and South: "I must prevent that. And so I need divisions for Italy and the Balkans. And since they can't be taken from any other place, apart from the transfer of the 1st Panzer Division from France to the Peloponnese, they will have to be released from the Kursk Front. Therefore I am forced to stop Citadel."

> " MORTAR AND ARTILLERY FIRE BEGAN
> TO FALL ON THE RIDGE, AND
> ## THERE WAS CONSIDERABLE MACHINE-GUN FIRE
> GENERAL JAMES GAVIN, U.S. 82D AIRBORNE DIVISION,
> SICILY, 1943 "

DID YOU KNOW

AT KURSK, FOR THE FIRST TIME IN THE WAR, A BATTLE WOULD BE FOUGHT ON THE RUSSIANS' TERMS, AND THE GERMANS WOULD PAY DEARLY. THE ATTACKING HEAVY GERMAN TANKS WOULD BE STOPPED BY 85MM ANTI-AIRCRAFT GUNS (USED IN THE GROUND ROLE), WITH 122MM AND 152MM HOWITZERS PROVIDING HEAVY FIRE SUPPORT. THE LENGTH OF THE RED ARMY FRONTLINE IN THE KURSK SALIENT WAS 300 MILES (450 KM) WITH A DEPTH OF 110 MILES (190 KM). INTO THIS AREA WERE DEPLOYED 20,000 ARTILLERY PIECES AND MORTARS, 6,000 ANTITANK GUNS, AND HUNDREDS OF KATYUSHA ROCKET LAUNCHERS. IN THE GROUND WERE UP TO 2,700 ANTIPERSONNEL AND 2,400 ANTITANK MINES EVERY MILE (1.6 KM). ABOVE ALL, IT WAS THE TENACITY OF THE ORDINARY RUSSIAN SOLDIER THAT WAS THE KEY TO SUCCESS AT KURSK. HE DUG IN TO HIS POSITION AND REMAINED THERE. HE WAS ORDERED TO REMAIN AT HIS POST, AND HE DID, OFTEN UNTIL HE WAS KILLED BY THE ENEMY.

Q What was the tank-busting version of the Ju 87 Stuka?

A The Ju 87G-1.

Q What was its main armament?

A Two 37mm Flak 18 cannon in under-wing pods.

Q Why did it have reduced speed and range?

A It was fitted with armor plating to protect the pilot and gunner when flying antitank missions.

Q On the Eastern Front, what was the objective of the Soviet Operation Rumyantsev that began on August 3, 1943?

A Its objectives were the destruction of both the Fourth Panzer Army and Sixth Army by reaching the Black Sea coast behind them.

Q What type of vehicle was the Soviet SU-76?

A A self-propelled gun.

DID YOU KNOW

THE APPEARANCE OF THE SOVIET T-34 TANK ON THE EASTERN FRONT IN 1941 WAS A NASTY SURPRISE FOR THE GERMANS. IN RESPONSE, DECEMBER 1941 SAW BOTH DAIMLER-BENZ AND MAN INSTRUCTED TO BEGIN DESIGNING A NEW, POWERFUL MEDIUM TANK. MAN EVENTUALLY WON THE CONTRACT WITH ITS DESIGN. THE RESULT WAS THE PANZER V PANTHER, WHICH INCORPORATED MANY FEATURES OF THE T-34, BUT WAS LARGER AND HEAVIER. FEATURES INCLUDED WIDE TRACKS FOR BETTER TRACTION AND IMPROVED CROSSCOUNTRY PERFORMANCE, A POWERFUL ENGINE, A POWERFUL MAIN GUN, AND SLOPING ARMOR FOR EXTRA PROTECTION. IN DECEMBER 1942, THE PANTHER AUSF D ENTERED PRODUCTION, THE FIRST MODELS LEAVING THE FACTORY ON JANUARY 11, 1943. THE PANTHER WAS ARMED WITH A NEWER VERSION OF THE 75MM KwK 42 L/70 GUN, WHICH WAS MOUNTED IN A HYDRAULICALLY POWERED TURRET. ITS WEAK SPOT WAS ITS SIDE ARMOR, WHICH WAS ONLY BETWEEN 1.57 IN (40 MM) AND 1.96 IN (50 MM) THICK, DEPENDING ON THE VARIANT. THE PANTHER MADE ITS COMBAT DEBUT AT THE BATTLE OF KURSK. BECAUSE OF TECHNICAL PROBLEMS, ESPECIALLY WITH THE TRANSMISSION AND SUSPENSION, MANY PANTHERS BROKE DOWN BEFORE AND DURING THE BATTLE. NEVERTHELESS, THE PANTHER'S PROBLEMS WERE IRONED OUT AND IT WENT ON TO BECOME ONE OF THE BEST TANKS OF THE WAR.

Q What was its main armament?

A One 76.2mm gun.

" AN INDESCRIBABLE PANIC STARTED.
MOTHERS GRABBED
CHILDREN AND RUSHED MADLY
AWAY
ELSE WENDEL, IN HAMBURG WHEN
BOMBED BY THE RAF IN JULY 1943 "

Q How many tank brigades did a Japanese tank division have?

A Two.

Q What was the caliber of the main gun in a Japanese Type 95 tank?

A 37mm.

Q The U.S. M3 light tank was called what by the British?

A The Stuart I.

Q What was its British classification?

A It was classed as a light cruiser tank by virtue of its armament and armor.

Q What type of vehicle was the U.S.-built M22 Locust?

A An air-portable tank.

Q Why was it never used by the U.S. Army?

A Because the army lacked an aircraft or glider to transport it.

> ## WE MUDDLED THROUGH THE FIGHTER ATTACK AND STAGGERED AWAY FROM THE TARGET
> CAPTAIN JOHN S. YOUNG, U.S. AIR FORCE,
> AUGUST 1, 1943

Q Who did use the M22?

A The British. They could transport it in their Hamilcar glider.

Q Why was a 75mm gun mounted in the right sponson on the U.S. Medium Tank M3?

A Because insufficient development work had been done on the problems of mounting a large-caliber gun in a revolving turret.

Q What was the vehicle called the Mine Exploder T1E4?

A A Sherman tank fitted with rollers, flails, and plunger rods to detonate mines.

DID YOU KNOW

THE PETLYAKOV PE-2 WAS ONE OF THE MOST IMPORTANT AIRCRAFT IN THE
USSR's INVENTORY, FIGHTING FROM THE BEGINNING OF BARBAROSSA
UNTIL THE SURRENDER OF GERMANY IN 1945. IT ENTERED SERVICE IN
AUGUST 1940 AS A MULTI-ROLE DIVE- AND ATTACK-BOMBER, HAVING A
CREW OF THREE AND BEING ARMED WITH FOUR 7.62MM MACHINE GUNS:
TWO FIXED FIRING AHEAD ABOVE THE NOSE; ONE AIMED FROM THE UPPER
REAR POSITION; AND ONE FROM A RETRACTING VENTRAL MOUNT. BECAUSE
OF ITS SPEED AND MANEUVERABILITY, GERMAN FIGHTER PILOTS FOUND THE
PE-2 DIFFICULT TO CATCH AND SHOOT DOWN. FROM AUGUST 1941, THE
EVEN-FASTER RECONNAISSANCE PE-2 VERSION BEGAN TO APPEAR OVER THE
EASTERN FRONT (THESE AIRCRAFT LACKED DIVE BRAKES AND WERE FITTED
WITH ADDITIONAL FUEL TANKAGE IN THE BOMB BAY AND HAD THREE
CAMERAS IN THE REAR FUSELAGE). IN TOTAL, 11,400 PE-2S OF ALL
VARIANTS WERE PRODUCED.

Q What type of vehicle was the U.S. M10?

A A tank destroyer.

Q What was its main armament?

A A 76mm gun.

Q A few M10s saw service with the British. What was their designation?

A 3i SP Wolverines.

Q What was the main armament of the Panzer III Ausf N?

A The 75mm KwK L/24 gun.

Q Which gun did it replace on the Panzer III?

A The 50mm KwK39 L/60.

Q The Panzer III Ausf N had a specific battlefield role. What was it?

A To provide close support for the heavier Tiger tanks.

> **I CALLED OUT: "CRASH LANDING! AS NEAR TO THE HOTEL AS YOU CAN GET IT!"**
> OTTO SKORZENY, DURING THE RESCUE OF BENITO MUSSOLINI

Q What was the Allied Operation Pointblank which was launched in June 1943?

A An offensive by British and U.S. bomber forces that would last until the 1944 cross-Channel invasion. U.S. strategy concentrated on daylight precision raids to destroy Germany's aircraft industry and air force. British attacks concentrated on night saturation bombing to undermine Germany's economy and morale.

Q Which British RAF squadron flew the "dambuster" raid in May 1943?

A 617 Squadron.

Q Which German dams were attacked by the British bombers?

A The Möhne, Eder, and Sorpe dams.

DID YOU KNOW

ON OCTOBER 31, 1942, THE SOVIET STAVKA ORDERED THE RAISING OF 26 RED ARMY ARTILLERY DIVISIONS. THE ORIGINAL DIVISIONAL ORGANIZATION WAS THREE HOWITZER REGIMENTS (EACH WITH 20 122MM HOWITZERS), TWO GUN REGIMENTS (EACH WITH 18 122MM OR 152MM GUN-HOWITZERS), THREE TANK-DESTROYER ARTILLERY REGIMENTS (EACH WITH 24 76MM GUNS) AND AN OBSERVATION BATTALION. AS WITH INFANTRY AND ARMORED FORMATIONS, THE ARTILLERY UNDERWENT NUMEROUS REORGANIZATIONS. IN APRIL 1943, FOR EXAMPLE, FIVE ARTILLERY CORPS HEADQUARTERS WERE CREATED TO CONTROL THE GROUPINGS OF ARTILLERY DIVISIONS AND, AT THE SAME TIME, A NEW DIVISIONAL FORMAT WAS ESTABLISHED: THE BREAKTHROUGH ARTILLERY DIVISION. THE NEW DIVISION COMPRISED: AN OBSERVATION BATTALION; A LIGHT BRIGADE (THREE REGIMENTS, EACH ONE WITH 24 76MM GUNS); A HOWITZER BRIGADE (THREE REGIMENTS, EACH ONE WITH 28 122MM HOWITZERS); A GUN BRIGADE (TWO REGIMENTS, EACH ONE WITH 18 152MM GUN-HOWITZERS); AND A MORTAR BRIGADE (THREE REGIMENTS, EACH ONE WITH 36 120MM MORTARS). IN ADDITION, TWO HEAVY HOWITZER BRIGADES (ONE OF FOUR BATTALIONS, EACH ONE WITH EIGHT 152MM HOWITZERS; AND ONE OF FOUR BATTALIONS, EACH ONE EQUIPPED WITH SIX 203MM HOWITZERS) WERE ATTACHED TO DIVISIONAL HEADQUARTERS. EACH DIVISION NUMBERED 11,000 TROOPS AND WAS EQUIPPED WITH 1,100 TRUCKS, AND 175 TRACTORS.

Q The RAF "dambuster" raid used special weapons against the German dams. What were they?

A Bouncing bombs.

Q Was the raid a success?

A Partly. Only the Möhne and Eder dams were breached. The specially trained squadron led by Wing Commander Guy Gibson lost eight aircraft. The raid caused some disruption to the German war industry, and it boosted civilian morale in Britain.

Q In the air war, what were Allied "shuttle" raids?

A Flying from a base in one country to bomb the target, then flying on to land at a base in another country.

Q What was the "window" system employed by Allied bombers over Germany?

A The dropping of foil strips to confuse German radar equipment.

Q Which German city was engulfed by a firestorm at the end of July 1943 following massive British air raids?

A Hamburg.

> **" THE MINUTE I WAS ON THE BEACH I FELT BETTER. IT DIDN'T SEEM LIKE EVERYBODY WAS SHOOTING AT ME**
> JOHN STEINBACK, SALERNO LANDINGS,
> SEPTEMBER 9, 1943 **"**

Q In the Pacific theater, what was Operation Toenails in June 1943?

A The U.S. offensive to retake New Georgia.

Q Who was the leader of the pro-Japanese Indian National Army?

A Subhas Chandra Bose.

Q Who commanded the U.S. fast patrol boat *PT-109*?

A The future U.S. president, John F. Kennedy.

DID YOU KNOW

GENERAL SIR WILLIAM SLIM (1891–1970) WAS AN IMPORTANT ALLIED LEADER IN THE FAR EASTERN WAR. SLIM HAD LONG-STANDING EXPERIENCE OF SOLDIERING IN THE FAR EAST, HAVING MOVED FROM THE BRITISH ARMY TO THE INDIAN ARMY IN 1919 AND RISEN TO THE RANK OF BRIGADIER BY 1939. THIS EXPERIENCE WAS TO STAND HIM IN GOOD STEAD WITH HIS MEN, WHO APPRECIATED BOTH HIS TOUGH YET PERSONABLE CHARACTER, AND HIS ABILITY TO TALK IN URDU AND GURKHALI AS WELL AS ENGLISH. HIS FIRST CAMPAIGNS IN WORLD WAR II WERE FOUGHT IN EAST AFRICA AND SYRIA, BUT IN MARCH 1942 HE WAS TRANSFERRED TO BURMA TO OVERSEE THE ALLIED RETREAT FROM RANGOON AS COMMANDER OF BURCORPS (SLIM WAS BY THIS TIME RANKED LIEUTENANT GENERAL). BURMA WAS TO BE HIS BATTLEGROUND FOR THE REST OF THE WAR. HE LED XV INDIAN CORPS DURING ITS DISASTROUS CAMPAIGN INTO THE ARAKAN, BUT OFFSET THIS DEFEAT BY STEERING THE FOURTEENTH ARMY TO VICTORIES IN THE ARAKAN AND ALSO THE CRUCIAL DEFEAT OF THE JAPANESE OFFENSIVE AT IMPHAL. IN JULY 1945, SLIM ROSE TO THE POSITION OF C-IN-C ALLIED LAND FORCES SOUTHEAST ASIA AFTER THE DISMISSAL OF GENERAL SIR OLIVER LEESE FROM THE POSITION.

DID YOU KNOW

Q Who became the head of the new South East Asia Command (SEAC) in August 1943?

A Vice Admiral Lord Louis Mountbatten.

Q Who was his deputy?

A Joseph Stilwell.

Q What were the objectives of SEAC?

A The geographical remit of SEAC was Burma, Malaya, Sumatra, Thailand, and French Indochina. SEAC's main objectives were to draw more Japanese away from the Pacific theater and support Chinese military efforts to the north of the zone. The decision was also made to bypass the fortified port of Rabaul, previously a key objective of Operation Cartwheel.

Q Following the successful conclusion of Operation Toenails in August 1943, what was the next part of U.S. strategy in the Solomon Islands?

A An amphibious offensive against Bougainville and Choiseul, planned for October/November 1943.

Q In Italy, what was the name of the German defensive line south of Rome, which was held until May 1944?

A The Gustav Line.

Q In September 1943 the Allies landed in Italy. At which port?

A Salerno.

Q Who was the Allied commander who issued orders for the evacuation of this port in the face of heavy German attacks?

A Lieutenant General Mark Clark.

" I PULLED THE PIN OUT OF MY GRENADE,
WHICH WAS STICKY WITH
SWEAT, AND LOBBED IT "
BERNARD FERGUSSON, CHINDIT, MARCH 1943

Q Where was the German Hagen Line?

A It was a defensive line on the Eastern Front, located just to the east of Bryansk.

Q On which river did the Germans intend to make a stand in the Ukraine in the autumn of 1943?

A The Dnieper.

> " THEY DROVE THE MEN ON, NOT JUST TO
> MAKE THEM WORK, BUT AS A
> ## CRUEL MASTER DRIVES A
> ## BEAST OF BURDEN
> JEFFREY ENGLISH, BRITISH PRISONER OF
> THE JAPANESE, MAY 1943 "

Q The Red Army established a bridgehead on this river in September 1943. Where?

A At Veliki Bukrin.

Q The inmates of which German extermination camp, located in Russia, mounted a revolt in October 1943?

A Sobibor extermination camp. Several Ukrainian guards and 11 SS men were killed and some 300 prisoners managed to escape, most of whom were killed by their pursuers. Those who had refused to join the revolt were all murdered.

DID YOU KNOW

ITALY'S MOUNTAINOUS TERRAIN WAS IDEALLY SUITED TO THE DEFENSIVE TACTICS EMPLOYED BY THE GERMANS TO HOLD BACK ALLIED FORCES TRYING TO PENETRATE THE THIRD REICH'S "SOFT UNDERBELLY." WITH NAMES SUCH AS GUSTAV, BERNARD, ROME, CAESAR, ALBERT, AND GOTHIC, THE GERMAN DEFENSIVE POSITIONS IN ITALY WERE TREATED WITH GREAT RESPECT BY THE ALLIED SOLDIERS AND COMMANDERS WHO HAD TO ATTACK THEM. UNLIKE THE FAMOUS SIEGFRIED LINE AND WEST WALL IN NORTHWEST EUROPE, GERMAN POSITIONS IN ITALY NEVER HAD THE SAME AMOUNT OF MATERIAL RESOURCES DEVOTED TO THEM. GERMAN COMMANDERS HAD TO MAKE MAXIMUM USE OF THE TERRAIN, MINEFIELDS, AND EARTHWORK DEFENSES. IMPROVISATION WAS THE NAME OF THE GAME, WITH THE TURRETS OF DISABLED PANTHER TANKS PRESSED INTO SERVICE AS FIXED PILLBOXES. THE KEY TO THE SUCCESS OF THE GERMAN DEFENSIVE LINES WAS THE SIGHTING OF POSITIONS ALONG NATURAL OBSTACLES, SUCH AS RIVERS AND HIGH MOUNTAIN RIDGES. EVERY APPROACH ROUTE WAS BLOCKED BY MINEFIELDS AND COVERED BY ARTILLERY OR MACHINE GUNS. CONTROL OF THE HIGH GROUND MEANT THAT GERMAN ARTILLERY FIRE WAS ALWAYS EXPERTLY DIRECTED ON TO ITS TARGETS.

211

Q What was the SS operation codenamed Harvest Festival?

A Following the rebellion at Sobibor, and to prevent further revolts, on November 3, 1943, SS Chief Heinrich Himmler ordered Jakob Sporrenberg, senior commander of the SS and the police in the Lublin district, to liquidate the Jewish forced labor camps. The operation was codenamed Harvest Festival. The SS murdered the prisoners at Trawniki, Poniatowa, and Majdanek camps, a total of 43,000 victims.

Q Which Soviet army liberated Kiev on November 6, 1943?

A The Thirty-Eighth Army.

Q What work was carried out at the Peenemünde center on the Baltic Sea?

A Rocket research.

Q Which projects were developed there during the war?

A The center developed a remote-controlled, pulse-jet-powered flying bomb (V1) and a faster, liquid-fuel model (V2) as terror weapons to undermine the morale of enemy populations.

Q Why did the Danish government resign at the end of August 1943?

A After refusing a German demand for the repression of "saboteurs." The Danish authorities had tried to avoid collaboration with Nazi Germany.

Q Which SS commander rescued Mussolini in September 1943?

A Otto Skorzeny.

Q Where was the Italian dictator being held prior to his rescue?

A The Gran Sasso Hotel in the Abruzzi Mountains, northern Italy.

Q Why did British forces land on the island of Kos in the Dodecanese in September 1943?

A The islands off southwest Turkey were a potential approach to southeast Europe and a base for air operations against German communications and oil resources in Romania. A victory there might also persuade Turkey to support the Allied cause as the threat of German air raids from Rhodes would be eliminated.

Q The British occupation of Kos was intended as a springboard for an assault on which island?

A The German stronghold on Rhodes.

Q How did the Germans retake Kos?

A A force of 1,200 German paratroopers landed on the island. Around 900 Allied and 3,000 Italian troops were captured. The Germans shot 90 Italian officers for fighting against their former ally.

213

DID YOU KNOW

STRATEGIC BOMBING—AIR OFFENSIVES AGAINST THE ENEMY'S INDUSTRIAL CENTERS AND POPULATION—USING FLEETS OF BOMBERS HAD BEEN CONSIDERED A WAR-WINNING FORMULA BY ITS PREWAR PROPONENTS. AFTER GERMANY BEGAN ITS FIRST MAJOR RAIDS AGAINST BRITAIN IN 1940, HOWEVER, ITS LIMITATIONS WERE EXPOSED. ALTHOUGH ATTACKS WERE HIGHLY DESTRUCTIVE, THEY FAILED TO PARALYZE THE ECONOMY OR UNDERMINE MORALE; INDEED, THE OPPOSITE SEEMED THE CASE AS THE POPULATION STEELED ITSELF FOR THE ONSLAUGHT. THE EFFECT OF ALLIED RAIDS ON GERMANY MET WITH SIMILAR RESULTS, ESPECIALLY AS BOTH BELLIGERENTS SUSTAINED HEAVY LOSSES DURING DAYLIGHT RAIDS WHERE THEY WERE EASILY TARGETED AND WERE FORCED TO MAKE LESS ACCURATE NIGHT ATTACKS. BRITAIN'S ANSWER WAS TO USE SATURATION BOMBING TO DESTROY HOMES AND FACTORIES ACROSS WIDE AREAS.

Q Who became chairman and president of the National Government of China in September 1943?

A Chiang Kai-shek.

Q Which atoll in the Gilbert Islands was captured by U.S. Marines at great cost in November 1943?

A Tarawa Atoll.

Q Which U.S. Marine division attacked Betio Island, Tarawa Atoll, in November 1943?

A The 2d Marine Division.

" A GERMAN WITH BLOOD
POURING DOWN HIS LEG POPPED
OUT OF A DOORWAY
AND SURRENDERED
Alan Moorehead, Tunis, May 7, 1943 "

Q Which two U.S. aircraft carriers were launched at the end of November 1943?

A The USS *Wasp* and the USS *Hornet*, both named after U.S. vessels sunk at earlier actions in the war.

Q How many aircraft carriers did the United States commission in 1943?

A Nine. The Japanese, suffering from severe industrial shortages, commissioned only two, these being conversions from existing vessels.

DID YOU KNOW

THE FIRST TROOPS OF THE U.S. 2D MARINE DIVISION WENT ASHORE AT
BETIO ON NOVEMBER 20, 1943, STRAIGHT INTO A HAIL OF BULLETS AND
SHELLS. BEACH RECONNAISSANCE HAD BEEN INACCURATE, AND MANY OF
THE "AMTRAC" AMPHIBIOUS VEHICLES GROUNDED ON A SHALLOW REEF,
LEAVING THE OCCUPANTS TO WADE ASHORE UNDER BLISTERING SMALL-
ARMS AND ARTILLERY FIRE. ON THE BEACH ITSELF, THE SOFT SAND MADE IT
DIFFICULT FOR THE U.S. SOLDIERS TO DIG IN. RADIO COMMUNICATIONS
BETWEEN U.S. UNITS BROKE DOWN, RESULTING IN 1,500 U.S. MARINE
CASUALTIES BY THE END OF THE DAY. HOWEVER, A BEACHHEAD WAS
ESTABLISHED THROUGH SHEER U.S. FIREPOWER, AND OVER THE NEXT
TWO DAYS THE MARINES FOUGHT THEIR WAY ACROSS TARAWA, THE
ENTRENCHED DEFENDERS CONTESTING EVERY METER OF GROUND TO
THE DEATH. A FINAL SUICIDAL CHARGE BY THE JAPANESE ON THE 22D
SIGNIFIED THAT RESISTANCE WAS FINALLY CRUMBLING, AND ON THE 23RD
THE FIGHTING FINALLY STOPPED.

215

Q Which Soviet city was recaptured by XXXXVIII Panzer Corps in November 1943?

A Zhitomir.

Q The German success was part of an offensive in the Ukraine designed to retake which major Soviet city?

A Kiev.

Q Did it succeed?

A No. The German offensive ground to a halt at the end of November 1943 short of Kiev.

Q Which German industrial plant was attacked by 290 U.S. B-17 Flying Fortresses on October 14, 1943?

A The Schweinfurt ball-bearings complex.

Q Was the raid a success?

A No. Sixty aircraft were lost and 140 damaged for little gain.

DID YOU KNOW

THE QUESTION OF WHY GERMAN TROOPS CONTINUED TO FIGHT THE RED ARMY WHEN IT WAS OBVIOUS THAT GERMANY WOULD LOSE THE WAR ON THE EASTERN FRONT IS AN INTERESTING ONE. THE REASONS WHY THEY DID SO WERE PROVIDED BY A SENIOR GERMAN OFFICER WHO FOUGHT ON THE EASTERN FRONT, GENERAL VON MELLENTHIN: "IN 1943, THE FLOWER OF THE GERMAN ARMY HAD FALLEN IN THE BATTLE OF KURSK, WHERE OUR TROOPS ATTACKED WITH A DESPERATE DETERMINATION TO CONQUER OR DIE. THEY HAD GONE INTO BATTLE WITH A SPIRIT NO LESS DETERMINED THAN THAT OF THE STORM TROOPS OF 1918, AND IT MIGHT BE THOUGHT THAT A WEAKENING OF MORALE WOULD FOLLOW OUR WITHDRAWAL FROM THE ILL-FATED SALIENT OF KURSK. ACTUALLY, NOTHING OF THE SORT OCCURRED; OUR RANKS HAD BEEN WOEFULLY THINNED, BUT THE FIERCE RESOLVE OF THE FIGHTING TROOPS REMAINED UNSHAKEN. THIS IS NOT THE PLACE FOR A DETAILED DISCUSSION OF THIS QUESTION, BUT IT IS OBVIOUS THAT THE CHARACTER OF OUR ADVERSARY HAD MUCH TO DO WITH THIS UNYIELDING SPIRIT OF THE TROOPS. THE CHURCHILL-ROOSEVELT DEMAND FOR 'UNCONDITIONAL SURRENDER' GAVE US NO HOPE FROM THE WEST, WHILE THE MEN FIGHTING ON THE RUSSIAN FRONT WERE WELL AWARE OF THE HORRIBLE FATE WHICH WOULD BEFALL EASTERN GERMANY IF THE RED HORDES BROKE INTO OUR COUNTRY." OF COURSE, A GERMAN GENERAL IS GOING TO EXTOLL THE VIRTUES OF HIS TROOPS, BUT MELLENTHIN PROBABLY SUMMARIZES ACCURATELY THE VIEW OF THE WEHRMACHT'S RANK AND FILE BETWEEN 1943 AND 1945.

THE RUSSIAN SOLDIER VALUES HIS LIFE
NO MORE THAN THOSE OF
HIS COMRADES
GENERAL VON MELLENTHIN, EASTERN FRONT, 1943

Q What change did this raid bring about in U.S. bombing tactics?

A The Americans halted unescorted, daylight raids due to high losses. Henceforth the bombers would be escorted by long-range fighter escorts.

Q What type of Royal Navy vessels attacked the German battleship *Tirpitz* in September 1943?

A Midget submarines, known as X-craft.

Q Which former Axis state declared war on Germany in mid-October 1943?

A Italy, on October 13.

Q Who were the "Big Three" at the Tehran Conference in November 1943?

A Stalin, Roosevelt, and Churchill.

Q At the conference, what date was set for the Allied invasion of France?

A May 1944.

217

Q Why was the American General Joseph Stilwell known as "Vinegar Joe"?

A Because of his aggressive and difficult personality.

Q In the Pacific theater, what was the "Tokyo Express"?

A "Tokyo Express" was the Allied nickname for the Japanese supply convoys running between Rabaul in New Britain and the Solomon Islands. The Japanese ships usually traveled via the Slot, the narrow stretch of water south of Bougainville that attracted violent naval battles.

Q What was the name of the airstrip on the island of Bougainville, which was made operational by the Americans in December 1943?

A Torokina.

> ❝ GERMANY NEEDS THE CONQUERED
> ## TERRITORIES OR SHE WILL
> ## NOT EXIST FOR LONG
> ADOLF HITLER, TALKING ABOUT THE USSR, JULY 1943 ❞

Q Which division spearheaded the U.S. invasion of New Britain at the end of December 1943?

A The 1st Marine Division under Major General W.H. Rupertus.

Q Why did the Allies wish to take New Britain?

A To isolate the vital Japanese naval and air facilities at Rabaul in the north.

DID YOU KNOW

HIDEKI TOJO (1885–1948) WAS THE POLITICAL POWER BEHIND THE PACIFIC WAR. THE SON OF A JAPANESE ARMY GENERAL, HE ENTERED THE MILITARY AND QUICKLY ROSE THROUGH THE RANKS. POLITICAL RATHER THAN OPERATIONAL APPOINTMENTS BECKONED. WITHIN THE ARMY HE SERVED AS THE CHIEF OF POLICE AFFAIRS AND CHIEF OF STAFF BEFORE BECOMING THE VICE MINISTER OF WAR THEN FINALLY MINISTER OF WAR IN 1941, THE SAME YEAR HE BECAME JAPANESE PRIME MINISTER. TOJO TOOK JAPAN TO WAR IN DECEMBER OF THAT YEAR BY GIVING THE ORDER TO ATTACK PEARL HARBOR, AND HE ADVOCATED A STRATEGY OF TOTAL MILITARY AND ECONOMIC WARFARE ON THE ALLIES, WHICH HELPED MAKE THE PACIFIC WAR THE MERCILESS FIGHT IT BECAME. AFTER THE JAPANESE DEFEAT ON SAIPAN IN JULY 1944, HE WAS FORCED TO RESIGN; HE MADE A FAILED ATTEMPT AT SUICIDE AFTER THE FINAL JAPANESE SURRENDER. IN 1948, HE WAS CONDEMNED TO DEATH FOR WAR CRIMES BY THE INTERNATIONAL MILITARY TRIBUNAL IN TOKYO, AND HANGED.

Q Which Allied leaders met at Cairo in November 1943?

A Winston Churchill, Franklin D. Roosevelt, and Chiang Kai-shek.

Q What was the main topic at the conference?

A They mainly considered postwar planning for China and Burma.

Q In November 1943 the British commenced a five-month bomber offensive against which German city?

A Berlin.

Q Which German medium tank made its combat debut at the Battle of Kursk in July 1943?

A The Panzer V Panther.

Q Many of these tanks broke down before they reached the combat zone. True or false?

A True. There were teething problems with the transmission and suspension systems.

Q Which German Stuka pilot single-handedly destroyed 12 T-34 tanks at the Battle of Kursk?

A Hans-Ulrich Rudel.

> **" A CITY OF ONE MILLION PEOPLE HAS BEEN DEVASTATED IN A MANNER UNKNOWN BEFORE "**
>
> JOSEF GOEBBELS, ON THE AIR RAID AGAINST HAMBURG, JULY 29, 1943

Q Which German battleship was sunk at the Battle of the North Cape in December 1943?

A The *Scharnhorst*.

Q What was the name of the British cruiser who finished her off with torpedoes during the battle?

A The cruiser HMS *Jamaica*.

1944

In the Pacific the Japanese suffered major defeats at the Philippine Sea and Leyte Gulf, while in Europe the Allies finally launched their invasion of France, codenamed Overlord. On the Eastern Front the Red Army shattered Army Group Center, and Allied bombers reduced Germany to rubble.

Q Who became commander-in-chief of Free French forces in North Africa in January 1944?

A General Jean de Lattre de Tassigny.

Q What battle was dubbed the "Stalingrad of the Italian Campaign"?

A The four-month battle to gain control of the monastery atop Monte Cassino in central Italy.

Q Why was this position so important to both sides?

A Because the German defenses around Monte Cassino guarded the route north to Rome.

> " OLDER MEN DECLARE WAR. BUT IT IS
> # YOUTH THAT MUST FIGHT
> HERBERT HOOVER, CHICAGO, JUNE 27, 1944 "

Q Which two rivers formed part of the German Gustav Line defenses in central Italy in early 1944?

A The Rapido and Garigliano.

Q Why did the Allies make an amphibious assault at Anzio in January 1944?

A The Allies were held up at the Gustav Line. To break the stalemate, the Allies tried to bypass the Gustav Line by staging an amphibious landing at Anzio in January 1944.

DID YOU KNOW

ITALY WAS ONE OF THE FEW THEATERS WHERE THE GERMANS DECIDED
NOT TO CONCENTRATE THEIR ARMOR FOR COUNTERATTACKS. WITH THE
TERRAIN ALL BUT PREVENTING THE MOVEMENT OF LARGE ARMORED
FORMATIONS, GERMAN COMMANDERS BROKE UP THEIR TANKS, ASSAULT GUNS,
AND ANTITANK GUNS INTO SMALL UNITS, USUALLY PAIRS, AND POSTED THEM TO
FORWARD STRONGPOINTS OR WITH COUNTERATTACK TEAMS. IN THE ITALIAN
TERRAIN, A HANDFUL OF HEAVY WEAPONS COULD PROVIDE FIREPOWER OUT OF
ALL PROPORTION TO THEIR SMALL NUMBER. DURING THE CASSINO BATTLES, A
HANDFUL OF StuG III ASSAULT GUNS AND MARDER III SELF-PROPELLED
75MM ANTITANK GUNS OPERATING WITH FORWARD GERMAN PARATROOP
STRONGPOINTS MADE IT IMPOSSIBLE FOR THE ALLIES TO TRY TO SPEARHEAD
THEIR INFANTRY ASSAULTS WITH TANKS. DURING REARGUARD OPERATIONS,
SMALL GROUPS OF TANKS ALSO PROVED VERY EFFECTIVE AT FORCING ALLIED
TROOPS TO DEPLOY TO MOUNT ASSAULT OPERATIONS. THE GERMANS WOULD
THEN QUICKLY RETREAT ONCE THEY HAD ACHIEVED THEIR AIM—DELAYING THE
ADVANCE—BEFORE THEIR LINE OF RETREAT BECAME THREATENED.

223

Q Why were the landings at Anzio the last major amphibious operation the Allies were to mount in Italy?

A Because of the need to move the bulk of their specialist craft and shipping to England to support the planned Normandy landings.

Q What was "Anzio Annie"?

A A German Krupp K-5 280mm-caliber railway gun.

Q Where did it operate from?

A A tunnel in the Alban Hills, south of Rome. It was wheeled out at night to fire barrages into the Anzio bridgehead before retreating underground during daylight to avoid detection by Allied aircraft.

Q What was Operation Carpetbagger that commenced in January 1944?

A Regular Allied airborne supply drops to partisans in the Netherlands, Belgium, France, and Italy.

Q Count Galeazzo Ciano, the former Italian foreign secretary, was executed by Italian fascists in January 1944. Why?

A His "crime" was to have voted with other fascists to oust Mussolini in July 1943. Ciano and his wife were lured to Bavaria in August 1943 following a report that their children were in danger. Having been promised safe passage to Spain, they were handed over to Italy's puppet fascist government.

Q What relation was Ciano to Mussolini?

> ## WHO HAS INFLICTED THIS UPON US? WHO HAS MADE US JEWS DIFFERENT FROM ALL OTHER PEOPLE?
> ANNE FRANK, APRIL 11, 1944

A He was Mussolini's son-in-law.

Q Who was the commander of the German Army Group North on the Eastern Front at the beginning of 1944?

A Field Marshal Georg von Küchler.

Q Why was he dismissed by Hitler in January 1944?

A For ordering the withdrawal of the Eighteenth Army in the face of the Soviet Leningrad Offensive.

Q Who replaced Küchler as commander of Army Group North?

A Walther Model.

Q Why was he nicknamed "lion of the defense"?

A Because after the Battle of Kursk, he conducted a magnificent fighting withdrawal in the Ukraine as his Ninth Army retreated with Army Group Center.

DID YOU KNOW

HUNDREDS OF THOUSANDS OF SOVIET WOMEN SERVED IN UNIFORM DURING WORLD WAR II. WOMEN HAD BEEN GRANTED FULL CIVIL, LEGAL, AND ELECTORAL EQUALITY IN JANUARY 1918 BY THE NEW BOLSHEVIK REGIME, AND DURING THE CIVIL WAR 74,000 WOMEN FOUGHT ON THE SIDE OF THE REDS, SUFFERING CASUALTIES OF 1,800. WHEN THE GERMANS INVADED THE USSR IN JUNE 1941, THOUSANDS OF WOMEN VOLUNTEERED FOR SERVICE (LATER THE SOVIETS DRAFTED UNMARRIED WOMEN). MORE THAN 70 PERCENT OF THE 800,000 SOVIET WOMEN WHO SERVED IN THE RED ARMY FOUGHT AT THE FRONT, WITH 100,000 BEING DECORATED FOR THEIR BRAVERY. IN ADDITION, KOMSOMOL, THE COMMUNIST YOUTH ORGANIZATION, MOBILIZED 500,000 WOMEN AND GIRLS FOR MILITARY SERVICE. WOMEN INITIALLY TRAINED IN ALL-FEMALE GROUPS BUT, AFTER TRAINING, WERE POSTED TO REGULAR ARMY UNITS AND FOUGHT ALONGSIDE MEN. ABOUT 30 PERCENT OF SERVICEWOMEN RECEIVED ADDITIONAL INSTRUCTION IN MORTARS, LIGHT AND HEAVY MACHINE GUNS, OR AUTOMATIC RIFLES. IN COMMON WITH MANY WOMEN IN UNIFORM, LUDMILLA PAVLICHENKO WAS TRAINED AS A SNIPER. SHE IS CREDITED WITH KILLING 309 GERMANS. LANCE CORPORAL MARIA IVANOVA MOROZOVA ALSO SERVED AS A SNIPER WITH THE 62D RIFLE BATTALION AND WON 11 COMBAT DECORATIONS.

Q Which Soviet city, under siege since 1941, was finally relived in January 1944?

A Leningrad.

Q The link up of the Red Army's 1st and 2nd Ukrainian Fronts at Zvenigorodka in late January 1944 trapped the German XI and XXXXII Corps where?

A The Cherkassy Pocket.

Q Who headed the Soviet secret police, the NKVD, in World War II?

A Lavrenti Beria.

DID YOU KNOW

THE GERMANS WERE INITIALLY SLOW TO MOBILIZE WOMEN, PARTLY DUE TO NAZI IDEOLOGY, WHICH VIEWED THE MAIN ROLE OF WOMEN AS BEING AT HOME BEARING CHILDREN. INDEED, INITIALLY NAZI LEADERS PROCLAIMED THAT THE USSR'S USE OF WOMEN SOLDIERS DEMONSTRATED THE SOVIETS WERE A WEAK ENEMY WHO WOULD EASILY BE DEFEATED. A LENGTHENING WAR AND HUGE LOSSES CHANGED THIS VIEW, AND BY 1944 THERE WERE 500,000 GERMAN WOMEN IN UNIFORM SERVING AS SUPPORT TROOPS (100,000 IN LUFTWAFFE ANTI-AIRCRAFT BATTERIES). AT THE END OF THE WAR, HITLER EVEN APPROVED THE RAISING OF ALL-FEMALE VOLKSSTURM BATTALIONS. IN ADDITION, YOUNG GIRLS OF THE *BUND DEUTSCHER MADEL* REPORTEDLY FOUGHT IN THE BATTLE OF BERLIN IN APRIL 1945.

> ❝ I HAD HOPED THAT WE WERE HURLING A
> WILDCAT ONTO THE SHORE,
> ## BUT ALL WE HAD GOT WAS
> ## A STRANDED WHALE ❞
> WINSTON CHURCHILL, ON THE ANZIO LANDINGS

Q What was the divisional title of the 5th SS Panzer Division?

A *Wiking.*

Q In February 1944, the Soviet NKVD began the mass deportation from their homelands of which Russian national groups?

A Chechens and Ingush.

Q Where were they deported to?

A Siberia and the Kazak steppes.

Q Estimate the number of people who died during the journey.

A Some 362,000 Chechens and 134,000 Ingush old men, women, and children were rounded up and packed on to 180 train convoys in the space of just over a week. Tens of thousands died during journeys which lasted up to two months. Half of all those deported perished.

Q Why did Argentina sever relations with Germany and Japan in January 1944?

A The Argentines uncovered a vast Axis spy network in the country.

Q The British Army's rifle in World War II was the SMLE. What do these letters stand for?

A Short Magazine Lee Enfield.

Q What was the rifle's caliber?

A .303in.

Q What was its magazine capacity?

A 10 rounds.

> " I CONTINUE CLOSING UPON THE
> FORTRESS, FIRING AT THE
> # CONTROL CABIN IN
> # THE NOSE
> HEINZ KNOKE, GERMAN FIGHTER PILOT,
> FEBRUARY 1944 "

Q What was the fire mode of the German Gewehr 41(W)?

A Semi-automatic.

Q Hitler supposedly coined the term *SturmGewehr* for the MP44 rifle. What does this term mean?

A Assault rifle.

DID YOU KNOW

ALTHOUGH NAVAL INFANTRY, SUCH AS THE BRITISH ROYAL MARINES AND THE U.S. MARINES, HAD ELEMENTARY AMPHIBIOUS SKILLS AT THE BEGINNING OF WORLD WAR II, IT WAS THE JAPANESE WHO TRULY PIONEERED AMPHIBIOUS TACTICS. FROM EXPERIENCE IN CHINA IN THE LATE 1930S, AND FROM THEIR OPENING CAMPAIGNS OF WORLD WAR II, THE JAPANESE DEVELOPED A SYSTEMATIC DOCTRINE FOR AMPHIBIOUS CAMPAIGNS, INCLUDING THE ESTABLISHMENT OF NAVAL AND AIR SUPERIORITY IN THE AREA OF LANDING; DETAILED INTELLIGENCE CONCERNING LANDING SITES AND ENEMY DEFENSES; AND SYSTEMATIC DISEMBARKATION OF TROOPS, AMMUNITION, AND SUPPLIES. THEY WERE ALSO CAPABLE OF NIGHTTIME AMPHIBIOUS LANDINGS, WITH SOLDIERS AND EQUIPMENT DAUBED IN LUMINOUS PAINT TO AID IDENTIFICATION. YET, DESPITE JAPANESE CAPABILITIES, THE UNDENIABLE MASTER OF AMPHIBIOUS WARFARE IN WORLD WAR II WAS THE U.S. AMERICAN AMPHIBIOUS LANDINGS WORKED IN THREE PARTS. AN AMPHIBIOUS FORCE WAS RESPONSIBLE FOR LANDING TROOPS ON THE BEACHES AND MAINTAINING THE FLOW OF RELEVANT LOGISTICS. PREPARATORY AND SUPPORT BOMBARDMENTS WERE PROVIDED BY A FORCE OF WARSHIPS SURROUNDING THE LANDING ZONE; FARTHER OUT AT SEA, FLEET CARRIERS AND OTHER CAPITAL SHIPS PROVIDED AIR AND SEA COVER FOR THE LANDING OPERATIONS—AND ALSO INTERDICTED JAPANESE REINFORCEMENT CONVOYS.

229

Q What was the British Army's main machine gun in World War II, the Korean War, and into the 1960s?

A The .303in Vickers.

Q What was the caliber of the U.S. M1919 medium machine gun?

A .3in.

Q The Czech ZB26 machine gun was known in British service as what?

A The Bren Gun.

Q Why was it so named by the British?

A By combining the first two letters from the original Czech factory that made the weapon (Brno) with those of the factory where it was made in Britain (Enfield).

Q What was this weapon's magazine capacity?

> " I BEGAN TO UNDERSTAND FOR THE FIRST
> TIME THAT IN WAR IT IS MOST
> ## OFTEN THE STRONG AND THE
> ## BRAVE WHO ARE KILLED
> HOWARD L. BOND, U.S. 36TH INFANTRY DIVISION,
> MAY 1944 "

A 30 rounds.

Q Which German machine gun was designed specifically for use by paratroopers?

A The FG42.

Q In the British Army, what rank did a single crown on a shoulder strap denote?

A Major.

DID YOU KNOW

As the war dragged on, it became increasingly more perilous for Hitler to visit his troops in the field. Air travel became too dangerous, and the fate of Japanese Admiral Isoroku Yamamoto, who was killed when his aircraft was ambushed by American fighters, was a salutary lesson in the problems caused by the loss of air supremacy by the Luftwaffe. Hitler retreated into a series of some 21 underground bunker complexes constructed in conditions of great secrecy. They were built around Germany to allow Hitler to remain protected when visiting each of the main battle fronts. Until the Soviets broke through to the Baltic coast in the winter of 1944, Hitler spent most of his time at the famous Wolf's Lair complex in the forests of East Prussia. Paranoid that the British would drop a division of paratroopers on the complex, Hitler ordered it to be protected by huge mine-fields and a specially trained élite defense unit, the famous *Führer Begleit* Battalion.

231

Q Which medal is Britain's highest decoration for "conspicuous bravery or devotion to the country in the presence of the enemy"?

A The Victoria Cross.

Q What is the difference between the British George Cross and the George Medal?

A The George Cross ranks next to the Victoria Cross, and is awarded mainly to civilians, i.e. a civilian Victoria Cross. The George Medal is awarded in circumstances similar to those required for the award of the George Cross, but of lesser merit. It is thus "junior" to the George Cross.

Q What was the main machine gun for all British tanks during the war?

A The 7.92mm Besa.

Q What was the smallest mortar in British Army service during the war?

A The 2in mortar, designated Ordnance ML2.

Q What was the Blacker Bombard?

A A British mortar designed by a Lieutenant Colonel Blacker, hence its name.

Q What was a PIAT?

A Projector Infantry Anti-Tank, a British antitank weapon.

Q What Swedish antiaircraft gun was used by both Allied and Axis armies during the war?

A The 40mm Bofors.

Q What was the name of the British A22 infantry tank?

A The Churchill.

Q In British service, what was a FANY?

A A member of the First Aid Nursing Yeomanry, a voluntary women's service.

Q Which British division had as its insignia a blue shield edged with red with a white eye in its center?

A The Guards Armoured Division.

DID YOU KNOW

THE NUMBER OF GENERALS IN HITLER'S ARMY HAD REACHED 2,242 BY 1944, NOT INCLUDING 150 LUFTWAFFE GENERALS AND THE SENIOR COMMANDERS OF THE WAFFEN-SS. SOME 40 ARMY AND 10 AIR FORCE GENERALS WERE PROMOTED TO COLONEL-GENERAL, OR FOUR-STAR RANK. HIGH RANK IN THE WEHRMACHT MEANT GOOD SALARIES: THE EQUIVALENT OF $100,000 WENT WITH THE RANK OF MAJOR GENERAL. LARGE HOUSES AND ESTATES WERE ALSO SHOWERED ON THE FÜHRER'S FAVORITES. HEINZ GUDERIAN, THE FAMOUS FATHER OF THE PANZER FORCE, WAS PROMISED AN ESTATE FOR HIS SERVICES TO THE REICH BY THE FÜHRER. IN SPITE OF SACKING HIM DURING THE RETREAT FROM MOSCOW, HITLER KEPT HIS WORD, AND IN JANUARY 1943 THE GENERAL WAS INSTALLED IN A 947-HECTARE ESTATE IN EASTERN GERMANY (NOW PART OF WESTERN POLAND). A GRATEFUL FÜHRER EVEN PAID FOR ALL THE GENERAL'S FURNITURE AND FARM MACHINERY. NOT SURPRISINGLY, GUDERIAN WAS EAGER TO RETURN TO HITLER'S SERVICE IN 1943 AS INSPECTOR GENERAL OF PANZER TROOPS. IN THE WAKE OF THE JULY 1944 BOMB PLOT HE SERVED HITLER AS OKH CHIEF OF STAFF. HE THEN CALLED ON HIS FELLOW GENERALS TO STAY LOYAL TO THE FÜHRER.

Q The insignia denoting Bellerophon astride Pegasus in pale blue on a maroon background was worn by which units?

A The British 1st and 6th Airborne Divisions.

Q What was the motto of the British Navy, Army, and Air Force Institute (NAAFI)?

A "Service to the Services."

Q In the Pacific theater, what was Operation Flintlock in January 1944?

A The U.S. invasion of the Marshall Islands.

WHEREVER WE WENT WE CAME UPON DEAD HORSES, SMASHED-UP VEHICLES, AND CORPSES

LEON DEGRELLE, CHERKASSY POCKET,
FEBRUARY 1944

Q What was the first phase of Operation Flintlock?

A Landings on Majuro Atoll and Kwajalein Atoll by U.S. Army and Marine Corps troops. The attack was supported by large numbers of U.S. land-based and carrier-based aircraft.

Q What were the next two islands invaded by U.S. forces during Flintlock, at the beginning of February 1944?

A Roi and Namur Islands. The two islands took two days to occupy and cost U.S. forces 737 casualties.

DID YOU KNOW

Armored vehicle production in Germany reached its peak in 1944, at just the time when battlefield losses were reaching their height. Panzer IV production rose only marginally to some 3,800, but Panther production surged ahead to 3,584, production of 623 Tiger Is was augmented by the building of 376 Tiger IIs, StuG III and IV production reached nearly 6,000, and some 2,357 of the new Panzerjäger IV with the L70 cannon were built along with 226 of the 88mm-armed Jagdpanther. These figures need to be considered against total losses in 1943 of nearly 8,000 tanks and assault guns, and more than 9,000 in 1944. This production surge allowed the frontline units just to keep their heads above water and gave Rommel a fighting chance of defeating the D-Day landings in June 1944.

Q Following the successful conclusion of Operation Flintlock, U.S. forces began preparing for Operation Forager. What was this?

A The capture of the Mariana Islands, which included the islands of Saipan, Tinian, Rota, and Guam.

Q What was the codename of the U.S. 5307th Provisional Regiment?

A Galahad.

Q This regiment had a more famous nickname. What was it?

A Merrill's Marauders. It was the U.S. equivalent of the Chindits, and had actually trained with Chindit units. Its nickname came from the name of its commander, Brigadier General Frank D. Merrill.

Q Which British units conducted Operation Thursday in Burma in March 1943?

A The Chindits.

Q What was the aim of the operation?

A About 9,000 men were deployed by glider in an area between Indaw and Myitkyina. The purpose of Operation Thursday was to harass Japanese forces to the south of Chinese and U.S. operations against Myitkyina, and cut the flow of Japanese supplies and communications heading north.

Q The Japanese launched an offensive in Burma and India which began on March 7, 1944. What was its codename?

A Operation U-Go.

Q Who led the offensive?

A Lieutenant General Renya Mutaguchi.

Q Which army did he command during the offensive?

A The Fifteenth Army.

> **A JAPANESE MACHINE GUN CHATTERS HYSTERICALLY, AND BULLETS CLACK AND CLAP OVERHEAD**
> JOHN MASTERS, CHINDIT, BURMA, MARCH 1944

DID YOU KNOW

THE WAFFEN-SS FOUGHT IN EVERY THEATER ON MAINLAND EUROPE, AND
BECAME INDISPENSABLE TO HITLER'S WAR EFFORT FROM 1943 ONWARD.
THE SEVEN ELITE WAFFEN-SS PANZER DIVISIONS BECAME KNOWN AS THE
"FÜHRER'S FIRE BRIGADE" BECAUSE HE RUSHED THEM FROM ONE CRISIS
FRONT TO ANOTHER TO "EXTINGUISH" ENEMY BREAKTHROUGHS. TO EQUIP
THEM FOR THIS ROLE, THEY RECEIVED THE BEST EQUIPMENT THE REICH'S
WEAPONS FACTORIES COULD TURN OUT. THEY WERE ALSO TOP OF THE LIST
FOR THE REPLACEMENT OF DESTROYED OR DAMAGED TANKS, FIELD GUNS,
AND ARMORED VEHICLES. IN ADDITION, EVERY EFFORT WAS MADE TO KEEP
THEM UP TO STRENGTH WITH TRAINED MANPOWER. THE MAJORITY OF THE
OTHER WAFFEN-SS DIVISIONS WERE EMPLOYED ON LESS CRUCIAL FRONTS,
IN LARGELY STATIC DEFENSE ROLES OR ON COUNTER-PARTISAN DUTIES. THE
REPUTATION OF THESE UNITS WAS MIXED, TO SAY THE LEAST. THE DIVISIONS
THAT FOUGHT WITH ARMY GROUP NORTH BESIEGING LENINGRAD AND
LATER DEFENDING THE BALTIC STATES, SUCH AS THE *NORDLAND*
PANZERGRENADIER DIVISION, ACQUITTED THEMSELVES WELL. THIS
DIVISION PLAYED A KEY ROLE IN SAVING THE EIGHTEENTH ARMY FROM
ENCIRCLEMENT AT RIGA IN SEPTEMBER 1944. THE SS *NORD* MOUNTAIN
DIVISION FOUGHT FOR THREE YEARS IN THE ARCTIC AS PART OF THE
GERMAN THRUST TO CAPTURE THE RUSSIAN PORT OF MURMANSK,
ESTABLISHING AN EXCELLENT REPUTATION ALONGSIDE THE ARMY'S ÉLITE
MOUNTAIN UNITS.

237

Q What was the objective of Operation U-Go?

A To spoil any Allied offensive moves in central Burma by crossing
into India, pushing Allied forces out of Burma in the process, cutting
the Assam–Burma railway used for supplying Stilwell's Myitkyina
offensive, and also occupying Imphal and Kohima and the flat territory
between (which was an ideal launch point for an Allied offensive). The
first part of the offensive involved the Japanese 33rd Division advancing
out and cutting the Tiddim-Imphal Road, a major Allied supply route to
Imphal, and trapping the 17th Indian Division.

Q Which British commander was killed in an air crash over Burma in March 1944?

A Major General Orde Wingate.

Q In April and May 1944, Japanese and British forces fought a bitter two-week battle at Kohima, at which location?

A The Tennis Court.

Q Which Japanese admiral was killed in an air crash at the end of March 1944?

A Vice Admiral Mineichi Koga.

" WE WERE TWELVE HOURS A DAY ON THE
TRAIL, AS A RULE—WHETHER
THERE WAS A TRAIL OR NOT "
CHARLTON OGBURN, MERRILL'S MARAUDERS, JULY 1944

Q Which fleet had he been commanding at the time of his death?

A The Combined Fleet.

Q On the Eastern Front, the capture of Kamenets Podolsk by the Soviet Fourth Tank Army at the end of March 1944 resulted in the encirclement of which German army?

A The First Panzer Army.

DID YOU KNOW

THE RAPID ADVANCE OF GERMAN ARMIES INTO THE SOVIET UNION IN MID-1941 RESULTED IN THOUSANDS OF RED ARMY SOLDIERS BEING CUT OFF BEHIND GERMAN LINES IN THE UKRAINE, BELORUSSIA, AND THE BALTIC STATES. MANY TOOK REFUGE IN THE FORESTS OF THE WESTERN USSR AND IN THE PRIPET MARSHES, THUS FORMING THE NUCLEUS OF A PARTISAN MOVEMENT. THE FIRST PARTISAN ACTIVITIES WERE SPONTANEOUS AND UNCOORDINATED, WITHOUT ANY ASSISTANCE FROM MOSCOW (BOTH STALIN AND HIS SECRET POLICE CHIEF, BERIA, WERE SUSPICIOUS OF ARMED BANDS OUTSIDE THEIR SPHERE OF CONTROL). HOWEVER, RECOGNIZING THAT PARTISAN DETACHMENTS COULD BE USEFUL, STALIN IN LATE 1941 BEGAN TO SEND CADRES BEHIND GERMAN LINES TO COORDINATE RESISTANCE. THE FIRST COORDINATED PARTISAN ATTACKS TOOK PLACE DURING THE WINTER OF 1941–1942, AND IN MAY 1942 THE SOVIETS ESTABLISHED THE CENTRAL PARTISAN STAFF TO DIRECT THE OPERATIONS OF AN ESTIMATED 142,000 PARTISANS OPERATING BEHIND GERMAN LINES. PRIOR TO THE BATTLE OF KURSK IN JULY 1943, THE CENTRAL PARTISAN STAFF ORDERED THAT ALL PARTISAN ACTIVITY BE DIRECTED AGAINST GERMAN COMMUNICATIONS IN THE CENTRAL SECTOR. THIS RESULTED IN 2,500 PARTISAN ATTACKS AGAINST GERMAN RAILROADS IN JUNE AND JULY 1943. SUCH LARGE-SCALE PARTISAN ACTIVITY MEANT THE GERMANS HAD TO DEPLOY SUBSTANTIAL FORCES IN THEIR REAR AREAS. IN 1942, 25 SPECIAL SECURITY DIVISIONS, 30 REGIMENTS, AND MORE THAN 100 POLICE BATTALIONS WERE INVOLVED IN ANTI-PARTISAN DUTIES. THERE IS LITTLE DOUBT THAT THE GERMANS AIDED PARTISAN RECRUITMENT. TREATING THE LOCALS AS SUB-HUMANS, RANDOM REPRISALS IN RESPONSE TO PARTISAN ATTACKS, AND LAYING WASTE WHOLE AREAS TO DENY PARTISANS SUPPLIES DID LITTLE TO ENDEAR THE GERMANS TO THE POPULACE. BY 1943, FOR EXAMPLE, TYPICAL ANTI-PARTISAN SWEEPS INVOLVED 10,000 TROOPS. ALTHOUGH SOVIET CLAIMS THAT PARTISANS KILLED 300,000 GERMANS DURING THE FIRST TWO YEARS OF THE WAR ARE EXAGGERATED, IT IS CERTAINLY TRUE THAT THE PARTISAN MOVEMENT MADE A SIGNIFICANT CONTRIBUTION TO THE SOVIET WAR EFFORT.

Q Why did the Germans occupy Hungary in March 1944?

A Ever since the Hungarian Army suffered huge losses around Stalingrad in early 1943, Hungary had been a lukewarm member of the Axis. Indeed, from April 1943 Premier Miklos Kallay had committed only a small number of poorly armed troops to the Axis war effort. Hitler received reports proving that Hungary had been clandestinely dealing with the enemy and, in mid-March, Himmler learnt from agents in Budapest that Kallay was advocating the sabotage of German military trains running through Hungary to German army groups on the Eastern Front. In view of all these things, and fearing that Hungary might conclude a separate peace, Hitler ordered the occupation of Hungary.

Q Which two field marshals did Hitler relieve of their commands on the Eastern Front in the spring of 1944?

A Erich von Manstein and Ewald von Kleist.

Q Why?

A He was irritated by the continual retreats in the Ukraine.

DID YOU KNOW

ABOUT 1,000 WOMEN AVIATORS WERE TRAINED AS FIGHTER AND MILITARY TRANSPORT PILOTS BY THE USSR IN THE WAR, 30 OF THEM BEING DECORATED FOR THEIR HEROISM IN COMBAT. THREE AVIATION REGIMENTS, THE 586TH WOMEN'S FIGHTER REGIMENT, THE 587TH WOMEN'S BOMBER REGIMENT, AND THE 588TH WOMEN'S NIGHT BOMBER REGIMENT (THE SO-CALLED "NIGHT WITCHES," LATER ELEVATED TO THE 46TH GUARDS BOMBER AVIATION REGIMENT) WERE STAFFED BY WOMEN PILOTS, ENGINEERS, AND MECHANICS.

MANY BOYS NEAR ME WERE HIT BY
SNIPER FIRE OR SHRAPNEL
FROM THE JAP MORTARS
RICHARD KENNARD, 1ST MARINE DIVISION, PELELIU,
SEPTEMBER 1944

Q The Packard V-1650 engine powered which single-seat U.S. fighter?

A The P-51 Mustang.

Q What type of aircraft was the Soviet Lavochkin La-5?

A A fighter and fighter-bomber.

241

Q Artem Mikoyan and Mikhail Gurevich were designers of what?

A These two Russians were famous aircraft designers.

Q What type of vehicle was the German Wespe?

A A self-propelled gun.

Q What was its main armament?

A A 105mm leFH 18M L/28 howitzer.

Q Who was the Allied general who requested the bombing of the monastery at Monte Cassino in February 1944?

A Lieutenant General Sir Bernard Freyberg.

Q Why?

A German troops had been sighted within the monastery walls, and there were enemy emplacements and strongpoints nearby.

Q Did the bombing kill the German defenders?

A No. Though much of the monastery was destroyed, the bombing did not destroy the subterranean chambers where the defenders were sheltering.

Q What was Operation Strangle, launched by the Allies in Italy in March 1944?

A An air campaign designed to disrupt German supply routes by bombing bridges, roads, and railways.

Q Who were nicknamed the "Green Devils of Cassino"?

A The German paratroopers who defended Monte Cassino.

> **"** IT WAS MOST THOUGHTFUL OF YOU
> AS AN OLD HARROVIAN TO CAPTURE
> ### ROME ON THE
> ### FOURTH OF JUNE
> HAROLD MACMILLAN TO GENERAL ALEXANDER, JUNE 4, 1944 **"**

DID YOU KNOW

TO SENIOR GERMAN ARMY COMMANDERS, THE WAFFEN-SS WAS A MIXED BLESSING. THERE WAS RESENTMENT THAT HITLER'S PRIVATE ARMY WAS SIPHONING OFF ITS BEST RECRUITS AND HAD THE PICK OF THE PRODUCTION FROM THE REICH'S ARMAMENT FACTORIES. HOWEVER, FIELD COMMANDERS GREW TO VALUE THE FIGHTING QUALITIES OF THE MAINSTREAM WAFFEN-SS DIVISIONS, IN PARTICULAR THE PANZER UNITS. WAFFEN-SS UNITS USUALLY CAME WITH SUPERB EQUIPMENT AND LAVISH SUPPLIES OF AMMUNITION, MAKING THEM A POWERFUL ADDITION TO THE FIGHTING POWER OF ANY ARMY HEADQUARTERS THAT HAD THEM ASSIGNED TO IT. FOR THEIR PART, WAFFEN-SS COMMANDERS WERE KEEN TO WIN THEIR SPURS IN BATTLE AND REGULARLY OFFERED UP THEIR UNITS FOR TASKS THAT ARMY OFFICERS HAD REFUSED. THIS RIVALRY BECAME LEGENDARY, AND NO WAFFEN-SS OFFICER WANTED TO BE SEEN TO FAIL ANY BATTLEFIELD MISSION. THE MORE GLORY THE WAFFEN-SS COULD GAIN AT THE EXPENSE OF THE ARMY, THE BETTER.

243

Q What was the purpose of the British 79th Armoured Division?

A To create specialist armored vehicles to defeat German fixed defenses, i.e. the Atlantic Wall defenses in France.

Q Who was the division's commander?

A Major General Sir Percy Hobart.

Q What was the task of the British Royal Navy's 30th Advanced Unit (30 AU)?

A To capture enemy prisoners, documents, and equipment.

> OVERPAID, OVERSEXED,
> ## AND OVER HERE
> British saying in 1944,
> about U.S. troops in England

Q What was a German S-boat?

A A fast torpedo boat.

Q At the beginning of May 1944 the Germans formed a new army group in France. What was it?

A Army Group G.

Q Which armies did it control?

A The First and Nineteenth Armies.

Q Who was the army group's commander?

A General Johannes von Blaskowitz.

Q In May 1944, the U.S. 82d and 101st Airborne Divisions carried out an exercise in Berkshire, England, as a rehearsal for their D-Day drops. What was the codename of this exercise?

A Exercise Eagle.

Q Which German battleship was damaged by aircraft at the beginning of April 1944?

A The *Tirpitz*.

Q The attacking aircraft flew from which British aircraft carriers?

A HMS *Victorious* and *Furious*.

Q Where did the attack take place?

A Altenfiord, Norway.

DID YOU KNOW

WITHIN THOSE COUNTRIES AND REGIONS OVERRUN BY THE GERMANS AND JAPANESE IN WORD WAR II THERE WERE THOSE AMONG THE VARIOUS POPULATIONS WHO WERE DETERMINED TO OPPOSE THE OCCUPIERS IN SOME WAY, OFTEN AT GREAT RISK TO THEMSELVES AND THEIR FAMILIES. THIS RESISTANCE COULD BE ACTIVE OR PASSIVE. PASSIVE RESISTANCE INVOLVED DEMONSTRATIONS, INDUSTRIAL STRIKES, AND SLOWDOWNS, THE PRODUCTION OF UNDERGROUND NEWSPAPERS AND LEAFLETS, AND WALL SLOGANS. ACTIVE RESISTANCE INVOLVED GATHERING INTELLIGENCE, ASSISTING ESCAPED ALLIED PRISONERS OF WAR AND SHOT-DOWN AIRCREWS, SABOTAGE, AND ARMED ACTION AGAINST OCCUPATION FORCES. THE DANGERS OF FIGHTING BACK AGAINST OCCUPIERS WERE EVER PRESENT, AND RESISTANCE MOVEMENTS WERE UNDER CONSTANT THREAT FROM ENEMY INTELLIGENCE, COLLABORATORS, AND INFORMERS, WITH TORTURE AND DEATH THE USUAL PRICE OF BEING CAUGHT. OWNERSHIP OF A CARRIER PIGEON, FOR EXAMPLE, WARRANTED DEATH BY FIRING SQUAD IN EUROPE.

Q Who was appointed to be commander of the Japanese Combined Fleet in May 1944?

A Admiral Soemu Toyoda.

Q A mass breakout of Allied prisoners of war took place at which German prison camp in May 1944?

A Stalag Luft III near Sagan, Silesia.

Q Was the escape attempt successful?

A No. After capture, 50 Allied airmen were shot by the Gestapo. Only three of the escaped prisoners—two Norwegians and a Dutchman—reached England.

Q What was the first Axis capital city to be captured by Allied forces in the war?

A Rome, by the U.S. Fifth Army on June 5, 1944.

Q What was the codename for the naval and amphibious element of the Allied invasion of France in June 1944?

A Operation Neptune.

" WE'RE GETTING KILLED ON THE BEACHES.
LET'S GO INSHORE AND GET KILLED
U.S. OFFICER ON OMAHA BEACH, JUNE 6, 1944 **"**

DID YOU KNOW

AS ALLIED AERIAL PHOTOGRAPHIC INTERPRETERS PORED OVER IMAGES OF THE FRENCH COASTLINE DURING THE SPRING OF 1944, THEY BECAME INCREASINGLY ALARMED AT THE SCALE OF THE CONSTRUCTION WORK UNDER WAY ON THE THIRD REICH'S WESTERN RAMPART. THEY WERE OBSERVING THE RESULTS OF FIELD MARSHAL ERWIN ROMMEL'S CRASH PROGRAM TO TURN THE COASTAL DEFENSES ALONG THE ATLANTIC COAST AND ENGLISH CHANNEL INTO A REAL OBSTACLE FOR ANY ALLIED AMPHIBIOUS INVASION. AFTER A TOUR OF THE DILAPIDATED GERMAN DEFENSES FROM THE BAY OF BISCAY TO HOLLAND IN DECEMBER 1943, ROMMEL WROTE A REPORT CALLING FOR THE FORTIFICATIONS TO BE REVAMPED. FOR HIS EFFORTS, THE HERO OF NORTH AFRICA WAS APPOINTED COMMANDER OF THE COASTAL REGION OF FRANCE. HE IMMEDIATELY ORDERED A HUGE CONSTRUCTION EFFORT TO STRENGTHEN WHAT SOON BECAME KNOWN AS THE ATLANTIC WALL. ALL MAJOR COASTAL TOWNS AND PORTS WERE TURNED INTO VERITABLE FORTRESSES, WITH HUGE CONCRETE PILLBOXES AND GUN EMPLACEMENTS POSITIONED TO PROTECT THEM. THE MONSTER GUN POSITIONS IN THE PAS DE CALAIS SYMBOLIZED THIS EFFORT TO CREATE "CONCRETE BATTLESHIPS" AT KEY PARTS ALONG THE ATLANTIC WALL TO PREVENT THE ALLIES SEIZING A PORT INTACT. THESE EFFORTS WERE COMPLEMENTED BY EXTENSIVE ENGINEERING WORK TO TURN LIKELY INVASION BEACHES INTO A DEATH TRAP FOR ANY ALLIED AMPHIBIOUS OR AIRBORNE ASSAULT. EXPLOSIVE-TIPPED STEEL AND CONCRETE TRAPS WERE PLACED OUT AT SEA, BELOW THE WATERLINE, TO PENETRATE THE HULLS OF APPROACHING LANDING CRAFT.

247

Q Who was commander-in-chief of Allied Expeditionary Air Forces during the D-Day landings?

A Air Chief Marshal Trafford Leigh-Mallory.

Q Who was commander-in-chief of Allied Expeditionary Naval Forces during the D-Day landings?

A Admiral Bertram Ramsay.

Q Operation Bagration was a Soviet offensive designed to destroy which German formation?

A Army Group Center in Belorussia.

Q Name the Allied D-Day invasion beaches.

A Utah, Omaha, Gold, Juno, and Sword.

DID YOU KNOW

IN JULY 1944, U.S. MILITARY LEADERS, THE JOINT CHIEFS OF STAFF, AND THE U.S. PRESIDENT MET TO DEBATE STRATEGIC OPTIONS FOR COMPLETE VICTORY IN THE PACIFIC. THOSE PRESENT DIVIDED THEMSELVES ROUGHLY INTO TWO CAMPS. GENERAL MACARTHUR ADVOCATED THE PHILIPPINES AS THE PRINCIPAL OBJECTIVE FOLLOWING THE CAMPAIGN IN NEW GUINEA, WHEREAS ADMIRAL KING (CHIEF OF THE U.S. NAVY) WANTED TO BYPASS THE PHILIPPINES AND CUT STRAIGHT TO THE ISLAND OF FORMOSA, SOUTH OF THE JAPANESE MAINLAND. BY TAKING FORMOSA, KING CONTENDED, JAPAN WOULD BE ISOLATED FROM HER RESOURCES IN THE DUTCH EAST INDIES. ALSO, FORMOSA WOULD BE AN EXCELLENT JUMPING-OFF POINT IN THE FINAL INVASION OF JAPAN, AND WOULD AVOID ANY WASTEFUL SLAUGHTER IN THE PHILIPPINE JUNGLES. MACARTHUR'S PLAN HAD A STRONG ETHICAL DIMENSION TO IT; HE BELIEVED THAT THE U.S. WAS UNDER A "MORAL OBLIGATION" TO RETURN TO THE PHILIPPINES AND LIBERATE ITS INHABITANTS. MILITARILY, HE ARGUED THAT IT WOULD NOT BE ADVISABLE TO LEAVE A LARGE JAPANESE PRESENCE IN THE REAR FOR A STRIKE TOWARD FORMOSA. THE OTHER KEY FIGURE IN THE DEBATE WAS ADMIRAL HALSEY. HE WANTED TO DEVELOP THE CENTRAL PACIFIC CAMPAIGN BY CAPTURING OKINAWA IN THE RYUKYU CHAIN, PART OF JAPANESE TERRITORY ITSELF, AND USE THIS AS THE LAUNCH PAD FOR THE INVASION OF THE MAINLAND. THE MOMENTUM WAS TOWARD MACARTHUR AND HALSEY'S PLAN, AND THE PRESIDENT AND THE JOINT CHIEFS OF STAFF GAVE THEIR ASSENT. FORMOSA WOULD BE BYPASSED.

A FEW MINUTES LATER WE SUDDENLY
WENT INTO THICK CLOUD
GENERAL MATTHEW B. RIDGWAY, COMMANDER OF THE
U.S. 82ND AIRBORNE DIVISION, JUNE 5, 1944

Q American troops landed on which beaches?

A Utah and Omaha.

Q List the reasons why American troops landing on Omaha Beach suffered heavy casualties.

A Allied bombers missed their target and dropped their bombs inland; the heavy seas meant all but five of the 32 first-wave tanks were lost before they reached the shore; the naval bombardment did not destroy the German defenses; and many landing craft stopped too far from the shore, which meant that when the troops jumped into the water many drowned.

Q Which U.S. unit stormed the Pointe-du-Hoc on D-Day?

A The 2d Rangers, commanded by Colonel James E. Rudder.

Q Who was the commander of Japanese forces on the island of Saipan when the Americans invaded in June 1944?

A Lieutenant General Saito Yoshitsugo.

Q Which U.S. divisions spearheaded the invasion of Saipan?

A The 2d and 4th Marine Divisions.

Q What was "The Great Marianas Turkey Shoot"?

A The Battle of the Philippine Sea, June 19, 1944?

Q Why was it called this?

A The Japanese lost two aircraft carriers and 346 aircraft to U.S. air and naval attacks.

Q The German Pistole 08 was more famously known as what?

A The Luger.

DID YOU KNOW

German anti-partisan operations in Russia were a mix of static defense and mobile offensive sweeps. Key bridges and major stretches of railroads could be secured only by the physical building of fortified support points, manned by a platoon of 20 to 30 men. Battalion-sized reaction forces were then based at regular intervals to patrol the main roads and railroads, ready to take the offensive against any partisan raids. Armored trains and small tank detachments were used to give security units overwhelming firepower. Air reconnaissance was used regularly to check railroad lines and roads for mines and other acts of sabotage. Areas of known partisan activity were ringed with support points to try to contain and stop the spread of hostile actions. Small patrols of *Jagdkommando*, or hunter, units were used to penetrate into partisan territory to gather intelligence and raid their bases. The services of the Gestapo were employed on captured partisans or their relatives to make them betray their comrades by leading German troops to their bases.

Q What was its magazine capacity?

A Eight rounds.

Q The Walther PP handgun was manufactured for German military service in two calibres. What were they?

A 7.65mm and 9mm.

Q When fighting stopped on the island of Saipan in July 1944, more than 30 percent of Japanese casualties had been suicides. True or false?

A True. The final death toll was high on both sides: 3,126 U.S. soldiers killed and 27,000 Japanese (including 8,000 suicides).

251

Q What was the next objective for the U.S. forces in the Mariana Islands after the fall of Saipan?

A The island of Guam.

Q When did U.S. forces invade Guam?

A July 21, 1944.

" YOU COULD READ CONCERN ON THE
GRIM, SET FACES AS THEY TURNED TO
PEER OUT OF THE WINDOWS
GENERAL MATTHEW RIDGWAY,
U.S. 82D AIRBORNE DIVISION, D-DAY "

Q U.S. Lieutenant General Holland Smith classed the conquest of which island as being the finest amphibious operation of the Pacific war?

A Tinian.

Q What happened at the Coworra prisoner-of-war camp, Sydney, in early August 1944?

A Japanese prisoners of war attempted a mass breakout. Three Australian guards were killed and 334 Japanese managed to escape, but Australian machine-gun fire killed 234 inmates and wounded 108 others.

Q Who commanded British and Canadian forces during the Allied invasion of France in June 1944?

A General Bernard Montgomery.

Q What was their immediate objective after landing in Normandy?

A The city of Caen.

Q What was the British Operation Goodwood in July 1944?

A General Montgomery's attempt to outflank Caen and open a route to Falaise.

❝ COUNTERATTACK BY JERRY FROM WOODS. MORTAR FIRE. 13 OF MY PLATOON KILLED OR MISSING
CORPORAL G.E. HUGHES, ROYAL HAMPSHIRES,
JUNE 14, 1944 **❞**

DID YOU KNOW

FRANCE'S ROLLING AND WOODED COUNTRYSIDE PROVED TO BE THE GERMAN ARMY'S ONLY ALLY DURING THE BITTER FIGHTING AFTER THE D-DAY LANDINGS IN JUNE 1944. GERMAN DIVISIONS BECAME EXPERT AT DISPERSING THEMSELVES IN WOODS, FARM BUILDINGS, TUNNELS, MINES, AND INDUSTRIAL SITES. ALL VEHICLES WOULD BE ADORNED WITH HUGE AMOUNTS OF FOLIAGE TO BREAK UP THEIR SHAPES AND MAKE THEM MERGE WITH LOCAL VEGETATION. THE GERMANS, HOWEVER, WERE DETERMINED TO AVOID BEING PARALYZED BY ALLIED AIR SUPREMACY AND DEVELOPED TECHNIQUES TO ALLOW THEM TO REMAIN HIDDEN AND STILL FIGHT. A SYSTEM OF CAMOUFLAGE HIDES WAS DEVELOPED, UNDER WHICH GERMAN UNITS WOULD OPERATE FROM CAMOUFLAGED BASES IN WOODS OR INDUSTRIAL BUILDINGS, JUST BEHIND THE FRONTLINE. UNITS WOULD EMERGE AT NIGHT TO REINFORCE AND RESUPPLY FRONTLINE POSITIONS. STRICT TRACK DISCIPLINE WOULD BE IMPOSED, SO ARMORED VEHICLES WOULD USE ONLY PREPARED ROUTES IN AND OUT OF THE HIDE, ON METALED ROADS SO AIRCRAFT COULD NOT SPOT TANK TRACKS ACROSS FIELDS.

253

Q In Normandy in 1944, U.S. forces fought the Germans in the so-called *bocage*. What was this?

A Normandy's distinctive terrain is known as the *bocage*. Modern intensive farming had yet to arrive in Normandy, with agriculture following much the same pattern as it had for hundreds of years before. Small farm holdings predominated, and this produced an interlinked network of small fields separated by ancient hedgerows. Crucially, these hedgerows had grown into thick barriers, reinforced by very high and thick earth banks.

Q Why was the *bocage* ideal for defensive warfare?

A Even the biggest German or Allied tank found these hedgerows almost impossible to pass through or over without specialist engineering or demolition equipment. Tank movement was effectively channeled along the few roads, making it easy for enemy antitank gunners to delay and hold up advances for hours or days at a time.

Q Which SS division was under constant French Resistance attack as it moved north from Toulouse to take part in the fighting in Normandy in mid-1944?

A The 2nd SS Panzer Division *Das Reich*.

Q Which French town was chosen by this SS division to be the target of a brutal anti-partisan reprisal action?

A Oradour-sur-Glane.

Q What happened at the town?

A The men were herded into barns, the women and children into the church, and the whole town was set on fire. Those who fled were machine-gunned. In total 642 people were killed, with only 10 managing to feign death and escape.

Q Which Waffen-SS tank ace stopped the British 7th Armoured Division at Villers-Bocage in June 1944?

A Michael Wittmann.

" I THEN THREW TWO GRENADES, WHICH WERE SUCCESSFUL IN ELIMINATING THE ENEMY

CAPTAIN JOSEPH DAWSON,
U.S. 1ST INFANTRY DIVISION, D-DAY **"**

DID YOU KNOW

FOR THE MAJORITY OF ALLIED TROOPS WHO ENGAGED THE GERMAN ARMY IN BATTLE IN NORMANDY, THE EXPERIENCE WAS THEIR FIRST TASTE OF COMBAT. THEY MIGHT HAVE ENDURED MONTHS OF INTENSIVE TRAINING IN ENGLAND BEFORE THEY WERE SHIPPED TO FRANCE, BUT NOTHING COULD HAVE PREPARED THEM FOR WHAT THEY WERE TO FACE. BRITISH, AMERICAN, AND CANADIAN DIVISIONAL, BRIGADE, AND BATTALION COMMANDERS WERE ALL LESS EXPERIENCED IN ALL-ARMS MECHANIZED WARFARE THAN THEIR GERMAN COUNTERPARTS. AT FIRST THEY ALL EMPLOYED RIGID TACTICS, WHICH LED TO THOUSANDS OF ALLIED CASUALTIES IN FRUITLESS FRONTAL ASSAULTS. THEY BELIEVED THEIR FIREPOWER WOULD OVERCOME THE GERMANS, AND THAT THERE WAS NO NEED TO USE THE TERRAIN TO COVER THEIR MOVEMENT OR TO TRY TO INFILTRATE BEHIND CENTERS OF RESISTANCE. THE ALLIES ALSO RELIED ON TOP-DOWN COMMAND PROCEDURES THAT MEANT THEIR INABILITY TO REACT TO SURPRISE GERMAN MOVES WAS A WEAKNESS. WHEN KEY OFFICERS WERE KILLED OR COMMUNICATIONS WITH HIGHER HEADQUARTERS DID NOT WORK, ALLIED ATTACKS OFTEN BROKE DOWN BECAUSE THERE WAS NO ONE TO TAKE THE INITIATIVE AND LEAD THE REMAINING TROOPS FORWARD.

255

Q **What was the codename of the U.S. operation that broke through German lines in Normandy in July 1944?**

A Cobra.

Q **Which general led the U.S. Third Army in France in 1944?**

A George Patton.

Q **Why had this general been publicly censured by his superiors the year before?**

A For striking a shell-shocked soldier in a field hospital in Sicily.

> " EVERY MILE WE ADVANCE THERE ARE
> DOZENS OF SNIPERS LEFT BEHIND US.
> ## THEY PICK OFF
> ## OUR SOLDIERS
> ERNIE PYLE, NORMANDY, JUNE 26, 1944 "

Q What was Operation Bagration in June 1944?

A The Red Army's offensive against Army Group Center.

Q Which German panzer army was destroyed during the first six days of Bagration?

A The Third Panzer Army.

Q At the beginning of July 1944, which German army, deployed east of Minsk, was destroyed following the Soviet capture of the city?

A The Fourth Army.

Q What was Operation Valkyrie, which took place on July 20, 1944?

A The assassination attempt on Hitler's life.

Q Where was it carried out?

A At Hitler's East Prussia headquarters at Rastenburg.

Q Who led the operation?

A Colonel Claus Schenk von Stauffenberg. He fled Hitler's head-quarters after planting the bomb (which failed to kill Hitler) but was shot later that day.

Q What was the Polish Committee of Nation Liberation?

A A Soviet organization formed from the NKVD-controlled Union of Polish Patriots. It was later known as the Lublin Committee and became the official legal authority, according to the Soviets, in liberated Polish territory.

DID YOU KNOW

THE SOVIET LEADER, STALIN, VIEWED THE WESTERN ALLIES WITH SUSPICION, OFTEN ACCUSING THEM OF POSTPONING THE SECOND FRONT BECAUSE THEY WANTED TO SEE THE USSR BLED WHITE. ALWAYS PUTTING HIS OWN INTERESTS FIRST, HE MADE EXORBITANT DEMANDS WHEN IT CAME TO LEND-LEASE SUPPLIES, AND PLANNED THE FINAL OFFENSIVES OF THE WAR WITH A RUSSIAN-DOMINATED POSTWAR EUROPE IN MIND. AFTER THE WAR HE QUICKLY MOVED TO CONSOLIDATE HIS POSITION BY REMOVING FAMOUS WARTIME COMMANDERS, AND SO FIGURES SUCH AS ZHUKOV, ROKOSSOVSKY, MERETSKOV, VATUTIN, AND KONEV DISAPPEARED FROM PUBLIC VIEW. HE ALSO DID NOT FORGET THOSE RUSSIAN NATIONALS WHO, IN HIS VIEW, HAD COLLABORATED WITH THE ENEMY. HE INSISTED THAT THE BRITISH AND AMERICANS ADHERE STRICTLY TO THE TERMS OF THE YALTA AGREEMENT, WHICH THEY DID, EVEN THOUGH THEY KNEW THAT REPATRIATION WOULD MEAN DEATH OR IMPRISONMENT FOR THOSE RETURNED. THUS, BETWEEN 1945 AND 1947, 2,272,000 SOVIET CITIZENS WERE RETURNED BY THE WESTERN ALLIES TO THE USSR. ONE-FIFTH OF THESE WERE EITHER SHOT OR GIVEN 25-YEAR SENTENCES IN THE GULAG.

Q The weapon designers R.V. Shepperd and H.J. Turpin created which famous submachine gun?

A The Sten Gun.

Q What was its caliber?

A 9mm.

Q What was its magazine capacity?

A 32 rounds.

Q The Japanese Rifle Type 38 was also known as what?

A The Arisaka Rifle.

Q Which organization rose in revolt against the Germans in Warsaw on August 1, 1944?

A The Home Army.

Q Who was its commander?

A General Tadeusz Komorowski, who commanded 38,000 insurgents in the city.

Q Which German commander was given the task of suppressing the revolt?

A SS General Erich von dem Bach-Zelewski.

Q Who was the fascist leader of Romania?

A Ion Antonescu.

"" UP AND DOWN THE BEACH AND OUT ON THE REEF, A NUMBER OF AMTRACS **AND DUKWS WERE BURNING**

EUGENE B. SLEDGE, 1ST MARINE DIVISION, PELELIU, SEPTEMBER 15, 1944 ""

Q In August 1944 the German Army in Normandy was encircled near which French town?

A Falaise.

Q What was the objective of Montgomery's Operation Market Garden in September 1944?

A An ambitious airborne operation to seize a series of strategic bridges in Holland, to allow the Allies to gain a foothold over the Rhine at Arnhem, and open a route for Allied tanks into the heart of Germany's Ruhr industrial region.

Q U.S. armored divisions were usually divided into three units, in which armor and infantry battalions were combined. What were these units called?

A Combat commands.

Q What type of artillery piece was the German 75mm GebG 36?

A A mountain gun.

> **I REMEMBER IT AS A CLAP OF THUNDER COUPLED WITH A BRIGHT YELLOW FLASH**
> HEINRICH BUCHOLZ, DESCRIBING THE BOMB ATTEMPT ON HITLER'S LIFE

DID YOU KNOW

THE SIEGFRIED LINE HAD BEEN BUILT IN THE 1930S IN RESPONSE TO THE FRENCH BUILDING THEIR FAMOUS MAGINOT LINE. THE GERMAN LINE STRETCHED FROM THE SWISS BORDER NORTHWARD TO NEAR THE DUTCH BORDER. IN THE "PHONEY WAR" PERIOD OF THE LATE 1930S, THE SIEGFRIED LINE HAD TAKEN ON ALMOST MYTHICAL PROPORTIONS, AS BOTH THE FRENCH AND GERMANS ATTEMPTED TO OUT-DO EACH OTHER IN THE PROPAGANDA WAR, CLAIMING THEIR RESPECTIVE LINES WERE STRONGER, BIGGER, AND MORE IMPREGNABLE THAN THOSE OF THEIR OPPONENTS. IN REALITY, THE GERMAN LINE WAS NEVER AS STRONG AS ITS FRENCH COUNTERPART, BEING MORE A SERIES OF FIELD FORTIFICATIONS FOR ARMY UNITS RATHER THAN A "CONCRETE BATTLESHIP" IN THE STYLE OF THE MAGINOT LINE. THE SIEGFRIED LINE BOASTED LONG LINES OF CONCRETE DRAGON'S TEETH ANTITANK OBSTACLES, PILLBOXES, AND HUGE BARBED-WIRE ENTANGLEMENTS.

Q In the U.S. Army, what were "tank-hunting teams"?

A Usually a tank battalion with an infantry company attached.

Q In the U.S. Army, what were "infantry-heavy teams" used for?

A Usually a group of infantry companies, they were used for attacks against towns and woods and for river crossings.

Q In Red Army service, what were Aerosans?

A A type of ski vehicle propelled by an aircraft engine. An armored version, the NKL-26, was produced for raiding operations in Arctic regions.

Q In the Pacific, the U.S. Navy's submarines experienced two main problems with their Mark XIV torpedoes. What were they?

A The depth-control mechanism of the torpedo was malfunctioning and directed the torpedo too far beneath its target (it ran at about 10–12 ft/3–4 m below set depth). Also, the torpedoes were equipped with the Mk VI magnetic influence exploder mechanism, an unreliable proximity detonator designed to explode the torpedo underneath a ship rather than on contact.

Q In the Pacific theater, where was "Bloody Nose Ridge"?

A On the island of Peleliu.

> " BY MIDDAY THE ENTIRE AREA
> RESEMBLED A MOON LANDSCAPE,
> ## WITH THE BOMB CRATERS
> ## TOUCHING RIM TO RIM
> GENERAL FRITZ BAYERLAIN, PANZER LEHR DIVISION,
> NORMANDY, JULY 1944 "

Q What were the three cornerstones of Lord Louis Mountbatten's Burma policy?

A Morale, monsoon, and malaria. Mountbatten raised Allied morale in Burma mainly through capitalizing on the victories at Imphal and Kohima, and promoting the idea that Japanese invincibility was a myth. "Monsoon" refers to his policy of maintaining the Allied campaign through the five-month monsoon season to enforce the Japanese collapse. As a corollary, he created the Medical Advisory Division to tackle tropical diseases such as malaria, which cost the Allies 120 men for every single battle casualty.

Q In October 1944 the Japanese launched Operation Sho. What was its objective?

A To crush the Allied landings in the southern Philippines using the whole Japanese Combined Fleet.

Q The operation led to which decisive naval engagement?

A The Battle of Leyte Gulf.

Q At that engagement how many aircraft carriers did the Japanese lose?

A Four: *Zuikaku*, *Zuiho*, *Chitose*, and *Chiyoda*.

DID YOU KNOW

IN SPITE OF BEING FIVE YEARS INTO A LONG AND BLOODY WAR, THE WEHRMACHT PUT UP AN AMAZING FIGHT IN NORMANDY IN 1944. WHILE SOME OF THE GERMAN ARMY'S GENERALS WERE DISAFFECTED WITH THE FÜHRER AND WERE ACTIVELY PLOTTING TO KILL HIM, THE RANK AND FILE OF THE FIGHTING TROOPS STILL BELIEVED IN GERMANY'S CAUSE. ROMMEL'S INFECTIOUS ENTHUSIASM RUBBED OFF ON THE TROOPS BEING TRAINED TO REPEL THE INVASION. HE WAS FAMOUS FOR HIS VICTORIES AGAINST THE BRITISH AND AMERICANS IN NORTH AFRICA; AND MANY OF HIS TROOPS, ALONG WITH THE DIVISIONAL OFFICERS, WERE CONVINCED OF THE LOGIC OF HITLER'S CLAIM THAT IF THE ALLIED INVASION COULD BE THROWN BACK INTO THE SEA, THEN GERMANY WOULD BE ABLE TO TURN ITS ATTENTION EAST TO FINISH OFF THE SOVIETS. "WHEN THE ENEMY INVADES IN THE WEST IT WILL BE THE MOMENT OF DECISION IN THIS WAR," SAID ROMMEL. "AND THE MOMENT MUST TURN FOR GERMANY'S ADVANTAGE."

Q Why was the Battle of Leyte Gulf in October 1944 so decisive?

A The final tally of Japanese shipping sunk was four aircraft carriers, three battleships, ten cruisers, eleven destroyers, and one submarine, with most other Japanese ships severely damaged. In addition, 10,000 sailors and 500 aircraft were also lost. The Battle of Leyte Gulf marked the undeniable collapse of Japanese naval power in the Pacific. From that point on, the suicide air strikes that had their inauguration over Leyte Gulf became an increasing feature of a desperate Japanese military that could no longer oppose the mighty U.S. Navy.

Q What does the Japanese term kamikaze mean?

A "Divine wind."

DID YOU KNOW

TIME AFTER TIME ON THE EASTERN FRONT DURING 1944, HITLER ORDERED CUT-OFF GERMAN FORCES TO FORM WHAT HE TERMED "FORTRESS TOWNS." HE BELIEVED THEY WOULD TIE DOWN SCORES OF SOVIET DIVISIONS THAT WOULD OTHERWISE BE FREE TO RAMPAGE WESTWARD. IN REALITY, WITH NO PANZER RESERVES AVAILABLE TO RIDE TO THE RESCUE, THE FORTRESS TOWNS BECAME DEATH TRAPS FOR THEIR GARRISONS. THE SOVIETS SIMPLY SURROUND-ED THE FORTRESS TOWNS AND WAITED FOR THE GERMANS TO RUN OUT OF FOOD AND AMMUNITION. THE SOVIET OFFENSIVE THAT DESTROYED THE GERMAN ARMY GROUP CENTER IN JUNE AND JULY 1944 DEMONSTRATED THE BANKRUPTCY OF THE FÜHRER'S IDEAS. WITHIN A FEW WEEKS THE RUSSIANS HAD SURROUNDED SEVERAL GERMAN ARMY CORPS IN ISOLATED POCKETS AT VITEBSK, ORSHA, MOGILEV, AND BOBRUISK. HITLER ORDERED THEM TO FIGHT TO THE LAST MAN. WHEN HE AT LAST ALLOWED THEM TO BREAK OUT IT WAS TOO LATE. ONLY A FEW THOUSAND MANAGED TO ESCAPE. MORE THAN 150,000 GERMANS WERE KILLED AND SOME 100,000 WERE CAPTURED. THE PRISONERS WERE LATER PARADED THROUGH THE STREETS OF MOSCOW BY THE VICTORIOUS SOVIETS.

EACH SPINNY AND COPSE CONTAINED ITS
DREADFUL QUOTA OF
DEAD GERMANS
JOHNNIE JOHNSON, RAF PILOT, THE FALAISE POCKET,
AUGUST 1944

Q **What was it applied to in World War II?**

A Volunteer Japanese pilots who crashed their aircraft into Allied ships. In the same way that typhoons destroyed Kublai Khan's fleets in 1274 and 1281, saving Japan from a Mongol invasion, it was hoped that the kamikaze would prevent the Allies from launching an invasion of Japan.

Q **When were the kamikaze first used?**

A The first mass attack of 55 kamikaze aircraft came on October 23–26, 1944, around Leyte, sinking five ships (including the carrier USS *St Lo*) and damaging 40 others, 23 severely.

Q **What was the rank of the officer who commanded a U.S. armored division?**

A Major general.

Q **In U.S. Army offensive doctrine, explain the difference between "Rat Race" and "Slugging Match."**

A The "Rat Race" was an advance to contact over open terrain, using tanks and infantry, in the face of minimal enemy resistance. The "Slugging Match" was a more deliberate operation against a known enemy position, in which combat commands attacked in close cooperation to provide mutual support.

Q What was the Slovak national uprising of August 1944?

A Since the summer of 1944 Slovak partisans of the Czechoslovak Army in Slovakia (18,000 in number) had been engaged in guerrilla activity against German targets, mainly in the central mountains. In response, the Germans moved 48,000 troops into Slovakia, prompting the outbreak of the Slovak national uprising in August.

Q On September 5, 1944, the USSR declared war on Bulgaria. What was the Bulgarian response?

A They surrendered at once.

> SPLATTERED EVERYWHERE WAS BLOOD:
> IT LAY IN POOLS IN THE ROOMS,
> ## IT COVERED THE SMOCKS
> ## OF THE DEFENDERS
> LIEUTENANT MACKAY, 1ST AIRBORNE DIVISION,
> ARNHEM, SEPTEMBER 1944

Q Who attended the Second Moscow Conference in October 1944?

A Winston Churchill, Joseph Stalin, and U.S. Ambassador Averell Harriman.

Q What was discussed at the conference?

A The USSR's entry into the war against Japan, postwar division of the Balkans, and the future of Poland. The main focus of the conference was Soviet influence in a postwar Eastern Europe.

DID YOU KNOW

THE JULY 1944 BOMB PLOT ONLY SERVED TO FUEL HITLER'S PARANOIA AND DISTRUST OF HIS GENERALS. INCREASINGLY, HE TURNED TO THE NAZI PARTY AND THE WAFFEN-SS TO RUN THINGS FOR HIM. THIS WAS BEST ILLUSTRATED BY THE APPOINTMENT OF THE HEAD OF THE SS, HEINRICH HIMMLER, TO RUN THE REPLACEMENT ARMY IN THE DAYS AFTER THE BOMB PLOT WAS FOILED. HIMMLER PROVED TOTALLY INEPT AT RUNNING THE SYSTEM OF TRAINING MANPOWER FOR THE FIELD ARMY AND MADE AN EVEN GREATER MESS OF THINGS WHEN HE WAS APPOINTED HEAD OF ARMY GROUP VISTULA IN JANUARY 1945.

Q In August 1944 the Allies began the assault on which German defense line in Italy?

A The Gothic Line.

Q Which German commander refused to carry out Hitler's orders to burn Paris to the ground in the fall of 1944?

A General Dietrich von Choltitz.

Q Why did British troops land at Patrai in the Peloponnese at the beginning of October 1944?

A Winston Churchill was determined to prevent a communist takeover in Greece.

Q Who fulfilled his promise "I shall return" by wading ashore in the Philippines in October 1944?

A General Douglas MacArthur.

Q Which Soviet spy was hanged in Tokyo in November 1944?

A Richard Sorge.

Q U.S. B-29 Superfortress bombers mounted their first raid against which Japanese city on November 24, 1944?

A Tokyo.

Q What was the name of the forest, south of Aachen, in which German and American forces fought a series of attritional battles in late 1944?

A The Hurtgen Forest.

Q What was the codename of the German offensive in the Ardennes in December 1944?

A Operation Watch on the Rhine.

Q What was the aim of the offensive?

A To punch through the Ardennes to capture the Belgian port of Antwerp, thereby splitting the British in Holland from the Americans in France.

Q Why was Watch on the Rhine initially successful?

A Because the attack had been planned in great secrecy it took the Allies totally by surprise, and initially swept away the weak American forces holding the frontline in the Ardennes. In addition, for almost a week the bad weather kept Allied air units on the ground and the German panzers were able to race westward. Finally, German commandos wearing Allied uniforms added to the panic among the green GIs trying to hold back the surprise Blitzkrieg.

Q Why did the offensive ultimately fail?

A Once the Allies recovered and brought their airpower and armored reserves to bear, Watch on the Rhine was doomed.

269

" OUR SHIPS HAVE BEEN SALVAGED
AND ARE RETIRING AT
HIGH SPEED TOWARD
THE JAPANESE FLEET
WILLIAM F. HALSEY, ON REPORTS THAT THE THIRD FLEET
HAD BEEN DEFEATED, OCTOBER 26, 1944 "

Q In the U.S. Army, what was a TALO?

A A tactical air liaison officer. TALOs were attached to ground units and were used to call down air strikes on enemy units.

Q Which Waffen-SS division was raised from Croatian Muslims, and which had its own Mullahs and Imans?

A The 13th Waffen-Gebirgs Division *Handschar*.

Q What was General Eisenhower's "Broad Front" strategy in northwest Europe in 1944?

A British and American armies would receive equal shares of supplies and advance in line abreast across France to the German border. This would keep up the pressure on the Germans along the whole of the Western Front and prevent them regrouping and launching a flanking counterattack against any exposed Allied spearheads.

Q What was the "Red Ball Express" that operated in France in 1944?

A 6,000 trucks moving along dedicated one-way roads from the Normandy bridgehead to speed supplies to the front to maintain the Allied advance.

> " EVERYONE IS BUSY SCRAPING
> THE BOTTOM OF HIS BOWL
> ## WITH HIS SPOON SO AS
> ## NOT TO WASTE A DROP "
> PRIMO LEVI, INMATE OF AUSCHWITZ, OCTOBER 1944

1945

IMPERIAL JAPAN AND NAZI GERMANY WERE FINALLY
OVERWHELMED BY A COMBINATION OF ALLIED
MILITARY AND INDUSTRIAL MIGHT. ALLIED BOMBERS
ROAMED AT WILL OVER ENEMY TERRITORY,
REDUCING DOZENS OF TOWNS AND CITIES TO
RUBBLE, CULMINATING IN THE DROPPING OF
ATOMIC BOMBS ON JAPAN IN AUGUST 1945.

Q Which extermination camp in Poland did the Germans evacuate in January 1945?

A Auschwitz. In sub-zero temperatures the Nazis evacuated more than 50,000 prisoners west toward Germany. Many thousands died from starvation or hypothermia in the march to other camps; others were shot when they failed to keep up. Most of the survivors ended up in other concentration camps: Bergen-Belsen, Buchenwald, and Dachau.

Q In late January 1945, the Germans created Army Group Vistula made up of the Second and Eleventh Armies. Who was its commander?

A SS chief Heinrich Himmler.

“ IF ONLY WE MIGHT FALL LIKE CHERRY
BLOSSOMS IN THE SPRING—
SO PURE AND RADIANT! **”**
ANONYMOUS KAMIKAZE PILOT, FEBRUARY 1945

Q What was the fate of the German cruise liner *Wilhelm Gustav* at the end of January 1945?

A Filled with civilian refugees from East Prussia, she was sunk by the Soviet submarine *S13* off the Hela Peninsula. More than 7,000 people drowned.

Q Which army invaded the Japanese-occupied island of Luzon in January 1945?

A The U.S. Sixth Army under General Walter Krueger.

DID YOU KNOW

GERMANY'S STRATEGIC POSITION IN JANUARY 1945 WAS HOPELESS: IN THE
WEST THE ALLIES WERE APPROACHING THE RHINE, IN THE EAST THE RED
ARMY MUSTERED OVER 400 DIVISIONS FOR THE DRIVE ON BERLIN, AND IN
THE SOUTH SOVIET FORCES WERE BESIEGING THE HUNGARIAN CAPITAL,
BUDAPEST. ONLY IN ITALY WAS THE FRONT STABLE.

Q The Allied advance to the River Rhine involved three operations
—Veritable, Grenade, and Lumberjack—what did each involve?

A Operation Veritable was designed to move Allied forces close to the
Rhine opposite Wesel. Operation Grenade would involve Allied
forces sweeping northeast from the River Roer to link up with the Veritable
formations, while the U.S. First and Third Armies taking part in Lumberjack
would move forward to reach the Rhine between Cologne and Koblenz.

Q What was the German Operation Bodenplatte in January 1945?

A A Luftwaffe offensive in support of the Ardennes Offensive, with
1,035 fighters and bombers attacking Allied airfields in Belgium and
southern Holland. The Germans destroyed 156 Allied aircraft but lost 277
of their own.

Q Give at least two reasons why the fight for the island of Iwo
Jima in February 1945 was so costly for assaulting U.S. forces.

A Japanese troops were pulled back into the interior where they sat
out the coastal bombardments and allowed U.S. forces to land
before engaging them from preprepared defensive positions. Around the
island were more than 800 pillboxes, bunkers, dug-in armored vehicles,
and 3 miles (4.8 km) of tunnels. The bunkers had an extremely low-profile
sloping face resistant to artillery fire. All pillboxes were situated to have
overlapping fields of fire; all beaches, and the slopes leading off them,
were zeroed in advance by Japanese machine guns, artillery, and mortars.

Q How did the terrain of Iwo Jima assist the Japanese defenders?

A Iwo Jima is a volcanic island, its convoluted rocky landscape full of caves, ravines, ridges, and other natural defensive positions. In one 1,312 ft x 1,968 ft (400 m x 600 m) area, U.S. Marines had to neutralize 100 individual defensive caves. The slope of the beaches was extremely steep with crumbly volcanic ash (the Japanese embedded antitank mines in the slopes), and U.S. Marines struggled simply to walk across such terrain carrying their 100 lb (45 kg) packs. Also, U.S. soldiers found in many places that the volcanic landscape was too hot to dig foxholes.

Q Which U.S. photographer immortalized the moment when U.S. Marines raised the Stars and Stripes on the summit of Mount Suribachi on Iwo Jima?

A Joe Rosenthal.

Q What was the main Soviet demand at the Yalta Conference held in the Crimea in February 1945?

A Stalin demanded a strong, pro-communist government in Poland to guarantee the future security of the USSR. As the Red Army controlled most of Eastern Europe, the British and Americans had little choice but to agree.

DID YOU KNOW

BY MID-1943, THE RED ARMY FIELDED SO-CALLED TANK ARMIES TO COMBAT THE GERMAN PANZER CORPS. THE CREATION OF THE FIRST TWO ARMIES— THE THIRD AND FIFTH—WAS ORDERED ON MAY 25, 1942. IN THEORY EACH TANK ARMY WAS MADE UP OF TWO TANK CORPS, ONE MECHANIZED CORPS, AND SUPPORTING UNITS—A STRENGTH OF 560 TANKS AND 45,000 MEN, THOUGH SOME WERE LARGER. IN JANUARY 1945, FOR EXAMPLE, THE THIRD GUARDS TANK ARMY HAD 670 TANKS, 43,400 TROOPS, 254 ASSAULT GUNS, 24 BM-13 ROCKET LAUNCHERS, AND 368 ARTILLERY PIECES.

" THE RAISING OF THAT FLAG ON SURIBACHI MEANS A MARINE CORPS FOR THE NEXT 500 YEARS "

JAMES FORRESTAL, FEBRUARY 23, 1945

Q Why did the Allies bomb the city of Dresden in February 1945?

A In response to a specific Soviet request for bombing German communications, and in particular with regard to the Berlin-Leipzig-Dresden railway complex.

Q Why did Syria and Saudi Arabia declare war on Germany in late February 1945?

A The rush to join the Allies stemmed from the announcement that only those states that declared war before March 1 would be invited to a conference in San Francisco on the proposed postwar "United Nations" organization.

275

Q Which bridge over the River Rhine was captured by American troops in early March 1945?

A The Ludendorff Bridge at Remagen.

Q Was it of use to the Allied war effort against Germany?

A No. The bridge had been weakened by demolition charges and it collapsed into the river 10 days after its capture.

Q The Soviet SU-152 assault gun was armed with which main gun?

A The ML-20 152mm gun howitzer.

Q Why did the U.S. wish to conquer the island of Iwo Jima?

A The island had to be taken for four reasons: the unescorted U.S. bombers flying from the Marianas to Japan were suffering heavy losses, and, therefore, airfields closer to Japan were needed for fighter escorts; Iwo Jima had two air bases and was only three hours' flying time from Tokyo; Iwo Jima was prewar Japanese territory, whose loss would be a severe psychological blow to the homeland; and the island was a necessary link in the air defenses of the Marianas.

Q What was the Burmese National Army?

A An independence movement fighting on the side of the Japanese.

" AMONG THE MEN WHO FOUGHT ON IWO
JIMA, UNCOMMON VALOR WAS
A COMMON VIRTUE
ADMIRAL CHESTER NIMITZ, MARCH 16, 1945 "

Q What was Operation Iceberg?

A The codename for the U.S. invasion of Okinawa.

Q Which were the two main elements of the Operation Iceberg U.S. invasion force?

A U.S. III Marine Amphibious Corps (6th Marine Division and 1st Marine Division) was on the left flank, with the objective of advancing to the west and up into the north of the island; while, beneath it, U.S. Army XXIV Corps (7th Infantry Division and 96th Infantry Division) began operations to clear southern Okinawa.

DID YOU KNOW

THE JAPANESE OHKA ("CHERRY BLOSSOM") WAS A ROCKET-POWERED PILOTED BOMB DESIGNED BY NAVAL ENSIGN MITSUO OHKA IN LATE 1944. EFFECTIVELY, THE AIRCRAFT WAS NOTHING MORE THAN A 2,646 LB (1,200 KG) WARHEAD WITH WINGS AND POWERED BY THREE SOLID-FUEL TYPE 4 MARK 1 MODEL 20 ROCKETS. TO DEPLOY THE WEAPON, IT WAS FIRST ATTACHED TO THE MODIFIED BOMB BAY OF A MITSUBISHI G4M BOMBER AND FLOWN TO WITHIN 25 MILES (40 KM) OF THE TARGET. ONCE RELEASED, THE OHKA'S ROCKETS WOULD IGNITE AND THE PILOT WOULD THEN FLY THE BOMB INTO HIS INTENDED TARGET. TO ENSURE THE UNSWERVING COMMITMENT OF THE PILOT, HE WAS SEALED INTO THE COCKPIT FOR HIS ONE-WAY TRIP.

Q **What was Nazi Germany's last offensive of the war?**

A Operation Spring Awakening at the beginning of March 1945.

Q **What was the objective of the offensive?**

A The German plan was to recapture Budapest by breaking through the junction of the Soviet Fourth Guards and Twenty-Sixth Armies, thereafter annihilating the 2nd and 3rd Ukrainian Fronts trapped on the west bank of the River Danube. The offensive was also designed to seize Hungary's oil supplies.

Q **Why was chief of staff Heinz Guderian against the offensive?**

A He wanted the divisions to be used for the defense of Berlin.

Q Which German forces were involved in Operation Spring Awakening?

A The Sixth SS Panzer Army (I and II SS Panzer Corps and III Panzer Corps), Sixth Army (IV SS Panzer Corps and Hungarian VIII Corps), and Second Panzer Army (XXXXIV and LXVII Corps).

Q Why was the plan totally unrealistic?

A The Germans had 430,000 troops, 5,600 artillery pieces, and 880 tanks and assault guns, supported by 850 fuel-starved aircraft, whereas the Soviets had 407,000 troops, 7,000 artillery pieces, 400 tanks and assault guns, and 960 aircraft. In the Stavka reserve was the Ninth Guards Army, while the 2nd Ukrainian Front lay to the south.

> **"**
> I STARED CURIOUSLY AT MY FIRST
> GERMAN CIVILIAN. HE WAS AN
> ## OLD MAN DRESSED
> ## IN SHABBY SERGE
> JOHN FOLEY, BRITISH TANK OFFICER,
> FEBRUARY 28, 1945
> **"**

Q The commander of the U.S. 4th Armored Division, Major General John S. Wood, had two nicknames. What were they?

A "Tiger Jack" and the "Rommel of the American forces."

Q The modern American Abrams main battle tank was named after which World War II commander?

A Lieutenant General Creighton Abrams, a tank commander in World War II and later chief of staff of the U.S. Army.

Q Major General Philippe Leclerc was the commander of which armored division?

A The 2nd Free French Armored Division.

Q Leclerc was a *nom de guerre*. What was his real name?

A Vicomte Jacques-Philippe de Hautecloque.

Q Why did he conceal his true identity?

A To protect his family in France, who lived in German-occupied territory.

DID YOU KNOW

WHEN IT ENTERED SERVICE IN JULY 1943, THE BOEING B-29 SUPERFORTRESS 10-CREW BOMBER HAD A RANGE OF 4,100 MILES (6598 KM) AND A BOMB LOAD OF 20,000 LB (9,072 KG). IT WAS AN ADVANCED AIRCRAFT—THE GUN TURRETS DOTTED AROUND THE FUSELAGE WERE CONTROLLED REMOTELY BY GUNNERS SITTING INSIDE THE FUSELAGE WHO AIMED THE WEAPONS VIA PERISCOPES. THE B-29 WAS IDEAL FOR THE VAST DISTANCES OF THE PACIFIC THEATER. FROM MARCH 1945, B-29S BEGAN OPERATIONS FROM FIVE BASES IN THE MARIANAS ISLANDS, CAUSING DEVA-STATION ON THE JAPANESE MAINLAND. ATTACKING AT NIGHT (PREVIOUSLY, THE B-29S HAD MAINLY CONDUCTED HIGH-LEVEL DAYLIGHT RAIDS), THE B-29S SCATTERED MILLIONS OF INCENDIARIES OVER JAPANESE CITIES—THE WOOD AND PLASTER CONSTRUCTION OF JAPANESE HOUSING MADE THE BUILDINGS INTENSELY VULNERABLE TO FIRE ATTACKS. THE FIRST SUCH FIRE ATTACK ON TOKYO CAUSED 80,000 DEATHS, A SIMILAR DEATH TOLL TO THAT CAUSED BY THE HIROSHIMA BOMB. SOME 3,970 B-29S WERE PRODUCED DURING THE WAR, SOME LATER SERVING IN THE KOREAN WAR.

Q The Soviet SU-152 assault gun used the chassis of which tank?

A The KV-1S heavy tank.

Q One of the Lend-Lease tanks supplied by the Americans to the Russians was referred to by Red Army personnel as the "grave for seven brothers." Which tank?

A The M3 Lee medium tank, because of its thin armor.

Q What was the only Soviet armored car manufactured during the war?

A The BA-64, which was based on the GAZ-67 jeep.

DID YOU KNOW

LEND-LEASE AID AS PROVIDED TO THE USSR BY BRITAIN AND THE UNITED STATES DID NOT INFLUENCE THE OUTCOME OF THE WAR ON THE EASTERN FRONT—WITHOUT IT, THE RED ARMY WOULD STILL HAVE BEEN VICTORIOUS. THIS WAS BECAUSE THE SOVIET UNION WAS ALSO ABLE TO GALVANIZE ITS VAST INDUSTRIAL RESOURCES TO PRODUCE TANKS, ARTILLERY, AND SMALL ARMS ON A SCALE THAT GERMANY COULD NOT MATCH. BUT WITHOUT ANY AID FROM THE WEST, THE SOVIET UNION WOULD HAVE TAKEN LONGER TO DEFEAT NAZI GERMANY, AND WOULD HAVE SUFFERED MANY MORE CASUALTIES DOING SO. BETWEEN 1943 AND 1945, WESTERN AID, SPECIFICALLY TRUCKS, RAIL ENGINES, AND RAIL WAGONS, ALLOWED THE RED ARMY TO MAINTAIN THE MOMENTUM OF ITS OFFENSIVES BY TRANSPORTING TROOPS AND SUPPLIES TO REINFORCE BREAK-THROUGH ARMIES, THUS DENYING THE GERMANS TIME TO ORGANIZE FRESH DEFENSE LINES AND ESCAPE ENCIRCLEMENTS.

THIS EVENING'S MOSQUITO RAID WAS
PARTICULARLY DISASTROUS
**FOR ME BECAUSE OUR
MINISTRY WAS HIT**
JOSEF GOEBBELS, 13 MARCH 1945 **"**

Q Which Nazi military award was intended to replace Imperial awards such as the Pour le Mérite?

A The Knight's Cross.

Q What type of weapon was the Soviet PTRS?

A A semiautomatic antitank rifle.

Q Lend-Lease aid to the Soviets included locomotives, boots, and field telephones. True or false?

A True. The Soviets received 1,860 locomotives, 11,181 rail cars, 15 million pairs of boots, and 422,000 field telephones.

Q What type of fighting vehicle was the German Panzer IV/70(V)?

A A tank destroyer.

Q What was the name of the U.S. M26 tank?

A The Pershing.

Q What was the main gun on the American M26 heavy tank?

A The 90mm Tank Gun M3.

Q What type of weapons were "Tallboy" and "Grand Slam"?

A Deep-penetration aircraft bombs.

Q What type of aircraft was the German Focke Wulf Fw 190?

A A single-seat fighter.

"THE BABY'S RIGHT THIGH HAD BEEN TORN OFF, AND THE LITTLE STUMP WAS WRAPPED IN RAGS
HANS GLIEWE, GERMAN SCHOOLBOY, DANZIG, MARCH 9, 1945**"**

Q What was Britain's first operational jet combat aircraft?

A The Gloster Meteor.

Q Who was its designer?

A George Carter.

DID YOU KNOW

THE HEAVIEST TANK PRODUCED BY THE GERMANS, AND POSSIBLY THE HEAVIEST TANK EVER PRODUCED, WAS THE MAUS, WHICH WEIGHED IN AT A MASSIVE 186 TONS (189 TONNES). DESCRIBED BY THE FATHER OF THE GERMAN PANZERS, COLONEL GENERAL HEINZ GUDERIAN, AS A "GIGANTIC OFFSPRING OF THE FANTASY OF HITLER AND HIS ADVISORS," THE MAUS NEVER SAW COMBAT. DR. FERDINAND PORSCHE PERSUADED HITLER TO ALLOW HIM TO START WORK ON THE MAUS IN THE SUMMER OF 1942. EVERYTHING ABOUT THE TANK WAS BIG. IT WAS TO HAVE THE BIGGEST GUN EVER MOUNTED IN A GERMAN TANK TURRET, A 128MM CANNON, ALONG WITH A 75MM SECONDARY ARMAMENT. THE FIRST FIELD TRIALS OF THE TWO PROTOTYPES GOT UNDER WAY IN LATE 1944, BUT THEY WERE NEVER ANYWHERE NEAR BEING READY FOR SERVICE BY THE TIME THE SOVIETS OVERRAN THE TANK TESTING RANGE AT KUMMERSDORF IN 1945. THE PROTOTYPES WERE ORDERED TO BE DESTROYED, BUT RUMORS PERSIST THAT AT LEAST ONE MAUS WAS CAPTURED BY THE SOVIETS.

283

Q The aircraft initially had a different name. What was it?

A The Thunderbolt.

Q The Meteor was a single-seat fighter, but what was the aircraft's first mission when it entered service?

A Chasing German V-1 flying bombs over southern England.

Q What was the wing armament of the Hawker Typhoon ground-attack aircraft?

A Four 20mm cannon.

> ## " THE MUZZLES WERE TRAINED ON BERLIN. ON THE FORTIFICATIONS OF FASCIST BERLIN—"FIRE!"
> GENERAL CHUIKOV, SOVIET EIGHTH GUARDS ARMY,
> APRIL 20, 1945
> "

Q Which German battlecruiser was towed to Gdynia and sunk as a blockship there in March 1945?

A The *Gneisenau*.

Q Which German light cruiser evacuated the coffin of Field Marshal von Hindenburg, which had been interred at the Tannenburg Memorial, in January 1945?

A The *Emden*.

Q Which two Japanese warships were the largest and most powerful battleships ever built?

A The *Mushashi* and *Yamato*.

Q Four such battleships were planned. What happened to the other two?

A The third, *Shinano*, was completed as an aircraft carrier, and the fourth was never built.

Q Which U.S. heavy cruiser transported components of the atomic bombs from San Francisco to Tinian in July 1945?

A USS *Indianapolis*.

Q Which Allied leader died of a cerebral hemorrhage in April 1945?

A U.S. President Franklin Delano Roosevelt.

Q Which Japanese army defended the island of Okinawa in April 1945?

A The Thirty-Second Army.

Q Why did the Japanese government cancel all education for schoolchildren above the age of six in April 1945?

A So that the young could be redirected into war industries to provide a boost to the Japanese labor force.

Q From which illness did President Roosevelt suffer all his life?

A Polio.

DID YOU KNOW

A MAJOR CONTRIBUTING FACTOR TO THE BATTLEFIELD SUCCESS OF THE GERMAN ARMY IN WORLD WAR II WAS THE FACT THAT ITS OFFICER CORPS WAS TRAINED IN WHAT IS NOW KNOWN AS MISSION ANALYSIS, OR *AUFTRAGSTAKTIK*. GERMAN OFFICERS OF ALL RANKS WERE TRAINED TO BE ABLE TO FIGHT WITHOUT DETAILED ORDERS, TO MAKE DO WITH JUST A BRIEF STATEMENT OF THEIR COMMANDER'S INTENTIONS. THE COMMANDER TOLD HIS SUBORDINATES WHAT HE WANTED ACHIEVED, NOT HOW TO DO IT. SUBORDINATE OFFICERS WERE EXPECTED TO BE ABLE TO THINK ON THEIR FEET AND ADAPT THEIR BRIEF ORDERS TO MEET THE REQUIREMENTS OF THE SITUATION ON THE GROUND.

DID YOU KNOW

THE JAPANESE BATTLESHIP *YAMATO* HAD A TOTAL OF 145 25MM ANTI-AIRCRAFT GUNS FOR HER FINAL OPERATION, A SUICIDE MISSION AGAINST U.S. INVASION FORCES AROUND OKINAWA IN APRIL 1945. WITH ENOUGH FUEL FOR ONLY A ONE-WAY TRIP, *YAMATO* WAS SPOTTED BY U.S. AIRCRAFT WELL BEFORE SHE REACHED HER DESTINATION. AN ATTACK BY MORE THAN 400 U.S. CARRIER AIRCRAFT LED TO MORE THAN 20 BOMB AND TORPEDO HITS. AT 14:20 HOURS ON APRIL 7, HER MAGAZINE EXPLODED, RIPPING THE SHIP APART AND SENDING HER TO THE BOTTOM OF THE PACIFIC. A TOTAL OF 2,475 CREW WENT DOWN WITH HER.

Q Was the British Royal Navy involved in the Okinawa operation?

A Yes. A large British carrier force under Vice Admiral Sir Bernard Rawlings operated against enemy positions in the Sakishima group.

Q Which British aircraft carrier was damaged by kamikaze aircraft off the coast of Okinawa in April 1945?

A HMS *Indefatigable*.

Q Who resigned as prime minister of Japan on April 5, 1945?

A Koiso Kuniaki.

Q Who replaced him?

A The 78-year-old Admiral Suzuki Kantaro.

Q In early April 1945, the USSR informed Japan that it would not renew its five-year neutrality pact with Japan. Why?

A Moscow stated the change in policy was a consequence of the Japanese alliance with Germany.

Q In early April 1945, the U.S. First and Third Armies linked up at Lippstadt to complete the encirclement of which economically important German region?

A The Ruhr.

Q What were the gradations of the German Wound Badge?

A Black—for one or two wounds; Silver—for three or four wounds; and Gold—for five or more wounds.

287

Q Which German award consisted of a vertical oval wreath of oak-leaves with a skull and crossbones at its base, and in its center a hydra with a broad-bladed sword plunging through its center?

A The Anti-Partisan Badge.

Q What was Germany's equivalent of the U.S. Jeep?

A The Volkswagen Kübelwagen.

> **MY FÜHRER, I CONGRATULATE YOU!**
> # ROOSEVELT IS DEAD
> GOEBBELS TO HITLER, APRIL 1945

> ## " THE SMOOTH GREEN TURF QUICKLY CHURNED UP INTO BLACK, TRACK-CLINGING MUD. ONE BY ONE THE CHURCHILLS SANK IN THE MUD "
>
> JOHN FOLEY, BRITISH TANK OFFICER, GERMANY, FEBRUARY 1945

Q What did the Soviet Tokarev 4M Model 1931 quadruple antiaircraft machine-gun mounting consist of?

A Four Maxim Model 1910 machine guns on a heavy pedestal mount with associated ammunition and water-cooling tank.

Q What type of vehicle was the Volkswagen Schwimmwagen?

A An amphibious jeep.

Q What was the German SdKfz 234/2 Puma?

A An eight-wheeled heavy armored car.

Q Which two Allied armies took part in the final campaign in Italy in the spring of 1945?

A The U.S. Fifth Army and the British Eighth Army.

Q Who was the Allied commander-in-chief in Italy in 1945?

A Field Marshal Harold Alexander.

Q Why did Hitler issue the decree on Demolitions on Reich Territory in March 1945?

A In response to the Soviets and Western Allies entering German territory.

Q What did this decree authorize?

A The destruction of "all military transport and communication facilities, industrial establishments, and supply depots, as well as anything else of value within Reich territory, which could in any way be used by the enemy immediately or within the foreseeable future for the prosecution of the war."

Q By what other name was the decree known?

A The Nero Order.

DID YOU KNOW

THE SCIENCE BEHIND THE ATOMIC BOMB IS RELATIVELY SIMPLE. A NEUTRAL NEUTRON PARTICLE HITS THE NUCLEUS OF A URANIUM ATOM, WHICH SPLITS INTO TWO FRAGMENTS: A KRYPTON ATOM AND A BARIUM ATOM. THE REACTION ALSO RELEASES AN ENORMOUS BURST OF ENERGY. ONE OR TWO FRESH NEUTRONS ARE RELEASED, SOME OF WHICH FIND OTHER NUCLEAR TARGETS AND REPEAT THE PROCESS. EACH SPLITTING OR "FISSION" CAUSES MORE—THE CHAIN REACTION. A RAPID CHAIN REACTION BECOMES A NUCLEAR EXPLOSION. HOWEVER, URANIUM HAS SEVERAL ISOTOPES, AND THE TRICK IS TO FIND A WAY OF ISOLATING THE URANIUM ISOTOPE U-235, WHICH HAS THE HIGHEST ENERGY FACTOR FOR THE DEVELOPMENT OF NUCLEAR POWER.

Q The final campaign in Italy centered on control of which valley?

A The Po Valley.

Q How did the Allies plan to defeat the Germans in Italy in the spring of 1945?

A The Eighth Army would attack westward through the Argenta Gap, while the Fifth Army would strike north, west of Bologna, thereby trapping the forces of the German Army Group C between the two.

Q Who commanded the British Fourteenth Army in Burma in 1945?

❝ IT SEEMS TO BE THE MOST TERRIBLE THING EVER DISCOVERED, BUT IT CAN BE THE MOST USEFUL
PRESIDENT HARRY S. TRUMAN ON THE ATOMIC BOMB, JULY 1945 **❞**

A General William Slim.

Q In Waffen-SS service, who were *SS-Helferinnen*?

A Female auxiliaries. They undertook clerical and administrative tasks.

Q What was the purpose of the SS-Kriegsberichter?

A This unit provided positive propaganda for Waffen-SS troops. Its members were in effect war correspondents.

DID YOU KNOW

BY LATE 1944, THE U.S. HAD MADE AMPHIBIOUS LANDINGS A FINE ART, HAVING LEARNT PAINFUL LESSONS ABOUT ISSUES SUCH AS BEACH RECONNAISSANCE AND THE EFFECTIVENESS OF NAVAL BOMBARDMENTS AT TARAWA AND SAIPAN. GENERAL MACARTHUR EMPLOYED AMPHIBIOUS WARFARE NIMBLY AT A TACTICAL LEVEL, USING SIMULTANEOUS MULTIPLE LANDINGS TO TRAP JAPANESE TROOPS OR BYPASSING HEAVILY DEFENDED JAPANESE POSITIONS BY LEAPFROGGING DOWN A COASTLINE. THE JAPANESE LEARNT EQUALLY PAINFUL LESSONS ABOUT U.S. AMPHIBIOUS SUPERIORITY, AND AT OKINAWA IN APRIL 1945 THEY DID NOT MAKE A COSTLY DEFENSE OF THE BEACHES BUT WITHDREW INTO THE INTERIOR WHERE THEY INFLICTED MASSIVE CASUALTIES ON THE AMERICANS. THE LESSON CAME TOO LATE, HOWEVER, AND U.S. AMPHIBIOUS TACTICS TOOK THE ALLIES TO THE VERY DOORSTEP OF THE JAPANESE HOMELANDS.

Q The German SdKfz 7 halftrack was used to tow which artillery pieces?

A The 105mm and 150mm howitzers and the 88mm Flak gun.

Q What were the "Shuri Line" defenses?

A A string of heavy Japanese defensive positions on Okinawa. These positions stretched across the island for roughly 24,000 ft (7,315 m) and included interlocking trench and pillbox systems, blockhouses, fortified caves, and strongly constructed bunkers.

Q Who took over when President Roosevelt died in April 1945?

A Vice President Harry S. Truman.

DID YOU KNOW

THE FINAL MEETING OF THE ALLIED LEADERS DURING THE WAR TOOK PLACE IN JULY 1945 IN POTSDAM, NEAR BERLIN. THE ALLIANCE HAD JUST WON THE WAR IN EUROPE. IT WAS STRAINED TO THE BREAKING POINT, HOWEVER. THE ALLIES MET TO PLAN THE OCCUPATION OF GERMANY AND THE POSTWAR WORLD. EACH NATION WAS MOTIVATED LARGELY BY SELF-INTEREST. THE UNITED STATES WAS REPRESENTED BY NEW PRESIDENT, HARRY S. TRUMAN. BRITISH PRIME MINISTER WINSTON CHURCHILL LEFT THE CONFERENCE MIDWAY THROUGH. HIS PARTY HAD BEEN DEFEATED IN A GENERAL ELECTION. THE NEW PRIME MINISTER, CLEMENT ATTLEE, TOOK HIS PLACE. IN MANY WAYS, SOVIET LEADER JOSEPH STALIN WAS THE WINNER AT POTSDAM. HE MANAGED TO SHIFT THE SOVIET BORDER WEST INTO POLAND. HE ALSO STRENGTHENED HIS INFLUENCE OVER EASTERN EUROPE. THE OTHER ALLIES HAD LITTLE CHOICE BUT TO LET HIM DO THIS. THE ALLIES ALSO DISCUSSED HOW TO END THE WAR WITH JAPAN. THE AMERICANS TOLD STALIN THAT THEY HAD A "NEW WEAPON" TO USE AGAINST JAPAN. THE WEAPON WAS THE ATOMIC BOMB. THE ALLIES ISSUED AN ULTIMATUM TO JAPAN DEMANDING ITS UNCONDITIONAL SURRENDER. JAPAN REFUSED, AND THE FIRST ATOMIC BOMB WAS DROPPED A FEW DAYS LATER.

Q Which famous U.S. war correspondent was killed in the Pacific theater in mid-April 1945?

A Ernie Pyle.

Q How was he killed?

A He was shot by a Japanese sniper.

Q Which capital city fell to the Red Army in mid-April 1945?

A Vienna.

Q Which Soviet fronts took part in the Berlin Offensive that began on April 16, 1945?

A The 1st Belorussian, 2nd Belorussian, and 1st Ukrainian Fronts. Their combined strength was 2.5 million troops, 41,000 artillery pieces, 6,200 tanks and assault guns, 100,000 motor vehicles, and 7,200 aircraft.

Q What were the German formations that defended Berlin against the offensive?

A Army Group Vistula (Third Panzer and Ninth Armies with LVI Panzer Corps in reserve—200,000 troops, 750 tanks and assault guns, and 1,500 artillery pieces) and the northern flank of Army Group Center (Fourth Panzer Army—100,000 troops and 200 tanks and assault guns).

Q Who commanded the Soviet 2nd Belorussian Front in 1945?

A Konstantin Rokossovsky.

293

Q Who commanded the Soviet 1st Belorussian Front during the Berlin Offensive?

A Georgi Zhukov.

" NO ONE KNEW WHAT HAD HAPPENED. A HUGE FORCE

HAD BEEN RELEASED ABOVE OUR HEADS

TATSUICHIRO AKIZUKI, RESIDENT OF NAGASAKI,
AUGUST 9, 1945 **"**

Q Why did Hitler order the arrest of SS chief Heinrich Himmler at the end of April 1945?

A He had been attempting to broker a peace deal with the Allies.

Q Who were the two key individuals who brought an end to the fighting in Italy at the end of April 1945?

A Karl Wolff, senior commander of the SS and Police in Italy, and Allen Dulles, head of the American Office of Strategic Services (OSS) in Switzerland. As a result of dealings between the two, Wolff and General Heinrich von Vietinghoff, German commander-in-chief in Italy, signed the instrument of unconditional surrender in northern Italy. The Swiss, the Allies, and many Germans and Italians in Italy had been concerned about a drawn-out campaign in Hitler's "Alpine Fortress," and the probable destruction of north Italy's industry.

> " YOU MAY SAFELY CALL
> # ME FRAU HITLER
> EVA BRAUN TO A MAID, APRIL 1945 "

Q On what date did Adolf Hitler commit suicide?

A April 30, 1945.

Q How did he end his life?

A He shot himself. His wife, Eva Braun, also killed herself at the same time by taking poison. Their bodies were then taken outside and cremated by the SS.

DID YOU KNOW

ON JULY 16, 1945, THE FIRST ATOMIC BOMB WAS EXPLODED AT ALAMOGORDO, NEW MEXICO, PRODUCING A BLAST THE EQUIVALENT OF 20,000 TONS (20,320 TONNES) OF TNT, SENDING A MUSHROOM CLOUD 40,000 FT (12,200 M) INTO THE AIR AND FUSING THE DESERT SAND INTO GLASS. THE U.S., HAVING ULTIMATELY INVESTED TWO BILLION DOLLARS IN THE MANHATTAN PROJECT, NOW HAD ITS ATOMIC BOMB.

Q **Why did Allied and German representatives meet in western Holland on April 28, 1945?**

A The Reichskommissar for the Netherlands, Arthur Seyss-Inquart, had offered the Allies the freedom to import food and coal into German-occupied western Holland to alleviate the plight of the civilian population if they would halt their forces. This led to a cessation of hostilities and saved the country from the ravages of further fighting.

Q **Who captured Italian dictator Benito Mussolini as he attempted to flee to Austria at the end of April 1945?**

A Italian partisans.

Q **Who was captured with him?**

A His mistress, Claretta Petacci.

Q **What happened to them after their capture?**

A On the orders of the Committee of National Liberation, Walter Audisio, a communist member of the Volunteer Freedom Corps, shot them both. Their mutilated bodies were later hung up in the Piazzale Loreto, Milan.

Q Which German general surrendered Berlin to the Red Army on May 2, 1945?

A General Weidling, commander of the Berlin garrison.

Q Josef Goebbels and his wife Magda killed themselves rather than be taken prisoner by the Soviets. But who did they kill first?

A Their six children.

Q Who did Hitler nominate as his immediate successor?

A Admiral Karl Dönitz.

DID YOU KNOW

WITH THE ALLIES ON THE RHINE AND SOVIETS AT THE GATES OF BERLIN IN THE SPRING OF 1945, HITLER ORDERED THE GERMAN POPULATION TO BE MOBILIZED EN MASSE FOR A FINAL *GÖTTERDÄMMERUNG*. THE GERMAN PEOPLE WOULD EMERGE VICTORIOUS OR DIE FIGHTING, DECLARED THE FÜHRER. DESPAIRING OF THE WEHRMACHT AND EVEN THE WAFFEN-SS, HE TURNED TO THE NAZI PARTY TO RAISE, ORGANIZE, EQUIP, AND LEAD THE NEW *VOLKSSTURM* MILITIA. OFTEN COMPARED TO THE BRITISH HOME GUARD, THE *VOLKSSTURM* WAS A SIMILAR DESPERATE MEASURE. OLD MEN, BOYS, AND FOREIGN REFUGEES WERE THROWN TOGETHER WITH FEW WEAPONS AND LITTLE IDEA HOW TO USE THEM, WHILE MANY OF THE LOCAL NAZI LEADERS OF THE *VOLKSSTURM* HAD LITTLE MILITARY EXPERIENCE. ACCORDING TO COLONEL GENERAL HEINZ GUDERIAN: "THE BRAVE MEN OF THE *VOLKSSTURM*, PREPARED TO MAKE ANY SACRIFICE, WERE IN MANY CASES DRILLED BUSILY IN THE PROPER WAY OF GIVING THE HITLER SALUTE, INSTEAD OF BEING TRAINED IN THE USE OF WEAPONS OF WHICH THEY HAD NO PREVIOUS EXPERIENCE."

> ❝ IT IS UNTRUE THAT I, OR ANYBODY ELSE IN
> ## GERMANY, WANTED WAR
> ## IN 1939
> HITLER'S "POLITICAL TESTAMENT," APRIL 1945 ❞

Q What was the Nazi Werewolf organization?

A A stay-behind resistance organization formed to continue the fight even after the Allies and Soviets had occupied Germany.

Q Who were its members?

A Only fanatical Nazis were allowed to join.

Q What was the German E-100 vehicle?

A A super-heavy tank.

Q Which vehicle was it intended to replace?

A The Tiger II (King Tiger).

Q What was its main armament?

A A 128mm cannon. Work on this vehicle was at a very early stage when the war ended.

Q In the Pacific theater, what was Operation Dracula in May 1945?

A The capture of Rangoon, Burma. On May 1, soldiers of the Gurkha Parachute Battalion were dropped south of the city, with a landing of the 26th Indian Division in the Gulf of Martaban on May 2. Rangoon was caught in a pincer movement between the southern advance and the 17th Indian Division advancing down from the north, which reached Pegu —40 miles (64 km) from Rangoon—on May 2. The Japanese in Rangoon realized their position was untenable and abandoned the city.

Q In one day—May 5—17 U.S. ships were sunk off Okinawa by mass kamikaze attacks. True or false?

A True.

> **" ETERNAL GLORY TO THE HEROES WHO FELL
> IN THE FIGHTING FOR THE
> FREEDOM AND INDEPENDENCE
> OF THE MOTHERLAND "**
> JOSEPH STALIN, MAY 9, 1945

Q On the same day the U.S. suffered its first civilian fatalities of the Pacific war. True or false?

A True. A Japanese bomb balloon, one of the hundreds released in the Pacific weeks earlier, killed six U.S. civilians—a teacher and five children—in Oregon.

Q How did U.S. forces at Okinawa celebrate the end of the war in Europe on May 9, 1945?

A In celebration of the final unconditional surrender of Germany, every U.S. naval gun and artillery piece on and around Okinawa fired a single shell at Japanese positions.

DID YOU KNOW

MICHINOMIYA HIROHITO (1901–1989) WAS THE LONGEST-REIGNING MONARCH IN JAPANESE HISTORY, TAKING THE THRONE IN 1926 AND KEEPING IT UNTIL HIS DEATH IN 1989. ALTHOUGH THE FIGUREHEAD OF JAPANESE POWER, WITH A QUASI-DIVINE STATUS AMONG HIS PEOPLE, HIROHITO'S CONTROL OVER THE EVENTS THAT LED TO WAR WAS LIMITED, DE FACTO POWER RESIDING IN THE CONTROL OF THE JAPANESE STATE BY THE MILITARY ESTABLISHMENT. RECENT RESEARCH HAS SHOWN THAT HIROHITO WAS ACTUALLY OPPOSED BOTH TO AN ALLIANCE WITH GERMANY AND ITALY IN THE TRIPARTITE PACT, AND TO THE JAPANESE WAR WITH THE U.S. HIDEKI TOJO WAS THE TRUE INSTIGATOR OF THE PACIFIC WAR, AND IT WAS HE WHO REJECTED A NOTE FROM PRESIDENT ROOSEVELT ON DECEMBER 6, 1941, THAT ATTEMPTED TO AVERT A CONFLICT. FOLLOWING THE DEVASTATION OF HIROSHIMA AND NAGASAKI BY ATOMIC BOMBS, HIROHITO BROKE WITH IMPERIAL PRECEDENT (TRADITIONALLY, THE EMPEROR IS PUBLICLY SILENT) AND ANNOUNCED ON RADIO ON AUGUST 15, 1945, THAT JAPAN WOULD ACCEPT THE U.S. DEMAND FOR UNCONDITION-AL SURRENDER. IN A FURTHER STEP, ON JANUARY 1, 1946, HE ANNOUNCED TO THE JAPANESE PEOPLE THAT THERE WAS NO DIVINE STATUS IN HIS OFFICE OR PERSON. BY SO DOING, AND FOR HIS ROLE IN CLOSING THE JAPANESE RESISTANCE, HIROHITO MANAGED TO ESCAPE ALLIED WAR CRIME TRIALS.

Q "Conical Hill" and "Sugar Loaf Hill" were fought over on which Pacific Island?

A Okinawa.

Q In May 1945 Chinese Nationalist troops captured the city of Nanning. Why was this so decisive?

A Nanning was only 80 miles (128 km) from the border of Indochina, and its loss meant that the Japanese Army in China was cut off from its forces in Burma, Thailand, Indochina, and Malaya.

> ## "
> ### CEASE FIRING, BUT IF ANY ENEMY PLANES
> # APPEAR, SHOOT THEM DOWN
> # IN A FRIENDLY FASHION
> WILLIAM F. HALSEY, MESSAGE TO THE U.S. THIRD FLEET,
> JAPAN, AUGUST 15, 1945
> "

Q What caused large-scale damage to the U.S. fleet off Okinawa on June 5, 1945?

A A huge typhoon. Thirty-five ships were damaged, including four battleships and eight carriers.

Q Name the two senior Japanese commanders who committed suicide as the battle for Okinawa drew to a close.

A The commander of the Japanese naval base on Okinawa, Admiral Minoru Ota, and the overall Japanese commander, Lieutenant General Ushijima Mitsuru.

Q The commander of the U.S. Tenth Army was also killed on the island. Who was he?

A Lieutenant General Simon B. Buckner.

Q Estimate Japanese and American losses incurred during the battle for Okinawa.

A The Japanese lost 100,000 dead, and nearly 7,500 Japanese soldiers surrendered. U.S. losses were 7,613 U.S. Marines and U.S. Army infantry killed, and 31,807 wounded. In addition, the U.S. Navy lost 4,900 seamen with 36 vessels sunk and 368 damaged. The air war over Okinawa was equally bitter. Japanese aviation losses numbered 8,000; 4,000 of these shot down in combat. U.S. aviation lost a total of 763 aircraft.

INDEX

302

MAIN

W9-CSN-056

APR 20 1989

$14.95

'90

'90

'90

MYSTERY

'91

'91

DEATH IN A DISTANT LAND

Also by Nancy Livingston:

The Far Side of the Hill
Incident at Parga
Fatality at Bath & Wells
The Trouble at Aquitaine

DEATH IN A DISTANT LAND

by

Nancy Livingston

St. Martin's Press
New York

Library of Congress Cataloging-in-Publication Data

Livingston, Nancy.
    Death in a distant land.

    I. Title.
PR6062.I915D4   1989   823'.914   88-30569
ISBN 0-312-02565-3

First published in Great Britain by Victor Gollancz Ltd.

First U.S. Edition

10 9 8 7 6 5 4 3 2 1

For Peggy
in friendship

DEATH IN A DISTANT LAND

Chapter One

It was so humid, condensation trickled down the outside of the cool windowpane in rivulets. Inside the hotel room, the whir of the air conditioner was loud, drowning sound from the television. The crowd on the screen, their faces contorted by shouting, could only whisper their excitement. Sweltering in the heat on the far side of the city they were intent on the same purpose as the two in the room, staring at a prison where a man was about to be hanged.

The shot on the screen changed to three small barred windows grouped immediately below the prison roof. Behind the bars, lights were switched on because dusk comes swiftly in Penang. As this happened the crowd gave an involuntary collective gasp.

There was a similar reaction from drinkers watching the same scene in a west London pub. Here it was only midday. There was a trace of summer heat in the pavements outside, enough to vaporize the current downpour. This dampness swept in uninvited as each new customer flung the door wide in his hurry to be out of the wet, and added to the fug. Here, the television was suspended from brackets above the bar; necks were cricked in an effort to see the screen.

"Serve him right." A fat woman feasted her eyes on the three small windows. She shivered deliciously, righteously safe, and tasted the gin in her mouth. "Serve him right, I say," she repeated mechanically. "That'll teach them a lesson."

"I doubt it." An inoffensive-looking man sitting near by couldn't bear to let the statement pass unchallenged. "Killing merely stiffens the resolve of those remaining not to be caught. There's two thousand years of proof if you care to consider the matter." But the barmaid intervened.

"Now then, Mr Pringle," she reproved peaceably. Subjects for aggravation were strictly defined: sex, second-hand cars and salaries. There were never any conclusions but arguments stayed within safe limits. What was on the screen lay outside her guidelines. "I don't know why they're showing us this, do you?"

"Blood lust," he answered sadly. "It increases the ratings whilst impressing ordinary mortals with the power of the State." As if to confirm his words the shot changed to the massed ranks of international news gatherers. Another quick cut and the lens had been refocused on more of the sweaty, expectant faces. "See how well those soft-drink sellers are doing?" he said. "I wonder what they peddled at the crucifixion."

In their luxurious Penang hotel room, the two men waited. They'd never met before today but both were members of the same organization, businessmen, seekers after profit and honoured for it in their respective communities. Secretly, they were two links in a chain that peddled death.

Neither was affected by the death agony inside the small prison cell because it was deserved: their organization had been endangered. A courier had behaved foolishly and been caught; he was paying the inevitable penalty, that was all. Zee, middle-aged and Chinese, listened to the commentary. After a moment or two he translated, his measured, high-pitched sibilance in sharp contrast to the excitement on the screen. "A few minutes more, apparently."

"What are they waiting for?" Ray Vincent was approaching forty, his once athletic physique beginning to blur. Thanks to his share of the profits, he enjoyed an indulgent way of life. That plus a lack of exercise had speeded up the decay. For Zee, his Western smells were offensive, the powerful deodorant, animal lanolin odour from the soap he used—the Chinese ignored them as politely as he could.

"There's been a request for a priest," Zee replied; "the man's a Catholic."

"That won't save him."

"No doubt he believes confession will save his soul."

Ray Vincent ignored the remark and reached for the whisky bottle. Fresh ice clinked inside his glass.

"Another orange juice?"

"No thank you."

8

"There's nothing he *can* confess to anyway. He spilled everything he knew the night they picked him up, not that it amounted to anything."

Mr Zee bowed in agreement. The organization was thorough. Contact was kept to the minimum: each courier knew the face but not the name of one other person, that was all. Neither Vincent nor Zee knew each other's true identity, only New York had that information.

Each had travelled independently to Penang as a result of a telephone call from New York. Zee waited patiently to be told why he'd been summoned. Vincent must be the executioner since he was not; had there been a reprieve, he knew Vincent would be under orders to kill, for the courier had panicked. He was no use to the organization after that; he had to be eliminated.

And as executioner, Vincent would have the instructions for Zee. The Chinese wondered where in the silky grey and apricot room a weapon had been concealed and whether the Englishman would still be capable of using it? That was the third stiff whisky.

Ray Vincent stared moodily at the screen. It was nine years since he'd last killed a man, nine years and a complete change of life style. He didn't want to remember that other self. He'd almost convinced himself it could be forgotten when the call from New York came, shattering a convenient illusion.

Knowing Zee was watching but careless of what he might report, Vincent drained his glass. He needn't worry any longer, the courier's neck was as good as broken, thanks to the State. And once he'd briefed Zee there was a good chance he could catch tonight's return flight.

"They want you to check out a possible replacement," Vincent said aloud. "He's staying in this hotel; that's why we're here."

"Ah . . ." Mr Zee understood and sucked in air.

"As soon as this farce is over—" Vincent gestured "—we'll take a look at him." On screen, film of the condemned man's parents weeping in their English slum, protesting their son's innocence, filled the delay. "Pa-the-tic." Vincent weighted the syllables impatiently. "He was guilty right enough. The dummy was caught red-handed."

He stopped speaking. The film had disappeared. They were

back live, at the prison, at the three prison windows. The camera zoomed in and isolated the one in the centre. There was no commentary now, nothing but stillness. Ray Vincent didn't move. On the other side of the world, in the London pub, customers were silent. Apart from Mr Pringle reading his *Guardian* everyone stared at the screen.

The silence affected him also for without looking up he asked quietly, "Mavis, d'you think you could switch that thing off?" The barmaid selected another button instead and her customers found themselves watching a snooker match. They looked at one another, outraged: they'd been denied their treat.

In Penang, Ray Vincent asked, "Is that it?" Mr Zee nodded.

"Yes, it's over."

"Good. Come over here."

From behind the curtain they gazed down over the balcony at the swimming pool and the sea beyond; a limpid blue pool separated by white-hot stones from a beach with sluggish grey waves. Around it, an aircrew shrieked and splashed noisily. Unaware of world events, dipping down in and out of continents for a day at a time, their lives spent in a capsule travelling from one swimming pool to the next.

One of the men, a steward, was poised on the springboard. Dark haired, not very tall, slimly built, his eyes were an unexpectedly deep blue against the tanned face. He made very little disturbance as he dived into the pool. As Zee watched, Ray Vincent nodded: "That's him."

"Have you ever considered taking a holiday in Australia?"

"No."

The inoffensive man was proud of that reply, succinct, well-rounded, impossible to misunderstand, but the barmaid shook her head. It was going to be difficult, she might've known. "I've always fancied going," she said firmly, to let him know the matter was as good as settled, "and Ollie Gorman knows a way of getting there cheap."

She'd got his full attention now. In The Bricklayers, Ollie Gorman's offers had, over the years, covered the full spectrum of larceny. "No." Mr Pringle repeated his refusal firmly. Mavis Bignell, however, knew the way not only to his heart but also to his loins.

Beneath the umbrella Mr Pringle groaned silently as her warm flesh nudged against his under his mackintosh. Lately, he'd discovered more than once that he wasn't as young as he thought he was. This evening, Mavis's thigh failed to stimulate him; was it the weather? Alas! Mrs Bignell mistakenly interpreted his sigh as capitulation.

"I'm glad you agree. The air in Australia's like wine, so they say, and you know what a few glasses of that does to you!" She gave a cheerfully lewd wink. "Besides, my friend Mrs Hardie has lost her grandson out there. I said we'd try and find him."

In Penang, the phalanx of news cameras pried out a final glimpse of dead bare feet lolling pigeon-toed over a stretcher and switched off their lights. Officialdom waited uneasily in the mortuary for the grisly ritual to be completed.

"An evangelist!" The man from the embassy whose training had not prevented nausea was grateful for any distraction.

"That's what he said, sir. He told the priest he hadn't thought about it during the trial but tonight he was sure there must be a connection. It was after he'd agreed to be a courier but before he'd actually started working for them; he was chatted up by this Chinese evangelist who claimed to be God's messenger."

"Oh, yes? Where was this?"

"In Singapore. This Chinese bumped into him, apparently quite casually. Offered to buy him a drink then told him details about himself, family stuff, things like that. He also hinted he knew the lad was about to make his first delivery."

"Wasn't he suspicious?"

"That's when the Chinese claimed to be God's messenger and have second sight."

"Good Lord!"

"He referred to the dangers of drug running but the lad pretended he didn't know what the Chinese was talking about. He told the priest he didn't believe he'd ever be caught."

"That's what they all say," the embassy man replied wearily. "It

11

certainly sounds like another member of the gang double-checking. We'll include it in the report . . . have you finished?"
The photographer took a final exposure. The mortuary attendant waited in the background, silent and alert, but gleaned nothing further.

In an office behind Macquarie Steet, Kev Macillvenny sat at his desk in a state of slow burn. Enormous hands stretched out in two huge fists of tense muscle. Below, his stomach strained against his trousers, a stomach that followed a continuous ever-increasing curve from his chest to his groin with no indentation between. "Those Pommie bastards!"

Long ago he'd learned to expect to be patronized; it was an integral part of every Pommie's character. Once, oh Glory! God had been on his side when a stupid Whitehall bastard had included a Latin quip in a telex. Not for nothing had Kev Macillvenny attended St Xavier's. He'd sent a forty-line reply entirely in Latin, every sentence ending with a question mark. There'd been absolute silence for weeks after that and he'd never received a reply.

What he couldn't understand was why? Jesuitical teaching hadn't eradicated Kev's essential faith in mankind, his belief as a trained officer of the law that if he and the Brits were on the same side, they should be able to work together.

Why dribble titbits of information when with the whole picture they might take out the gang altogether? What did it matter who got there first, Whitehall or Macquarie Street? Such was Kev Macillvenny's naivety. His fists tightened again in another angry spasm.

Macillvenny's aide Charlie watched the mottled flesh in front of him darken and guessed the cause. He waited for Kev to recover. Sod the Brits. Why worry? There were other ways of finding out what you needed to know.

"There's nothing else come in, you've checked?" As always, Macillvenny was prepared to give the Poms one last chance.

"Nuthin'." Charlie believed in husbanding his resources. Monosyllabic except when under stress, he leaned against a shady bit of wall watching the sun beat down on Kev's bald patch. There was so little hair left you could see the pattern of veins in the skin. Jesus, how long before the silly bugger's blood pressure exploded because of those Poms? Charlie's conscience stirred faintly; he was fond of the old man. "Don't matter, does it, Kev?" he asked, conciliatorily. "We've got hold of the same information."

"That's not the point!" Injured pride replaced Kev's fading anger. "They should've told us. Out of politeness."

"Yeah, well . . ."

"We're both trying to stop the same racket, right?"

"Yes, Kev." The arguments never changed; Charlie was bored.

"So why can't they be frank with us?" There was no answer to that. "What've we got?" Charlie handed him a filched photostat of the embassy man's report. Macillvenny stared morosely at the line: "Previous contact, Chinese evangelist", and the details that followed. "Where would you disappear if you were this bloke and knew you might've been blown?"

"I reckon I might stick around. Singapore's a place any Chinese could hide up in." Kev eyed him thoughtfully.

"You think *they*'d take that much risk? That organization runs a tight ship."

"So where's the risk? We know he'll have a respectable front, some kind of business cover. And he must be a key fella, sent in like that to check the bloke's nerve. So he made a mistake? That bloke's been taken care of but they'll need a replacement—and they'll want *him* given the once-over, too. No, wherever the guy is, he'll lie low for a while, but I reckon he'll be back."

"Any description? Did the bloke give the priest any details?"

"Nah. Guess he'd got other things on his mind."

In a room in Whitehall, Anthony Pelham-Walker gazed out at the rump of the Duke of Wellington's horse. It was his least favourite object. It filled the window frame, but because this room was allocated to holders of Anthony's position, it followed he was stuck with it.

A desk man to the point of constipation. Anthony Pelham-Walker occupied both position and office by reason of attrition. He'd bored his superiors so often over the years they'd promoted him out of self-defence, to rid themselves of his company.

13

Now with a status that meant he lunched alone at his club and with younger, brighter men to do the work of the department, Anthony Pelham-Walker reigned in solitary mandarin splendour. He signed what was put in front of him and incorporated the clever younger men's opinions as his own in finicky memos that were ignored but occupied his days with their composition.

Unfortunately this placid existence had suddenly come under threat. In the dark small hours in his loveless marriage bed Pelham-Walker had been smitten with an awful, undeniable truth, as blinding as that which occurred on the Damascus road: his life, his entire *raison d'être*, was completely meaningless.

For most mandarins, an Alka-Seltzer next morning would've redressed the balance but Anthony Pelham-Walker drank sparingly. On waking, the thought was still there and he knew it wasn't a bad dream. It refused to go away. Like toothache it nagged, occupying his mind to the exclusion of everything else. By late afternoon—he was always the last to leave despite having nothing to do—he was desperate.

It was at that point Crispin Sinclair walked into the room, not so much a clever man as a high-flier determined to reach the top of his grade in as short a time as possible. Which was why he used every opportunity to ingratiate himself. "Oh, you're still here, sir, good . . . A file has been sent over . . . For Information Only, but I thought you ought to see it."

It was the only file that had arrived on his desk that day and Anthony Pelham-Walker seized it with trembling hands. Was there still some small task, some justification for the gong that in the fullness of time would undoubtedly be his? He pored over the sheet it contained, running his finger along the words.

Dear God, thought Crispin, I thought even in Cambridge they learned to read. Batman suddenly looked up, his eyes shining, and Crispin felt distinctly uneasy. "A nugget of information, Sinclair!"

"A—minuscule—nugget, sir?" Crispin replied tentatively; and none of our business anyway, he thought. He'd only brought it in to make the stupid bugger feel important. "I'm afraid, at this stage, we cannot put it higher than that," he added judiciously.

"Has it been acted upon?" Good Grief!

"Not in so many words, sir . . . it's been fed into the computer, analysed and so forth but acted upon—no." Sinclair forced himself to give a confidential smile. "I fear, even in our department, we consider there's very little more that can be achieved—at this stage." And he certainly wasn't going to screw things up by offering inane suggestions to Scotland Yard, he'd got his career to think of. "One cannot see any possible way in which anyone could—act—at present?" Pelham-Walker nodded agreement. Crispin swallowed with relief. For a moment he thought Batman had lost the rest of his marbles.

"So what happens next?" asked Pelham-Walker, his shoulders beginning to droop.

"We wait, sir. We'll be told, naturally, if this particular oriental gentleman crops up anywhere else." He gave a gay, confident laugh. "We haven't bothered the Australians with it because, frankly, we don't consider it all that important."

"Oh, I quite agree. As you say, we must wait and see. But keep me informed." Pelham-Walker handed back the file a mite reluctantly, Crispin considered. As he left the office he glanced at his watch. Good Lord, he'd nearly made himself late!

Chapter Two

In matters of the heart, Mavis Bignell had until the advent of Mr Pringle been a gallant loser. But after their first encounter when she, naked and deputizing for the usual model, faced Beginners in Oils, Mavis realized that at last Fate had taken a hand.

For one so well endowed by nature the years of waiting had been a trial. Of course there were always those ready for "a bit of a nibble" but they got short shrift. Mavis came from a background where "saving oneself" was ingrained. Herbert Bignell had been a terrible disappointment but she didn't seek consolation elsewhere. As well as pride in her reputation, Mavis was also convinced that someday "Mr Right" would come along.

When on that fateful evening Mr Pringle had been so overcome, so overwhelmed by the mass of sculpted pearly-pink flesh and the Titian triangle, Mavis's sense of values underwent a sea-change. She watched the quiet, inoffensive stranger attack his canvas with demonic energy. She'd never met an artist before but no doubt about it: this was it, this was Real Life! His picture, a remarkably thick composition, was finished in three hours flat; they carried it between them up to Mrs Bignell's bedroom where, as she modestly described events afterwards, Mr Pringle had swept her off her feet.

If they'd been drawn together out of loneliness—for Mr Pringle's beloved Renée had died not long before the late, unlamented Herbert—romance quickly replaced it. Once or twice Mr Pringle suggested matrimony but Mavis declared she preferred the status quo. "In my experience, marriage can kill love stone-dead. People get careless about hurting one another's feelings. I couldn't bear that to happen to us."

All the same, she had to admit these days life was a little dreary. The sparkle had disappeared from their relationship. It seemed to her as if Mr Pringle had withdrawn into a melancholy world of his

16

own and being of a naturally cheery disposition herself, Mrs Bignell found it dispiriting. When she heard Ollie Gorman offering his cut-price tickets to Australia the same day she herself had had an enormous unexpected stroke of luck, she knew it must be "a sign"; she and Mr Pringle would shake the dust off their feet and enjoy themselves.

It had taken longer than she'd anticipated; Mr P had held out against all manner of persuasion. Tonight she'd wheedled him to accompany her to Mrs Hardie's, ostensibly to comfort her friend over the missing grandchild. What Mavis had omitted to mention was that she'd invited Ollie Gorman too, and this was weighing on her conscience.

As they stepped over the threshold, Mr Pringle shrank from the overhearty greeting. "Come on in, squire, don't be shy. We're all friends in here." Ollie's florid red face dwarfed the tiny kitchen. Half-hidden, the neat small shape of Mrs Hardie bobbed out round the side of him.

"It is kind of you to come round—" she began.

"Of course it is, but what did you expect?" Ollie Gorman demanded. "At The Bricklayers, we know Mr Pringle. If he says he'll come, then he will, he's not the sort to let you down. He's Mavie's friend, after all." Ollie leered.

"Now just one moment . . ." Mr Pringle was shocked; had he been inveigled here on a false premise? "If you and Mrs Bignell wish to discuss her travel arrangements, I must point out she will be flying to Australia alone. I shall not be accompanying her, I simply cannot afford to." Mavis's departure was an established fact and the date chalked up above the bar. The darts final between The Bricklayers and The White Hart had been postponed in consequence.

"You haven't agreed—yet—" Ollie Gorman smirked with elephantine subtlety "—because you haven't let me tell you how inexpensive it is. Shall I tell him now, Mavie? Is your friend ready for the shock of a lifetime or should we steady his nerves first?"

Mrs Hardie recognized the prompt and hastened in with her line. "Would you like a drink, Mr Pringle? From a bottle of sherry? Mr Gorman was kind enough to bring one."

"Ollie, dear, not Mister. Like I said, we're all friends here."

17

"I'm afraid I haven't got proper glasses."

"Would you like me to pour?" Mavis asked.

"Oh, would you!" The flustered hostess hid behind Ollie again. "I'm afraid I'm not used to doing it."

"Tell Mr Pringle about Ben," Mavis suggested tactfully. Mrs Hardie glanced automatically at the photographs on the mantelpiece.

"It's over six months since I heard from him. Gary took him to Australia without telling Linda—just collected Ben from outside the school one day. I was away visiting friends at the time. Of course Gary and Linda had split up by then."

Mavis handed Mr Pringle his sherry. "Gary always wanted to go back to Australia but Linda refused to go with him."

"That wasn't the only thing they argued about." Mrs Hardie was candid in her betrayal of her daughter. "He and Linda used to have hundreds of rows. I don't know how Gary put up with it as long as he did."

"What I can't quite understand—" Mr Pringle was less polite than usual. He preferred dry Spanish sherry and what Ollie Gorman had supplied was a sickly, dark brown substance "—is why his mother—Linda, isn't it?—hasn't tried to secure the boy's return through the proper channels."

"It costs too much." Mrs Hardie sighed. "She did go to a solicitor. She made an appointment but when she come home she told me it wasn't any use. They'd got joint custody, too, you see." She sighed again. "It didn't do me no good either. I've been stuck with her ever since Gary went. She moved back just when I was all set to go to one of them warden places. I'd got my name down and there was a vacancy."

"As regards Ben—" Mr Pringle clung to the point "—surely your daughter should be the one to go and search for him?"

"I told you," Mrs Hardie repeated patiently, "we can't afford it, either of us."

"Show Mr Pringle that last postcard you had," Mavis suggested. It was produced from a worn handbag.

"You can read it if you like," Mrs Hardie told him.

It was a view of a small Australian town. The roads were wide, the buildings bright, clean and single-storey. Across the plate-glass

18

window of an ice-cream parlour on one corner of the crossroads someone had scribbled an arrow in biro.

"'Dear Gran, '" Mr Pringle read on the back, "'We are in Bathurst eating banana splits. Dad and me come here this morning from Sydney. Love, Ben. XXX'"

"Gary's a truck driver. He wrote when he first went saying he'd send for Linda and me as soon as he and Ben got fixed up somewhere," Mrs Hardie told them sadly, "but we never heard from him again. In that letter Gary said the Australian sunshine would do Ben good." The grandmother was near to tears. "I hope it has . . . I thought I could trust Gary."

"I'm very sorry," Mr Pringle said helplessly. In the small room, the emotion was disturbing. "If there was any way I could help . . . but I simply cannot afford to accompany Mrs Bignell to Australia, much as I wish to do so." Ollie Gorman looked as though he was about to spring to life but Mavis frowned; nevertheless, the time had come for her to confess.

"You could afford it if you let me treat you."

"That's impossible." Mr Pringle was embarrassed that she should say such a thing in front of strangers. Besides, as a retired member of Her Majesty's Inland Revenue he was extremely conscious of the rules concerning gifts.

"I didn't tell you before—I cashed in my Premium Bonds and put them on the Derby," Mavis said quietly. "They hadn't done anything for years, it seemed a waste leaving them where they were."

"I tried to give her a tip but it was a good job she didn't listen," Ollie announced. "Mavie was right and I was wrong—and she put it all on the nose, she's a goer all right."

Despite his aversion Mr Pringle had to ask: "What happened?"

"It won, sixteen to one. I made just over two thousand pounds, two thousand and forty eight to be exact." Years of mental arithmetic enabled him to work the sum out backwards.

"Good grief! You put all that on a horse!"

"I was very careful which one I chose." Mavis was huffy. "I didn't pick any old horse—this one had nice eyes. I didn't tell you at the time because I knew what you'd say."

Two thousand pounds! "You should invest it in life insurance,"

Mr Pringle murmured faintly, "and include the interest in your next tax return—"

"Blow that for a laugh," his lover replied vigorously. "I've always wanted to visit Australia and I want you to come with me. There's no fun going on your own."

"And when you hear how little it'll cost you—" Ollie couldn't restrain himself any longer, his bracelet clanked against his watch as he seized Mr Pringle's arm "—you'll wonder why you never considered going there before."

Chapter Three

It was one of those pairs of small brick-built cottages that crop up unexpectedly among the dunes and industrial hinterland on the far side of Heathrow. Long ago they'd been homes to families who scraped a living from these gravel pits and marshes; now they were bought by those who needed a base close to the airport.

The dark-haired steward, Evan Jones, lay on his divan bed, smoking duty-free cigarettes. He wore an old vest and jeans. The room was bare of furniture apart from the bed, one chair and some packing cases. The area round his bed was neat; clean clothes were folded in their temporary storage boxes, ash from his cigarette was tipped meticulously into the container in his hand, and the coverlet on which he lay was tucked in at the corners with precision.

The rest of the room was strewn with debris, tools, decorating equipment and tiles, laboriously imported box by heavy box after trips to Rome. Piled in a heap in one corner were souvenirs, ready to adorn the half-finished Spanish-style bar.

Upstairs the two bedrooms were completely bare. In the bathroom the towels were from hotels where he'd stayed. Ashtrays had international names. Nowhere was there the stamp of Evan himself: the cottage was a rag-bag of junk, collected by a scavenger who'd flown round the world and seen nothing of it except hotel rooms, bars and swimming pools.

The steward had been stripping wallpaper when the second phone call came. He'd made no effort to continue, fear had paralyzed him. The hand holding the cigarette still trembled. Despite his instinctive tidiness, some of the ash spilled on to the floor. Above, wide-bodied jets made the ground vibrate, and less than a mile away motorway traffic kept up a constant roar. He wasn't aware of any of it. Evan Jones was far too terrified: he was trapped.

Yesterday when the first, expected message came, he'd asked the anonymous voice to relay one back for him. He'd worked it out very carefully indeed, written it down. Even so his voice shook as he read out the words. The caller hadn't spoken, he'd hung up. That was when Evan realized his hands were wet with sweat.

He tried to convince himself it was going to be all right; the silence proved it. Whoever *they* were, they'd accepted his assurances and were prepared to release him from bondage. He'd even managed a few hours' sleep after he'd drunk enough whisky.

Today the telephone mocked him. The latest in crazy technology, a scarlet plastic shape with a gold cord, it was designed to be an amusing accessory on the Spanish bar. When he'd answered it an hour ago, the tinny voice had destroyed his peace of mind for ever. That red toy was no longer a phone but a bomb that had blown his life apart. There would be no more sleep.

Confirmation of the threats the caller had made arrived in the post: photographs. Evan Jones stared at them again, horribly fascinated by the irrefutable evidence they contained.

It was a sequence of three pictures. The first, slightly fuzzy, had been taken in a hotel room moments after he'd lifted the first consignment from its hiding place. Too late, Evan remembered the sudden unexpected arrival of a chambermaid coming in with a laden trolley. The second, snatched from a car that must've been following him, showed Evan making a prearranged drop in Sydney. The last, inside a Hong Kong nightclub, was much clearer; he'd been facing the concealed camera that time, a stupid happy smile on his face as he accepted the wad of notes.

Evan sobbed aloud, cursing himself for being a fool. When *they* first approached him, he'd been wildly excited as well as indignant. His immediate reaction had been to report what had happened, but after an hour or two he began to consider the matter. Supposing he only did a couple of trips, then refused? The money would certainly be handy—how could *they* force him to go on?

He would keep his side of the bargain, he'd given them his word; he'd never tell a soul. Nor would there be anything to incriminate their organization—the irony of that finally hit Evan. The stranger who'd first spoken to him in Penang was quite right when he'd said there would be no way he could identify them. Every contact had been by phone. Evan had only met one other person but he didn't know his real name. It was safer that way, the man claimed.

Three trips, that's all Evan had decided; three, maybe four, then he'd chuck it in. He congratulated himself on his strength of will. There could only be a minimal risk in three trips.

To date, it had been seven. Evan needed the money because he'd been taken off the profitable transatlantic run with its dollar expenses and sent east instead, where allowances were much smaller and currencies unstable. The rate of exchange against the rupee was ludicrous, you couldn't pay the gas bill with those.

Lying on the divan, he found himself thinking of his family in Wales. Fourteen of them and he the only one with a job. My God, how proud they'd been when the airline took him on, treating him like some bloody hero. And then when he told them he'd bought a house . . . Oh hell! They wouldn't be cheering when they got to hear about this!

He flung the photos aside. He'd promised Mam she could come here for a holiday, too. He wanted to prove that he'd arrived. To show her their family could feel proud. What a joke! Evan looked about. He'd have to do the place up quickly and sell it. He'd even have to give up his precious job and disappear, lose his identity, if he wanted to be truly safe. Maybe he'd never escape them, ever!

Suddenly he was on his feet. Fear had gone. Instead, he was very, very angry. There must be a way out. All those months without work—was he going to give up without a fight? Stop being so bloody feeble-minded! Forget about being caught, just bloody well think of a plan!

Evan plugged in the kettle—coffee would settle his stomach if his hands stopped shaking long enough to make it—and unfolded a large sheet of paper. Thin black lines criss-crossed in a dense geometric pattern. Down one side were flight numbers and across the top, days of the week. It was the company's eastern flight schedule for the next three months.

Evan picked up his duty roster and out of habit checked his next departure and flight details one more time. Tomorrow, Monday 31st, leaving Heathrow on Flight 974 at 1000 hours GMT. Wait a tick . . . Evan ran his finger down the thin line, across, and down again. A night-stop at Abu Dhabi; but the flight out of there the

23

following morning had an asterisk—it was a charter! Christ, there might just be a way out after all. *They* had assumed he would be on a routine ten-day Sydney terminator but he would be outside the regular route pattern once he picked up that charter!

For the first time since the tinny voice destroyed his peace of mind Evan Jones began to breathe easily. This might be his only chance, he must use it carefully. If he loused it up this time, he could be a goner.

It had taken several weeks for Ollie Gorman to come up with a pair of tickets, after all. Their date of departure had been put back three times. It all depended, Ollie explained, on there being spare seats on charters, but Mr Pringle didn't believe it. He fully expected to be turned back at Heathrow or, worse still, have to pay extra before the airline would accept them. He made the mistake of confiding his gloom to Mrs Bignell and she reacted extremely sharply.

They had gone round for a final visit to Mrs Hardie, to collect one or two photographs of Ben and a letter to give to her young grandson in the unlikely event that they find him. Mr Pringle was very doubtful but Mavis continued optimistic. "You never know" was her constant refrain.

Mrs Hardie, neat in her sensible trouser suit, perched birdlike on a corner of her kitchen table and poured them tea. Gone was the shy awkwardness of their first encounter. On her own, mistress of her kitchen, she chatted happily. "Isn't it exciting, you're off at last! And it's ever so kind of you to take the trouble. I'm ever so grateful."

"I'm afraid we can't promise—" Mr Pringle began but Mavis interrupted.

"You haven't heard anything, I suppose? Since we were here last?" Mrs Hardie shook her head and gave a fierce sniff. "Never mind, dear. Is this the latest photo you have of Ben?" Tears were swiftly, unobtrusively wiped away.

"Yes. Taken at school last year, that's why he's in uniform."

Mr Pringle sipped his tea. There were more family photos on the walls. One was of Ben when he'd obviously taken a tumble and had a hefty plaster cast on one leg. Others, from the nineteen-fifties as

24

far as Mr Pringle could judge from the length of the shorts, showed a much older youth with the same startling blue whites to his eyes. The family resemblance between the two was strong.

"That's Ben's uncle." Mrs Hardie spoke softly and her voice trembled a little. "Linda's brother. He'd have been thirty-seven next birthday . . ."

"I'm sorry." The implication was obvious. "Was it—an accident?" Mrs Hardie sighed.

"Not really. We'd been expecting it but it still came as a shock." In the silence Mr Pringle looked again at the dead youth then at the picture in Mrs Bignell's hand.

"They're extremely alike."

"Yes." Mrs Hardie's voice sounded flat as if the possible loss of her grandson as well as her son was too much to bear. Mr Pringle wondered uneasily if he could speed their departure. He'd no intention of raising false hopes in Mrs Hardie concerning Ben. He tried to signal to Mrs Bignell but she had their brochure in her hand.

"Would you like to see our itinerary, dear? It should be the holiday of a lifetime." Mr Pringle's heart sank; from experience he knew this could take a very long time indeed. Ever since he'd capitulated and agreed to be treated, Mavis's ideas had continued to expand. It usually began with a phrase he'd learned to dread: "As we're going all that way, it seems silly not to . . ."

Since their first visit here when he'd finally given in, their holiday had expanded from just over two weeks to six. He had to admit it was possible to see a great deal of Australia comparatively cheaply and how silly it was to go all that way and not see as much as possible, but he was beginning to wonder whether he would survive the trip.

Under pressure, Ollie Gorman had admitted he'd no idea who their fellow travellers would be. Scientists of some sort, he thought, travelling to Australia via Bangkok.

"We stay in Thailand for a couple of days, then we go by train all the way down through Malaysia to Singapore." Mrs Bignell's eyes were warm as she conjured up the picture. "Ever so romantic. Past all those rubber plantations Somerset Maugham used to write about."

"Oh, yes?" Mrs Hardie's books came from a different shelf in the library.

"Then we pick up a flight at Singapore for Sydney—I'm really looking forward to that. We go with these scientific people all the way up Australia. You know how they have Greyhound buses in America? Well down there they call them Wallabies."

"I always get sick on a coach," said Mrs Hardie. "What happens at night? D'you stay in hotels?"

"We camp out under the stars."

"Camp!" Mrs Hardie couldn't believe it. "You ever done any, Mavis?"

"I shall be all right." Mrs Bignell was adamant. "Mr Pringle once put up a tent during the war, didn't you dear?"

"The brochure assures us that the tents 'are simplicity itself, and help is available should it be required'," he protested, but Mrs Hardie shook her head.

"I don't like the sound of that. Those brochures are full of lies. You read it in the papers every day. I hope you'll be comfortable. I wouldn't fancy it. Have another cup of tea before you go?"

"According to our itinerary, on one of the days we stop for lunch in the town where Ben sent his postcard. Bathurst."

"Do you?" Mrs Hardie was attentive.

"Yes, and I thought we'd go to that ice-cream place—" Mavis broke off because someone had entered the kitchen.

"Oh, there you are Linda." Mrs Hardie didn't seem particularly pleased to see her daughter. "This is Mr Pringle who's going to look for Ben."

The woman who came into the room took Mr Pringle by surprise. She was tall and fleshy with a mass of blonde hair and without the spare delicate build of her mother, nor the distinctive blue eyes of her dead brother. As Linda greeted each of them in turn, Mr Pringle had the feeling she was making an effort to subdue her personality. He could imagine her enjoying a knees-up at The Bricklayers much more easily than living in this finicky neat kitchen full of knick-knacks.

"How do you do? We will do our best to find your boy although I fear that cannot be much. Australia is such a very large country

26

. . ." Mr Pringle was embarrassed. Mrs Bignell, as usual, was overconfident.

"Don't you worry, Linda. If anyone can find him, Mr Pringle can. We're going to Bathurst and we'll ask in the ice-cream parlour. If I show them Ben's photo, someone might remember."

Linda glanced at it briefly. "Yes, they might." She sounded as unconvinced as Mr Pringle. He felt inward relief; unlike Mrs Hardie, Linda obviously realized their chances were slim.

"I wish I thought it likely . . ." he began and she looked at him in understanding.

"Don't worry . . . You'll do what you can, I expect."

Mrs Hardie's small shoulder blades hunched against any suggestion of defeat. "You will try," she pleaded.

Mrs Bignell stood up, cramming photographs, letter and brochure into her handbag. "You leave it to us," she replied. "Australia may be a big place but there aren't many people in it, it said so in *Reader's Digest*."

The paragraph was on the front page. Headed "Drug traffic hits new high!" what followed was a vitriolic attack on the attempts of New South Wales's authorities to stem the flow. Charlie read it on the ferry over from Manly. Looked like Kev's blood pressure was in for another bad day.

Chapter Four

"This aeroplane's got an upstairs."

"Mmmm . . ." Mr Pringle didn't care, he still felt ill. The effort of following five thousand other people the eight miles to a departure gate, then climbing into this Odeon cinema, of being herded to a seat that squashed the coins in his pockets into the flesh of his buttocks, had defeated him. He was hemmed in by strangers, he couldn't move—he couldn't breathe! Half a mile away, someone was waving an oxygen mask. Mr Pringle was desperate for air. Never before had he experienced such claustrophobia—and how could an Odeon transport this mass of bodies half-way round the world? It was ridiculous!

Mavis had solved the problem of her seat; she'd refused it. "Look, dear, these are for anorexics," she said cheerfully. "Where's the one I've booked?" The stewardess had been in the job too long.

"The width of an economy seat was laid down in the Warsaw Convention of 1948, madam."

"We were all thinner in 1948," Mavis told her coldly, "we still had ration books." She was magnificently arrayed in fuchsia and stood her ground. She pointed to the distant front cabin. "What about one of those? They look much wider." The stewardess was outraged.

"Madam, that is the First Class!"

The line of those waiting to be seated now snaked back as far as the tarmac. The purser made frantic hand-signals. Despite her fury the stewardess had to give in. "As a temporary measure, may I suggest that you sit in the lounge for take-off?" Mrs Bignell smiled, satisfied. She turned to Mr Pringle.

"See you later, dear, when I find where they've hidden the bar."

Alone, he stared out through yellowing cracked Perspex in the

28

porthole and tried to forget everything he'd ever read about pressurization failure. At a rough guess, there were fifty-eight rows of elderly cripples between him and the emergency exit, so why worry? He couldn't escape.

Music was available to soothe his fears but even as he reached for the headphones, a voice from the Tannoy informed those on the port side that their speakers were no longer working. Mr Pringle wondered gloomily if they'd had any similar problems with the engines?

"You go up this spiral staircase and you come out on the first floor," Mavis continued.

By some miracle they'd become airborne after all and had stayed aloft long enough for the first meal to be flung at them. The inevitable queues formed outside the lavatories. So much for emergency procedures—Mr Pringle could no longer even see the fire exits because of the anxious throng. Mrs Bignell, flushed and happy, fought her way through to where he sat in the rear cabin.

"It's nicer upstairs, less crowded," she reported.

"Any bedrooms?" His internal organs had been dangerously compressed for too long. "A bunk would do."

"There's only this place they call the lounge. Very shabby. The plastic's peeling off the walls and the stuffing's come out. You can see right through to the metal. The captain's sitting up there. Claims he's got an upset tummy." Mr Pringle was immediately awake.

"Who's flying this blessed thing then?"

"Colin."

"Who the hell's Colin?"

"Ssh!" Mavis never failed to be shocked by language. "He's the first officer. I've been chatting to him while he had his supper. Steak and kidney. He said he was glad of a bit of company. He showed me how some of the little levers worked—"

"What!"

"Keep your voice down. It's perfectly safe to sit in the cockpit provided you don't pull any of the knobs. *Colin* says the skipper's shamming. He says he's in a sulk because he's been passed over for promotion." Mr Pringle closed his eyes. "Mind you, it's Colin I feel sorry for." Mavis was solemn. "D'you know, his wife's two-

29

timing him with a British Caledonian first officer. Every time Colin takes off from Heathrow, the other one's winging in from Gatwick—isn't it a shame? He was nearly crying when he told me about it."

So was Mr Pringle. This dilapidated two-storey cinema, hurtling through space in sole charge of an emotional cuckold . . . "How can one man eat supper, fly the thing and keep a lookout?"

"Oh, they don't bother looking. Colin says the speed these things travel, you wouldn't even see the one you hit. Well, ta-ta dear. We'll be in Abu Dhabi soon, that's where the crews change over." She bent lower and murmured, "If the next steward's friendly, maybe he'll let me stay in the upstairs lounge."

They disembarked into a hot dry night and straggled across to an artificial air-cooled oasis. Mr Pringle gazed down from under a vast mosaic palm tree at fellow travellers round the fountain below. Mrs Bignell had disappeared to strip off some of her clothes. "I plan to peel off the layers as we go," she'd told him. The thought helped distract him from the terror of flying.

From his vantage point, it looked as though others should be encouraged to follow her example. Some passengers were still in suits and ties. One carried a mac and another, inexplicably, an umbrella. It was so British it was embarrassing.

"There we are . . . that's better." Her jacket was gone but the silky pink skirt remained, topped by a sleeveless, low-necked flowery blouse. Mavis now sported exotic earrings and a scarf wrapped turban-style round the vivid hair.

"I say!" said Mr Pringle and Mavis puffed out her magnificent chest.

"I'm glad you like it. I think I'll go back to the aeroplane, dear. See if I can find the new crew. Would you like to join me if there's another spare seat in the lounge?" He shook his head.

"No thank you. If possible, I shall try and sleep on the next leg."

There was an armed Arab guard barring the exit back to the aircraft. Mr Pringle watched Mavis approach, saw the man's glance descend to her chest . . . and remain there, transfixed. If Mavis's figure was more suited to a bygone era in the West, here at least it was appreciated.

They chatted; the man laughed and stood aside to let her pass.

30

Evan Jones had worked out his plan very carefully indeed. He went through it again as he set out champagne glasses for the first-class customers. It all depended on one as yet unknown factor.

A passenger had come back early, he could hear her climbing the stairs. Like an overblown peony she stood before him, smiling plumply. "Hallo, dear, I'm Mavis. Shall I give you a hand? I'm used to bar work and I can't stand the thought of being idle all the way to Thailand." It was fate, thought Evan.

Mr Pringle tried to sleep. He ignored the offer of duty-free cigarettes, the second dinner and the four-gallon jug of boiling coffee that hovered dangerously close to his ear. The lights were lowered and gangsters began shouting at one another on the screen (noiselessly for those on the port side). He closed his eyes. Someone touched his arm. A steward in a tuxedo leaned over to pass him a glass. "From Mavis." The young man's eyes were very blue against the tanned skin. "One of her margaritas . . . She's the life and soul of a party going on in the first-class lounge—want to come?" He'd got an engaging grin. Mr Pringle smiled in response.

"Thank you, but no. Please tell Mrs Bignell I'm glad she's enjoying herself." The steward laughed.

"She's doing that all right—the other passengers are loving it. She's teaching some Americans to sing 'Roll Out the Barrel'."

On her way to freshen up as dawn flooded the cabin, Mrs Bignell paused by his seat. She looked bright-eyed and happy. "Hasn't it been a lovely flight? Did you manage to sleep?" Loyally and because she'd treated him to the ticket, Mr Pringle lied and said that he had. "I've found out about the people we're travelling with, these scientists going to Australia."

"Oh, yes?"

"There's forty of them but this was the only aircraft they could charter. That's why there were spare seats for blokes like Ollie to sell."

He was astonished. "Sounds very high-powered. What exactly do they do?"

"They're phonies."

31

"Pardon?"

"That's what it says on the labels, FONEs. I presume that's how you say it. It stands for 'Friends of Nuclear Energy'."

"Then why are they going to Australia? Surely they don't have nuclear energy down there?"

"That's what I thought. Rum, isn't it."

After joining the queue for a wash, she had more to impart. "It's highly secret. To do with the government. One of the wives told me."

"If it's a secret . . . ?"

"She's had a tiff with her hubby. She says she doesn't care any more who knows about it. You see, when they left for the airport this morning he managed to reverse the Volvo over their pet rabbit. She said the only memory she'll carry round Australia is of her children, screaming over this nasty mess lying in the road—"

"Yes, yes." He'd been looking forward to breakfast. "So what sort of secret mission is it?"

"Well . . ." Mavis squeezed in beside him to keep it confidential. "You know how people tried to stop firms burying nuclear waste at home—got up petitions, that sort of thing—then it was election time and the government decided none of the sites were really suitable because they'd all got voters living in them?"

"Yes?"

"Then they wanted to bury it under the Irish Sea but people were worried about what it might do to the fish?"

Mr Pringle nodded: "Understandably so."

"Well that's what this is all about. These scientists are visiting Australia, hoping to find a suitable place to dump the waste down there."

"You're joking!"

"No, I'm not. As part of the bicentennial celebration of the founding of Australia, the lady said."

"Good grief!"

"Her husband's told her if they do find somewhere suitable, he might be given the Queen's Award to Industry."

Bangkok was heavy with a torpid heat that sapped Mr Pringle's strength. He was thankful all he had to do was struggle on to an

32

air-conditioned bus. His fellow travellers, still in their suits, looked even worse than he did. Mrs Bignell settled beside him. "The crew are staying at the same hotel, isn't that nice? I've invited Evan to join us when we go sightseeing tomorrow."

He remembered the lilt in the voice. "Is Evan the steward?"

"He's a lovely boy." She watched as the last of their party climbed into the coach. "What a miserable looking bunch of sods these scientists are. Fancy sending them on a good-will mission."

"Is that what it's supposed to be?" Mr Pringle hoped the Australians would understand.

The road into the city was a highway, raised up, with traffic streaming past on either side: Thai people on scooters or driving small battered lorries, who smiled and raised their hands in greeting. Conditioned by years of sullen London faces Mr Pringle lifted his timidly in reply. They passed hoardings covered in exotic curved script—he couldn't understand a word. At every street corner, in front of skyscraper offices, were tiny shrines decked with flowers where devout passers-by knelt to pray.

He was in the abroad, no doubt about it, in the mysterious, beguiling East, the downfall of so many foreigners. He squeezed Mrs Bignell's hand. "Isn't it marvellous? We've actually got here!"

She saw the gleam in his eye. After her all-night partying, Mavis was tired. My word, she thought, I hope I can manage to keep up. "What we both need first," she said firmly, "is a kip."

The hotel was a vast dark cavern with heavy wooden ceilings. Everywhere, a mass of tourists eddied: Germans, Dutch, and, it seemed, thousands of Japanese. He and Mavis were stranded in a sea of people, anchored to their suitcases.

"Hi, you two OK?"

"Oh, Evan—can you sort out which is our room?" The steward nodded at Mavis, made his way confidently to the reception desk and returned with a couple of forms.

"Fill these in and give me your passports." He grinned at Mr Pringle's expression. "It's perfectly safe, honest. Everyone has to hand them in out here."

"I see."

"Look," he said, returning with their key, "I'm sure you're

bushed right now but when you want to go and eat, there's a marvellous place just across the road—let me show you." As they walked back into the blinding sunshine, Mr Pringle suggested hesitantly that he might like to join them. The young man shook his head.

"Not tonight, thanks. You go and enjoy yourselves. We'll meet up tomorrow, after breakfast, and 'do' the town. 'Bye."

"Isn't he nice." Mavis watched him go. "Who says all young people are yobs nowadays—Evan's such a polite boy." They began to walk towards the lifts. Mr Pringle's thoughts had already reached the seventh floor.

"I wonder if our room will have a double bed?"

Chapter Five

The day had satiated them. It had begun easily enough, on the river. They had sailed to where a canal branched off and old women in boats, protected from the blistering heat by vast coolie hats, hawked vegetables and watermelons. Mavis was entranced. Today, abandoning pink for shades of caramel and orange and framed by her sunshade, she was, Mr Pringle thought happily, his own exquisite tropical bloom.

All the commerce of the city had been on that river. Young bloods whizzed past in "hot rods", the vast engines anchored to their flimsy boats by nothing more than shafts. The wash from huge barges lumbering up and down rocked their motor launch. Everywhere there were contrasts: Western-style hotels facing wooden houses across the Chao Phya, concrete buildings interspersed with the delicate shapes of pagodas.

In the afternoon, the pace quickened. They were dazzled by porcelain palaces studded with jewels, temples roofed in marble, by innumerable statues covered in gold, guarded by strange mythical beasts and crowned by the omnipresent Garuda bird.

Finally, in a temple containing a reclining Buddha nearly fifty metres long, Mrs Bignell threw in the sponge. "I'm sorry, dears, I can't manage another step, my feet are so swollen." She lifted one daintily for them to inspect. "I'll never get my shoes back on as it is."

In the taxi, she and Mr Pringle promised themselves they'd come back tomorrow, commiserating with Evan who had to fly home to England instead. That evening the three of them sat in an open-air restaurant amid Greek columns, soothed by fountains choreographed to Beethoven, Bizet and the Beatles. It was kitsch, it was delightful. Mavis paused in the midst of her satay to demand: "Isn't this—magic!" and Mr Pringle readily agreed. He raised a solemn glass.

35

"To the swift quadruped with compelling eyes."

"What I still can't get over—" Evan returned to an earlier theme "—is those blokes renovating the statues today, surrounded by gold leaf and jewels. Each box must've been worth a fortune— what's to stop any of them pinching the lot?" Mr Pringle felt a slight irritation that Evan should ruffle their mood. He quoted their guide's response to the same question: " 'Who would want to rob the Lord Buddha?' " But Evan scoffed: "Almost everyone I know . . . and talking of Buddhas, what about that other one made of solid gold? How big would you say it was—fourteen, fifteen feet?"

"Something like that." Mr Pringle wanted to relax and listen to the music. "I don't think I've ever seen a more serene face." Evan stared at him.

"Serene! Imagine what you'd get for it? I didn't see any security, did you? Fancy keeping a king's ransom in some shabby old temple in a back alley!" Mr Pringle sighed.

"They have a different set of values here. I'm shamefully ignorant, I admit, but their religion obviously brings tranquillity rather than greed. Perhaps theirs is a better way?" Evan's eyes were suddenly hard.

"You know something? All that'll disappear the minute someone works out it's worth his while to nick the thing, bet you anything you like." Mr Pringle wasn't a gambling man and such an attitude disturbed him.

"I'm sad to hear you say so."

"Well, I like it here." Mavis pushed away her empty plate. "I like the people, the place—the food's smashing. It's been a lovely day so don't let's spoil it." Evan twirled the stem of his glass.

"It's OK for some . . . I know too much about poverty." Mr Pringle thought it prudent not to hear.

"I do wish you'd let me take your photo, Evan," Mavis protested. "I wanted to show them at The Bricklayers: 'Look what I managed to pick up—and he never even asked for a tip!' "

"No way." Evan was sunny again. "By the time you two get back you'll have forgotten about me. Holidays are like that. Hope the ones I took of you come out all right, though."

36

"Give me your address anyway." Mrs Bignell scrabbled in her bag for a pen. "I want to send you a postcard when we get to Australia." Mr Pringle listened indulgently. He agreed with Evan, theirs was an ephemeral acquaintanceship, then he chided himself; he hadn't allowed for Mavis's kind heart. She wouldn't forget the boy.

The steward dictated an address in Carmarthen. "I've got a place near the airport," he explained, "but I haven't been there long. The postman sometimes forgets I live there, so I send most of my mail home to Mam. She looks after it."

"I won't send a rude one then." Mavis winked. "Not if your Ma's going to read it first." Evan picked up Ben's photo from among the debris on the table.

"This the kid you're hoping to find? What amazing eyes. Looks a bit skinny, though."

"Poor little mite," Mavis agreed. "Always in and out of hospital, the accidents he's had. Let's hope Australia has done him some good after all. Now what was your aunty's address in Sydney?" Mr Pringle groaned, silently. Not more vanished relatives! She must've caught his mood because she said quickly, "Evan was expecting to go to Australia. He didn't realize he'd only get as far as Bangkok because of the charter."

"It's aunty's birthday." The steward was apologetic. "If you could send the parcel for me, that's all. It'll be too late by the time I get to England—and I promised Mam. Here—" He pulled out a five-pound note "—this is to cover the postage—I insist," for Mr Pringle was beginning to murmur a protest. "Take a taxi from the hotel to the post office, there should be sufficient. I've already addressed it—it's just a few books, if Customs want to know," he added, "some paperbacks aunty can't buy in Australia." Then to Mavis, "Thanks again for helping me out."

"That's all right, dear, thank *you* for a lovely day!" Wine and exercise had left Mrs Bignell feeling mellow.

"Well—" Evan looked at his watch "—if I'm to make that five a.m. call . . ." He rose and stretched out his hand, "Thank you again." Mr Pringle shook it politely, mindful that it was the steward who had found them a guide and organized the day. He must stop feeling jealous of the young, it was the worst sin the old could commit. He watched with scarcely a qualm as Evan kissed Mavis's hand.

"D'you want to give me the parcel now?" she asked.

"If it's not too much trouble?"

"Of course not. Back in about five minutes, dear."

On his own, Mr Pringle listened to the music. The fountains rose and fell to a melody he recognized vaguely as of his own time and culture, plaintive but insidious. Was that all they could offer this beautiful land? Nothing but songs extolling a greed for sex? It seemed a poor return for all the pleasure he'd had today.

Chapter Six

They were lethargic next morning, heat had sapped the desire to do
more sightseeing. "Just a little stroll," Mavis declared; "that'll be
enough for me. Then a rest before we leave for the station."

As they stood on a footbridge above Petchburi Road watching
the lunch-hour chaos below she said, "He'll be half-way home by
now."

"Who, Evan?" Mr Pringle looked at his watch and tried to
grapple with time zones. "More than that, I think. He could be
landing soon." Mavis sighed.

"Odd, isn't it? On the other side of the world already and last
night we were all having dinner together. Nice boy . . . lovely
manners. Comes of having a Welsh mother, I expect." Mr Pringle
wasn't really listening. He was more interested in the lack of
aggression among Thai drivers despite the pressure of traffic. Had
London once been the same? He couldn't remember it.

"I need to go back and finish my packing," he reminded her.

"I did it for you while you were in the shower, dear. Let's find
somewhere that sells sandwiches. They warned us in the brochure
there might not be much food on the train."

There was only one coach-load for Bangkok station, the rest of the
charter having dispersed to Bali or, in the case of a quiet grey-
haired group, to one of the graveyards on the River Kwai. They
were, Mrs Bignell discovered, the only additional people accompanying the Friends of Nuclear Energy. She looked at her
fellow travellers disparagingly.

"Don't they look seedy? They wouldn't influence me—I don't
know about the Australians." Mr Pringle watched them climb
aboard. It was certainly true the group had a scruffy air and an
obstinacy concerning dress he'd observed before among the

39

British abroad. It was as if patriotism demanded they cling to flannel, collars and ties in spite of the tropical climate, to demonstrate a national identity. Unfortunately it made them a hot, unprepossessing bunch.

At the station, their leader checked off names on a list. "Pringle and ah . . . Bignell. Not members of our party, I think?" There was more than a hint of condescension.

"We're definitely not friends of nuclear energy if that's what you mean, so don't try and give us any badges," said Mavis firmly. The leader stared at her in horror.

"Madam—that information is classified!"

She returned his gaze, blandly. "Then you've had a little leak, haven't you? One of the sort your lot are always claiming can't happen."

It had taken longer than usual to pay in the bar takings at Crew Briefing because there was a queue. By the time Evan had finished and reached his old Metro in the pound, he was bone-weary. It was not only the time change with skin and mouth dry after hours of flying: he felt drained because of the irrevocable step he'd taken; there was no going back.

He hadn't slept during those few hours before the call came in Bangkok. He'd tried to convince himself there'd be no risk; nothing could go wrong. Mavis would do what he'd asked. By the time *they* found out, she'd be half-way across Australia.

Dare he risk driving to the cottage and having a shower? He desperately wanted to, and a pot of tea? No, no—for God's sake, what if he arrived too late? He had to get to London before those damn civil servants disappeared for the weekend. Panic made him grip the steering wheel—steady, steady . . . !

Evan threaded his way on to the roundabout and turned east along the M4. He wasn't going to the police. That would mean giving himself up. He'd be banged up in a cell as soon as he told them what he'd done and that would be the end.

But in Whitehall there was a department set up to protect citizens who found themselves in difficulties abroad. A liaison of civil servants to negotiate between the innocent and those foreign powers whom they'd inadvertently offended. If anything went wrong, Evan comforted himself with the thought, that department would rescue Mavis Bignell. Any niggling doubts he pushed to one side.

He would admit to them that he'd agreed to be a courier—"played along" was the way he'd describe it. He'd hand over the photographs as proof. It was essential to make them believe everything had been deliberate, from the beginning; a single-handed attempt to bring drug peddlers to justice. This last act involving Mavis Bignell was, he'd claim, born out of expediency just as he was preparing to make a clean breast of it. Until he'd forced the gang to send the photographs, he'd got no proof and once he had that, one false move and he was a dead man. The knowledge that he still could be made the sweat break out once more.

He'd hand over some of the money, that couldn't be avoided. He'd admit to three trips, that was all . . . he hadn't been foolish enough to pay all of it into the bank.

Everything depended on convincing Whitehall to set the necessary trap in Australia. Until that was sprung, Evan Jones would need police protection round the clock. A "safe house", that was what it was called. Somewhere with a bed where he could sleep for twelve hours!

He was breathing more easily, concentrating because of his tiredness, but with each mile growing in confidence. Stick to the plan, forget everything else; it was going to be all right.

The leader of the FONEs, a physicist, was called Protheroe. Once on the train, Mr Pringle managed to convince him Mrs Bignell meant no real harm by her remark. He bought the man a warm beer in the old-fashioned restaurant car with its windows wide open to the humid air.

Protheroe's shoulders were bowed down by the thousand and one irritations caused by herding colleagues plus their spouses on a good-will mission. Mr Pringle was sympathetic. He told of similar tribulations caused by citizens engaged in tax evasion. The physicist recognized a kindred spirit.

"One can't be too careful, Pringle. You see we haven't revealed the purpose of the mission to the Australian government, not yet. I

41

don't mind telling you, that good lady of yours gave me a fright when she came out with the name like that. The trouble is, some of the wives in our party—they don't understand what the word 'secret' means."

"I don't think Mrs Bignell told anyone else . . ." Mr Pringle wondered about Evan but dismissed the idea.

"Thank God the sightseeing part is nearly over," complained Protheroe. "Tackling the natives is going to be tough as it is. The Australians are so *childish* about all things nuclear." It took another beer before Mr Pringle could excuse himself and return to the icy cool of their sleeper.

Mavis and he sat facing each other on the brown vinyl seats, watching lush vegetation slide past. The train travelled at a leisurely speed enabling them to gaze their fill at villages built on stilts, with walkways over irrigation canals, fringed by traveller's palms.

Occasionally they ambled through a station that might have come from some pre-Beeching line: single-storey, low-roofed, cream-painted with a verandah. In one, a saffron-clad monk helped dispel any notion they were back among the shires.

At dusk they went over a level crossing where children guarding water buffalo waved to them, and Mavis sighed with pleasure. "Isn't it wonderful," she murmured, "all those rice paddies and rubber plantations." Truth to tell, Mr Pringle was finding mile after mile of it soporific but wouldn't dream of saying so. The beer had left him feeling drowsy.

She examined the sleeping arrangements. "When they unfold these bunks, that top one's going to be a bit too close to the air conditioning for comfort. You'd better sleep down below, in mine." She gave him a knowing look. "I've always fancied trying it on a train, haven't you, dear?"

My word, he thought, twice in two days! He'd do his best, a man couldn't do more.

It had been several weeks since Anthony Pelham-Walker had experienced his revelation of futility. He'd almost given up hope. Five months to go to retirement and still nothing. He lay awake wondering if he dare beg his Maker for a dispensation; some small

42

task that would give meaning to his life. They hadn't been in touch for years; had communications in that direction finally been severed?

But the boon was granted without a single prayer, delivered not by God's messenger but Crispin Sinclair. As he grasped its significance, Anthony Pelham-Walker felt his heart begin to pound.

Crispin wanted to scream; it was bad enough being caught just as he was leaving the office—but for Batman to sit reading the unwanted statement again and again . . .

"We should have handed him over rather than listen to him," Crispin said plaintively. "But the chap's Welsh. He charmed his way in then refused to budge until we'd taken it all down." Anthony Pelham-Walker looked up.

"What?"

"I'll telephone Scotland Yard, shall I?"

"Certainly not." No one was going to cheat him of this.

"I'm sorry, I don't quite follow . . . ?" Had Batman finally cracked?

"Jones came to us," Pelham-Walker insisted, "asking for our help—"

"But it's not ours to give, sir." Sinclair was shocked. "Quite frankly, the sooner we let the proper authorities have him, the better." He glanced furtively at his watch. He was going to miss the next train as well!

"These tourists, where are they now?" Crispin checked his notebook.

"Their train should reach Padang Besar in a couple of hours—which is why I really do feel we should contact the police."

"No!" Pelham-Walker was striding about the office. Crispin looked on helplessly.

"But what about the risk, sir? What else can we do?"

"Don't you realize what day it is, Sinclair, and the time?"

"Friday, sir. Twenty-seven minutes past six. Approximately."

"Exactly. We are the only ones left in Whitehall? Am I right?"

"Yes, sir, but in Scotland Yard there are lots of people—"

Anthony Pelham-Walker brushed this aside.

43

"He came to us," he repeated. "He wants *us* to intercede; that means you and I, Sinclair, or rather I alone. The matter is too delicate."

"Begging your pardon, sir, he wants us to act way outside our remit!" By way of reply, Anthony Pelham-Walker reached inside a drawer and flung his passport on to the desk.

"According to Jones's statement—" He picked up the paper again "—these tourists stay overnight in Penang before continuing to Singapore. After twenty-four hours there they fly to Sydney where Jones was due to hand over the package?"

"Yes." Crispin's eyes were drawn to the passport. What the hell was Batman up to? Forcing himself to look away he said, "Jones says he's made deliveries in Penang, Singapore and Sydney. Once he arrived there'd be a phone call to say where he should make the drop. They must have several couriers to keep the route supplied. Jones claims he doesn't know of anyone else but that's to be expected.

"In the normal way his roster for this trip would've included eight-hour stopovers at Abu Dhabi, Bangkok where he picked the stuff up—"

"From the dressing-table drawer in his hotel room," Anthony Pelham-Walker murmured. Crispin assumed this was a question.

"I think that has to be true, sir. Apparently, the crew are always allocated the same rooms in that particular hotel. Who better than a member of staff both to hide the stuff and keep tabs on the courier?" He took another furtive peek at his watch. "Don't you think—as time is not on our side, sir . . . ?" Anthony Pelham-Walker was once more engrossed in the statement.

"Jones states that he decided from the beginning to act—in the public interest—to bring these wicked men—"

"That's where the statement becomes a work of fiction, obviously," Crispin interrupted confidently. Pelham-Walker looked at him coldly.

"You think so? Tell me, is Jones not concerned for his own safety? After what he's done?"

"He's asked for police protection."

"He must have it, Sinclair. You must contact Scotland Yard and arrange it. As for the rest, that is down to me . . . What was the

44

name of that tourist again?" Crispin gaped. "The name?" Pelham-Walker repeated curtly.

"Oh . . . Mavis Hilda Bignell. Jones saw her passport. Look, sir, don't you consider we should simply contact the duty officer. . .?" To his dismay, Batman shook his head.

"We are the correct authority, Sinclair. This department was created for this type of contingency." Anthony Pelham-Walker leaned across, full of enthusiasm. "It's why we must act!"

"You mean—send a telex?"

"Act, man, act! What good is a piece of paper? It didn't help Chamberlain."

"You don't mean . . . ?" Crispin Sinclair allowed the full horror to show on his face.

"Book me on a flight that connects with the one those tourists are catching out of Singapore."

"But what d'you intend to do?" Batman was transformed. He barked his thoughts like an actor playing Monty.

"Assuming this woman gets through . . . no reason why she shouldn't . . . Jones stresses she's no idea what's in the package, she'll behave innocently enough . . . She'll need protection only when she reaches Australia. That's when *they* will try and relieve her of it and where *we* will be waiting."

"We?"

"I. Plus the Australian police, of course. Notify them of my ETA and that we require their co-operation." He's loopy, thought Crispin, he's blown a gasket, gone round the twist, nutty as a fruit cake!

"Oh, and Sinclair—" Batman was wagging a finger "—that message must be in code. Any murmur outside these four walls and I shall hold you responsible."

It was late morning and the sun was at its zenith. It beat down from above and was reflected upwards from the concrete platform at Padang Besar. They waited, all of them crowded into the one small patch of shade by the Immigration shed. They had been told to leave the train while compartment doors were locked and Customs officers worked their way along the carriages, examining the luggage.

45

The heat was so fierce it had stopped all conversation; that, and the monster poster that faced them. Underneath a six-foot-tall hangman's noose, against a black background, the message was simple:

BE FOREWARNED
DEATH FOR DRUG TRAFFICKERS
UNDER MALAYSIAN LAW.

The same words, printed in red, showed up starkly on the immigration forms as, one by one, they shuffled closer to the metal grille to hand these over in exchange for the return of their passports. Protheroe, his head protected by a hanky, called out the names. "Mr G D H Pringle . . . Mrs M Bignell . . ."

They moved forward, pressing against the grille to be out of the sun. Official faces smiled in welcome. Mr Pringle smiled back and accepted his passport gratefully, tucking it away in his pocket. "Bignell, please . . . ?"

It wasn't the Immigration officer speaking, it was one of the uniformed Customs men. He called out again as he stepped down from one of the carriages, "Which one is Bignell?" Slung from his shoulder was Mavis's overnight bag. The zipper was undone; on top where everyone could see it was a square brown-paper parcel with an address in Byers Street, Enfield, Sydney NSW. "Open this, please."

Blood pounded through Mr Pringle's veins. The moment in time was frozen as everything became dreadfully clear. Something danced in front of his eyes, not spots but a hangman's noose over a gallows.

Ray Vincent was categorizing last year's house sales when the phone rang. It was the direct line. He heard the long-distance echo behind the familiar cough.

"It's OK, Janice, we can finish these later." As the girl glanced at the clock, he laughed. "Point taken. Why don't we tackle them first thing Monday?"

"Thanks, Ray." There was a swirl of skirt above the leather boots and she was gone.

46

Vincent murmured, "Hold on a moment," and listened. In the outer office there was the rustle of a mac, the word processor was switched off and the street door opened. As the Yale lock clicked shut, he murmured, "Yes?"

"Our reluctant friend didn't arrive at Singapore. His flight was changed."

"Shit!"

"Deal with it." That was all. Ray Vincent pushed the button for the dialling tone and tapped out a number from memory.

"Crew information?"

Evan had never felt so weary or exhilarated. They'd believed him, it was going to work! Provided Mavis wasn't picked up—and why should she be?—he was safe!

It was dusk; he switched on his headlights. He couldn't remember if he'd reset his watch when they landed this morning but what did that matter? It was nearly over.

The man in Whitehall had taken his statement then gone away to consult someone, presumably. He'd returned to ask for the photographs then, after another interminable wait, came back in a temper and told Evan to make himself scarce.

Excitement confused Evan. Had the man been sympathetic? He couldn't be sure. They were about the same age, him and the Whitehall bloke, but what different worlds . . . He shrugged as he thought of the sophistication and expensive suit. The man hadn't been particularly interested when Evan described where he'd be hiding. For Whitehall had been unable to offer protection even though Evan pleaded desperately.

"Go somewhere safe," the man kept saying. "Go sick, stay out of sight, you'll be perfectly all right. Leave a number where we can contact you."

Evan told him he'd be staying with Mam and gave the number of the chippy. He'd tried to make the product of a public school understand that in their street it was the only telephone. He'd had to repeat the number—excitement made his accent incomprehensible. Now he was on his way home, the safest place he knew.

He'd picked up details of his next trip at Crew Briefing: Cairo on the sixteenth. He'd collect a few things from the cottage then drive

47

through the night to Carmarthen. On the sixteenth, if Whitehall gave him the go-ahead, he'd drive directly to Heathrow and pick up the flight. After tonight, he'd avoid the cottage like the plague until he knew it was safe, until he read in the papers they'd picked up the men in Sydney; that's when he'd be sure. In Whitehall, they'd promised to keep him informed. That chap had been decent; the more he thought about it, the more Evan was sure. It was going to be all right; he was free!

"What I still can't understand," said Mavis, "is why they were all such old books."

"So you said before," Mr Pringle answered shortly. Terror and heat had taken its toll. They had finished their train journey at Butterworth and dragged their cases the short sticky walk to the terminal. Now, on an ancient crowded boat belonging to the Star Ferry line, they were crossing to the island of Penang.

Mr Pringle hadn't had the courage to confess his imaginings at the Customs Post. As the wrapping had been torn off the parcel, he'd fainted clean away. People assured one another loudly it was because of the heat but when he'd opened his eyes, expecting to find Mavis in handcuffs, she'd been splashing him with eau-de-Cologne. Beside her on the platform was a pile of worn paperbacks. After that, all Mr Pringle wanted to do was howl and disappear into a big dark hole—if only he could control his heartbeat!

Mavis waited placidly for him to recover. It was his own fault, she'd warned him often enough. At his age, she'd told him, you can't expect to be at it every night but whenever they went on holiday—would he listen? No, he would not. Serve him right. She hadn't felt like it in Bangkok because she'd been tired; she'd wanted the first time to be when they were on the train because it was so much more romantic. Like Somerset Maugham, she thought vaguely.

It was quite dark as Evan turned off the motorway and threaded his way through the lanes. He began to wonder if he would have left Singapore by now, had he been on the scheduled flight? It was too much effort to work out the time difference.

He looked hazily at the clock on the dash and noticed the red light shining fixedly. Christ, he must need petrol badly; it'd begun to flicker on his way into London. It made him nervous, wasting more time. He joked feverishly with the garage cashier as if needing to impress her with the memory of his visit.

He bumped down the track to the two cottages and switched off the engine. His next-door neighbour, an air-traffic controller at West Drayton, hadn't returned because his lights weren't on. Evan toyed with the idea of waiting in his car until the man reappeared but that was stupid. His neighbour might be working nights, not due back until the morning.

He must stop being twitchy. Grab clean jeans and some sweaters then drive like the clappers until he got to Wales. Brisk, eager to be on his way, Evan unlocked the front door.

Anthony Pelham-Walker told the car to wait; there was just enough time to pack a case before driving to Heathrow. As he approached the front door, he could see the lights were on; Fiona was having one of her parties.

Years ago the pretext had been furthering his career but once she'd realized she'd married a failure, Fiona dropped all pretence and invited her own friends instead.

It seemed to Anthony Pelham-Walker that every evening he returned to find his drunken wife making a fool of herself. He recognized it was partly his fault; she was disappointed in him. He hugged to himself the thought that all that was about to change, but as he ran downstairs, suitcase in hand, he felt compelled to drop one tiny hint. He was no longer the dull fellow she railed at, day after day; he had become—operational.

"I'm going outside, Fiona. I may be gone . . . some time."

"Well, piss off then!"

Chapter Seven

The elegant room in Penang, with its pale grey walls and silky bedcover, soothed them both. Below their private balcony the swimming pool beckoned. It didn't take Mr Pringle five minutes to get into his bathers but Mavis was trying on her new costume.

As he waited, he picked up one of the paperbacks that had shortened his life expectancy; a copy of *The Mousetrap* with a picture of the original London cast on the cover. He examined another by Nevil Shute. "I wouldn't have thought there was any problem buying these in Australia?"

"Neither would I," Mavis called from the bathroom.

"What d'you intend doing with them?"

"Sending them, like I promised. I've kept the wrapping paper and that's got the address on it. It shouldn't be difficult to parcel them up again . . ." She emerged. "What d'you think?"

"I say!" She'd talked about the bathing suit, described it as "an investment"—that meant she'd paid too much for it but all the same . . . "My word, Mavis!" Clinging fabric sculpted her body, lifting the proud breasts, emphasizing the surprisingly small waist, and burst into a cascade of emerald-green pleats over her milk-white thighs. Mavis smoothed the garment, satisfied.

"I think it was worth it."

"Worth it? You're a proper bobby-dazzler in that thing! Come on. I want to show you off to Protheroe."

In her painfully clean kitchen, Mrs Hardie made the first pot of tea of the day and let it brew. She took pride in her housekeeping. It was terrible the way Linda went about things. That mug, for instance. Ever since her daughter moved back in, Mrs Hardie had shut her eyes against its vulgarity—a naked woman's body with a handle on the back—disgusting! Mrs Hardie always used pretty

50

china with a delicate honeysuckle design. It added to the flavour of the tea.

Pulling her sash tight, she picked up both mug and cup. Her quilted cotton dressing-gown was ankle length but the synthetic lining drooped lower. Taking care, Mrs Hardie began to climb the stairs. Behind her the letter-box snapped shut. A gaudy postcard, possibly from Mavis Bignell, fluttered down. Without thinking, Mrs Hardie turned, caught her foot and fell.

Scalding liquid soaked the quilting and burned her shoulder and breast. She lay very still, too sick to cry out, the picture of a Thai temple dancer on the floor beside her.

"Ma . . . ? Oh God, what've you done!" Linda looked down on the fragile heap, one leg bent under at such an awkward angle. There was a flurry of cheap nylon lace as she ran downstairs. "What happened?"

"It was an accident. Ah!" Linda had attempted to lift her. "My leg!" moaned Mrs Hardie, "I think it's broken. I should've gone to that warden place when they offered . . . they've got no stairs there."

Crispin Sinclair's lover, a Grade Three at the FO, was having an extremely bad time. There was no doubt Big Bear was in one of his moods. Their weekend had been ruined. Big Bear got home too late for them to leave for the country and after that he'd spent the rest of the evening on the phone.

"What I bloody well can't understand is who's behind this charter," Crispin grumbled petulantly. "It sounds as if it's organized by British Nuclear Fuels but when I spoke to them, they denied all knowledge of it."

"Is it important?"

"Of course it is! Batman's on his way to Ockerland to join it. I'm supposed to send him the details—The Friends of Nuclear Energy, whoever they're supposed to be."

"Oh, you mean the FONEs." His Grade Three lover paused, the slice of toast half-way to his mouth.

"You've heard of them?"

"Yes but it's classified . . ." But his clearance was lower than Crispin's so it didn't take long.

Mavis sat in the shade by the pool with her new friend. They'd got as far as first names and photographs. "This is the little boy we're hoping to find while we're out there." Jean Protheroe resumed her glasses.

"You don't see many with rickets nowadays," she said. Mavis examined the photo more closely.

"His grandma never mentioned rickets."

"I think I'm right. I used to do health visiting . . . This is our conservatory, Mavis. Kenneth said 'Blow the cost, you only live once. Order whatever takes your fancy.'"

"Very nice!" The late Herbert Bignell had never made such an offer in his life.

At the deep end, Mr Pringle was equally fascinated by Protheroe's strategy for dumping nuclear waste.

"You say there are suitable sites already out there?"

"Yes, plenty. Quite big ones. What's more," Protheroe said cheerfully, "they're already contaminated. Where we tested the bomb in the fifties—remember?"

"Ah, yes . . . but doesn't the Australian government want Britain to go in and clean them up?" Protheroe shook his head vigorously.

"No point, none whatsoever. Cost us millions of pounds to do that—and why bother when we *need* somewhere for all our bally waste."

"But," Mr Pringle began tentatively, "won't the Australians object?"

"Thought of that." Protheroe was positively jovial. "Came up with a solution the Australians are bound to find acceptable." He whispered in Mr Pringle's ear, "Give the contaminated land back to the Aborigines!" Mr Pringle was mystified. "The black fellas are always demanding land," Protheroe explained. "They claim it was stolen from them in the first place."

"Yes, but surely . . . ?" Mr Pringle couldn't think of a tactful way of asking the question. "Won't there be a danger of—radiation?"

"Possibly." Protheroe measured his words judiciously. "One can't be one hundred per cent safe whatever the precautions,

52

with nuclear waste." Mr Pringle saw he'd been misunderstood.

"What I meant was if the land is radioactive already and the Aborigines take it over, won't the Australian government be worried?"

"I doubt it." Protheroe was hearty. "I doubt it very much indeed. They never have been before."

Mr Pringle was speechless, but Protheroe called back as he splashed across the pool, "Killing two birds with one stone *and* making a profit—wouldn't be surprised if that isn't worth a gong in the birthday honours!"

In Farnham, Ray Vincent sat very still. Moonlight spilled over the desk and on to the floor. He'd have to leave the darkened office soon or Adele would begin to wonder. There was the telephone call as well, to New York, but for the moment everything was too much effort.

He'd called in here to scrub himself clean and shred his shirt and slacks. The scraps were in a box which he'd burn with the garden rubbish tomorrow. The light-weight jacket and trousers he'd changed into didn't keep him warm. Despite his efforts his body trembled in another spasm.

He was out of condition. He'd needed a Scotch before he left, another tumblerful when he got back. Automatically he reached to put the bottle back when he noticed the stains on the label. They were black under the moonlight but daylight would turn them red. He needed to stuff the bottle in the box with the rest. He hadn't the strength, his arms were leaden. "Come on, come on!" he muttered. The trouble was, the business wasn't finished.

"Your mother's worried about going back to your house which has stairs, that's the problem. She keeps saying she's had the offer of sheltered accommodation and wants to go there while she's still got the chance. Frankly, my dear, I'd jump at it if I were you. It's one of the few remaining ones that are run by the council. The rates are quite reasonable."

"No thank you, Sister. I'd much rather Mum came back home. I'll look after her."

Hospital visiting was nearly over and the sister still had her report to finish. All she should be concerned about was how soon they could discharge a patient. There was no reason to keep Mrs Hardie in provided she would be cared for.

"Are you sure you can manage? I know she's not heavy but your mother will need help with the lavatory for several days yet."

"Oh, yes." Linda forced herself to smile. "I'm sure she'd rather be at home. Among her own bits and pieces." Sister glanced at her watch.

"I'll talk to doctor about it." Most daughters would leap at the chance of subsidized, sheltered accommodation for a widowed mother. Should she point out the advantages once more? This woman looked as if she was the type for boyfriends rather than a stay-at-home. The bell rang for the end of visiting, putting a stop to their conversation.

Chapter Eight

The train arrived in Singapore at night and passengers queued to file past a dog behind a grille at the end of the platform. Three of them arrived together: Mr Pringle, Mavis and a student with a back pack. The dog barked suddenly. Mavis jerked to a halt and the other two cannoned into one another. The dog barked again.

"I shouldn't make a fuss of it," Mr Pringle warned, "it's probably been trained to bite." He watched in surprise. The dog was up on its hind legs, pawing frantically at the grille. "Hello? What's it doing that for?" Customs officers converged and within seconds the contents of the student's back pack were spread on the counter. Delicacy made Mr Pringle hold back; the young man's private life was no concern of his but an officer beckoned impatiently.

"I think they want us to go through, dear." They shuffled forward, close to the mesh. The wheels on Mrs Bignell's suitcase caught in the concrete and Mr Pringle bent to free them. Above his head the student was saying "There's only two left, for Chrissake!" as squashed sweet-smelling cigarettes were discovered in a jacket pocket.

Inches away from Mr Pringle's face, the dog barked frantically, saliva dripping from its jaws. He was offended. "I like dogs," he said, slightly hurt. He followed Mavis on to the concourse as the student plus back pack were ushered through an ominous-looking unmarked door.

In the taxi to the Orchard Hotel he was full of memories. "I used to have a tortoise when I was a boy . . . now those were difficult creatures to train."

"Perhaps that dog was hungry," said Mavis. "I know I am."

55

Singapore was bursting with wealth, full of fantastic buildings that looked as if they'd been put up only yesterday. After Bangkok, the contrast was startling. They left the bags and went in search of food. Orchard Road was full of skyscrapers and opulent restaurants. "D'you think we can afford to eat here?" Mavis shouted above the traffic.

"If we find somewhere modest . . . A little snack perhaps?"

Inside a hamburger bar, Mr Pringle grappled with the exchange rate. "Thank goodness we're not staying long!"

"Tomorrow morning we're going on a short tour of the city, including Raffles, then straight to the airport."

"Fine. I wouldn't mind an early night, either." But when they returned to the hotel, it was full of police: the Protheroes' room had been burgled.

Next morning, Mr Pringle asked, "Was much taken?" He'd felt diffident about joining the rest commiserating with the Protheroes over breakfast.

"Joan's not sure," said Mavis. "Everything was in such a mess. All their clothes chucked on the floor and trampled on—she was terribly upset. Hang on a minute, dear, I want to see how he does this."

They were in Raffles Hotel; they'd watched a scratchy video of the Japanese surrender set to Elgar. Now, in the Tiffin Room, an equally elderly bartender was demonstrating a gin sling. Mavis took a professional interest.

"Not that we have much call for those in The Bricklayers," she sighed, "but you never know."

On the aircraft to Sydney she had more news. "They've sorted themselves out and Joan doesn't think anything's been taken after all—isn't it odd?"

"Very. I bet Protheroe's upset."

"Oh, he is. He's convinced there's a mole from Greenpeace trying to sabotage their mission."

In England, there was another little leak of the sort that couldn't happen when the phone rang in Kenneth Protheroe's office. The voice was warm, Australian and male.

"Hi, this is Lenny. Coach captain on Wallaby Tours—'Hop with us from State to State' and all that. I'm phoning from Sydney, New South Wales, love." The amber nectar of his tone reminded Protheroe's secretary, Miss Wilson, of sunshine and everything else that was missing from her life.

"Yes?" she answered cautiously.

"Listen, love, this FONE party—any idea what it stands for?" Lenny asked innocently. "You see we got this logo on the side of all our coaches, it's a wallaby, right? And he's talking to a duck-billed platypus—and the point is, in the balloon sticking out of the wallaby's mouth, we like to put somethin' about our passengers, right?"

Miss Wilson understood. Not only that, Lenny's phone call had interrupted dark thoughts as to why her boss had been too mean to invite her to join the junket. There'd been plenty of spare seats.

"Last month we had 'On hire to the Rotarians of Toowoomba'," Lenny continued cheerfully. "We do it with big red stick-on letters, see, and I thought wouldn't it be nice if we could do somethin' like that for the Poms." He waited.

Serve Protheroe right, thought Miss Wilson savagely. Why shouldn't she be out there with this sexy Paul Hogan character instead of sitting here in a dingy office? There was a whistle in the earpiece. Minutes were ticking by on Wallaby Tours' phone bill. "Hi, darlin', you still there?"

No one had applied that word to Miss Wilson for years. "Have you a pen?" she asked.

In Macquarie Street, Kev asked, "Do you know what this is all about?" He waved the telex. Charlie shrugged.

"Some Pommie bastard comin' out on a free trip."

"Yeah, but why this particular bastard? This . . . Pelham?"

"Christ knows."

"And why," said Kev Macillvenny, aggrieved, "does the stupid so-and-so insist we turn out to meet him on a Sunday? Doesn't he know we got taxis in Australia? And a five-day week?"

*

57

Linda smiled brightly as she pulled up a chair. The metal legs scraped the polished vinyl. "I've brought you some magazines." They weren't the sort Mrs Hardie liked, with knitting patterns and recipes. "You'll never guess—I've managed to get the garden weeded ready for when you come out. It looks really nice now. You'd miss not having a garden, you know you would."

"I don't want no more stairs, Linda."

"Look, supposing I ask them at the bank . . . see if I can get a loan and have a lav put in downstairs, will that do?"

"But why can't I have a little flat? Sister says I'd get priority because of my accident. On the ground floor."

"Listen, Mum." Linda's voice trembled a little. She leaned forward so that other patients couldn't hear. "I don't want to leave while there's a chance Ben might come back. I want his room to be there, ready. I don't want the authorities pointing the finger, saying I haven't got anywhere suitable. You know they would if I was living in a one-bedroomed place. That's all I could afford if you give the house up."

"Why didn't you tell me that was the reason?" Mrs Hardie asked in surprise. Linda sniffed.

"I didn't realize you were that serious about the warden place, I suppose. Look, I'm sorry if things have been, you know . . . I'll try a bit harder when you come home, all right? Oh, this arrived today." Linda reached in her shoulder bag. "Mavis must be nearly at Sydney by now."

His private phone rang. There was the familiar echoey cough. "Just a minute." Ray Vincent closed the door to the outer office. "Yes?" His fleshy face was drawn, he'd lost his confident air.

"He didn't tell us everything . . ." Vincent swallowed. "They couldn't find it, Ray . . ." The caller waited for him to speak but he remained silent.

"We've told 'Parker' to meet you there . . ." This was a shock. Vincent tried to sound calm.

"OK."

"Make sure he tells you this time. . . before you deal with him." There was a click then the tone, so much louder than the

58

whisper had been. Ray Vincent lit a cigarette and wasted over a minute smoking it before he opened the door and called, "Going to see a client about a property, Janice. Back by lunch time."

Chapter Nine

They flew in low over Botany Bay which seemed a bad omen. After they'd taxied to a halt, a granite-faced native leapt on board and sprayed them with tear-gas against contamination. Mr Pringle wondered nervously what other welcoming rituals awaited them in God's own country.

They passed through the usual formalities but Mrs Bignell's thoughts were elsewhere. As they emerged on to the concourse, he had to ask twice if she could remember the instructions concerning their coach.

"Oh, sorry, dear . . . I wasn't paying attention. According to the brochure it should be parked somewhere to the left once we get outside." She hesitated as if about to speak again but Mr Pringle was already moving towards the exit.

Lenny and Pete were on their hunkers in the shade. Their two vehicles proudly sported the new device. Against sparkling white paintwork, each wallaby told each platypus:

WE'RE TAKING
THE FRIENDS OF NUCLEAR ENERGY
ROUND AUSTRALIA!

Protheroe was the last to emerge. Others stood aghast. "Oh, no!" he cried. "No, no, no! Take that down at once!" Pete paused in rolling a cigarette.

"Isn't that typical?" he said in disgust. "All that work and them Poms aren't even grateful."

From the shelter of the building, Anthony Pelham-Walker watched them. He'd had plenty of time to regret his impetuosity. Between the Middle East and India he'd begun to draft his resignation on the back of a sick-bag but now, for the first time, he felt his spirits begin to lift. It was all turning out just as Evan Jones had prophesied, so why worry? Mavis Hilda Bignell had gone through Customs without any fuss. There she was now, climbing aboard the coach. All he had to do was tag along—and accept the plaudits afterwards. The Australian police would deal with any unpleasantness; he would simply sit back and wait.

He came to his senses; the first coach was ready to leave. Where was his own transport? Briefcase tucked under his arm, he stepped out from beneath the canopy.

Inside the Toyota, Kev Macillvenny said in disbelief, "That can't be him, can it? Not that dapper little nut?" Charlie groaned. "Strewth! You gotta be jokin'?"

"Only one way to find out . . ." Kev heaved his bulk out of the car and strode across. "Mornin'. You Pelham? Hear you decided to pay us a little visit."

Anthony Pelham-Walker stared: shirt-sleeves? When the man was on duty? "I gather Sinclair managed to contact you," he said coldly. "Have you a car? We need to follow that coach."

The voice, like the attitude, was public-school insensitive, designed to put down all who heard it. It made Kev's toes curl and the hairs on his forearms bristle. "How 'bout puttin' me in the picture, Pelham? Just what the hell's goin' on?"

Pete and Lenny, supervised by Protheroe, removed some of the lettering. The sign now read:

WE'RE TAKING

THE

ROUND AUSTRALIA!

Pete was still resentful. "You lot don't have to worry 'bout secrets, not in Sydney. We know all about Pommie spies, we gotta book on the subject—"

"Once and for all, we are not members of MI5!" hissed Protheroe. Pete looked round the sweaty, travel-stained group.

"They should've told you back home, we don't *need* no more convicts—" Lenny grabbed his arm.

"Cool it, will you!" He gave Protheroe a tight, brief smile. "If you'd like to join your good lady, we'll get started," and shoved Pete towards the other coach.

"How was I to know he got no sense of humour?" demanded Pete. "Calls himself a Friend, don't he?"

In the Toyota, Anthony Pelham-Walker finished his explanation tiredly, "In short, a passenger aboard that first coach has, unknown to her, two kilos of heroin in her luggage."

"Bloody hell! And you let her take the risk of travelling with it?"

"Justifiable, in my opinion," he said defensively. "As you can see, she hasn't been picked up. Look out, they're off!" At the wheel, Charlie squirmed.

"Mister, we ain't rookies, you know." He slid into the line of traffic.

"What I don't understand, Pelham, is why you're here?" asked Kev. Truth to tell neither did Anthony Pelham-Walker any more. How could he explain to this huge man with the flabby belly the blinding self-knowledge that had brought him so low, or the certainty thirty-six hours ago that this voyage would bring fulfilment?

As a partial truth, could he plead extenuating circumstances? As it had been after four p.m. on a Friday, Whitehall had been empty and he the only suitable person available? Better not; that information was privileged.

"Why weren't we notified through the normal channels?" Kev persisted. "All we got to do is keep tabs on this lady and pick the guy up when he shows, right? Do we know anythin' else?"

"I've given you all the information we were able to glean," Pelham-Walker said curtly. "Don't let that woman out of your sight and we should learn the rest for ourselves."

Charlie smarted at the clipped authoritative tone: "Yes, sir!"

On the seventh floor of the Koala Hotel, Mr Pringle stood on the balcony, enchanted. "You can just see Sydney Harbour bridge—look!"

"Yes . . ." Mavis was unpacking their suitcases and sorting out

62

laundry, but her thoughts were elsewhere. "You remember that dog, the one in Singapore?"

"What about it?"

"Do they always bark like that whenever there's the slightest trace of something?" A tiny cloud, no bigger than a man's hand, threatened Mr Pringle's sky.

"Why d'you ask?"

"When Evan gave me that parcel of books for his aunty, he remembered he'd brought her some flour as well. Stone-ground, wholemeal. You can't get it out here, apparently."

Mr Pringle felt dizzy suddenly and his knees began to buckle just as they had at the border post.

"Flour . . . ? Evan gave you . . . ?"

"Yes, in two plastic bags. I hadn't got room so I packed them with your things. The dog must have smelt it."

"Me! It was barking at me?" Mr Pringle was back inside the room, clinging to a chair.

"At your suitcase," she corrected. She caught sight of his face. "Don't get upset, dear, it's only flour. I didn't like to tell them their dog was barking over nothing, they might've been offended."

"Mavis—where's that 'flour' now?"

She lifted out his carefully folded shirts. There, at the bottom of the suitcase, between his sandals and *Hints On Camping For Scouts*, were two thick plastic bags, each full of a buff-coloured coarse powder. When he tried to speak, Mr Pringle found it difficult.

"How much would you say there was?"

Mavis considered. "They look the same as the ones I buy in Sainsbury's, about two pounds in each." She was puzzled by his expression. "You feeling all right, dear? Evan told me this flour was specially ground by someone he knew . . . his aunty has difficulty finding any."

"I'm not at all surprised," whispered G D H Pringle, hoarsely.

He'd been lying there so long, time had ceased to exist. Next door the air-traffic controller had come home and gone away again, back to West Drayton. There was no way Evan could attract his attention, his bonds were too tight.

The telephone wasn't the only red object in the room. There were splashes on the bare plaster and rolls of wallpaper. There was so much blood, a constant, dark red trickle, flies were buzzing in it.

He never knew there could be so much pain. His body was a screaming mass of agony. His brain couldn't cope, he kept fading in and out of consciousness, each shallow breath pushing death away ever more feebly. It couldn't continue: the will to live had nearly disappeared just as each gasp sucking in oxygen added to the endless pain, increasing the dark red wetness that oozed through the sodden rags.

He'd been so stupid, holding out like that—but then his plan had been stupid, too. He hadn't allowed for the snakelike speed of the organization when one of its members stepped out of line.

Evan had phoned his contact from Heathrow and recited the words he'd been practising all the way home. "When I realized I was on this terminator, I gave it to this tourist. She's tubby, reddish sort of hair, part of a charter travelling to Sydney. They're staying at the Koala—" His contact tried to interrupt at that point but Evan pressed on. "No, listen—*she* thinks I've given her a birthday present for my aunt—I gave her a parcel as well, with an address I copied off a pamphlet. All you've got to do is tell Sydney to collect the stuff. The charter arrives there Sunday so she can't post it." But his contact had phoned New York immediately instead.

It was so unfair! Only a few more minutes, he'd have been on his way to Wales. But the fair-haired bastard had got here first; he'd been waiting for him.

Throughout the tearing hacking at flesh and bone, Evan had clung to one idea: don't tell them everything. Keep something back. Give his saviours in Whitehall time to set the trap.

It wasn't saving him, it was costing him his life, that was the irony. They'd left him here to die. Slowly. Each time numbness forced him to move, the bleeding started up again, and the pain. . .

The axe was still there and beside it, thick with flies, two objects that looked like an old pair of gloves but which had once been a part of him.

And he'd thought he could cheat them! He was expendable. Three trips? There was no escape except death.

The door opened but Evan was no longer aware of sounds. It was the light across his face that made him open his eyes. There were two of them this time; the first, the one who'd done this to him, leaned over loosening the bonds. His pungent body odour was made even stronger by excitement. "Tell us the name this time or you'll die for it."

The second man was a thin black shape against the light. He giggled, high-pitched uncontrollable laughter. "We're going to show you what we do to naughty boys, holding out on us like that!" He moved closer and bent down so that Evan could see what he had in his hand—Oh, Mam! He'd tell them the name—Mavis Hilda Bignell—not that! Please!

It wasn't likely to be a long vigil outside the Koala Hotel but Kev and Charlie hadn't left anything to chance. They couldn't let this innocent Bignell dame risk her life. OK, so she'd been dumb, agreeing to help the steward like that, but she still had the right to protection.

It wasn't likely she'd be attacked. They'd wait until she and her partner were out somewhere then turn her room over. And boy, would that guy get a surprise! Charlie had three men posted on their floor.

Trouble was, this stupid Pom Pelham hadn't asked the steward the right questions. Charlie glowered at him in the driving mirror. Sleeping in the back, eyes closed, mouth open, twitching and making noises in his sleep. How could anyone criticize the Bignell lady when there were blokes like him in charge?

Charlie eased his spine against the back of the seat. One or two of the Poms had wandered past the parked car, guidebooks in hand. A notice in the foyer reminded all members of the FONE group their first meeting with the media was at six p.m.

Maybe whoever was coming to collect would assume Bignell would be attending it? Jesus, had they got to wait that long! Despite himself, Charlie yawned. He'd been planning a Sunday on the beach with an Esky full of cold Foster's.

From the back seat he suddenly heard the high plummy voice.

"There goes her friend, Pringle. According to Jones, he's not involved." They watched him wandering aimlessly, comparing the plan in his hand with the names of the streets.

"So why isn't she with him?" asked Kev.

"Perhaps she's taking a nap," said Pelham-Walker who badly wanted one himself.

"Oh, for Chrissake—look what he's carrying! Does he really think it'll rain?" Charlie's incredulity was loud.

"Why not? He's British," Pelham-Walker replied sharply.

She wasn't asleep, far from it, because they'd had a fearful row. Not the normal sort of tiff at all but a full-blown shouting match. Mavis still quivered at the memory. Despite the way the dog behaved in Singapore, she refused to accept Mr P's suggestion—it just wasn't possible, not with a nice boy like Evan.

She admitted to a soft spot: neither she nor Mr Pringle had children of their own and sometimes Mavis experienced maternal yearnings. On this occasion it had been those blue eyes, the way Evan had smiled at her and his lovely manners. He'd looked so smart that day in Bangkok. Mrs Bignell also had a weakness for short-sleeved stripy shirts with buttoned-down collars; Mr Pringle thought they were cissy.

But it wasn't as if Mr Pringle knew for certain—he was as ignorant as she was. Even when they made a tiny hole in one of the plastic bags, he couldn't be sure what the stuff was. Mavis was furious at the injustice of it. He hadn't let her sniff or taste, he said that would be far too dangerous. Admittedly the powder had got a funny sort of smell, but that was all. As neither of them went in for all that health food nonsense, who was to say it wasn't wholemeal stone-ground flour? She pushed aside her doubts. If it came to choosing between a barking mongrel or Evan Jones, the boy got her vote every time.

Mr P had marched off without apologizing, to get rid of it. He'd tried pouring some down the lavatory but the smell had made them queasy. It still lingered even though they'd opened the windows. Fortunately, there was a breeze which ought to do the trick. Mrs Bignell sat at the dressing-table pondering what to do next.

It was a nuisance, discovering it was a Sunday. There were postcards to send as well as the parcel. She looked at it, idly; Byers Street, Enfield, Sydney. "I wonder if they've got a tube or buses," she thought; then more vigorously, "If they have, I'll damn well take it there myself. His aunty's going to have one present on her birthday."

Mr Pringle wandered along Oxford Street and into an empty commercial quarter. He'd solved the problem of carrying the powder easily enough. He never travelled without a plastic mac. It was dun-coloured as its predecessor had been and the one before that. It had been bought at the same gents' outfitters he always patronized and if the design had varied one iota from the first mac Mr Pringle had purchased there in 1949, he would've been dumbfounded.

Like all the others, it had two large pockets with flaps. While Mrs Bignell scoffed, Mr Pringle put a plastic bag of 'flour' in each, securing the flaps with Sellotape from his camping kit. He'd refolded the mac neatly so the bulging pockets didn't show and announced his intention of taking a walk.

"If anyone asks, you can tell them I have the powder. That should ensure your safety." As he'd said this he'd felt incredibly noble.

"The only one who's likely to, is a little old Welsh lady who's been looking forward to a few wholemeal scones!" Mavis replied derisively.

At first, he'd toyed with the idea of dropping both bags into some municipal waste-bin, but dismissed it. Their fingerprints were all over the plastic and besides, that wouldn't destroy the stuff. Mr Pringle intended to get rid of it once and for all. As to what would happen when the traffickers found out . . . terror blurred his vision and made him stumble.

Anger had faded. He shouldn't have shouted. It wasn't in Mavis's nature to be disloyal and she believed in Evan Jones. If Mr Pringle hadn't been so tired—or frightened—he might have behaved more rationally. Fear dominated him now, making him glance back over his shoulder.

Those men in the car outside the hotel had given him a scare but they hadn't looked up. He'd armed himself with Mrs Bignell's camera to look more convincing as a tourist—if only his knees would stop wobbling! Perhaps the disguise was unnecessary? None of the passers-by turned to look. Mr Pringle concluded, not for the first time, that he really was the sort of chap other people ignored.

He passed an attractive modern building with a fountain, but hurried on when he saw it was a law court. He was descending rapidly towards the harbour. Between him and the water were trees, some sort of park. Mr Pringle walked into the Botanic Gardens, looking for somewhere to dispose of the powder, and ahead, against a perfect sky, he saw the unmistakable silhouette of the Sydney Opera House.

He was thirsty. It was hours since the last plastic cup of orange juice on the aircraft. He climbed the long flight of steps with the rest of the visitors and walked round the outside, admiring the silvery white domes despite his worries. On the far side, built out over the harbour, was an open-air café with tables, chairs and umbrellas. Children were eating ice-cream; their parents had pots of tea! In an instant Mr Pringle had joined the queue.

He sat at a table nearest the railing. If only he could empty the two bags into the harbour . . . but he could, couldn't he? Provided he was careful, what was there to stop him? The first seagull landed on the chair beside him.

It was the biggest bird he'd ever seen, until the next one joined it. Mr Pringle looked around; there were seagulls everywhere, huge, red-eyed monsters, swooping on titbits before customers had finished eating, arrogant bird-terrorists demanding ransoms.

Mr Pringle had never liked gulls. These terrified him. Never mind, they couldn't interfere. Summoning his courage, checking to make sure no one was watching, he took out his pocket-knife. He made a couple of slits through the pocket into the bag and began to shake the contents into the bay.

For her little outing, Mrs Bignell dressed in her floral two-piece. It was bright, herbaceous and gave her courage. She needed a bit of that, on her own in a strange town. But they'd been ever so helpful downstairs. One of the receptionists had taken her outside, and explained the route. Now she was on her way to the railway station at Circular Quay.

"That's her," said Pelham-Walker suddenly.

"You mean—that seed-packet lady?" Charlie asked.

"Yes."

Kev was older than Charlie and his tastes were more mature. He gave a deep-throated, appreciative growl.

"Look—she's off somewhere. We'll have to do something soon or we'll lose sight of her!" cried Pelham-Walker. Kev swallowed a retort.

"She's not got the stuff," he observed calmly. "That handbag's too tiddly, unless it's the parcel, but that looks too small as well—"

"She's getting away!"

"Think you can manage all by yourself, Charlie?" Kev smirked.

"Aw, shove off!"

Thank God none of the fellas were around to watch him tail a red-haired woman dressed in all the colours of the rainbow—it was embarrassing!

Enfield was further than Mavis anticipated. After the city, Sydney suburbs were monotonous, nothing but mile after mile of bungalows interspersed with shops. Some slums, too; she hadn't imagined there'd be any of those in Australia. Never mind, the weather was gorgeous.

Wanting to be friendly, Mavis remarked on this to a fellow passenger. The woman stared before saying as it had bloody well been the same for the past nine months, when did *she* think they could expect a decent drop of rain? Which just went to prove, thought Mavis philosophically, some people are never satisfied . . . All the same, her feet were killing her. She'd definitely take a taxi back.

The bus journey was more interesting. One or two of the shop-fronts reminded her of childhood holidays in south coast resorts, queuing up for Liguorice Allsorts. Apart from the weather, she could've been back in England—"Byers Street!"

There were single-storey dwellings as far as the eye could see. One or two were old-fashioned, clapboard built with faded ochre corrugated roofs. Mavis checked the number on her parcel—it was

69

the green-painted wooden one with that huge tree in the front garden. She walked up the three steps and, in the absence of a bell, rattled a rusty fly-screen.

Charlie watched. Mrs Bignell grew impatient. She checked the number against the one on the parcel and rattled the screen again. After another pause she walked along the verandah, peering in at the windows. "Lady, I hope you know what you're doin'," Charlie breathed. He waited until she'd disappeared round the side of the house before running like crazy to the end of the block, down the next street and vaulting over a locked gate—he was in the grounds of some clubhouse. Keeping low, Charlie covered the scrubby grass at speed and peered through a crack in the boundary fence. The Bignell woman was at the back of the property now, shouting through a half-open door. From where he stood, Charlie could hear: "Hallo? Are you there? I've brought a birthday present from Evan."

The breeze was much stiffer now, whirling rubbish in among the white tables and chairs. The Sunday visitors had gone, including the man who'd sat beside the rail. Only the waitresses remained to witness the kamikaze gulls. "Did you ever see anything like it? Look at that, I don't believe it! That bird dived straight into the water!"

"It must've broken its neck?"

"Yeah, I reckon—hey, what about those two, ripping each other's feathers out?"

"Jacqui, over there! On that table!"

"Oh, my God, what a mess!" As the sun went down leaving only cold and darkness behind, they continued to watch the mayhem, unable to tear themselves away.

Mr Pringle arrived back first. He sidled past the open door where Protheroe was conducting the meeting and into the lift. He too had a peace offering: a bottle of brandy. In their room, he found Mavis's note: "Gone to deliver parcel. Back soon."

G D H Pringle's blood ran chill in his veins. She still refused to accept the truth and had gone to meet those drug traffickers, face to face. Why, they might even now be torturing her! Images flashed past, each worse than the last, of all Mr Pringle had read of their dreadful practices. He must phone the police! If they went immediately, they might still be in time to save her. The address? What was the address on the parcel?

He seized the waste-basket but it was empty. Mrs Bignell had used the same wrapping after all. He racked his tired brain but couldn't remember any of it, not even the name of the street. As he stood there, impotent and helpless, tears began to fall. "Oh, Mavis . . . !"

Behind him, the door rattled impatiently. "Open up, dear. It's me, I'm back."

"She was out anyway."

"If she ever existed."

"I left the books. And a note."

"Did you mention the flour?" he asked anxiously. Mavis shook her head.

"I thought I'd better not, to be on the safe side. Mind you, I still don't believe you but I want to give Evan a chance. I'm going to write to him."

"All right." He'd agree to that, for the sake of reconciliation. Both were of an age and sensibility to know how important this was, not to be hurried nor glossed over in trite phrases.

Mr Pringle wondered again whether he should stress how cruel drug traffickers could be. Mavis looked so relaxed, sitting there in her pretty dress, drinking brandy, why spoil the mood? Besides, he could explain to the police if the need arose.

"It definitely wasn't flour," he insisted weakly. "You should've seen what it did to those gulls!"

"Yes, well, if anyone does turn up we can tell them there's a whole new lot of addicts flying round Sydney harbour."

"Mavis, it may not be that simple. Drug dealers are extremely ruthless! Two kilos of heroin or cocaine, whatever it was, must represent an enormous sum of money—"

"Serve them right," Mavis countered stoutly.

"Mavis—" His small stock of courage had ebbed away "—let's tell the police now, for our own protection?" She shook her head.

"No. We've got to give Evan a chance. I'm going to write to him

71

at his mam's and tell him if he has been led astray, he's got to go straight from now on. I'm not going to tell him we've got rid of the flour—he's more likely to take my advice if he thinks we've still got it and could hand it over to the authorities."

"I hope you're right." Mr Pringle was much less sanguine. "What did you say in your note?"

"I wrote it in Welsh," she said smugly. "If his aunty really does live there, she'll understand."

They puzzled over Charlie's copy of it in Macquarie Street: "MANY HAPPY RETURNS, YACKYDA, FROM A FRIEND OF EVAN!"

"So what does it mean, Pelham?"

"I've told you, I haven't the least idea," he repeated for the twentieth time. Kev picked up the list of titles.

"Forensic are checking the books. If it's a code, let's hope they can break it. Why don't you phone your office, Pelham? Tell 'em to put the pressure on Jones? Get some results for a change."

Anthony Pelham-Walker's petulant mouth set in an obstinate line. "There's absolutely no point in telephoning before ten a.m. Monday at the earliest—"

"Jesus wept!" muttered Charlie. Kev left an eloquent pause.

"So all we got," he said eventually, "is two facts: number one, she's still got two kilos in her luggage; and number two, no one's made contact yet—check Charlie?"

Charlie shook his head emphatically. "No phone calls, no one visited the room. We know she didn't have nuthin' with her this afternoon except that parcel and a tiddly little purse . . . It's still got to be there."

"And she's got to be protected."

"Right," Charlie agreed.

"What happens now?" Anthony Pelham-Walker demanded. "It was my intention to be on the return flight this evening. I really can't go on sitting here, waiting for something to happen . . ."

Kev glared and he shrivelled into silence. "If you want to get on the flight, Pelham, be my guest. I'm telling the truth when I say Charlie and me would be glad if you did . . ." He waited hopefully but Pelham-Walker made no reply. "However," Kev continued,

72

"if you want to stay with us instead, I suppose we can't stop you doing that either."

Anthony Pelham-Walker had every intention of staying. What was the point of returning empty-handed with the additional problem of explaining away two thousand pounds of tax-payers' money wasted on a ticket to Australia? Realizing Pelham wouldn't budge, Kev turned his back and consulted Charlie instead.

"What's their itinerary?"

"They're coach-camping with these FONE people as far as the Red Centre. After that, the party splits up."

"It'll take a few days to get that far. Know what I reckon? As they haven't made the pick-up here in Sydney, I guess the plan is to do it somewhere quiet, on one of the campsites. It'd be so easy to rob a tent, some place where there weren't too many police around." Charlie nodded.

"So we go along?"

"Right. The Bignell lady still has the stuff but she doesn't know what it is. We'll have to assume that Jones told her to leave that message at Byers Street—who lives there anyway?"

"An Asian couple. Seems like they're away for the weekend." As Kev raised his eyebrows, Charlie nodded in agreement. "Could be a lead. We're checking on it. Meanwhile—" He jerked his head "—which of us gets to share a tent with him?"

Chapter Ten

"What I'm looking forward to now, apart from seeing the countryside of course," said Mavis, "is finding Mrs Hardie's grandson." Hope sprang as optimistically as ever after a good night's sleep.

Mr Pringle didn't share it; he'd had nightmares, full of terrifying images of dead seagulls, torn and bleeding, floating in Sydney harbour. He'd also woken to the certain knowledge that someone, somewhere, would come in search of those two plastic bags.

"According to the brochure," Mavis reminded him, as they walked towards the lift, "we can start the search for Ben today. We're due in Bathurst for lunch."

Anthony Pelham-Walker, too, was feeling sombre. The spurt of energy which had caused him to leave England precipitately had disappeared, leaving cold reality behind. He'd behaved irrationally and that wouldn't be forgiven in Whitehall.

As he shaved, he tried to analyse and quantify. He'd assumed could he but witness the hand-over of drugs, protect an innocent female and order the arrest of the unknown malefactor, he could return in triumph. How childish! And look what it had cost? In an era of ministerial purges when expenses were being cut through the bone to the marrow! He might be close to retirement but he'd be lucky to hang on to his pension after this!

There was a thud against the door. He opened it and picked up the newspapers. If he'd felt doom-laden before, today's headlines made him suicidal:

"POMS TO DUMP RADIOACTIVE MUCK HERE!"
"AUSSIES SAY 'NO' TO BRITS' NUCLEAR WASTE!"
"GET OUT AND STAY OUT—FONES' COVER BLOWN!"

74

Comprehension was swift. "Oh, Lord," muttered Anthony Pelham-Walker. His predicament had got worse. Never mind trying to creep back home and explain, far better disappear into the outback for a while until the fuss had died down.

Jean Protheroe, white, shaken, told them about the newspapers. "It's brought on Kenneth's asthma!" she whispered. "I'm going up to our room to find his inhaler." Mavis was mystified.

"Surely everyone guessed the idea might not be popular?"

In the dining room, scientists gathered in anxious groups. Understanding had penetrated even the most academic: here in Australia, the natives didn't want to glow in the dark.

Mr Pringle read the headlines. He didn't care what happened to Protheroe. If the FONEs wanted to split atoms, they should take responsibility for cleaning up the bits afterwards. He reached the back page and sighed with relief: not a word about dead gulls polluting Sydney harbour!

As he sipped his coffee a much comforting thought occurred: if Protheroe had succeeded in alienating the locals, maybe the police would travel with the coach, to protect the party? Oh yes, that was a lovely idea! That way he and Mavis would be completely safe.

Mrs Hardie was awake. They'd dimmed the lights but she hadn't taken the pill to make her sleep. The ward was quiet. Nearer to the nursing station, an accident victim moaned despite the drugs. She'd have plenty to cry about once she saw herself in a mirror, thought Mrs Hardie sympathetically.

Beside her locker, the suitcase Linda had brought was packed ready. All she had to do in the morning was put in her nightdress and washing things. The crimplene trouser suit and frilly blouse were on the chair; tomorrow, Mrs Hardie was going home.

Although eager, she kept remembering the conversation with the welfare lady. Yet again Mrs Hardie had turned down the offer of a flat. "I can't keep promising you one," the woman told her worriedly. "I don't know when there'll be another."

It was true. Occupants at Brierly Court often found a new lease of life inside the comfortable well-planned flatlets. "There'd be companionship," the welfare lady told her. Mrs Hardie understood:

Linda. She was going back to sharing with her daughter. It hadn't worked before. If it didn't this time, Mrs Hardie might be stuck with it.

She hadn't been fair, she told herself. Look what her daughter had had to put up with? Most girls would've gone off the rails, losing Ben and Gary at the same time. And Linda was making the effort these days. She'd visited at least three times. She'd cleaned the house, ready for the home-coming. The living-room sofa had been turned into a bed, the hospital was lending a commode and she'd promised to look after her mother.

"I shall manage," Mrs Hardie told herself; "I owe it to Linda to try again. Anyway, we'll have to stay put, so Ben'll have a place when Mavis brings him back."

Their departure from the hotel had been quick and furtive. Scientists scurried out, convinced that hordes of Australians were after their blood, but the street was empty. It was early and the public hadn't had time to react. Rather embarrassed, removing dark glasses and turning down their collars, the Friends of Nuclear Energy took their seats. Mr Pringle and Mrs Bignell were half-way down Pete's coach. Each day passengers would rotate, Lenny ordered, thus everyone got a turn in the front seat. Protheroe had objected. He'd assumed that seat was his.

Today, apart from Lenny and Pete, plus a trainee driver, there was also the cook: Sheri. She would accompany them throughout the journey, Mr Pringle learned, and he thought this an excellent idea. Sheri was nubile, she wore a sleeveless T-shirt and very short shorts. Much of her golden flesh was available to admire. Not that he was being disloyal to Mavis. Memories of their quarrel were still vivid—he was anxious not to upset *her* in any way—but a little variety never did anyone any harm, especially at his age.

The sight of tightly rolled sleeping-bags above their heads was exciting. In the bowels of the coach behind their luggage were the tents. How would he compare with his fellow explorers once they were out in—The Bush?

Mr Pringle's emergency camping pack was with his pyjamas: penknife, coiled twine, needle and thread, spare tent-peg, matches, candle, torch including spare batteries, a twin-pack of soft

76

lavatory paper (pink, in deference to Mrs Bignell) and last, but most important of all, his old scouting manual—G D H Pringle was prepared. He wouldn't mind betting the nuclear physicists weren't. The ability to blow up the planet didn't necessarily equip a man for survival on its surface.

From her window seat, Mavis's contentment increased with every kilometre. The air was so clean and sparkling out here, as if someone had peeled away the dirt and damp; she could see for miles. They drove out of Sydney, past graceful small terraces with ornamental iron balconies. These gave way to industrial suburbs but as they reached Parramatta elegant houses began, surrounded by trees and paddocks. The highway narrowed and began to climb. In the distance she could actually see the Blue Mountains!

Pete had read the morning papers. He didn't like the sound of this party at all. These bloody Poms wanted to screw up Australia! "Mornin' folks. Like to tell you about the amenities on the coach. You'll have noticed the toilet down the back. It's got chemicals in it. Right now, it's clean. If it gets used, we've got to add more chemicals . . . which is OK in New South Wales, we got modern roads. Further out, Stuart Highway for instance, the surface is really bad. Full of holes. But that toilet is there for your convenience, if you really need it. Once we're in the bush, we use a gunny shovel. That's G-U-N-N-Y, for shovelling shit."

Behind him, in the Wallaby Tours uniform of dark red shorts, navy socks and white open-necked shirt, Charlie grinned. The badge on his pocket described him as a trainee-driver. As far as Lenny and Pete were concerned, he'd been put there by the government to keep an eye on the FONEs. Pete gave it as his opinion that this was a bloody good idea. Charlie waited for the next titbit from Pete. From their faces he could see that a few of the passengers were beginning to revise any romantic notions about the outback.

Pete changed the subject. He'd made them anxious about their bladders, now he wanted to stir them up a bit. "This trip's nice and easy, folks," he announced ruminatively. "Plenty of spare time in the schedule. Maybe we could make a detour, visit those contaminated sites you're interested in. . . Would you like that?"

77

There was a worried consultation down the back, a pretence at examining maps and itineraries. It was one thing to describe radioactive land as "suitable for our purpose", none of them had envisaged setting foot on it. Naturally it would be perfectly safe, they told each other, but that was no reason to change the route. Pete watched through his driving mirror. "Just testing," he murmured.

Protheroe seized the mike and reminded them the great camping adventure would begin in earnest tomorrow. Tonight would be their last in a comfortable bed, in a motel in Coonabarabran.

They were climbing higher and higher. On either side, skeletal-grey eucalyptus, the bark hanging in shreds, framed the vastness beyond: from horizon to horizon, nothing but thickly wooded mountains. Above the tree-tops in the heat, the blue gum haze merged into an infinity of sky.

"Big, isn't it?" said Mavis. Bigger than she'd expected; had *Reader's Digest* misled her? Surely not?

In the Toyota, Anthony Pelham-Walker gazed uneasily at the view. He'd telexed the necessary instructions to Sinclair before they left, to proceed immediately to Wales and contact Jones. So far the scientists here had been unable to fathom the message. And Charlie had drawn a gloomy blank in Byers Street.

"Couple got back in the early hours . . . Japanese. Missionaries. It's church property, rented out to whoever needs it. We've checked them out." Kev snorted.

"If Jones knew Byers Street was in Enfield, maybe he'd made drops at another house?" He and Charlie had looked at Pelham-Walker and he'd been forced to admit that Jones hadn't been asked the question.

"I—we didn't enquire about—drops."

"Jesus—didn't you ask him anythin'?" Kev demanded.

How could he defend his lack of expertise? Of course he hadn't known what questions to ask, his department weren't interested. Their task was to extricate stupid fools like Jones from foreign jails then hand them over to the police. *They* did the questioning.

Anthony Pelham-Walker felt himself shrinking, like Alice. He had to assert himself or he'd fall down the nearest rabbit hole. "I

78

think," he said slowly, "I should have gone on the coach, rather than Charles." Kev shifted the gum in his mouth.

"You handle a gun, Pelham?" The shock made him gasp. "You don't mean—he's armed?"

"What d'you think this is, for Chrissake? A picnic trip? Those people want their drugs back, they want to stop the rot started by Jones and if that Bignell lady gets in their way, they'll try and kill her."

The two coaches drove in convoy into Bathurst, past spacious properties. Horses grazed in outlying fields but the town itself was small and compact. Both Mavis and Mr Pringle, still making comparisons with England, expected a city. "Bathurst ends at the bottom of that street," said Mavis in surprise indicating the burnt brown-grey plain. "It's amazing how wide the roads are considering that's all there is."

"Wide enough for a bullock cart to turn." Mr Pringle had been reading the literature.

"Oh, look! There's the place!"

The coaches had pulled up beside open parkland in the centre where Lenny told them they would picnic. It was at the main intersection and as he looked in the direction of Mrs Bignell's hand, Mr Pringle found himself gazing at the view on the postcard.

There were the same stubby lamp-standards down the middle of the street, their white globes like giant blobs of ice-cream, the same cars parked at an angle to the kerb and, on the corner facing them, the ice-cream parlour itself. It was as immaculate, clean and shiny as the postcard and Mr Pringle, having come so far, blinked to discover it was real.

"What d'you want to do?" he asked awkwardly. He hadn't discussed tactics. All along he'd thought it so unlikely they'd find the parlour; he hadn't allowed for the Australian scale.

Bathurst looked sizeable on the map because for many, many miles there was nothing but isolated farms. It was definitely a town, however, the hub of a widely spread community, full of shops, churches, pubs and services, sheltering from a midday sun under canopies that stretched out over the pavements.

Beside the coaches, Protheroe was organizing a queue: lunch

was nearly ready. It had been a smooth operation. Lenny and Pete put up tables, Sheri set out salad and fruit. On a portable grill, hamburgers were sizzling. Breakfast was a distant memory and Mr Pringle discovered he was peckish.

"Shouldn't we eat first?" he suggested feebly.

"Eat?" Mavis stared. "After coming all this way? We're going over there to ask questions and show them Ben's photo. You can have a cornet if you're that hungry."

"Hallo . . . ?" Charlie shielded his eyes. "Take over for me will you, mate?" Pete flipped the hamburgers expertly.

"Come and get it, folks. Grub's ready."

Chapter Eleven

Rain swept across in sheets, rippling over the pavements and filling the gutters. It washed the fronts of the houses, the sash-windows, the steps up to the inset front doors and ran down the brickwork. It poured endlessly on to black roofs making the slates gleam, but the sheer volume of water couldn't eradicate the hopelessness; it was a desolate place.

Crispin Sinclair watched sullenly as the torrent blotted out the view. Reaction in Whitehall this morning, when they'd discovered what Batman had done, ranged from incredulity to complete indignation, but to Crispin's shocked surprise the guns had been turned on him as well. Why hadn't he reported what was going on? Why fall back on the lame excuse of "acting under orders"? Why not use his initiative? Or hadn't he got any? His answers had obviously been judged unsatisfactory and the remainder of the interview was equally unpleasant.

Now he'd been ordered to sodden old Wales to rescue his reputation because of that stupid telex from Sydney. What was worse, if he didn't succeed in squeezing every last scrap of information out of Jones, it would count against him at his next assessment. Damn and blast!

Crispin peered through the windscreen: what a place! No wonder Evan Jones preferred to travel. He switched the wiper to its fastest speed and looked along the row of houses. They were all so—neglected. People should make an effort to help themselves, he thought irritably. A few thou' spent on refurbishing and this street could be transformed. You saw it happen in London all the time.

He started the engine and coasted along, pulling up short of the actual house. Living rooms fronted directly on to the pavement. Through several windows he could see televisions with bodies

81

slumped in front of them, watching endless rubbishy movies. In the middle of the afternoon! Crispin's antipathy increased. Why not get out and do something? Pulling his belt tight, he made a dash for the drab front door.

"Yes?" The girl was about twenty and the resemblance to Evan was strong. Hair fell across her forehead in the same dark wave, the eyes were blue but what a pallor she had. No international traveller this. She hugged the shapeless cardigan protectively across her breast. "Yes?" she asked again.

"I'd like to see Evan Jones if he's at home."

"Evan?" She looked blank. Crispin experienced a flash of anger: had the idiot given a false address?

"Evan Jones," Crispin repeated as to a half-wit. "He's an airline steward. I understand his family live here?"

"Yes, we do but Evan isn't home. He's away somewhere." Blast! Rain was seeping in through Crispin's fashionable Italian leather shoes.

"Look, d'you think I could come inside? If Evan isn't here, I'd like to speak to his mother instead." The girl was shivering and doubtful. "Here's some identification . . ." Crispin fished out his driving licence and staff pass. The girl shrank even further from the official-looking stamp.

"You can come in, I suppose. Mam's out. It's Monday. She's down the Social Security."

He waited in the dank front parlour. In this house the television was in the kitchen-cum-dining room at the back. He caught a quick glimpse as the girl opened the door from the passage on her way to make tea. He saw people look up—there were four or five in that back room but none of them was Evan Jones. The ceiling light was on. It emphasized the gloom beyond the window and shone on their pale expressionless faces.

Crispin Sinclair retreated to the unlived-in parlour. What purpose did the room have? An uncut moquette suite, regimentally placed, and a battered upright piano with lacy material draped over the top. There was even a metronome—did anyone ever play? Everything reflected an earlier era, especially the furniture, obviously deemed too good to be thrown away. The room would never be used but held in readiness for Christmas or funerals.

Everything was too damn clean. His shoes had already left marks on the semicircular rug; he could scarcely take them off. There was nowhere to put them except on the hearth. A few spots of soot sullied the tiles, washed down in the deluge, proof there had once been a fire. Like the girl, Crispin shivered. Probably no heat in here since last Christmas. The grate was filled with red paper roses.

"Two sugars, you said?"

"Please."

"I'm sorry, there aren't any biscuits."

"I'm not hungry. Really." As soon as he'd finished here, he'd find the best hotel and have the largest steak on the menu. He smiled. "Lovely cup of tea." She didn't respond.

"Why d'you want Evan? There's nothing wrong, is there?" Her twenty-year-old face looked suddenly older, as if expecting trouble.

"I met him recently. We had a chat. As I was passing through Carmarthen . . ." That was a mistake. Nobody "passed" by this street. He saw her withdrawal. "Well, to be honest, Evan told me all about his 'mam'." Crispin tried to make the imaginary conversation sound warm and intimate. "Said if I was ever anywhere near here, to come and look her up." The girl was still dubious.

"I can give Mam a message if you like?" Crispin smiled again.

"I knew you must be Evan's sister, but no, thank you. I'm not in any hurry. Tell me, where d'you think he might be?" She shrugged.

"Mam might know. I can't remember. I think she said it was Bangkok this time, or Hong Kong. Somewhere out there." The girl couldn't care less; she'd as much chance of seeing either city as flying to the moon.

"When I met him in London, a few days ago, Evan had just returned from Bangkok." It wasn't any good, he couldn't interest her in that. "Doesn't he come back here between trips then?" Crispin asked casually. "I remember him mentioning that he did."

"Sometimes. He's got a house near London. Near the airport, anyway. He's doing it up. He says we can go and stay with him when it's ready." There was a little animation at the thought of the treat. "Evan's there more often than here because of getting it straight."

If he was there now, he was being plain bloody stupid, thought Crispin contemptuously; at least in this tight community he'd have had the protection of his family. Should he cut his losses? It was obvious the steward hadn't come back to Wales as he'd promised he would.

"When was the last time you saw your brother?" The girl frowned. Days hadn't much relevance in her life, they followed one another in an uneventful pattern.

"On Sean's birthday," she decided. "He was here then."

"What date was that?"

"Last month. The fifteenth." That settled it. Crispin Sinclair glanced at his watch. He'd have to hurry if he were to get a decent lunch before returning.

"Look, I think I will leave a message after all . . . time's getting on. Please tell your mother I was asking after Evan. And if he does come, would you ask him to call." He gave her his card. "He can leave a message at that number any time." A thought occurred. "Has anyone—any of Evan's other friends been here recently?" She wasn't as stupid as he'd first thought.

"You're from the police, aren't you?"

"What makes you say that? I'm not, as a matter of fact—"

"Is he in trouble?" she persisted.

"No, of course not. I wanted to see him about his new house, actually. I can get building materials at trade discount. Evan was really keen when I told him and I wouldn't want him to miss out." It sounded a reasonable excuse to him but whether the girl believed it was another matter.

"I'll tell Mam you've been." She wanted rid of him. A man in smart clothes with a posh accent was outside the norm, not to be trusted. "She might be a long time because of the buses."

"Yes, of course. Thank you for the tea." She was already in the passage, pulling her cardigan round her before opening the door.

"I'm sorry I missed your brother."

"If Evan's back, he'll be at his house," she repeated. "He and Mam have fixed a date for her visit and I know he wanted to get it finished before then." Crispin decided to give Evan Jones a piece of his mind if that was the reason. Nothing but a wild-goose chase, coming here.

"I'd like to catch up with him before his next trip. Maybe I'll drop by his place. Holt's Farm Cottages, wasn't that it? Down a mile and a half of unmade lane, according to your brother."

The girl looked at him obliquely. "I don't know about the lane; I've not visited it yet."

Careful, he thought. A stranger going to all that trouble? In this street, men in suits probably meant debt-collectors from Carmarthen or Swansea. He paused on the step. "I'm often travelling on the M4," he shouted, above the rain. "Your brother's house isn't much of a detour." But she wasn't interested in that either; she'd already shut the front door.

In Heathrow, the final call for the missing British Airways passenger to Sydney echoed over the Tannoy: "Mr Ray Vincent, proceed to Gate 31 *immediately* for embarkation." The disembodied voice had all the charm of an angry nanny.

He approached Customs unhurriedly and waited until his bag had disappeared into the maw of the X-ray machine before stepping through the scanner. When the buzzer sounded, he automatically took his cigar case out of a breast pocket and handed it over. The Customs man glanced inside before returning it.

At the departure gate, the ground hostess hissed angrily as she saw the missing passenger unzip his overnight bag in response to the officer's request. A gaudily coloured box with gift paper and label lay on top of some clothes.

"I didn't bother to wrap it, I thought you might want to see inside," the passenger said diffidently.

"Quite right, sir. 'To Wayne on his eighth birthday, love from Uncle Ray'—I see." In the cardboard box, dark grey pieces of moulded fibreglass lay in a plastic tray ready for easy assembly. The Customs man looked at the sheet of instructions. "These get more realistic every day, don't they?"

"They do indeed."

"No bullets?"

"No." Ray Vincent smiled. "They make me nervous . . . besides, it's amazing how easily kids can damage themselves, even with toys." The officer shuffled the lid back on and invited the passenger to close up his bag.

"How right you are. Have a pleasant trip."

"Thank you."

Ray Vincent followed the ground hostess's angry back up the aircraft steps. As a design, the weapon was precision-made, Swiss perfection with the few remaining metal parts carefully disposed of within his bag. He'd be glad when the Swiss solved the problem of the bullets though, being a non-smoker.

He fastened his seat-belt and closed his eyes, willing himself to forget. Adele hadn't believed his excuses. "Why now, why today? It's not that long since you told me you wouldn't have to go back East. You never said a word last week when I bought two tickets for the barbecue."

"I didn't know last week, it only cropped up this morning." She'd become even more suspicious.

"When did they call? You said a phone call from New York—"

"At the office. First thing this morning. You can ask Janice if you don't believe me." He cursed himself for admitting too much; there'd been too many slip-ups, he couldn't afford any more.

They hadn't spoken during the drive to Heathrow. Adele slid into the driving seat without offering to kiss him goodbye. "You'll phone? As soon as you know when you're coming back?"

"As soon as the deal's signed, promise. It shouldn't take long, the conveyancing side is all tied up—" But he needn't have bothered because she ignored it.

"I suppose you want me to keep the P-O-N-Y a secret until you return."

"What, and ruin Amy's birthday! Lord, no . . ." He'd bent to hug his plump little daughter who wrinkled her nose as she always did.

"You smell nice, Daddy." Adele immediately contradicted her.

"If you want my opinion, you use too much. It's very strong, Ray." He'd tried to smile. He'd stood in the shower until the water ran cold but he hadn't been able to wash away the memory, not this time, of the hot smell of blood.

"Would you like me to bring you more opals? To match the necklace?"

"I thought you said you'd only be away a couple of days? You'd have to go back to the mine to do that. Will you be away that long?"

The Tannoy calling his name had interrupted and he tried not to sound relieved. "Listen love, must go. Take care—" But Adele was already pulling away from the kerb. He heard Amy wail, "You promised we could wave Daddy's plane goodbye, you promised!"

Sugary music stopped, another nanny told him the flight time and altitude and the vast machine hurtled down the runway. Ray Vincent switched off his reading light and pulled down the blind. A steward was making his way through the cabin with the inevitable champagne cocktails.

He and Zee had made a mistake, using Jones. The organization didn't tolerate mistakes. They'd sent Parker to help him obliterate that mistake . . . the memory of what had happened made Vincent grip the arms convulsively. Parker had actually enjoyed doing it. *He'd* wanted to be quick but Parker insisted on doing it his way. . .

The steward was offering him a drink; Vincent shook his head, breathing hard to regain control. Easy . . . easy. He had the name, he knew where to find her, all he had to do was finish the job, his way. Then it would be over—please God let this be the last time!

"That's Gary, all right." The friendly woman serving in the ice-cream parlour nodded at the photo in recognition. "Taken in England, was it?" Mavis Bignell was delighted.

"Yes, a few years ago. Gary is Ben's father. How marvellous you remembering them. Have you seen them recently?"

"Ben, that's his kid's name, is it?" The woman topped the two knickerbocker glories with dollops of cream. Watching her, Mr Pringle began to feel queasy. Mavis searched through the pile of photos for one of Ben, but when she showed her the friendly woman shook her head.

"Sorry, love. It's nice and clear, you can see what he looks like all right, but I don't remember the kiddie at all. It's not likely I would have met him, is it? Gary used to be a truck driver. They don't allow them to carry passengers."

"Ben sent his grandma a postcard from Bathurst." Mavis found it in her bag. "Look, he's marked this place."

"Oh, yeah . . . We sell those. Maybe Gary bought it here? Or at the post office?"

"Read the message," Mavis urged. "Ben says he had an ice-cream." The woman reached for her spectacles. She wasn't as young as Mr Pringle first thought; blonde hair had been dulled by middle-age and constant exposure to the sun emphasized the wrinkles as it did for so many women out here.

"Did the kiddie write this?" she asked.

"Yes," replied Mavis. "His grandma, my friend Mrs Hardie I was telling you about, she got it from him a few months ago."

"Well, I haven't seen Gary for a long time." The woman broke off to attend to another customer. "Yes? What'll it be?"

"Coke," said Charlie.

"I told you it wouldn't be difficult," Mrs Bignell whispered conspiratorially. "Ben must've come here with Gary. Maybe Gary kept him out of sight? Because of the rules about passengers?"

"Possibly. I shouldn't get too excited. We don't want to arouse false hopes in Mrs Hardie."

Mr Pringle plunged the long spoon in as far as the bright green jelly. He'd leave the cherry till last like he always did.

"Must be all of six months since Gary was here." The woman had returned. "He'd been laid off, poor fella. He was hoping to find work up country." She sighed. "It's not easy nowadays. Too much competition. And Gary had stayed in England too long, he'd lost his contacts."

"It was his wife who was the problem," said Mrs Bignell. "Linda. Did he tell you about her?"

The woman behind the counter didn't reply. Instead she said, "Gary always told me he was willin' to turn his hand to anythin'."

"Perhaps he went on a sheep station?" Mr Pringle's knowledge of Australia was sketchy and the woman laughed in a kindly way.

"You need an awful lot of skill to handle sheep, it's not somethin' you can pick up easily. No, I reckon Gary's in the Northern Territories. Maybe Katherine. Or Alice. They're always advertising for workers up in there, 'cause it's too bloody hot. People can't stick it for long."

Mavis and Mr Pringle had a brief discussion. They would send another postcard to Mrs Hardie, Mavis decided, and Mr Pringle dissuaded her from writing "Hot on the trail!"

"It's extremely unlikely we will find the boy. He's of school age. His father must have arranged that he live somewhere permanent in order to attend one. Gary could hardly take the child along when looking for work."

"And Gary was broke." The woman behind the counter was sad. "He was down to his last few dollars. He was hitchin', which ain't the best way to travel in this country."

"Perhaps we should leave a little something?" Mavis enquired delicately. The friendly lady suddenly went pink.

"No need," she insisted. "If Gary turns up again, he'll be looked after." And Mr Pringle had to kick Mavis on the shin to stop her asking any more questions.

It wasn't going to work, Mrs Hardie admitted it to herself, not ever. She was certain of it now. The house hadn't been cleaned, not by her standards. Immobile on the sofa, the cast on her leg anchoring her to the downstairs back room, she gazed at polish smears, dull brass and dust. Linda had attempted to clean. On the mirror above the fireplace there were streaky marks and the distinct imprint of her fingers where she'd held it steady. She'd used one of those aerosol things. They made everything worse in Mrs Hardie's opinion.

It hadn't taken long for her to drop back into her old habits, either. Mrs Hardie's mouth twitched. The table lamp was on, she could see the clock. Two a.m. and her daughter still wasn't in. When she did return, she'd probably be drunk. Mrs Hardie scolded herself vigorously for not accepting the welfare lady's advice. Fancy letting Linda talk her out of it—all that nonsense about needing a garden for Ben to play in—as if Gary would give the boy up even if Mavis and her friend did manage to find him.

Oddly enough, the garden was the one thing Linda had tackled. Through the window Mrs Hardie could make out the rockery against the solid darkness of the trim lawn.

In the warden flats, you didn't have to worry about gardening; all that was taken care of. As soon as the home help came tomorrow and after Linda had gone to work, Mrs Hardie would ask her to make that phone call. To the welfare lady. Surely *she* wouldn't have reallocated the vacant flat already?

It was very late but Crispin Sinclair decided to break his journey after all. Better that and have all the answers ready for the inevitable inquisition tomorrow morning.

His irritability increased as he bumped down the track—it wasn't doing his suspension any good at all—that Jones could be so stupid as to stay where he could be found! The chap didn't deserve any help.

The two cottages were in darkness, which was a blow. Crispin banged on each front door in turn then, deciding he would leave a note because Jones was obviously out boozing somewhere, searched for a stick to push the Filofax page through the letterbox. Passing the back door, he tried the handle and found it wasn't locked.

The air-traffic controller drove the last few yards much more carefully. He travelled the lane often and knew the potholes. There was a movement ahead—someone was leaving the house next door. Had Jones finally returned? It was dark, he didn't recognize the silhouette.

The controller turned into his own parking space and switched off the ignition. Odd, the stranger hadn't moved. He still leaned against the open door front, almost clung to it. The controller could see clearly now that it definitely wasn't Jones.

For a moment or two, he stayed where he was. Silly to be so cautious, no doubt, but these cottages were isolated. Winding down the window he called, "Is Evan back? Have you seen him?" Almost as an afterthought he added, "I've got a bone to pick with him. He must've let some food go bad, the smell's been awful lately." He broke off. Whoever the stranger was, he'd turned away and was vomiting frantically into a patch of grass.

90

The controller left his car and hurried across. The stranger, whey-faced and shaking, was on his knees. When he looked up there were tears streaming down his face. "Police. . .quick as you can. For God's sake, don't go in there! Close the fucking door!"

Chapter Twelve

The further they were from Sydney, the more Mr Pringle's courage returned. He questioned Mrs Bignell gently, he didn't want to rekindle their quarrel, but he had to know how much she'd told Evan.

"I said we were hoping to find Ben."

"Did you describe our route in detail?"

"I don't think so . . ." She answered slowly. "I said we were sharing a coach with the FONEs—we had a laugh about that. Why d'you ask? You're not still worried about that powder, whatever it was?"

"Yes, I am. Whoever it belongs to is bound to come for it." Mavis looked at the miles of empty road ahead and the bare landscape on either side.

"He'll be a bit conspicuous if he does . . . all the same, there aren't many police about, either. Tell you what, dear, I promise not to pick up any more strange men. Even if a gorgeous bit of crumpet tries to chat me up, I shan't even listen. Now I can't say fairer than that, can I?" He hadn't the heart to insist the matter was serious.

They arrived at their destination, Coonabarabran, and the El Paso Motel. As their coach turned into the car-park, Mavis said approvingly, "Very Spanish."

The FONEs liked it, too. A familiar landscape of trees and green hills had been left far behind. Once beyond the Great Dividing Range, they'd begun to appreciate how vast and hostile this land was; mile upon mile of meagre vegetation following years of drought. Coming from England it had to be experienced to be understood. Here they were back in civilization where there were hot showers and comfortable beds.

The motel was single-storey with a steep red-tiled roof and deep white arches concealing the reception buildings. On either side, conifers cast dark shadows. "They've got a proper restaurant, it says so on the sign. D'you think there'll be a band?"

"Goodness, I doubt it!"

Protheroe was already marshalling his troops. Tonight, the FONEs were scheduled to meet members of the public. As Friends they were about to preach on the benefits of nuclear disposal and "sound out local opinion", as Protheroe put it. Mr Pringle thought it prudent if he and Mavis distanced themselves.

"You never know, they might have a band . . ." Mrs Bignell sounded wistful. She waited as Charlie and Len unloaded the baggage. Trundling her suitcase, she followed Mr Pringle to where Protheroe was handing out the keys. "Herbert and I used to go to the Palais regularly, on Latin-American nights."

It wasn't often that the late Mr Bignell was referred to and Mr Pringle listened attentively. "If Herbert hadn't needed a partner for the *pasa doble* competition, we might never have got together," she sighed; "and when he turned up that evening, in white tie and tails, that was it. I'd never seen anyone dressed like Fred Astaire before. I only found out afterwards they belonged to his uncle who was a mason. Herbert was a good dancer, though," she said loyally. "We did get as far as the final eight." Mr Pringle was silent for a moment, in tribute.

"I'm afraid I don't dance."

"No, I know." For Mavis, this was no consolation. "Still, there's one or two FONEs come without their wives," she said, brightening, "and they're not dangerous, so if there is a band, I think I might wear my red lace."

Anthony Pelham-Walker's confident air had disappeared. Alone, apart from Macillvenny, in a vast burnt-out wilderness, he'd no one to blame but himself; he longed, though, for the familiar protection of the department. Kev tried to interest him in the sights.

"See those white parakeets? Typical they are . . ." Pelham-Walker yearned for a humble sparrow. "We'll be drivin' past the Warrumbungles tomorrow," Kev went on. "Thirteen million years ago they were formed, after a huge volcanic explosion."

What were Greenwich or Whitehall compared to that? The sight of ordinary houses and streets in a town was suddenly as reassuring as a lifebelt to a drowning man.

Kev booked rooms at the Country Comfort Motel. Pelham-Walker let him take charge. He watched apathetically as Kev phoned first Charlie, then the office in Macquarie Street. With nothing to interest him, Anthony Pelham-Walker found his thoughts drifting homeward towards Fiona: what would she get up to while he was away?

Unpleasant possibilities flooded his tired brain—he must get back at once! What on earth was he thinking of, wandering aimlessly round this benighted country? Kev's voice broke through his confusion: "Give me that bit again?" Anthony Pelham-Walker felt depressed. He no longer wanted to hear of any developments, he wanted to go home.

"That's great," said Kev. "Send the bloke a message from me. Tell him I think he deserves a medal. Anything else?" He frowned. "Nothing more . . . ?" He swivelled round. "What's your fella's name again?"

"Sinclair. Crispin Sinclair."

"Yeah . . . anything come in from Sinclair?" He replaced the receiver, obviously displeased. "What's Sinclair think he's doing? He's had enough time."

Anthony Pelham-Walker forced himself to consider the return journey to Wales. "We should hear something soon," he agreed, "unless they're resurfacing the M4. They often do at this time of year." Kev worked out the implication for himself.

"You don't mean Sinclair's gone by car? Why not hire a plane?" Anthony Pelham-Walker tried to bridge the gulf.

"In England . . . in my department . . . no one hires an aircraft without special permission from the Minister, which could take months, and in Sinclair's grade, wouldn't be granted for any reason whatsoever. It'll be difficult justifying a journey to Carmarthen at 31.3 pence per mile as it is."

"But Pelham . . . we're all of us trying to break up a drug racket."

"We're trying equally hard at our end, believe me, Macillvenny. Any criticism—"

"At 31.3 pence per mile!"

"If we can't prove we're cost-effective, we risk being wound up altogether."

"You can't be serious! My God Pelham, that's terrible." Kev was stunned by the parsimony. "How in hell are you supposed to catch villains under those conditions?"

"I honestly don't know," Pelham-Walker said wearily. "Fortunately that is seldom my concern."

"Cheer up. We may have had a bit of luck. One of your Customs officers was on the ball. A passenger for Sydney turned up at Heathrow with one of those 9mm semi-automatic Heckler & Koch plastic pistols. Had it in pieces like an assembly toy but your bloke spotted it. He knew the sort of gun that *should* have been in the cardboard box because his kid's got a similar one. When he picked it up, it felt too heavy, that's what made him look closely. No identification, all carefully removed. Smart of the officer to think of checking that. Fortunately, Heathrow made the decision not to intercept but to send us a signal. They've circulated those departments who might be concerned, including ours of course. Nice to have some co-operation from the mother country once in a while." The sarcasm was ignored.

"Is the passenger known to you?"

"They're still checking him out," Kev replied. "He's a businessman who visits Sydney occasionally, name of Vincent. Says in his passport he's an estate agent—which he's not. You don't need that sort of pistol in the property business.

"Your bloke didn't spot any ammunition but maybe Vincent's got training bullets concealed someplace."

"What are those?"

"If he's a pro, and with a gun like that what else could he be, he needs to practise."

They were into realms that Anthony Pelham-Walker had only read about, and not in interdepartmental memos. He was very frightened indeed. "Do you think he might be carrying real bullets as well?" he asked tremulously.

"We'll find out when he gets here," Kev grinned. He looked at his watch. "Take-off was o-nine-thirty British Summer Time . . . Twenty-two hour flight—he should get here early tomorrow. Our

95

blokes will be waiting. By then, we should have off the computer everything there is to know about Ray Vincent."

"According to Lenny," said Mavis, "tomorrow morning we're going to see the koala. It lives in a national park not far away from here." Despite the lack of a band, the evening hadn't been a disappointment. First there was the discovery that Mrs Bignell's favourite drink, port, was not only available, it was manufactured in quantity in Australia. After that, with so many varieties to sample, the El Paso restaurant had taken on a roseate glow.

For Mr Pringle, the sight of his fellow countrymen setting forth on their mission had provided a memory to treasure. Protheroe's instruction had been to "blend in" with the local population and the scientists had done their best. Trousers had been abandoned but not brown socks and buckled sandals. Shorts revealed the forced rhubarb pallor of British knees. Heads were topped with inappropriate Australian hats and, worst of all, Protheroe sported a T-shirt with a saucy emu on the chest.

As they trooped outside he called, "Remember, our hosts this evening are the Lions of Coonabarabran," and they sallied forth; Daniels, every one.

Lenny and Pete watched incredulously. "Are they in disguise?"

"Yeah," said Pete, "they're pretendin' to be Kiwis."

"You know," said Mavis as they went back to their room, "I'm getting a bit fed up with those FONEs, they're giving the British a bad name. I wish we'd decided to travel independently; we could look for Ben properly on our own." Mr Pringle had indulged in sufficient port to make him reckless.

"There's nothing to stop us hiring a car. We could catch up with the coaches later on. Pete and Lenny are travelling in easy stages." Mavis hugged him, eyes shining.

"We can talk to the ice-cream lady again? You know the sort of questions to ask. There wasn't nearly enough time this morning." Already Mr Pringle was regretting his gesture.

"It's a long way back to Bathurst."

"Yes, but the roads are so much quieter out here. And I'm sure that woman knew Gary."

"She may not be willing to tell us," he warned.

"Oh, you'll manage." Mavis squeezed his arm. "It's amazing how you can coax people when you want. Come on, let's find out about hire-cars." Mr Pringle remained where he was.

"Mavis, there is a serious problem if we do go it alone."

"You mean—because of the powder?" He nodded.

"At least Protheroe and his lunatics give us a degree of protection. Alone with me, your life could be in danger."

He looked so grave, Mavis shivered. "You're not just trying to frighten me?"

"I've concealed my fears until now for the sake of our holiday, but the risk is there. In my opinion, it's a serious one." She considered for a moment or two.

"Well, if I went back without doing my best, I'd never forgive myself." Mr Pringle accepted this with a sinking heart.

"I think we should try and rejoin the coach during their stay at Ayers Rock. That gives us nearly three days for our search."

"Oh, yes, I don't want to miss that. They said in *Reader's Digest* it was the eighth wonder of the world."

"Ah," he murmured, "they so often do."

Kev picked up the receiver: "Yes?"

"It's me," said Charlie. "Change of plan this end. The seed packet's going back to Bathurst to look for that kid she was talking about. Pete's fixing up a hire-car deal for the two of 'em right this minute. They're leaving early tomorrow."

"Stick with her," Kev ordered. "Offer to drive if you can. We'll follow."

"Right." Kev replaced the receiver.

"We're heading back, Pelham," he said. "This could be interesting."

"Oh yes?" Another long day on the road . . . with another Chinese take-away at the end of it? Why was it at the opposite ends of the earth the food was always the same?

He was leaving to return to his own room when he had a sudden thought. "Missionaries?"

"Pardon?" asked Kev.

"You said, the house in Byers Street was occupied by missionaries."

"They're genuine. We checked them out."

"But wasn't there a priest involved when that chap was hanged in Penang?"

"My word, Pelham, so there was!" Kev stared. "Better watch out. Could be you got a talent for this type of work after all."

In the El Paso Motel, Mr Pringle examined Ben's last postcard again. He looked at the message. What had the friendly woman said? "Did the kid write this?"

Had she really no idea where Gary had hidden the child? Their relationship was, Mr Pringle guessed, a close one. Was she protecting a lover who'd kidnapped his only son?

He added the postcard to the photographs of Ben. Top of the pile was the most recent. He could understand why Mrs Protheroe had suggested rickets. The boy had the same fragile bones as his grandmother and the thin legs were slightly bowed. The blue eyes were compelling, such an intense colour, the whites reflected it.

Perhaps the film had had a blue tint? Mr Pringle's snaps often turned out a funny colour. He yawned and stretched. "Ready for bed?"

"Yes, I am." Mavis fixed him with a stern gaze. "And we'll save our strength tonight if you don't mind."

After his recent exertions, he was only too glad to comply.

In England it was half-past ten in the morning. The home help let herself back in. "How d'you get on?" asked Mrs Hardie eagerly.

"The welfare lady said she can't promise you another flat but she will come round and talk to you about it. I told her where she could find the key and when you'd be on your own; she said to say she quite understood. She'll be round by the end of the week."

The girl glanced at the clock. "If I get a move on, I can do the bathroom as well as the kitchen before I go."

She disappeared and Mrs Hardie limped across to the mantelpiece. None of the ornaments had been done. The girl hadn't been trained; all she did was flip a duster and leave it at that. The sooner

Mrs Hardie had a place of her own where she could do the cleaning properly, the better. As she hobbled back to the sofa, the girl called from the kitchen, "You're nearly out of washing-up liquid, did you know?"

Chapter Thirteen

"They heckled Kenneth!" Jean Protheroe was tearfully angry. "He'd set aside time for questions but they wouldn't even let him finish his speech!"

"How rude!" said Mavis.

"Dear me," murmured Mr Pringle. He tried to appear sympathetic as he continued to load their luggage plus tents and sleeping-bags into the hire-car.

"Kenneth's got a migraine this morning as well as asthma. It's the strain, you know. He kept telling them about the benefits but they refused to listen."

"What—benefits?" Mr Pringle paused, mystified.

"Becoming world leader in the disposal of nuclear waste, of course," Mrs Protheroe replied, tartly. "Australia could be ahead of the Japanese for once if only they'd listen."

"But isn't the government here against—" Mr Pringle began, then winced as Mrs Bignell stepped on his foot.

"The Australians have elected a government that's hand in glove with big business, so they're bound to understand the benefits." Mrs Protheroe spoke with conviction. "Which is why it was so surprising when one of the natives began shouting abuse."

Seeing his expression, Mavis explained, "I think Jean means one of the black ones don't you, Jean? An Aboriginal native."

"Yes. I'd no idea they let them out of their compounds. I thought they stayed in designated areas, going walkabout whenever their goats had eaten all the pasture . . ."

Jean Protheroe had a clear bell-like tone and Mr Pringle glanced round nervously to ensure neither Lenny nor Pete was within earshot.

"We didn't imagine for a moment *they*'d be invited to the meeting, to make trouble for Kenneth."

100

"I think it's the bedouins who have goats, Jean, not the Aborigines." Mavis looked at Mr Pringle for confirmation. He threw discretion to the winds.

"Surely the whole purpose of your visit was to arrange for the disposal of nuclear waste beneath Aborigine homelands? Under those circumstances are they not entitled to ask questions, and protest?"

Jean Protheroe's expression changed; this was one of those whingeing lefties the Prime Minister was always warning about! "I don't think you've understood, Mr Pringle. Kenneth and his colleagues have travelled all this way to explain to a backward people how their empty deserts can be made profitable. What's more," she warmed to her theme, "FONE are prepared to retrain any natives who live on those sites to handle the waste under a special YTS scheme. They'll be able to earn their living whilst remaining in their compounds. The Australian government are bound to see the advantages and the Japanese are queueing up to be the first to bury their plutonium. But we need support to make these simple people understand—and now you're deserting us." She made it sound like a crime.

"Only for two days," Mavis protested.

Mr Pringle asked mildly, "If the natives become radioactive, will they still be allowed to go walkabout?" Fortunately Charlie arrived in the nick of time.

"You folks ready to leave?" He turned to Mrs Protheroe. "We'll be meeting you again at Ayers Rock."

"Possibly not," she said darkly. "Kenneth may decide to cancel the tour altogether." She strode away and Charlie opened the passenger door for Mavis.

"Would you like me to drive?" he asked politely.

"Oh, would you, dear? It would be easier for us if you did. How kind of Pete and Lenny to spare you."

"We need a few things for the coach. Pete wants me to pick 'em up in Bathurst."

In such a small town, thought Mr Pringle, how odd? He sat in the back and wondered about Charlie. He hadn't been at Kingsford Smith when they'd arrived but then neither had the cook, Sheri. Of course they hadn't, they weren't needed that day, either of them; there was no need to worry. Charlie was an employee of Wallaby Tours not part of a drug syndicate; he'd be a useful ally if anything occurred, young and strong. Ought Mr Pringle to explain there could be a problem? Should he, in fact, take Charlie into his confidence?

Mavis was chattering away telling him of their search. Mr Pringle decided to remain silent. She'd assured him again last night that Evan knew nothing other than that they were travelling with the FONEs. Surely now they'd departed from that itinerary, he and Mavis would be even more secure?

A cold wind blew down the Carmarthen street, whipping up discarded greasy wrappings from outside the chippy. The middle-aged woman holding the door open a crack spoke quickly out of chilly nervousness, "Yes, what d'you want?"

The young WPC said gently, "Mrs Jones? Can we come in, love? It's. . .personal." The woman, dark-haired, blue-eyed with a tired tense face, sensed something even colder than the wind in the way one of them couldn't meet her gaze.

"Not all of you." She wanted to delay whatever it was as long as possible. "There's too many with only me and Lesley here."

The CID man who'd been avoiding her suddenly looked up; she saw the pity in his eyes. "We haven't done anything wrong," she whispered. Her heart was thumping as the policewoman spoke again.

"No, it's nothing like that. It's about Evan, love."

Crispin Sinclair was in his flat, suspended from duty until the results of police enquiries were known. He couldn't stop shivering. He knew he wouldn't sleep despite the pills his lover had given him. "The department kept insisting it was *my* responsibility," he repeated; and his lover replied automatically, "Yes, you said. Bloody nerve."

"They claimed I'd let the fool walk into a trap—I kept telling him to go to Wales—"

"Yes, I know."

"They said I should have handed him over to the police straight away—"

102

"Well you should. We both know that."

"Don't you start!" The youth looked wounded.

"All I meant was, if it hadn't been for Batman, you would've gone to them, wouldn't you? The police?" There was a pause. "Well, wouldn't you?"

"Oh, shut up!" Crispin shivered so violently this time his lover became alarmed.

"I'll get you some cocoa . . . How about a hot-water bottle, that might help?" From the kitchen, he called out, "Here . . . have you replied to that telex yet? The one Batman sent from Sydney?"

"Shut up about the blasted telex. What the department really wants is for me to resign!" The youth stood in the doorway, cocoa tin in hand.

"Yes, you said. Poor old bear. What a bloody nerve!" Without warning, tears began coursing down Crispin's face.

"It was so awful! They'd bashed him to pulp with that hammer—blood and brains everywhere!" His lover's gorge began to rise.

"Oh, for Chrissake, heart!" It was no use, he'd always been sensitive; he dropped the tin and dashed to the bathroom.

The British Airways flight taxied to a halt at Kingsford Smith and passengers began to disembark. Scrutinizing them from the arrival building were two immigration officials. Inside, waiting on the concourse, were airport security guards and, in an unmarked car outside, the police.

At Immigration desks, each official knew the name: Ray Vincent was to be allowed through as far as the concourse to see whether anyone contacted him, before being taken in for questioning.

From their vantage point, the officials watched the crowd gather in the arrival hall below. Two 747s had arrived simultaneously which meant there were several hundred milling about.

Radio contact between the tower and the BA flight had worked perfectly. The purser indicated unobtrusively as Ray Vincent descended the steps, a member of the ground staff followed the passenger into the arrival hall and now, as the officials watched from the viewing gallery, brushed past casually as Vincent joined the waiting crowd.

"That must be him. On the left—light-coloured mac, carrying a navy overnight bag!"

"Got him." The second man moved to a wall phone and passed the information through to Passport Control.

Below, passengers stood patiently behind white lines and approached Immigration singly or in pairs when beckoned to do so. Gradually, the mass of bodies shuffled forward. Not until Ray Vincent was at the front did the two watching him make a move.

As he stepped up to a desk and they heard their colleague say "Good morning, Mr Vincent," they slipped past screens and took up position on either side of the concourse, ready to identify him to the guards. There were now four people to watch every move Ray Vincent made.

The first guard spoke into his radio: "Suspect has arrived at Passport Control. Coming through any minute now."

"Check."

By the carousel, the crowd waiting for their luggage was three to four deep. The two guards moved closer in.

"Business or pleasure, sir?"

"A bit of both, I hope." Ray Vincent's entry document was in order. The officer stamped his passport and returned it. "Enjoy your visit. Your luggage will be arriving shortly."

"Many thanks." Vincent gave an easy smile but instead of moving forward, went towards the transit desk, increasing his speed to a brisk trot. He pushed his way to the front, cash in hand. "Excuse me . . . sorry. Look, any chance of the next flight to Brisbane? My wife's terribly sick." The accent was Australian and the clerk scarcely looked up as he referred to his screen.

"Sorry to hear that. Will club class suit?"

"Fine, thanks. The name's Walsh, John Walsh." Ray Vincent was already peeling dollars off the roll. "Keep the change—give it to charity."

"Thank you, sir." The clerk called after him, "Last call was five minutes ago, I'll tell them you're on your way—TAA 464, Gate 15, Mr Walsh!" People waited sympathetically as the clerk confirmed it over his mike to ground control.

It took nearly four minutes for the Immigration official to get from his desk to a guard, another two minutes for them to reach the transit desk and a further minute to establish what had happened. By then, the aircraft containing "John Walsh" was taxiing toward the main runway.

The first officer had to complete his take-off checks before he could attend to the signal from the tower and pass it to the chief steward. He and the purser checked the seating plan but Ray Vincent was no longer in club class, he was recovering his nerve in one of the tourist washrooms.

Something had gone badly wrong! He'd planned every move—it had been damn tight because the BA flight had been behind schedule, but he'd made it, thank God! But why had those guards been on the look out? He was hyped up, he always was on a job, and when the man brushed past he knew the reason instinctively. Experience got him through the rest of it—but why?

Mirrors reflected the fleshy face, the gut that was beginning to be noticeable. Ray Vincent gripped the wash-basin. Why were they looking for him? They couldn't possibly connect him with Jones. What the hell had gone wrong? The infinite mirrored reflections were taut with fear.

After five minutes, he'd got his breathing under control. There was probably some damn-fool explanation. He'd get on with what he had to do; there wasn't time to worry about anything else.

He folded his poplin mac in a tight small roll, unzipped his bag and began. He exchanged his British passport for an American one concealed in the stiffening at the bottom, packed the cardboard box in its gift paper, flushing away the original label and replacing it with one that read "To Philip from Uncle Greg".

He sprayed his fair hair grey, combed it flat and parted it on the opposite side.

Changing his shirt and tie for a T-shirt, he put on a seersucker jacket bought in San Francisco. Finally, he stuck a scrap of bloodstained lint and plaster to his jaw.

When cabin staff banged on the door and told him they were approaching Brisbane, Ray Vincent limped to an empty seat at the back of the rear cabin.

He was among the first tourist passengers down the steps and across the tarmac, putting on blue-tinted glasses against the glare of the Brisbane sun. The slight limp and hunched shoulders didn't prevent him keeping up with the crowd.

The TAA terminal was cool and airy with rows of grey seating and plants hanging from the high-tech rafters. The elderly American limped with the rest past more security guards who were scrutinizing them again. He hadn't imagined it, they were looking for him! Ray Vincent kept an even pace, instinct again, but his heart beat painfully.

It was an internal flight, there were no formalities. He was free to walk outside and join a bus queue.

He waited until all those in the line for taxis had been driven away. When the next vacant cab drew up, the "American" appeared to change his mind, hailed it and disappeared.

The driver chattered occasionally. His passenger listened, looking to right and left as though a stranger in the elegant city. His blue glasses had thick lenses; they added years to his age as did his hesitant speech. Ray Vincent peered uncertainly at the address in his diary. "Canberra Hotel?"

"Sure. It's in Ann Street. Not smart, but nice and central."

"Good . . . Don't find walking that easy . . ."

The Canberra was a warren of three hundred cramped, old-fashioned rooms. When, an hour later, Ray Vincent walked through reception a second time, none of the desk clerks paid attention.

He was an anonymous businessman now, sufficiently tanned to pass for an Australian, in a short-sleeved shirt and tie. The cardboard box was inside a salesman's zip-case with a company logo across one corner: Leigh Plastics. Blue-tinted glasses had been exchanged for bifocals with thick tortoise-shell frames, and the shaving cut had vanished.

He still had difficulty controlling his breathing—he was too old for the job. Out of practice. He'd ask to see them in New York, do a deal. Pull out. Did anyone ever get to retire? Would they allow him to? Careful planning had got him this far but could he keep it up?

Even though he was sure he wasn't being followed, Ray Vincent

106

automatically doubled back twice on the short walk, coming out at the back of the coach station before dodging the traffic on North Quay and crossing the bridge. He bought a paper from a newsstand. On a bench overlooking the river Zee waited for him.

"Look, something's gone wrong."

"They are angry in New York," Zee said. "Very angry." The blood pumped even faster. Zee slid his evening paper across the seat between them. It was open at the foreign news page. "Jones has been found."

"So?" Vincent was aggressive. "We knew he would be. There's nothing there—" He stabbed the brief paragraph "—to connect him with *us*."

Zee then asked, "So why d'you insist something is wrong? Here . . ." A small plastic box slid across under cover of the paper. Ray Vincent opened the lid without looking at it and ran a finger over the contents to reassure himself. Could he risk telling Zee about the security guards waiting at Kingsford Smith? If New York really was angry . . . The Brisbane sun no longer felt warm.

"They say you and Parker went crazy."

"Listen, don't blame me—that maniac actually enjoys what he's doing!" Pent up fear made Vincent garrulous. "You weren't there—when he'd got hold of that hammer, the saliva was oozing out!"

"It was your operation. All identification should have been removed and the body hidden where it couldn't be found." Vincent didn't speak. Zee watched him check the yellow label on the box. "Six dozen 88-grain, hollow-point configuration, as you requested," he said automatically. He never raised his voice even though it could scarcely be heard above the traffic on North Quay.

Vincent's hand closed over the cold bullets. Of course he and Parker should have obliterated all traces! He'd slipped up. Parker had only been sent in because he'd failed originally to get the information out of Jones. Another mistake—and New York didn't permit those. The hard edge of the plastic box bit into his palm.

"This is their itinerary." Zee pulled out a copy of the FONEs' travel plan, stained and covered with cigarette ash, obviously retrieved from a waste bin. He passed it across, aware as always of the other's Western smell.

Ray Vincent said dully, "What's going to happen?" Zee immediately distanced himself.

"I leave here tonight for good."

"Where are you. . . ?" But Vincent bit back the question. Zee wouldn't tell him, it was against the rules. Zee stood, tucking the paper neatly under his arm.

"According to the English newspapers, Jones was found by a contact from the British Home Office." He watched as the implication sank home.

"Oh, Christ!" Vincent stared at Zee, fear making his stomach lurch and his voice hoarse. The double-crossing Welsh bastard! That was why they'd been on the look-out. "I haven't got a chance!"

Zee asked simply, "You have what you need?" Vincent nodded dumbly. "New York also said . . ." He hesitated.

"What?"

"Remember your daughter, Amy." Zee walked away across the bridge and Ray Vincent watched him go.

They were alone but Mrs Hardie and the welfare lady talked quietly, like conspirators.

"It's not the same flat, that one's gone. This is on the corner of the block. It's nice but it doesn't get quite as much sun. You'll have to give me a definite yes as soon as you can. D'you want time to think it over?"

Mrs Hardie shook her head vehemently. "I should have said yes last time."

The welfare lady was full of regret. "It hardly ever works . . . a married daughter returns home, starts sharing a kitchen . . . there's bound to be friction. I had hoped you'd be nicely settled by now. Is your leg healing all right?"

"Yes . . ." Mrs Hardie looked at her fearfully. "There's nothing wrong, I start therapy next week."

"Good. Now, what about your daughter, have you told her?"

"No, and don't you say anything, neither."

"But—the tenancy here can't be passed on, you know. This is a three-bed unit; Linda wouldn't qualify."

"I'll tell her once it's definite. She interfered last time. I don't want to miss my chance again."

"We'll wait until the paperwork's complete. It'll take about three weeks. They always redecorate, too, so it's nice and clean. I know how fussy you can be." She laughed again, not unkindly because this was one of the few aspects of her job that gave pleasure: another unwanted old person about to be rehoused satisfactorily.

"The previous tenant left a cooker, a fridge and so forth. Why not give yours to Linda? It might soften the blow when you break the news."

"Yes, all right." Mrs Hardie remembered the angry scenes last time. "I want to do what I can." She was relaxing by the minute; all she had to do was keep the secret a little bit longer.

"Fine." The welfare lady was anxious to be off. "I'll keep in touch."

Crispin Sinclair lay in bed doped with sleeping pills watching his lover pack. "What you doing that for?"

"Don't be a prat!"

"What?" He tried to focus fuzzy thoughts. "What d'you mean?"

"You saw the news."

"So? The police have told the media, what about it?" The youth spun round.

"I'm getting out because I don't want my head bashed in with a hammer." Crispin stared at him. "Think about it!" the youth shouted. "Work it out for yourself. *They*'ve just told everybody that poor Welsh bastard was discovered by 'a representative of the Home Office'."

"They didn't give my name—"

"Everyone in the department knows it was you—that information isn't classified. How long before those friends of his, the ones that killed him, decide you might know something?"

"They wouldn't turn up here!" Crispin Sinclair was open-mouthed. His lover shoved a stack of compact discs on top of his clothes and fastened the suitcase. "Don't be ridiculous!" Crispin struggled out of bed and followed him into the hall. "You can't mean it?" The youth turned, his hand on the Yale lock.

"If I was you, heart, I'd get these changed for something big and heavy. Fix a chain. Tell them downstairs your life's in danger—" He broke off because Crispin was laughing at him. "Suit yourself," he snarled and slammed the door behind him.

Chapter Fourteen

It took all day to return to Bathurst, partly because in Dubbo, where they stopped for tea, Mavis insisted on showing Ben's photo in every café she could find. People were kind, but none remembered seeing the boy. As they resumed their journey she said thoughtfully, "I suppose I could be asking in the wrong sort of place. Lorry drivers don't stop in the middle of towns, do they, because of parking?"

"That's right," replied Charlie.

"Perhaps we should ask at transport cafés instead?"

"Depends what time you plan on gettin' to Bathurst. You given any thought to where you're going to sleep tonight?"

The question sounded innocent enough but much to Mr Pringle's chagrin, by the time they drove into the town Mavis declared she preferred another motel rather than a tent. When he protested she said simply, "Charlie's been telling me about the spiders. Did you know there's one that can give you a fatal bite? A horny funnel red-back, wasn't that what you said it was, dear?" In the driving mirror Charlie's face gave nothing away. Not having read *Reader's Digest*, Mr Pringle couldn't dispute it.

"That spider's only active in this particular area," Mavis said placatingly. "It's safe to use campsites in other places."

Charlie was relieved it had been so easy. Guarding the seed packet inside a motel room was the way he wanted it. He'd think of another excuse tomorrow, depending on where they ended up.

Dropping the pair outside the parlour, he circled the town until he saw Kev's Toyota. Kev was waiting for him. "I've booked three rooms at the hotel across the way. They're going in the middle one. Where are they now?"

"Eating ice-cream and tryin' to find out about that kid. What's the problem?"

111

"Vincent's on the loose. He dodged them at Sydney and caught a plane to Brisbane, but they didn't pick him up when he landed there."

"Shit! Do we know anything about him yet, like whether there's a connection?" Kev shook his head.

"No, but we're not taking risks even if there is no way he could get to Bathurst today. Stay with them, Charlie. There's bad news from London, too. Jones has been found murdered. Pelham's on the phone now, tryin' to find out all they know about that as well as Vincent. Dammit, someone somewhere must know about him."

The short-sighted American tourist registered as Greg Fischer checked out of the Canberra Hotel in Brisbane less than three hours after he'd registered. A noisy group of sales reps milling around the foyer distracted the cashier's attention. It was only later he noticed the short length of the visit, and that Fischer had paid for a full twenty-four hours.

Despite his limp, Fischer moved quickly down Ann Street to the coach station. His feet tapped an inexorable rhythm on the pavement; Amy, Amy . . . God help anyone who laid a finger on her!

Inside the coach station, he locked himself in a cubicle in the gents'. When Ray Vincent emerged, he wore neat Australian slacks and a sports shirt purchased that afternoon in Leichhardt Street. Some of his other clothes, including his English raincoat, he disposed of in a garbage can together with the remains of the cardboard box and wrapping paper. The 9mm pistol was now reassembled inside the slim salesman's briefcase and the thick tinted glasses had been exchanged for the tortoise-shell rims. He walked out of the back of the coach station and hailed a cab to the airport.

"Yes, sir, can I help you?"

"Judd, passenger for Broken Hill. I telephoned earlier."

"Ah, yes, Mr Judd, I have your reservation. Your flight leaves in half an hour."

Ray Vincent bought an evening paper and a cup of coffee. He badly wanted a drink. Tired taut nerves reawakened aches and pains in his neglected body. He needed a week's hard work-out in a gym—instead he'd got nothing but travel ahead. And at the end of it. . . ? He put that thought firmly out of his mind as he'd trained himself to—if only he could do the same with Amy. He forced himself to read the paper.

Nothing more about Evan Jones, which wasn't surprising. He checked the FONEs' itinerary again. Tonight they were due at Gilgandra, tomorrow, Wilcannia, within driving distance of Broken Hill. There'd be barely half a day before he met up with Mavis Hilda Bignell. Not long but his plan was ready. When it was over, he'd catch the next direct flight home, he wouldn't stop until his daughter was in his arms.

"Ansett announce the departure of their flight AN62 to Broken Hill calling at Bourke . . . ." Ray Vincent swallowed the rest of his coffee.

The friendly lady wasn't behind the counter. Mavis and Mr Pringle consumed banana splits and considered the problem. "I wonder if that new waitress knows Gary was the other lady's boyfriend."

"Go very carefully, Mavis. The other lady might not want the fact generally known."

Mrs Bignell waited until the waitress brought them tea before introducing the topic. "We popped in here yesterday. We were trying to find out about a little boy called Ben. This is his father. I think your colleague knows him?"

The girl glanced at the photograph and gave Mavis an old-fashioned look. "You mean Gary."

"Oh, you know him?"

"Couldn't help knowing him. I rent a room in Joyce's flat. Gary used to stay when he was passing through. . .it isn't a big flat."

"Did you ever meet Ben, his little boy?" The girl shook her head, looked at the proffered photos, and shook her head again.

"Didn't know he had a kid, to be honest. A wife, yes, back in England, that was the problem."

"He's divorced now," Mavis confided. "I hope your friend Joyce likes children because he's brought Ben—"

"Divorced? Gary? Oh, Jeez . . ." The girl sat abruptly and stared at Mavis. "When did that happen, for God's sake?"

"I'm not quite sure," Mavis admitted. "Before he came back to Australia."

"So how about that . . ." The news had obviously surprised her. Mr Pringle asked tentatively, "Do I take it, er, Joyce hadn't heard?"

"You take it," the girl said tonelessly. "In fact she'd given up hope of ever seeing him again. Did you tell her he was divorced when you saw her yesterday?"

"No," said Mr Pringle slowly, "I don't believe we did. We talked about the child rather than his parents."

"Maybe that was why Joyce cried most of last night, with you coming and talking about Gary and all." At their blank looks, she said, "You know where Joyce has gone today, don't you?"

"No?"

"She's left for Hobart. She's getting married on Saturday to a bloke she met through a dating agency, he's in pesticides." The girl fingered the photo. "He's dark, though. . .'fact, he's the nearest Joyce could find to Gary, know what I mean?"

"Oh, dear!" Mavis Bignell was sad. "That doesn't sound very promising."

By the end of half an hour, Mavis had polished off a "Wicked Lady" and come to terms with the situation. "Gary may have heard about Joyce's engagement, perhaps that's why he hasn't called, or maybe there was some other reason, but whatever it was, he must be earning his living. He's probably still driving lorries."

"Road trains," Charlie corrected. He'd rejoined them and was drinking the inevitable coke. "That's what they call the big long-distance trailer trucks out here."

"Ben must be at school," Mr Pringle pointed out. "A child doesn't travel round during term time."

"Ben missed such a lot of schooling at home," sighed Mavis, "because he was sickly." The waitress picked up another photo.

"He looks a frail little thing. How old d'you say he was?"

Mr Pringle brooded. The pictures were fanned out in front of him. Were there special schools out here, for sickly children? Could Gary afford to send his child to one? The waitress

114

confirmed Joyce's remark yesterday, that Gary was always "flat broke".

He looked up and found Charlie watching him. "I was thinking. . ."

"Yeah?"

"If one had a child requiring medical attention . . . the bills would be very heavy for a man like Gary."

"Could be," Charlie was non-committal. "He'd qualify for benefits—"

"Yes, but he might not know about those, not yet. And he'd be pretty desperate if he couldn't support the boy. Suppose he decided to foster Ben on a temporary basis, until he got a home together. How would Gary go about that?"

In the thirty-seater aircraft, Ray Vincent was beside a young mother with a pretty dark-haired daughter on her knee. The woman wore a sundress with panties underneath but little else and Vincent was uncomfortably aware of her body. He hadn't been in Australia long enough to become acclimatized; he thought of Adele instead, would she be safe as well as Amy?

The little girl had the same soapy smell Amy always had after her bath. She was about the same age but thinner and yellowy-tanned by the sun.

"Oh, Jesus!" The mother looked at him apologetically. "Sorry. I keep feeling sick. Kelly, stop bothering people!" Beneath the clinging cotton jersey of her sundress the nipples stood out. Ray Vincent made himself look her in the face. The child was wriggling to get down.

"Is your daughter shy of strangers or will she sit on my lap?"

"Are you sure you don't mind?" He smiled.

"I've got one of my own." It was against every rule, talking to strangers!

"Oh, well . . . if you're sure. Kelly, would you like to sit on the gentleman's knee?"

The little girl's hair was soft. She leaned docilely against his chest, a thumb in her mouth.

"I found out this morning I was pregnant," said her mother. "I was dreading flying after that."

"Congratulations."

"Yeah . . . Phil'll be pleased. We've got a farm. He wants a boy."

"What if it's another girl?" The mother smiled, her face softening.

"I shan't mind, I guess. Kelly, take your thumb out, darling."

For some time they didn't speak. The stewardess brought round small square trays of regulation sandwiches. Vincent and the woman took it in turns to eat.

"What's your little girl's name?" It was the child and it caught him off guard. Before he could stop himself, Ray Vincent heard himself say "Amy. . ."

After that, it was too late.

"There's one other thing you could try," said Charlie. Mavis sat beside him, dejection making her red curls droop.

"What's that, dear? I thought we'd phoned every single blessed adoption agency you knew in Sydney. I don't think I could go through explaining to anyone else today."

"No, not the kid, the father. You reckon he's still a truck driver, right?"

"As far as we know," said Mr Pringle.

"So why don't we ask them to call up on CB radio? All the truckers use it. Someone must know about him?"

"That's a good idea. Tomorrow," said Mavis, "when I've got my energy back, we'll find a nice-looking lorry driver and ask him to speak to his friends."

"Truckers. Out here that's what we call 'em."

"Well, yes . . ." said Mavis.

In Kev's room they were holding a council of war. "All we know for certain," said Kev, "is, number one: Evan Jones gave the seed packet two kilos of heroin and she still has it. Did you manage to get anything out of her?"

"Not a thing," Charlie admitted. "I tried. Asked about people she'd met on the flight, people who had contacts in Sydney, people who asked people to take things out for their friends—all she wanted to talk about was the kid.

"I know when he was born, when he first broke a leg,

116

everything. What she didn't want to talk about was how an airline steward gave her two bags of stuff and told her someone would be round to pick it up." Charlie took a pull on his beer.

"What about her partner?" asked Pelham-Walker.

"I thought Jones told you he wasn't involved?" Kev frowned.

"That's correct. But as they're obviously so close . . ." The motel walls didn't insulate the three of them from Mavis's laughter nor the occasional joyful chortle from G D H Pringle.

"At their age," said Charlie sourly, "it's disgusting."

"One day," Kev was stern, "*you*'ll be grateful you can still manage it. *If* you can. After wearing them tight jeans that strangle your balls for most of your life. Now, number two: Sydney can't tell us anything more about Ray Vincent 'cept what it has in his passport—and that he's been in Singapore a few times. Last visit when that guy was hanged in Penang."

"Oh yeah?" Charlie was alert. "Wasn't there a hint that guy might be reprieved?"

"My department had hopes initially," Pelham-Walker waved a deprecating hand. "There were insufficient grounds for an appeal, I fear."

"No," said Kev. "What Charlie was meanin' is why Vincent was around at the time the guy might have been let out. The organization don't have much time for blokes who get caught." He looked at Charlie who drew a thumb across his neck. "Right."

Pelham-Walker felt sick. "Surely not!"

"Look, get it out of your head Vincent's in real estate, Pelham. Not while he's carrying that gun, he isn't. Brisbane are still tryin' to find him, by the way. And we got no result on Byers Street except it's always been let to missionaries."

"I see."

"So what's the news your end?"

"Evan Jones was brutally murdered—in stages apparently."

"You mean he was tortured?" Anthony Pelham-Walker shied away from such an unpleasant word. "The poor bastard," Kev grumbled. "Didn't the bloody fools your end realize he was our only witness? Why the hell couldn't you protect the poor bugger?" Pelham-Walker patted his mouth with a handkerchief.

"I have done what I can to help," he said, attempting dignity. "I

117

have instructed Crispin Sinclair to find out what he can about Ray Vincent. It isn't his field, of course, but he will do his best."

"Any idea who killed Jones yet? Any names?" asked Charlie.

"That sort of evidence takes weeks or months to sift through." This made Kev angry.

"They must act quicker 'n that! We don't want the same thing to happen to the Bignell lady."

"I don't see how there can possibly be a connection. Two men were involved in Evan Jones's case. Traces of saliva and sweat found at the cottage—"

"Two? Pelham, d'you think for once in a bloody while you could tell me the whole of the information, 'stead of keeping little titbits back!" The roar unnerved him. "We been lookin' for one bloke—now you tell me there's two of 'em!"

"I'm so sorry, I never thought . . ." Anthony Pelham-Walker flapped his hands helplessly. He was dishevelled after two days on the road. Any lingering aura of Whitehall authority had completely disappeared. The eyes were dull in his thin face and the tightly pursed mouth twitched constantly. "I fear I'm not exactly suited . . . My milieu, my *métier* even, is to be situate in an office, away from unnecessary pressures. I'm much more accustomed to making rational decisions after consideration of all known facts—"

"Yeah?" sneered Kev. "Like not to offer protection to Jones? Well there's no bloody office and it was your decision to involve yourself, not mine, Pelham. You are in this now, whether you like it or not, and we're all the protection that Bignell lady's got, apart from Charlie, so start doin' some of that rational thinkin' you're good at, and do it quick!"

Suddenly the bronze equine buttocks, Greenwich, even a drunken Fiona, became very desirable objects. Anthony Pelham-Walker was saved from further wrath by the telephone.

"Yes? Oh, great!" Kev's left fist clenched with frustration. "Well, keep tryin'. Whatever you do, don't give up because we gotta find him . . . Yeah, yeah . . . It's a hard life!" He banged the receiver down. "Bloody Queenslanders!"

"What's up?"

"They think they gotta a lead on Vincent at a hotel in Brisbane but he checked out four hours ago."

"Did he leave a forwarding address?" asked Pelham-Walker, interested.

Dear God, don't let me kill him! Kev's knuckles cracked under the tension.

In their comfortable room Mavis couldn't sleep. The other bedside light was still on. "What are you doing?"

"Looking at the pictures of Ben. In over half of them he has some injury or other."

"I told you, he was always having accidents. Mrs Hardie visited that hospital ward—"

"Was there ever an investigation? As to why?" Mavis rolled over and looked at him.

"You mean—whether it always was accidental?" Her eyes grew round. "Mrs Hardie doted on him, he was her only grandchild."

"No, I meant his parents, Linda and Gary." She sat up indignantly.

"That's a bit strong, isn't it? What you're suggesting?"

"Child abuse isn't unknown. Everyone claims it was an unhappy marriage."

"Yes, but not because of Ben. Gary worshipped the boy."

"And—Linda?" This made Mavis uneasy.

"Linda liked a good time, not staying at home. Mrs Hardie was always baby-sitting, or Gary. He didn't go drinking much." She considered the implication but shook her head. "I think you're wrong. I can't see Linda deliberately injuring her baby."

"Just a thought," Mr Pringle said mildly, "Because Ben seems to have been so remarkably unfortunate."

"I've been awake, too, thinking about that powder. You still think someone might come for it, don't you? I was wondering about Charlie actually."

"Good heavens!"

Mavis sighed. She didn't like to think ill of anyone with such muscular brown legs. The way men wore shorts all the time out here was lovely! Then she remembered how she'd been beguiled by Evan's blue eyes. What a blasted nuisance it was, growing old. It made you lose your marbles, gave you a weight problem and stopped you enjoying yourself. When she spoke again, she sounded irritable.

"The truth is I don't know if I'm right. But I got to turning over in my mind what you said at Sydney. After we'd had that bit of a spat. 'Be suspicious from now on . . .'—d'you remember?"

"Yes, I do."

"Well Charlie only joined the trip that morning and you could see Pete hadn't met him before, the way they shook hands. Then today, while you were zizzing away in the back, he asked me ever such a lot of funny questions. More hints, really. About people I might have met on the trip."

"Oh dear." Mr Pringle had almost forgotten about it because of Ben. Now, fear returned in abundance. He'd be lucky if he managed a wink of sleep after this. "I wonder if we should contact the police after all?"

"Not on your nelly," Mrs Bignell said stoutly. "We're giving Evan a chance to go straight first. And anyway, just suppose he—Charlie—is the police?"

"Oh, crikey!"

"Not that I think it's very likely," she added comfortably. "I think he's more likely to be one of *them*, come for the powder like you said. Whatever he is, I think we should be very careful and keep our distance, don't you?"

"Absolutely."

Bother! thought Mavis. She'd been honest but it hadn't done her any good. Wasn't that always the way? All the scrumptious things in life were bad for you, like cream cakes. Then she remembered with a sense of shame that she was already beloved, and cherished, and had no further need of handsome young men. "Tell you what," she offered in expiation, "how about a cup of tea? There's milk and digestives in the fridge. You stay where you are, I'll make it."

When she leaned over to put the cup on the bedside table, her breasts were close enough for him to kiss. As he thanked her, Mr Pringle murmured gently, "You will take great care, won't you, Mavis?"

Chapter Fifteen

Crispin Sinclair made the one-way race circuit of Farnham a second time, looking for an empty space. In the end he surrendered and drove into a car-park. There was a lunch-time jazz session erupting from the foyer of the Redgrave Theatre. Elderly ladies pushing shoppers from Sainsbury's across to the bus-stop walked past the noise with disapproving sniffs.

"They require," Batman had said, "information concerning a Mr Ray Vincent, a British subject working as an estate agent. They need a photograph and any other details you can discover. Vincent is in Australia at present . . ." He paused but decided against giving his subordinate further information. "This time, Sinclair," he added sharply, "I shall expect results."

"Yes, sir. Is there any chance you'll be returning shortly? There has been a certain amount of—speculation—in the department—" But Batman had hung up. Sod him, thought Crispin, leaving me to face the music.

The flat oppressed him. Ever since lover-boy's departure the sound of the phone gave him the jitters and he refused to answer the door unless the caller's voice was one he knew. He'd be safer looking for Vincent; outside he'd be anonymous.

There was no R Vincent listed as an estate agent. A bored telephonist commented, "He's probably trading under another name. D'you know if he lives in the Greater London area?"

"Quite likely, I'd say."

"Shall I transfer you to Directory Enquiries? His home number might be easier to trace?" But this time there were hundreds of R Vincents. Crispin phoned his ex-lover at the FO.

"I thought you'd have been killed by now."

"You left some of your discs behind. I'll smash them if you don't get me some information."

121

"Bitch!"

"I want an address and phone number from the passport office or Australia House. This chap renewed a visa recently."

In the end, his lover could only come up with the name of a town. Crispin scratched his initials on each of the discs before putting them in the post.

He pushed open the door of the *Farnham Advertiser*. "I wonder if you happen to have photographs of one of our local celebrities?" He smiled charmingly at the middle-aged lady behind the counter. "It's his wedding anniversary next month. Some of us are planning a *This is Your Life* kind of thing. I've been detailed to find pictures for the album."

"We might have." She'd opened an old-fashioned card index.

"It's Mr Ray Vincent. He's an estate agent. You don't happen to know him yourself, by any chance?"

At the Orano Windmill Motel in Gilgandra, the FONEs settled down to enjoy their final night in comfortable beds before going camping. The tour was to proceed after all. Protheroe knew that to justify the subsidized cost, he had to return with proof of their efforts. On the other hand, there was no point in being unnecessarily heroic.

"From now on, there will be no public meetings which the press can gatecrash. We shall hold informal gatherings in the bush," he announced.

"Outback," murmured one who was better informed.

"Ah, yes. Outback. When we get to the campsites or isolated settlements we can offer to answer any questions the locals may have . . . Reassure them, that kind of thing. These meetings will be logged of course but will be impromptu to avoid any further adverse reporting by the, er, media." Fellow physicists nodded. To a man, they understood.

"Adam Lithgoe" stood under a shower for several minutes. Wearing only a towel, he padded quietly along to the hotel laundry room and took his clothes out of the machine. A housewife would've thrown up her hands in horror; new, white T-shirts now had blotchy stains from the seersucker jacket.

Ray Vincent appeared satisfied. He didn't hang them to dry outside, though, but on a line in his room. Dressing in business clothes once more and with opaque sunglasses, he set off to make a few necessary purchases. He had to visit a bank, which made him edgy because it meant leaving a record of the transaction, but there was no way round it, he needed a hefty amount of cash.

In a sports shop, the assistant was sympathetic over the loss of his binoculars. "Can't put anything down nowadays . . . folks just aren't honest any more. These are nice and neat. Useful as night-glasses."

"Fine."

Ray Vincent worked his way along the street, mentally checking off his list. When the last item was purchased he ate a hefty steak at a snack-bar before returning for another long shower; he hated not to be clean. The stubble on his chin was itchy now because he hadn't shaved since yesterday. He resisted the urge to scratch as he checked out.

"That was a short visit, Mr Lithgoe." The receptionist smiled in a friendly fashion. Ray Vincent grimaced.

"Summons from head office. You know how it is . . ."

Once outside, he moved smartly to where his final purchase, a rusty Volkswagen, was parked. Checking a compass against the map for a few miles, to be certain it was accurate, he drove west out of Broken Hill.

Mrs Hardie was using metal crutches supplied by the hospital and catching hold of each familiar piece of furniture. It was late and only the day following the welfare lady's visit but she was in a fever to complete her arrangements. Ollie Gorman filled her kitchen as usual. She sat, for safety's sake, leaning the crutches against the table.

"You're doing marvellous," he assured her loudly, "and you're looking so well. Now—" A notebook was in one hand, a stubby pencil in the other "—as I see it, what you need is a van with a Luton top—that's the boxy bit above the driver—where we put the beds."

"Bed," Mrs Hardie corrected him. "I'm only taking the one. I'm leaving the rest for Linda."

123

"All the same, you'll need a Luton if you're going to take that sideboard."

"Yes." She wouldn't part with it; not much had survived her marriage but her mother had saved every penny to give her that.

"Lovely piece of furniture . . ." Ollie spoke automatically as he totted up figures. "Now, we got a choice. If it's a weekday, it'll have to be two small vans—I'll have to pay one of the drivers the going rate, can't lay my hands on two vans you see." He sucked in air at the size of the total. "Fifty-eight, say sixty-five with beer money. If it was a Sunday, now, my brother-in-law'd do it. He can borrow his boss's van. It's big, only need the one. That'd work out much cheaper."

"I don't want anything illegal."

"He'd replace the petrol." Ollie was wide-eyed. "Engines ought to be used every day otherwise the batteries go flat. Thirty quid. Say, thirty-five, to cover incidentals."

"All right."

"These bits and pieces of yours . . . little ornaments, photos and such. We couldn't be responsible for the packing. Can Linda give you a hand?"

"Linda mustn't know," Mrs Hardie said quickly. "I told you before."

"So you did," Ollie pacified her. "I'd forgotten."

"It's important."

"OK, I'll remember. But can you manage?"

"Yes . . . I'll ask my home help. She doesn't mind earning a bit extra." Ollie Gorman's glance had strayed across to the mantle-piece.

"I see Mavie's keeping you well supplied with postcards. Has she come across Ben yet?"

"No . . ."

"Never mind, she'll keep trying. We got a pc from her at The Bricklayers. Said she'd been picked up by ever such a nice young man on the aircraft. Old Pringle'd better watch out." Ollie leered. "That bar isn't the same without Mavie, you know. Even the beer tastes flat. Your Linda's been in plenty . . . enjoying herself."

"Listen, Ollie, you will be careful what you say? Not even a hint?"

"Cross my heart and hope to die. When d'you want the job done?"

"I should know by the end of the week."

"So what's the seed packet decided to do today?" Charlie stood in the open doorway of Kev's room from where he could watch the restaurant unobserved.

"Pringle's been doing the sums. I heard him say they could afford one more day in the hire-car then they got to catch up with the coaches. They were discussing looking for this Gary character rather than the kid, they reckon he might be easier to locate."

"Sounds reasonable," said Kev. "The kid's most likely back in Sydney if his father's on the road."

"*If* he's still got a job. Anythin' from Brisbane yet?"

"Nuthin'." Kev was disgusted. He switched off his electric shaver and came to stand behind Charlie. "So . . . one more day then they rejoin the tour?"

"Looks like it."

"When she'll be where *they* expect to find her . . . and a long way from home, where I think they'll come out into the open and go for it."

"You don't think . . . I mean, she's no idea what could be comin' to her, Kev."

"She's the only bait we've got. We can't let her in on it, she couldn't act the decoy convincingly. She'd start havin' the vapours every time she saw a strange man. Besides, you'll be up there with her."

"Yeah."

"With me and Pelham right behind you."

Jean Protheroe marvelled at the flat arid landscape. Fifty-seven miles according to Pete, with a rise of only seventeen feet. Worse than Lincolnshire. Blazing heat made the window hot to the touch and showed up the grey under her auburn rinse. "How long could a man survive out there, Kenneth?"

"Depends how much water he had in his billy-can," he said playfully. "Notice the mirage?"

"One can scarcely miss it, it's gone on for miles. Are we stopping for coffee today?"

"Somewhere called Cobar. It's a copper town."

"As long as it has air conditioning, that's all I ask."

He waited in the Volkswagen, screened from view behind scrubby spinifex. Ray Vincent wore shorts and one of the mottled T-shirts. Dust from his all-night drive covered his hair and clothes as well as the car. Sweat caked it deep into the wrinkles on his face, etching a pattern of weariness.

He saw the moving billowing dust, the glint of red and white—it must be them, they'd finally got here! As both coaches swept past, he scanned the passengers, gripping the binoculars fiercely.

The only red-head was in the second coach. He picked up the sugar and slipped along unobtrusively, keeping in the deep black shadow of verandahs until he was close to where they were parked.

It was too hot for coffee. Across the street was the Western Hotel with the longest verandah in New South Wales, according to Pete. They began to drift across. As soon as the first disappeared inside, momentum increased. "It's open!"

"Mine's a lager, two if we've got time."

"Two? I could drink the place dry!"

"Goin' for a slash and a cold coke, mate," said Pete.

"Right. Sheri and me'll clear this lot then we'll join you." Lenny began stacking unwanted urns and crockery back into the belly of his vehicle. Ray Vincent moved swiftly and unscrewed the filler cap on the adjacent coach.

In the pub, Pete was discussing the route ahead with Protheroe. "We can stay in Wilcannia if you like. See what you think when we get there. Or we can push on to Broken Hill."

"Anything wrong with Wilcannia?"

"We-ll . . ." Pete was reluctant to do his country down. "It used to be an important sort of a town . . . all that's changed. It's got a kind of hopeless feel to it nowadays."

"We can reach it in time for a late lunch?"

"Sure. Sheri's got everything organized. We can keep goin' as long as you like."

126

"Let's see it, then decide." Protheroe looked at his watch. "Time ladies and gentlemen, if you please."

They went in convoy, Lenny in the lead. From time to time he and Pete chatted over their radio. The horizon stretched endlessly ahead, Cobar had disappeared. Outside, the sun reached its zenith.

"She's coughing a lot, mate . . . snatching, too."

"Muck in the carburettor?"

"Nah . . ." The engine surged then missed and Pete pressed his foot down. "Somethin's odd though."

"Want to stop?"

"You keep goin'. You and Sheri see to the dinner. I'll nurse the old girl along."

The coach bucked under the pressure of his foot then juddered to a halt. "Just goin' to take a look, folks. Maybe a 'roo's got jammed in the works."

There was nothing on the horizon except the disappearing dust that was Lenny's coach, and the flies.

"Can't he leave the fan on to keep it cool! That might help." Up and down the coach, frantic arms holding *New Scientists* flailed ineffectually.

"It's so hot! Absolutely stifling!"

Lying in the road beneath the crankshaft, Pete saw feet wander past. "Hey! Come back." He slithered out wiping the oil from his face. "It's dangerous to wander off. If you must come outside, stay in the shade."

Ten minutes driving time behind, Ray Vincent turned off the highway and drove along a dried-up river bed. Silver-white ghost gums shielded him from view. When he judged he'd travelled far enough, he stopped, took up the binoculars and crawled to the level of the road.

The FONEs were huddled in a narrow strip of shade beside the coach. The emergency barrel of water was out and the driver was shouting at them to sip, not gulp each precious cupful. Ray Vincent slithered back down behind the protecting scrub and doubled back to his car.

He took out his own two-gallon can, soaked a towel and

wrapped it round his head. He wet his lips but didn't swallow and settled down to wait.

In Wilcannia, lunch was nearly over. They lolled under trees in the drab municipal park. One or two sat on the swings. Lenny checked his watch again; over an hour. Time to find out what was happening.

"OK, folks, if you've finished, there's the Darling river in that direction. Plenty of wild life if you like that kind of thing but keep out of the sun. The bar's open in the hotel over there. Any problems, see Sheri. Back soon as I can."

Pete was struggling to keep discipline. "Please do as I ask. None of you are used to this kind of heat. Please, folks . . . Come back inside and I'll run the fan for five minutes. Keep as still as you can to conserve energy."

"Can I have some more water?" He looked at his watch.

"None yet, sorry."

"Why can't you call the AA or something?" asked Protheroe angrily. The chorus was taken up.

"Surely you can use that radio to speak to a garage!" Pete tried not to grin because his lips felt ready to split.

"Maybe you haven't noticed . . . we don't have that many garages. Lenny'll be here soon."

When the other coach eventually pulled up, some of the FONEs ran across half hysterically, desperate to be cool. Lenny crouched down beside his partner.

"What's the trouble?"

"Dirty fuel, I reckon. Which is bloody odd considerin' she's been goin' all right. She went sweet as a nut up to Cobar."

"So it's a breakdown job?"

"I'd say so. You'll need to get those Poms out of the sun pretty soon. Can't tow this old girl as well." Lenny knew he was right but it didn't make it any easier.

"Protheroe'll wet his knickers. I'll see what's available to come out from Wilcannia. You stayin' here?"

"Yeah," Pete growled. "Might as well start emptyin' her. I'll leave the radio switched on."

"Right. Got enough water?"

"Yeah."

Ray Vincent felt dizzy. He tried to focus on what was happening through the heat haze. Passengers were climbing aboard the other coach which reversed and set off back towards Wilcannia. Great!

He swallowed the cupful of water he had beside him in the scrub, he could afford the luxury this time, and not bothering at concealment ran back to his car.

His watch felt loose on his sweaty wrist. He paused to tighten it and didn't notice Pete dip underneath the coach once more.

The Volkswagen roared to a halt beside the luggage compartment. Vincent was out, tugging at the handle. It took him by surprise because it wasn't locked. He didn't stop to think but flung the flap upright against the side of the coach and began heaving suitcases on to the road.

"Good of you to stop, mate—" Pete froze as Vincent swung round. "Bloody hell—!" The wrench caught him on the side of the neck and his head crashed against the unyielding metal coachwork. Pete's legs folded and his body tipped forward into the dust.

"Christ!" Ray Vincent wanted to keep on hitting, to annihilate the knowledge in Pete that he'd seen him. He kicked the body on to its back; eyes stared upward, seeing nothing. He gave the head another hard blow and began emptying the suitcases.

Sweat blinded him; it wasn't here! Wreckage was strewn over the road. Clothes were heaped among the slashed luggage. She'd got the stuff with her, it was the only possible explanation. Worse, she obviously knew what it was, otherwise she'd have it in her suitcase. Jones had sworn he hadn't told her—a man facing death doesn't lie. But the steward hadn't picked a stupid old tart, he'd found one that had her wits about her.

Ray Vincent bundled the wreckage into the hold in a fury. Inside the coach he slit open every remaining package but it wasn't there either. He didn't want to kill her; he'd gone to all this trouble to avoid it, but now. . .she'd signed her own death warrant.

A crackle on the radio brought him to his senses. He rushed out, leaping clumsily into the road. The Volkswagen still throbbed and, as a last vicious gesture, Ray Vincent kicked the driver's body so that it lay in the full glare of the sun.

He drove recklessly until the outskirts of Wilcannia. There was no other choice of route, he had to go through it. Instinct made him slow down. He'd have to go back to Broken Hill and risk being recognized. Ray Vincent was forced to consider his alternative plan. He had to get ahead of the tour which meant driving day and night as far as Port Augusta. That was the only way to gain enough time.

Sweat soaked the plastic seat. He'd planned to do it without killing because a bullet could hamper his escape. The organization were angry because the route had dried up but even they agreed, once Jones was dead, there was no point in killing the woman. Not after Vincent had been able to assure them Jones knew nothing more. Vincent's task was to retrieve the two kilos and get out leaving no traces.

Then Zee had told him about the Home Office connection. Jones hadn't said a word about that. What else had he managed to withhold despite the agony? If Parker hadn't gone berserk, they could've got it out of him.

Ray Vincent cursed savagely. Another corpse and his luck could run out. Amy! Had he killed that dumb idiot of a driver? His skull was cracked, enough to stop him talking. Long enough for Vincent to find the woman. She had to die.

The police officer eased his gut out of the driving seat and stood, elbows resting on the roof. The farm dog was announcing his arrival loudly enough.

A young woman pushed open the mesh door and called, "Yes? I'm bathing my little girl." He walked across slowly. This property was remote and he didn't want to make her nervous.

"Mrs Chrissie Cartwell?"

"That's right."

"My ID, Mrs Cartwell." He waited. She examined it carefully. Inside, he could hear the little girl splashing about.

"I'll wait out here if you prefer, Mrs Cartwell."

"No, it's OK. I'm in the kitchen." She went ahead of him,

sweeping her daughter up in the towel and lifting her out of the tin bath. "What's the problem? My car insurance?"

"I believe you were on a flight from Brisbane to Broken Hill coupla days ago? We're checking all the passengers on that flight."

"My word! That was a full load."

"It was, Mrs Cartwell. Luckily 'bout twelve of 'em came from the same firm. Makes life easier. Now according to this—" He showed her the photostat of the seating plan "—you were in a window seat, 8A, with your little girl on your knee, right?" The woman nodded.

"Boy, I felt crook that day."

"What about the passenger in 8B, name of Judd?"

"He helped me with Kelly."

"Remember anythin' about him? What'd he look like, for instance?"

"God, what is this? Was he a rapist, or what?"

"Not as far as we know." The policeman tried to keep it avuncular. "Just been told to find out all we can. What colour hair, can you remember?"

"Fair, I think . . ." Chrissie Cartwell pushed her own out of her eyes and reached for Kelly's nightdress. "Yes, he was fairer than you."

"Tall?"

"Not very. Middling like Phil, my husband. Broader though. He looked—like he enjoyed his food a lot."

"A gut you mean?" She laughed.

"Well . . ."

"I get it, not as big as mine. Did he look like an outdoor sort of fella?" Chrissie frowned.

"He might've been once, with that build. I think he was some kind of salesman. He'd got one of those zip-up briefcases. To do with plastics, I think."

"That's real observant of you, Mrs Cartwell." He was about to ask another question when there was a shout.

"He was smelly!" Kelly was peeping over her mother's shoulder. "Smelly man!" she yelled again. Chrissie Cartwell laughed.

"Certainly was! I told you I was feeling crook? Some of those

131

men's toiletries, they really set me off. Kelly's the same. Takes after me, except she's not pregnant." The officer nodded sympathetically.

"Any idea what it was? What brand?"

"No . . . it was woody, sort of musky. Powerful. Oh, and another thing—he'd got a daughter, too. Told Kelly her name was Amy. That any use?"

"Sure." He waited patiently as Chrissie Cartwell searched her memory for a final item that eluded her.

"Yes, that was it . . . he seemed like a proud father. He was really fond of that little girl."

"It's been a lovely day. I'm only sorry we haven't come across Gary but you never know—" Mavis was as optimistic as ever "—with all those lorry drivers calling each other on their CBs, we still might. I gave them our whereabouts."

Yeah, thought Charlie gloomily, just about the whole of Australia knows where you're goin', lady, so let's keep our fingers crossed.

"One of them told me he'd come across several Pommies driving those road trains."

"Poms," Charlie corrected, "or Pommie bastards, that's how we say it." Mavis took it in her stride.

"It's an interesting language, isn't it, full of subtle nuances? And it's very kind of *you* to do all the driving, dear." In the cool of the morning, Mrs Bignell had changed her mind about Charlie. He couldn't possibly be a drug trafficker and she couldn't see him as a policeman. He was simply a driver who knew the road far better than they did. "Mr Pringle's catching up on his beauty sleep!" she murmured.

He'd done nothing but sleep, the randy old sod! Charlie glanced in the mirror. Mr Pringle's head was tilted back and his mouth open. When he wheezed occasionally, his moustache twitched. He'd been like that for the best part of three hundred and fifty miles.

It was dusk and far behind he could see Kev's headlights. At the last roadhouse, they'd managed a snatched urgent conversation. "Whoever it is, he's out in the open—Pete's been attacked, I've been talking to the police at Wilcannia."

132

"Christl!"

"Can't stop—she's looking this way. Lenny's takin' the rest of 'em to the campsite at Broken Hill, that's where we'll go next." Charlie did a quick calculation.

"That's a bloody long way!" But Kev had disappeared.

When she was told, Mavis didn't object. Another long drive would be lovely. There would be a full moon later on, very romantic. She'd done her best to find Gary, her conscience was clear; from now on she could simply sit back and enjoy her holiday.

The coach had been towed away. They drove unwittingly over the stretch of road where the flying doctor's aircraft landed earlier. When they paused for a meal in Wilcannia, they learned all about it in the pub.

It was a beer-swilling place where Aborigines sat drinking silently, watching others who simply passed through. Charlie kept his eyes on Mavis Bignell's face as the bartender gave them the details then, making his excuses, he went to stand in the urinal next to Kev.

"She was genuinely upset. No sign she's worked out what the bloke was really lookin' for."

"Good," said Kev softly. "He's bound to try again. Tomorrow they're travelling to Coober Pedy; day after that, Ayers Rock. That'll be his last chance. After that, the Poms are due to go home."

"You still reckon it's this Vincent bloke?" Kev shrugged.

"Dunno. The office are sending all they've got to Woomera. That's tomorrow's coffee stop. We might find somethin' interesting waitin' for us. Meanwhile, Charlie my son, you just keep your eyes peeled as far as Broken Hill."

"Yeah . . ." Charlie indicated Pelham-Walker hidden in a cubicle. "The mother country come up with anythin'?"

"Give 'em a chance. They're probably down to usin' bikes by this time, to save the pennies."

An embarrassed police force had done their best. The FONEs had been soothed, Protheroe was deferred to and a forty-seater coach put at Lenny's disposal. The red and white Wallaby vehicles would be left in Wilcannia and Charlie's was already being repaired.

133

What mattered was that the rest of their holiday should be as smooth as possible because nothing like this had happened before and they were anxious to avoid bad publicity.

After the first burst of anger, the British told each other vandalism was the same all over the world. Their belongings were stowed temporarily in paper sacks. Once they were in Broken Hill, they'd been told to purchase new luggage and the state would foot the bill.

"Generous, really," said Protheroe, "all things considered. I doubt whether we'd have done the same for any Australians visiting Bournemouth."

"No one would attack a coach in Bournemouth!"

"I don't know . . . These days."

"I think we should organize a whip-round," Jean Protheroe insisted. "From what Lenny told me, Pete's in a bad way."

Outside the operating theatre in Alice Springs, Pete implored with his eyes but couldn't speak. "A Volks'," he begged silently. "He was driving a Volks'." The anaesthetist picked up a needle.

"Just a prick, you'll hardly feel a thing." Ten seconds later, Pete was unconscious.

They drove into Broken Hill at sunset. Ochre soil and scrub had given way to bungalows surrounded by lawns and trees. As usual the contrast was startling. Further into town there were shacks close to the mines and, on the far side, the campsite itself.

There was excitement, voices had a confident ring. Hearing them, Lenny managed a smile. "Maybe you'd like Sheri and me to show you how to pitch the first tent?"

In the scramble to unload, sleeping-bags, tents and airbeds were tossed out feverishly. Beyond the mêlée, Sheri had started up the barbecue and the fragrance of grilling steaks added to the urgency.

"We pitch them in a line," Lenny instructed. "Each shares two pegs with the next tent and so on. No gaps, right? You connect the centre pole, push it up the middle to support the roof—and there you are."

It was so simple: a heap of canvas transformed into a modest sentry-box of a dwelling in a twinkle. Lenny hammered home four pegs and it was done. Scientists and physicists looked at one another in amusement: how could their combined Oxbridge talents fail to cope with that?

Protheroe began the rout by shouting at Jean. Up and down the site, others followed suit, bawling, yelling, seizing mallets, grabbing inflatable mattresses and disputing possession of sleeping-bags. Bedlam reigned as a half-crazed army of generals issued commands to mutinous spouses.

When it was over, the line of tents snaked uncertainly, sagging roofs a drunken silhouette against the night sky. Arriving a few hours later when all was quiet, Mr Pringle surveyed it and shook his head. He began erecting their tent as quietly as possible. Mrs. Bignell sat on a stool in the moonlight to watch.

"I do think you're clever," she whispered. "Ours is the only one that's upright. But why is the opening on the opposite side to everyone else?"

"I fancy none of them have noticed they're facing east. Sunrise is about five a.m." He held open the flap and she crawled inside.

"I'm so glad you're not a nuclear physicist, dear."

Charlie clambered into the empty hold of the coach where he was to sleep. Lenny lay there waiting, smoking a cigarette. "We've got somethin' to discuss." Charlie groaned.

"Can't it wait?"

"No it bloody well can't!" Lenny hissed. "Someone nobbles a coach, nearly kills my best mate, all because somethin's happenin' that I don't know about. And don't give me any crap about it's these Poms and their silly ideas upsettin' a nutcase, because it bloody well doesn't add up! So what's going on?" Charlie told him.

At the finish, Lenny stubbed out his cigarette. "You bastards owe me one coach and driver and one hell of an apology—"

"I'll drive," Charlie said quickly. "I'll do Pete's share."

"Too right you bloody will," Lenny agreed, "and you'll pay compensation if the poor bugger dies." He looked at Charlie speculatively. "You forgot to tell me the important bit, didn't you?" Charlie didn't reply. Lenny leaned across.

135

"What you forgot to say was—that wasn't the end of it. This maniac's gonna try again. Isn't he?"

In their tent, Mr Pringle waited until he heard Mavis's regular breathing before easing himself out of his sleeping-bag. Thank heavens he'd managed to doze earlier. In Wilcannia, he'd been too shocked by the news to speak. Seeing that Mavis hadn't grasped its significance, he'd decided not to upset her. Tomorrow, in private, he would persuade her they must go to the police. Tonight he would defend her against all comers.

G D H Pringle wasn't a brave man. He'd no intention of engaging an attacker, but he could raise the alarm if necessary and to do that meant staying awake. He sighed. It was the only way. At least he could look at the stars.

Pulling on a sweater and with his scout knife, Mr Pringle unzipped the flap and went outside. Alas for heroism! Up and down the row, the FONEs were wide awake in the unfamiliar surroundings, reliving earlier acrimony or acting out marital fantasy.

Sitting there, it became impossible to concentrate on the universe. Who on earth was addressing his soulmate loudly as "Mrs Piggybum"? Surely not that elderly academic who was always complaining about the food?

As he shook his head over other embarrassments, wondering how on earth they would face each other in the morning, there was an explosive shout. Mr Pringle seized his knife but it was only Protheroe, savaged by mosquitoes. He erupted out of his tent at the other end of the line, knocking down the pole. Mr Pringle watched sadly as sagging rigging gave way and domino effect took over. Irate tousled heads began to emerge. At least Mrs Bignell was safe, he reflected.

Chapter Sixteen

The inquest into the unlawful killing of Evan Jones was soon over without revealing any of the details the press were so eager to hear. One witness, Crispin Sinclair, exhibited a skill in avoiding pitfalls which brought forth praise.

"Most satisfactory . . ." The atmosphere inside the limousine taking him and the acting HOD back to London was cordial.

"Thank you, sir."

"Despite Pelham-Walker's aberration, I think we can claim the department has salvaged its most precious possession ... its reputation." Crispin remained modestly silent.

There was a suggestion of a cough from the official, a clearing of the throat that heralded a delicate matter for discussion. "Re the subject of Pelham-Walker—and this must go no further, Sinclair."

"Yes, sir?"

"A decision has been taken which, given the circumstances, was inevitable I fear . . ."

Evan's mother and sister were driven home by sympathetic police. The WPC lingered in the chilly hall. "You will stay with your mam. You won't leave her on her own?" Evan's sister nodded.

"She hasn't been left since it happened." The policewoman looked relieved.

"At least they've released the body for burial. Maybe she'll find some comfort, being able to grieve properly."

"The doctor gave her some pills." The daughter was doubtful. "She's been like a zombie since . . . I don't think she knows what's going on."

"Poor thing," the WPC murmured. "I'll keep in touch, love. As soon as there's a hint they've got the men who did it, I'll come round. OK?"

The girl returned to where her mother sat in the kitchen. "Would you like a nice cup of tea, Mam?" Her mother roused herself.

"That was him, wasn't it? That found Evan? The last person to see him alive?"

"That's right." The girl waited. Eventually her mam said, "I just wanted to be sure."

It was an early start at Broken Hill. Mr Pringle's social standing had risen a couple of points; theirs was the only tent which hadn't collapsed during the night. If Mrs Bignell hadn't been so obdurate concerning the police, he might have relished the situation even more.

"Look, dear, we can't be sure it was one of the drug people who wrecked the coach. Why did he hit Pete on the head if he was? Jean Protheroe said the police thought it was straightforward vandalism, they were very apologetic about it."

"Mavis, we must tell someone!"

"All right," she capitulated. "I'll finish that letter to Evan. When we get to Coober Pedy we'll find a post-office and after that—if anything else happens—we'll tell someone. That do?"

It was a compromise but it didn't make his cornflakes taste any better.

His nerve was shaken again when they paused for coffee at Yunta, a hald with two roadhouses and six small dwellings. Mr Pringle was determined not to let Mrs Bignell out of his sight but having sampled ice-cream in one café, she decided it might taste even better on the other side of the road. Mr Pringle lingered behind, anxious for a private word with Lenny.

"This youngster my friend is so anxious to trace . . ."

"Yes?" Since Charlie's revelation about Mavis Lenny's manner towards both of them was guarded. Fortunately Mr Pringle appeared unaware.

"The boy enjoyed poor health and had missed a great deal of schooling. Would the authorities out here insist he attend a remedial school in the circumstances? And would there be a way of finding out once we return to Sydney?" Lenny's eyebrows rose.

138

"Search me," he admitted honestly. "You could be right, but I'm blessed if I know who to ask—hallo? Looks like your friend's found herself a pal over there—"

What happened next took him completely by surprise. Mr Pringle shot across the road at twice the speed he would expect from a man his age, and stood panting between Mrs Bignell and a bewildered truck driver.

It was less of a shock to see Charlie already there, one hand inside his jacket, but Lenny still swore. That Bignell lady was dynamite; the sooner this whole trip was over, the better. Lenny had screwed a promise of compensation for Pete's injuries out of Charlie in return for co-operation, but thank God there were only three more days to go.

"Yes?" gasped Mr Pringle. The truck driver was massive and towered over him.

"I was only askin' if she was the party looking for the Pom. She fitted the description and this is the Wallaby Tours outfit, ain't it?"

"It's all right, dear. This isn't about you know what . . ." Mavis was stopped by his expression as Mr Pringle whipped round. "I mean, it's about Gary," she finished lamely. She smiled up at the driver. "Have you found him on your CB?"

"Not exactly. Not many Poms drivin' road trains, nowadays. There's one we all know 'bout, though. Got his own business in Perth. He uses other Poms as truckers when he can."

"How far's Perth from here?" asked Mavis. He was astonished.

"'Bout two thousand five hundred kilometres due west."

"Oh, dear." Even Mavis realized it was impossible.

"That can't be Gary," Mr Pringle insisted. "He hadn't got a job when he came back, remember." He turned to the trucker. "I'm sorry if I appeared abrupt. One of our coaches was involved in an incident yesterday." The huge Australian was already shaking his head.

"Shockin'," he told them. "Never heard anythin' like it before . . . Everyone's been talkin' 'bout it. Been on the national news and everythin'."

"The other Pommies?" asked Mavis. "Are any of them nearer than Perth?"

"Yeah, that's what I came to tell you 'bout. One of 'em was headed for Coober Pedy last night. You might find it's him when you get there." Mavis glowed.

"How splendid! Would you like an ice-cream? I was just going to have another one." Charlie watched them disappear. Now why did old Pringle react like that if he didn't know about the stuff? It didn't add up.

He was still brooding about it when he joined Kev during the tea-stop at Woomera. They were at the disused launch site, dotted with concrete plinths each topped with an empty rocket. The site symbolized more than a forgotten era to the FONEs. Physicists wandered among the defunct exhibits crying aloud in happy recognition. "Those things were goin' to protect Australia once upon a time," said Kev. "Now look at 'em. Just scrap metal."

"Yeah." Charlie hadn't reached the age of nostalgia. "Listen, Kev—"

"Later, Charlie, when we're at Coober Pedy. We've not got much time before the coach leaves and there's this mass of stuff come from Macquarie Street. Pelham's bloke finally got permission to use a carrier pigeon, too. Look at these." Kev pulled photographs out of a pile.

"So that's what Vincent looks like nowadays?" Charlie began to read the caption: "'Father Christmas doesn't fail the children! Popular local figure Mr Ray Vincent, seen here with his daughter Amy, stepped into the breeches (literally) when a colleague was struck down with flu. Mr Vincent, past President of the society, took over the red robe rather than disappoint the children.'"

"It ties in with this report come in from Brisbane." Kev thrust it into his hand. "A woman passenger claims the man sat next to her talked about his daughter, Amy."

"Yeah, but Kev, this won't help identify him, not with the whiskers. Ah, that's better . . ." Charlie stared at the next photo, of a group of golfers. An arrow identified a fleshy-faced, fair haired man. "Looks as if Santa Claus has changed quite a bit from his visa mugshot."

Kev compared the one supplied by Immigration. "Clever bastard . . . just a few changes. This must've been taken when he was twenty pounds lighter, had more hair—"

140

"But why would Santa Claus need a 9mm pistol?"

"He was headed in the right direction." Kev stabbed the Brisbane report. "Could've been there, waiting for when the coaches drove into Wilcannia. Just his bad luck the seed packet wasn't on one of them."

"He picked the right coach, too," Charlie pointed out. "She and Pringle travelled with Pete. Do we know for certain why the engine was playing up?"

"Not yet," said Kev. "We're going to have to assume . . ." And Charlie nodded.

"Until we hear different, I'd say it's Santa."

There was a strangled cry from across the room. Both men turned. Anthony Pelham-Walker was clutching a signal and holding the desk for support. "I've been—dismissed!"

"Aw well, Pelham—" Kev tried to make it sympathetic "—it was a risk you took, comin' out here when it wasn't your problem."

"You don't understand—I must get back at once!"

"They're not likely to stop your pension, are they?"

"The honours list!" It was a moan from the heart. Charlie didn't understand.

"He's frightened he won't get a gong," Kev explained. "Listen Pelham, stick with us, mate. We can't leave you here, you'd be marooned. If anything's gonna happen, it's got to be during the next three days. Besides, when we get to Ayers Rock, that's where you can catch a plane."

Sixty kilometres out of Alice Springs, an old truck was parked within a circle of termites' nests, a straggling insect-made Stonehenge, each hollow segment nearly five foot tall.

Ray Vincent had spent six hours in Alice. He'd checked into a hotel, showered, then visited a bank. It set his teeth on edge when he had to do that—he hated leaving any traces—but he needed money. He'd bought the truck for cash; it was battered but it was adequate. He'd driven this far into the bush, checking his compass constantly, because he needed to disappear.

The heat was frightening. Would the tyres last? He'd only got three spares and the thorns between the rocks were needle sharp.

He forced himself to leave the car and pace several metres in each direction to check his isolation. Once he was satisfied, he rested. The driving cabin was an oven. He wrapped his sleeping-bag round his head for more protection. He was dehydrating as he sat there, but on this job you went by the clock; he wasn't due for the next sip of water.

The Heckler & Koch P9S was reassembled and inside the binoculars case. He'd taken the spring, screw and remaining metal parts out of the handles of his overnight bag after the last airport X-ray machine. When he'd killed the Bignell woman, he'd ditch the pistol altogether. It was too much of a risk to smuggle it back into England.

He slit open the cigars and loaded the training bullets; they didn't give the right "feel" but he didn't want to waste live ammunition. Now that he was ready, he allowed himself a sip of water before measuring out the range.

Powdery brown dust covered his trainers. When he stumbled, Ray Vincent deliberately wiped his hands on his shorts. He'd had to become a businessman again in Alice Springs but by the time he got to Ayers Rock, he wanted to be back inside the role of an ageing drop-out. People went out of their way to avoid bums, from middle-class indignation.

Vincent jammed the target in the bole of a ghost gum. The plate, ten inches in diameter, had been taken from the hotel where he'd rested for those few hours. He strode back to the twigs at the fifty-metre mark, hefting the gun from hand to hand, letting the strength and power filter through his nerves to his brain. It was irksome having only two magazines but more would've been risky. He'd allowed himself more time for target practice, to compensate.

He reached the mark. Without a pause, pushing the slide home as he spun round, he aimed at the device in the centre of the plate, "Telford Territory Motor Inn".

The plastic bullets gave no recoil. He emptied both magazines then waited, listening for the slightest disturbance in the surrounding bush. A pair of galahs rose and flapped lazily away. Silence. Ray Vincent walked forward to examine the plate, and immediately felt sick. It was cracked, that was all. He'd caught it twice on the rim, two out of thirteen, and only three days left!

*

If the scenery that day reminded Mrs Bignell of Mars, her first view of Coober Pedy was completely lunar. The vast Pimba plains had been empty of trees. Brown earth and scrub gave way to reddish dirt with yet more tufts of spinifex, but as they approached the town they could see not a trace of green, simply piles of shale, craters with mysterious ventilation shafts growing out of the sides, and ramshackle entrances opening on flights of steps that led underground; Coober Pedy sat astride undiscovered layers of opal.

They circled the low hills, some topped with shanty-type houses, until they came to a halt in a dusty open square. Opposite was what to Mr Pringle looked remarkably like a blockhouse.

"Sorry, folks. It's too windy to risk the tents." The FONEs stared at the billowing grey clouds. Dust had seeped inside the coach, they could taste it on their skin. "Sorry about the lack of a motel, too. They're plannin' on buildin' one here sometime. Meanwhile, they got this alternative accommodation . . ." and Lenny gestured across the square.

It was worse than any squaddies' hut, half tunnelled out of a disused mine, with double-tier metal bunks less than a foot apart. As shrieks of dismay began, Charlie looked round satisfied; he couldn't have planned it better himself. Only one narrow entrance? The seed packet would be snug and safe in here all night.

Amid the wailing and disbelief, Jean Protheroe's voice was loudest. "First you kill the family pet, now you reduce me to this!" As she paused to draw breath, Lenny said innocently, "Did you know they sell opals? The shop's in the cave over there."

Mavis didn't join the frenzied rush; she shook the nearest metal frame. "It's only for one night," said Mr Pringle encouragingly. One of the springs pinged and rust spattered on a spiders' nest below. "I don't think those can be the dangerous variety, at least I hope not."

"It's not the creepy-crawlies," Mavis said flatly, "even if they are twice as big as those at home; it's these bed-frames. None of them are up to my weight. And we'll all be in here together!"

"How about a little something from the shop?"

They walked along a passage hewn out of sandstone, breathing

143

cool clean air gratefully. Lights glinted on quartz crystals still embedded in the rock. At a crossroads, branching galleries led in several directions, to coffee and souvenir shops, to wooden front doors with brass handles. "They really do live underground." Mavis was amazed.

"Not surprising when you consider the outside temperature."

"I wonder if Gary is behind one of those doors?"

The jewellery shop was doing a roaring trade in *bijoux* peace-offerings following the disastrous camp at Broken Hill. But what about tonight? Mr Pringle wondered. Would the world's leading scientists cope any better in a Stalag?

He saw with surprise that Mrs Bignell was by an open showcase. Ahead of her, Mrs Piggybum and her mate were already being served. Mr Pringle knew a desperate man when he saw one. "You've never worn jewellery before, Jessie!" the mate quavered; and she answered sharply, "No, because you're always too mean to give me any." Protheroe's quest for a suitable nuclear waste site was, Mr Pringle decided, producing an unexpected fall-out.

He came to attention. It was Mavis's turn and the assistant offered her a ring which she slid on her finger. "What d'you think?" He thought it very large but dared not say so.

"How about the dark one with the red sparkle in the middle?" It was much, much smaller. The assistant gazed in respectful admiration.

"Isn't it the most wonderful stone? They only find black opal like that once in a lifetime."

Oh my goodness! And he'd invited Mavis to try it on! Would they accept his pension book by way of a deposit? Mrs Bignell lifted the fiery perfection from its velvet bed. It stuck—it wouldn't go over her knuckle! Glory be!

"We can have it altered," the girl was saying. "When d'you leave?"

"Tomorrow, first thing in the morning," he gabbled. Mavis put the ring back and sighed.

"I shouldn't be tempting myself in here at all. What I'm really looking for in Coober Pedy is a Pom called Gary," she told the girl, "a long-distance driver. You haven't come across him, by any chance?" The girl relocked the showcase.

"Have you asked at the church? There's over forty nationalities in this town. They come and they go but most visit the church sooner or later."

Outside it was already dusk; the wind had died and in the stillness, Lenny was describing the wonders of the night sky.

"That's Betelgeuse. And Orion—on its side from your point of view. Tomorrow, at Ayers Rock, it'll be marvellous. Not many lights to dazzle your eyes."

"We know our way around the heavens," Protheroe began pompously.

"Yeah but d'you know what's beneath them as well?" Lenny shifted dust with the toe of his boot. "Under that, for instance?"

"More rock of course."

"Deep down, there's water. Enough to make the desert fertile. But if we pump too much out, we'll damage the whole ecological cycle for ever."

"Every schoolboy knows that!"

"What I'm getting at, is that you want to dump radioactive muck down there. Down the old mine-shafts. I heard you discussing it on the coach today."

"It'll be perfectly safe! Encased in glass and concrete designed to withstand hundreds of years—"

"If the stuff's so bloody safe, go stick it down a pit in your own backyard!"

Mr Pringle and Mavis sat for a minute or two; silence was instinctive. The church was another empty dug-out at the end of a tunnel. A few rows of folding chairs faced a cavity in the rock containing a wooden hitching post that was the altar. Behind that, a thumbstick with a horizontal branch made the cross. Decoration was the most primitive Christian sign of all, the fish, carved on the rockface behind the cross. After all the dust and heat, the church was an oasis.

Only one other person was there. Mavis stirred and spoke quietly into the void, "Is it difficult to find someone in Coober Pedy?"

"Depends if he wants to be found." The man considered Mavis

145

before adding, "Quite a few come here to get escape, for various reasons. Nobody asks questions."

"It's not personal, it's on behalf of a friend of mine."

Mr Pringle waited patiently as she went through the rigmarole. Was this stranger a priest or a sinner seeking forgiveness? There was no way of telling.

"Did the boy write this himself?" The stranger's question broke through his reverie; it was the same the friendly woman had asked on their first day in Bathurst. Mr Pringle leaned forward. "What makes you say that?"

The stranger explained. "The writing on this postcard, the shape of the letters . . ."

Of course!

When the stranger had finished looking at the photographs and handed them back, it was obvious what his occupation was. "If you find the father, tell him to bring the boy here. We have services for the sick. There have been cures."

In the last bar they found in Coober Pedy, the bartender looked faintly interested before he returned the picture of Gary. "Had a Pom in here a while back . . . couldn't get a job. He was a driver."

"It's as bad here as it is back home," Mavis said indignantly.

"Took him on for a coupla days. He paid for his tucker cleaning out the bar. Used to sleep in the corner over there. Quiet sort of fella."

"Was his name Gary?" The bartender shrugged.

"Who knows? No one asks in Coober Pedy. Ain't that sort of town."

Later, in the lower bunk, Mr Pringle wondered apprehensively if anything would befall him during the night? No other lady loomed as dangerously or as low.

His brain was racing now; it had been dulled by the heat but the stranger in the church had provided the necessary stimulus. The same doubt that had been at the back of Mr Pringle's mind, echoed by the friendly woman in the ice-cream parlour, provided the key.

He listed the questions he needed to ask Mrs Bignell tomorrow morning. When he knew the answer to those, they might be a little nearer finding Ben.

146

At least it had taken his mind off drug trafficking. And with FONEs in every bunk, the squalid blockhouse was a solid, impregnable mass of human discomfort. Mavis would be quite safe tonight; even the spiders had fled.

Chapter Seventeen

The level of water in the second plastic container was low but not dangerously so. Ray Vincent had marked off the hours on a stick with the same precision as the intervals between target practice. He varied the range, from fifty down to twenty-five metres, and his success rate had improved.

Sunset would soon be over. He moved quickly, making a rough bed of blankets inside the truck. The days when he'd learned to be a survivor out in the dark were long gone. He was soft with too much good living and the heat had sapped his energy, more than he'd anticipated. That killing affected him, too. He tried to shut it out but it was there whenever he closed his eyes—and it frightened him every time to remember how much he'd enjoyed it!

He'd been disgusted by Parker's behaviour but it was no use pretending—that surge of excitement had been just like the first time.

For Christ's sake, stop imagining things! It was a job, that was all, a job and nothing else. Let your mind rip like that and you were trapped in a circle with no beginning and no end. Pointless. Ray Vincent looked at his watch: time to eat.

He had kept his memory in separate compartments, ever since the first time. He'd been thirteen years old. Last night, Pandora's box had sprung open throwing out swirling kaleidoscopic violence. What had loosened the tight control? It frightened Ray Vincent that he couldn't understand when all he wanted to do was try and forget.

During the night he'd heard death screams from unknown creatures. Beneath his feet the ground pulsated with life that burrowed away from the sun. Animals and reptiles fighting both the heat and each other. Vincent wanted to be back in familiar terrain; he'd grown too old for this game.

Perhaps that's why forbidden thoughts returned to disturb him? Of the first time he'd watched human life disappear in a rattle of breath. He'd never forgotten it, just shut it away. Last night it came back; he'd had to relive each frozen second. Only then, when the memory was complete, could he sleep; it was always the same.

When he'd met Adele he'd tried to erase the past. After Amy was born, he'd made even greater efforts but it hadn't worked. Last night he'd experienced the same elation he'd known at thirteen— the feeling of absolute power that had blood pounding and intoxicated the senses—and he'd surrendered to it! That supreme moment when you knew you had stamped out life for ever. Despite Parker's brutality that feeling had consumed him when Evan Jones's eyes turned dull.

There was no excitement now, nothing but weariness. Ray Vincent had one chance left, that was all. There'd been too many mistakes and nowhere to hide. New York provided identities, passports, credit cards, supplied the cash and called the shots. He was forever their creature and the world wasn't big enough once you made mistakes.

He ate quickly, spacing out food with sips of fruit juice. He was filthy and the stubble on his chin was caked with dust. The only relief was an icy aerosol spray each time he changed his clothes.

Tomorrow he'd bury his dirty ones with the rest of the debris, before heading south down the highway. It meant a dawn start to be at the tourist resort near Ayers Rock by early afternoon.

The FONEs were due there in the evening. They'd be travelling north. According to their itinerary, they were due to stay two days; ample for his purpose.

He was fixing up an insect net when a movement caught his eye. For a few seconds, Ray Vincent held his breath. Softly, he slid a hand into the map compartment and reached for the gun. In a second he'd eased up the catch, pushed home the slide and fired.

It was perfect. He responded automatically to the recoil. No need to waste a second shot, he'd hit the target. In the fading dusk he bent down to examine it closely.

What had been a living creature was splattered over a wide area. This time Vincent hadn't used a plastic bullet but one from Zee's box, copper-jacketed, hollow-point, designed to mushroom on impact with flesh, and with a velocity of twelve hundred feet per second and sufficient power to kill a stag.

He'd blasted the tiny creature apart. From the head, he tried to gauge the size. The delicate pink lizard had scroll-like folds of flesh round its grey eye. Ray Vincent measured from the centre of the skull to the tip of the elongated nose with his finger. Say about nineteen centimetres overall. Like the gun in his hand, it was a perfect design, honed by billions of years of evolution to play its part in this harsh land; a beautiful, living creature. He'd hit it from, say, twenty-six metres? Not bad. Ray Vincent returned to the truck knowing he would sleep.

He woke with a start: Amy. No, he must not think about her until it was over—but he caught sight of his watch. Of the date on his watch. Back home it was Amy's seventh birthday. Christ! He'd forgotten it was today!

He'd never done that before—never been away on any of her previous birthdays. He'd got to find a phone, to tell her he loved her. Adele would never forgive him if he didn't.

After Coober Pedy, Yulara tourist resort would be heaven, the FONEs declared. How civilized to be in a tent once more! And with two days to explore Ayers Rock. Nothing to beat the rock, Lenny declared, nothing in the whole wide bloody world. Mr Pringle was inclined to think it might be true.

There was another reason why he and Mrs Bignell rejoiced: today it was their turn in the front seat. What bliss to contemplate the endless highway stretching ahead and watch vistas unfold. On a practical level, it also meant the Protheroes were at the back of the coach alongside the toilet.

Mavis was more than ready to admit she'd grown tired of Kenneth Protheroe. "I don't know how Jean puts up with it, day after day."

"Perhaps she's fond of him?"

"No, I don't think so. Not after what he did to the rabbit." She was in her floral blouse and fuchsia skirt, in honour of the occasion, and wore the tiny opal studs Mr Pringle had presented to her at breakfast.

150

"A small consolation because we didn't find Gary."

"They're lovely," she told him. "Let's face it, we didn't really expect to. That Pommie driver in Coober Pedy turned out to be called Gareth, with a wife in Liverpool, did I tell you?"

Lenny climbed into the driving seat and saw the flowery profusion. "My word!" Mavis blossomed.

"It's going to be a lovely day, I can feel it in my bones. Rather hot, I expect, but you can't have everything, can you?"

They turned off the main highway and began heading west. Here, views became much more green, trees, bushes, even the scrub, but the earth itself was red. Where growth was sparse the ground was ochre colour, but beneath the shade of Casuarina trees it become red as blood. Ahead, gouged out of the land, the carefully graded dirt-road stretched to infinity.

Suddenly, to the left and framed by trees, a solid dark shape appeared on the skyline. Protheroe couldn't contain himself. He raced to the front of the coach, camera at the ready, fat bottom blocking the view, deaf to everyone's protests.

Lenny waited until the roll of film was finished. "Got what you wanted?" he asked cynically.

"Magnificent, thanks!" Protheroe turned to face his colleagues. "Some of you may not know, Ayers Rock is a boulder, separate from the earth's crust," he lectured, "and like an iceberg, the greater part of it is buried beneath the sands of the desert."

"Don't you think you'd better wait until we get there?" Lenny sounded laconic.

"Pardon?"

"That ain't Ayers, that's only a little rock, Mount Conner. 'Bout another thirty kilometres before we gets a glimpse of the biggie."

Golly, thought Mr Pringle, if that was "little", what on earth was the other one like?

In the Yulara resort a short distance from the rock, a dusty Toyota and an old truck arrived within minutes of one another. In the Toyota, two men were arguing. "Look, Pelham, I don't want to share a tent any more than you do—"

"I fail to comprehend why we cannot spend the night in an hotel."

"I told you, there's a conference goin' on at the Sheraton." Kev indicated the dusky rose-coloured building with high-tech aluminium sails to protect it from the heat. "They've got delegates from forty countries. Plenty of headaches for security and the police. They can't spare anyone to help out. Which means until somethin' breaks, it's down to you, me and Charlie. Now let's have a beer and get the tent up."

In the Visitors' Centre, the grubby figure looked out of place. Ray Vincent was itching to be outside, merging with the mixtures of types and nationalities on one of the campsites. In this elegantly cool interior, flanked by screens and arrangements of grasses, he was conspicuous. "Can I help you?"

"I want to make a long-distance call." He spoke quietly but it was still too loud. Other visitors might pretend to be deaf, that was all. They weren't travel-stained as he was but he daren't waste time in a shower. Already Amy would be in bed, probably crying herself to sleep because he'd forgotten.

He had to restrain himself from hurrying across to the Perspex dome. He seized the receiver. "Hi, Adele? Wake the birthday girl up, tell her Pop wants to give her a great big kiss."

"Ray . . . is that you?"

Despite the thousands of miles, he was there beside her in the room. He could see her face. He knew what had happened. "What's wrong?" He didn't have to ask because he knew. He had to hear her say the words. Until she did, it wasn't real.

"What's happened?" It was difficult to breathe, to keep his voice steady. When Adele spoke, the words would be printed in his brain for ever and he would share her agony.

"Where is she, Ray?" The voice was a tired shadow from hours of weeping. "They said you would know. I've been waiting . . . I haven't been to the police. They said Amy would be killed if I did that . . . Who are they, Ray? Who's Parker? What have they done with my baby?"

The terror was so great his body hunched tight to stop himself screaming. "It's all right, Adele . . . promise. They'll bring her back . . . As soon as I've done what they want . . . It'll be all right . . . Darling, I love you!"

He shouldn't have said that. Anger and fear burst from her in one great wave of hate that swamped and choked him so that he put out a hand to stop himself being knocked over by it. When he tried to speak, he found she'd rung off.

Mavis spotted it first. This time there was no mistake. The most massive rock she'd ever seen in a vast flat plain. Huge though it was, that rock had turned on its side in a prehistoric ocean, back in the Dreamtime.

"It's incredible," she whispered.

"Yep," said Lenny fondly. "That's it, that's the biggie."

"Are we stopping?"

"Not right now," he replied. "I want to show you the Olgas first."

"If they're bigger than that," Mr Pringle protested. "I don't think I can cope."

"The Olgas are a group of boulders. None of them's larger than Ayers but together they are. The black fellas have the same sort of beliefs about them. The Olgas are part of their legends but I don't find them as spooky."

"You're right," said Mavis slowly. "Ayers has an atmosphere, even from here. It's very powerful."

"That's what the black fellas say. It's their place of mysteries." Pete glanced in his mirror at Protheroe, back on his feet to re-establish his superiority. "It's been here since the Dawntime, according to them. I hope it lasts a while longer."

"Surely no one would interfere—" Mr Pringle saw his glance and understood the implication. "Oh, dear . . . let us hope not."

The Olgas were half an hour away across the desert. In the clear late afternoon light they saw the huge features of the Dying Kangaroo Man, as the Aborigines dubbed him millions of years ago. The stone glowed dark red, sculpted by nature and full of pain. Even the scientists fell silent at the sight of it.

At the foot of the Olgas, like ants they scurried about in an effort to come to terms with the phenomenon. For Mr Pringle, each vast stone had been weathered in curves so that the whole took on the form of a slumbering female megalith, awaiting the call of her god.

It was a relief to be offered fruit squash; to climb back into the

153

protection of the coach. For Lenny insisted they return for the greatest experience of all: the few precious moments when Ayers Rock comes alive with all the colours of the setting sun.

When it was over, Mavis couldn't find words to describe it. They were at the campsite at Yulara and she watched Mr Pringle rig their tent. "I'd no idea it would be like that . . . that article didn't prepare you at all . . . Would you like me to give you a hand, dear?"

"No thank you." Mrs Bignell's efforts with guy-ropes were well-meant but lacked cohesion.

"Red, purple, blue . . . and over so quickly. Kenneth Protheroe didn't get the film in his camera. I heard Jean shouting at him. 'All this way,' she was yelling, 'and you manage to miss it!' "

"I fear his has not been a particularly successful trip. What are the plans for this evening?"

"After we've eaten, the coach will take us to where the pubs are. That's where the truck drivers go as well as everyone else."

Yulara had been built twenty kilometres away from Ayers Rock in a scooped out depression of the land and carefully landscaped. Linked by a drive, the area contained hotels, camping areas separated by hummocks, a swimming pool, shops, visitors' centre and an amphitheatre.

In the middle and tall enough to screen even the hotels, was a lookout from which everyone could gaze his fill at the rock.

As he climbed to the top to look at the view, Mr Pringle decided the complex was the best answer yet to the problem of tourism. Buildings were a dusky ochre to blend with the desert. Each had the same futuristic aluminium sails, strung above the roofs to deflect the sun. Very little would be visible outside the area, he decided.

He caught a glimpse of the thatched roofs of an earlier settlement much nearer the rock. Too near, he thought. This was one place on earth where Man should respect God's mysteries.

He remembered with a start he was supposed to be protecting Mrs Bignell. There were still some questions to be answered, too. On the coach, she'd refused to be distracted from the sights.

She was unpacking inside the tent. Charlie squatted near by, inflating the airbeds. Mr Pringle nodded to him and crawled through the flap. "About Mrs Hardie's son—" he began.

"Oh, not again, dear! I told you all I knew this morning. He died before I met Mrs Hardie and she doesn't like talking about it."

"His death was not entirely unexpected?"

"I don't think so, no . . . like I said, she goes out of her way to avoid mentioning it. And I never pry."

"Of course not," Mr Pringle paused to let the ruffled feathers settle. "In the photographs on her mantelpiece, I noticed how much Ben and his uncle resemble one another."

"Yes," Mavis agreed. "It's the blue eyes, I think, it makes the whites so clear."

"What about ill-health? Was Mrs Hardie's son prone to sickness?" She considered.

"I'm not sure, dear. As I say, I can't remember her talking about it."

"But when Mrs Hardie's son died, was there an inquest?" This time she was truly shocked.

"Are you suggesting that my friend, Mrs Hardie—"

"I suggest nothing. Can you answer my question?"

"If there'd been any hanky-panky we'd have heard about it at The Bricklayers," Mavis said firmly and turned her back on him. Mr Pringle retreated.

Outside, the sandy soil was blood-red under the lamps. It seeped between his toes. Back on the knoll he looked at the distant black mass of the rock and, near at hand, the resort with the line of the drive picked out in arc-lights.

He watched a bus make the circuit of the drive, picking up passengers. There were other coach parties and families in camper vans, tents dotted about and tourists sleeping in their cars. Everywhere lights twinkled among the trees.

As Mr Pringle turned for a final look at the rock, he saw a shape on the edge of the ridge. It was near enough to make his blood run cold. When it howled, he gave a nervous involuntary yelp.

In the dark, the dingo brought to the surface all the disquietude; he was in an alien land, in a desert beside a primordial rock. What was worse, there were unknown dangers threatening Mrs Bignell but she still refused to go to the police. "Tomorrow," she'd promised, "as soon as that letter's in the post."

155

Suddenly there were other dogs silhouetted on the ridge; the pack was assembling, drawn by the aroma of so many barbecues. Mr Pringle experienced an acute desire for human company and hurried back down towards the tents.

"Guess you're not used to this kinda life, Pelham?"

"At home, the climate is unsuitable."

"Yeah . . . we keep everythin' ready in the garage. At weekends, we just fill up the Esky and go where the fancy takes us. It's the great outdoors all right. The kids love it."

"Fiona and I decided against having children."

You would, you mean old poofter, thought Kev. Catch you wanting to share . . . He flipped the steaks on the griddle and walloped on chilli sauce with a lavish hand; proper man's food.

Anthony Pelham-Walker watched in irritation. There was surely no need for all this nonsense—why not take a table at the Sheraton and eat in a civilized manner?

He made no attempt to help clear away either but waited for the main business to begin. Kev spread out the papers from Macquarie Street. "Now . . . let's sum up what we know so far."

They were opposite the tents that housed the FONEs. Kev had pitched theirs so that surveillance was a simple matter. Charlie would watch from the other side where he, too, had an unimpeded view.

Kev sorted telexes into neat piles. "According to immigration, Vincent has blue–grey eyes, height five-ten. Seems he's visited five times during the last six years. Occupation: Estate Agent. Home address: Farnham, in the county of Surrey. Wife: Adele . . . married seven years, one child, Amy. That's all."

"Apart from a 9mm pistol."

"Yeah . . . even out here, real estate ain't that rough. What've you got?"

"According to Sinclair, Vincent set up the agency, apparently from scratch, five years ago. He provided all the capital himself. His previous occupation was listed as 'Security Adviser'."

"Covers a lotta possibilities, Pelham." Kev pulled the tag off another can of beer. "Anythin' else?"

"Sinclair has had difficulty tracing anything more than seven or eight years previously. Vincent bought his present house—again for cash—on the outskirts of Farnham and joined various clubs in the area, presumably to establish himself in the community."

"He'd just got married," Kev pointed out. "What sort of a place is this Farnham, in the county of etc?"

"An old market town, increasingly occupied by London commuters of a high-earning capacity. Houses are pricey."

"So about seven years ago, this bloke appears with his new wife . . . and plenty of cash. The dates tie in with the increase in traffic our end, when the organization really got started and we had the first big surge. Heroin was available all over the place. Did Sinclair come up with anything about the second mystery man who killed Evan Jones?"

"I fear not. It's not his field."

"Yeah . . . another desk fella."

Anthony Pelham-Walker ignored him and stared at the photographs. "It's possible the second man is here also, having evaded Immigration's watchdogs. Have you had these circulated?"

"Yep—and it is possible," Kev agreed. "If so, you, me and Charlie might be in for some nasty shocks the next coupla days." Pelham-Walker swallowed. "However . . . as this Vincent character is our only lead—because according to Macquarie Street no one else has connected him with a job—I suggest we concentrate on him. *Someone* has to contact the Bignell lady and relieve her of those two packages."

He picked up the Brisbane report once more. "Passenger confirms male subject, early forties, wearing heavy glasses, etc, etc . . ." He skimmed through the rest. "Remarks of special interest: subject uses perfumed unguent and referred to daughter 'Amy' in affectionate manner." He tossed the report across. "If it was Vincent, he's slippin'."

He folded his arms in a manner that was now familiar to Pelham-Walker. "Why would an old ex-pro who's losin' his grip come all this way? Why not use an operative based here?"

"Perhaps because he's personally responsible?" suggested Pelham-Walker.

"Could be, Pelham . . . So where's he hidin'? What d'you think?

157

Is our man in the Sheraton over there, getting ready to make his move?''

If he is, thought Anthony Pelham-Walker bitterly, it was thoroughly unjust.

In a lean-to made from groundsheets strung between ropes attached to the truck, Ray Vincent lay between his blankets.

Sleep was impossible: Parker had Amy. It was his only thought and it burned a hole in his brain. Nothing else mattered except what Parker might be doing, just for the hell of it. Parker who'd wielded that hammer . . . who'd laughed so excitedly. What would Parker begin to do to a seven-year-old girl?

It had to be tomorrow. He daren't waste more time. He would phone New York and demand that Parker release her, he'd risk another call to Adele, he'd catch the first plane to New York if that's the price they demanded, but please God, let Amy still be safe!

That morning there was another postcard from Mavis and a brown envelope from the DHSS. Mrs Hardie limped back to the kitchen and opened the envelope first. A form confirmed the allocation of sheltered accommodation and gave a date two weeks hence when Mrs Hardie could expect to move in. Underneath, the welfare lady had scribbled a message urging her to let Linda know "at the earliest opportunity".

Nothing like the present, Mrs Hardie thought shakily. She'd make the tea first. Maybe she'd be strong enough after a nice hot cuppa.

Linda was bleary-eyed. She drank thirstily from the vulgar mug. These days she scarcely bothered to greet her mother in the mornings. It was the booze, Mrs Hardie realized that. Linda spent most evenings at the pub. According to the home help, there were empty bottles in the dustbin. Gin and Campari, that's what this daughter of hers drank. Proper alcoholic's brew that was. Mrs Hardie put the DHSS form on the worktop. "I've had this today."

"What?" Linda drank her tea and stared out of the window.

"It's confirmation of a place. I've accepted this time. You'll not stop me whatever you say. I've told the welfare it's definite." Linda turned away from the window and refocused on her mother.

"What are you on about?"

"If you ring and ask, they'll tell you what's available. You'll have to move, this is family accommodation. The welfare lady's expecting you to call. I said I thought you'd want two bedrooms . . ." Mrs Hardie's voice and courage faltered.

"I'm not moving because of Ben. You know that. We've been over it hundreds of times!" Linda was already shouting and her mother backed away.

"Linda, he's not coming back. Gary won't let him go, you know he won't. Even if Mavis manages to find them—"

"I'm not moving from this house!"

The shriek stunned Mrs Hardie. When she recovered, she said quietly, "You'll have to, Linda. They won't let you stay on. You haven't got enough priority. There's another family due to move in here—"

"No!" Linda had her mother by the shoulders, shaking her, forcing her to understand, "I'm not . . . leaving . . . !" The metal crutches crashed to the floor. Mrs Hardie clung to the worktop.

Her daughter's face was inches away from her own. She couldn't escape the staring, pleading eyes. Linda was willing her to understand. Mrs Hardie shrank away, the stale breath adding to her sick fear.

"I'm not leaving, Mother . . . Ever. Because of . . ." Linda hesitated, looking past her mother at photographs on the mantelpiece.

Mrs Hardie seized the pause. "Because of what, Linda? What are you trying to tell me?"

Eyelids drooped over the protuberant eyes. Everything about her daughter was suddenly flaccid. When she spoke, she was exhausted.

"You know. You're running away because you've no guts . . . but it's your fault as much as it's mine."

This time, Mrs Hardie shut her eyes.

As the moon rose, they howled; every dingo in the pack adding to the hideous, mean wailing. In their tent, at the end of the line, it was unnerving. Mrs Bignell snuggled up, warm and curvaceous, and reached out a hand. Mr Pringle's hopes were immediately raised. "That emergency haversack of yours, dear. . . ?"

"Yes?"

"You haven't got a tin of Mr Dog in there by any chance? One or two sound as if they could do with a nibble."

Chapter Eighteen

In the cool of the early morning, Mrs Bignell vanished into the laundry room of the shower block and Mr Pringle obediently hoisted a washing line. It was a time for pottering, for catching up with postcards, posting Evan's letter and visiting the police.

To his surprise, Mavis had capitulated without further argument. "We'll find a pillar box then the police station. I expect they've got one in the Visitors' Centre—although I doubt whether the police here will be interested. They'll probably insist we go to the ones in Sydney on our way back home."

"Possibly. But it will be a relief to tell someone. Look at this newspaper, the report of some Customs haul in the UK, nothing to do with us but it mentions the street value of one drug." He indicated the Australian headline.

"'Heroin valued at £200,000 a kilo!'" Mavis was incredulous.

"You see why I'm so anxious, if that's what it was?"

"Yes, I do . . . How wicked . . . two hundred thousand pounds." It made her very thoughtful as she gathered her bits and pieces for washing.

Mr Pringle began a solitary breakfast. None of the FONEs were about. Charlie went past on his way to have a shower. Apart from that, Mr Pringle was alone in the dining area. From the other side of the camping lot, screened by the Toyota, Kev watched him through binoculars.

"Mind if I join you?" asked Lenny.

"Please do." Mr Pringle waited until he'd pulled up a stool. "I was beginning to wonder where everyone was."

"Sulkin' in their tents."

"Oh?"

"Yeah . . . seems like there was an altercation at the Sheraton last night," Lenny drawled. "Protheroe organized another of his

161

meetin's—'Extending the hand of friendship and profit'. Invited anyone who was interested to learn how much profit could be made out of nuclear waste."

"What went wrong, weren't they interested?"

"Too right they was interested!" Lenny waved the piece of sausage on his fork. "Over at that hotel there's a conference goin' on. International CND. There're representatives from forty different countries havin' a pow-wow 'bout the Nuclear Menace. They turned up and they was very, very interested. There was what you might call an exchange of ideas."

"Oh, dear!"

"Them FONEs looked sick as parrots by the time they got back last night. All the same—" Lenny looked along the line of tents "—they can't stay sulkin' in there. They'll fry when the sun gets up. My word, look at that!"

Mrs Bignell had returned and was pinning up her washing. Fluttering in the breeze it sent an exotic signal that warmed cockles deep inside Mr Pringle; silk and satin underwear in lavender, purple, whisper-pink and pearl, the message was unmistakable, utterly feminine and inviting.

"My word!" said Lenny again. "Them's her campin' frillies?"

"Oh, yes." Mr Pringle felt like a sultan. "My friend doesn't believe in lowering her standards because we're in a desert."

"You two comin' on the trip to the rock? Coach leaves at ten-thirty 'stead of two o'clock. I thought it'd be better than climbin' in the heat."

Oh bother, thought Mr Pringle. Mavis came across, all fresh and sparkling in her marigold outfit. Lenny explained the change of plan.

"I don't suppose it'll matter, will it," she asked expressively, "if we post that letter this afternoon?"

"But we're not going to put off—the other matter?" Lenny had gone for toast and marmalade but Mr Pringle remained cautious.

"As soon as possible," Mavis agreed. "As soon as we get back from the rock, we'll go and tell them."

Anthony Pelham-Walker had been detailed to be a messenger-boy. He hadn't been ordered about like this since he was a fag. It

162

made him very angry but Kev insisted. He trailed back wearily from the Centre and flopped down beside the Toyota.

"Aw, there you are, Pelham. Breakfast's nearly ready." Macillvenny was doing it deliberately, he thought: bacon, sausage, tomatoes, fried bread and a slithery fried egg to top the lot. "Now, what's the news this mornin'? Anything happened back there?"

"I made those enquiries you suggested," he replied stiffly. "No more telexes from Sydney. However, long-distance calls made via the operator yesterday included three to England."

"And?" But Anthony Pelham-Walker didn't work as speedily as that.

"I have my address book." He produced it from his blazer pocket. "Fortunately one of my wife's relatives lives in Aldershot which is next door to Farnham . . . the codes may be similar."

Kev's chewing slowed then stopped. Pelham-Walker's finger fumbled down the page. "Yes, here we are . . . the Beresford-Smiths. How odd." He looked up, surprised. "I think we must assume the caller *was* ringing Farnham. One of these three has a code which is precisely the same—0252—it's a most unlikely coincidence someone else would be calling Aldershot."

"Most unlikely . . ." Kev agreed. "Vincent's here, all right. It's got to be him. The bastard's somewhere on this site—and he's come for the stuff!"

Mrs Piggybum was doing her hair, winding the grey plait round her head and stabbing home the hairpins. Once it had been a thick blonde tress that had had Porky boy in paroxysms. In those far-off days she'd been his little "Swiss miss". Porky boy had changed, much to her regret, he'd become stringy and grey, like her coiffure.

She'd never altered her style, she still wore dirndl skirts. Not now of course, not in the desert. For this holiday she had trousers, bought from Help the Aged, shapeless and comfortable.

Mrs Piggybum had seen the exotic flags on the washing line, fluttering shamelessly. It caused indignation and pain inside the shrivelled academic chest to think that Mrs Bignell could even afford such garments. Expensive scraps of satin and lace—what about her moral obligation to the Third World!

163

All the same . . . curiosity got the better of Mrs Piggybum. Seeing no one about, she approached the washing with discretion.

It was difficult to judge who had the greater shock. As the man emerged abruptly through the tent flap, Mrs Piggybum squealed. He was nothing better than a tramp! "What d'you think you're doing? That tent doesn't belong to you!" Strong, upper-class, and no-nonsense.

"I was hoping to find Mavis Bignell." Clipped and just as authoritative.

"You'll probably find her—"

"What are the plans for the day? Are you going to the rock?" The questions were rapped out and she answered instinctively.

"Some of them are. The coach leaves at half-past ten. Who shall I say was asking. . . ?" But the man was striding away. Typically Australian, no manners whatsoever.

Still in a huff, Mrs Piggybum resumed her quest. Like every other woman—and several of the men, come to that—she had an overwhelming desire to know the exact size of the brassière . . . Damn! She wasn't wearing her glasses.

Anthony Pelham-Walker resigned himself to his final day in the appalling heat. The first connecting flight was tomorrow and, by God, he'd be on it. He ignored the excited chatter between Kev and Charlie. This business had nothing more to do with him, he should never have got involved.

But what was the point in rushing home? His job had gone, his chance of glory. If life had been pointless before, he'd made it doubly so by coming here and losing any hope of a title.

That was the only reason Fiona had stuck by him. She'd probably consulted the most expensive divorce lawyer in London by now—one who would suck him dry. What a prospect! Disgrace and poverty, all because he'd imagined his life meaningless!

Mrs Bignell had her sunshade as well as her dark glasses. The coach wasn't full because some of the FONEs had decided to go swimming instead. As they drove, she kept remembering the newspaper headline. "Those two bags . . . four hundred thousand pounds!"

164

"Try not to worry. We'll go to the police first thing this afternoon. About Mrs Hardie's son, Billy . . ."

"Yes, dear?"

"Can you remember any reference she made? She must've talked about him occasionally." Mavis frowned.

"I think she told me once he was better off dead, something like that. She was upset. She was crying when she said it." Mr Pringle looked grave. It was a judgement he'd learned to mistrust.

"Those photographs she has; Ben resembles Billy in several respects. They have the same vivid blue-white eyes, their limbs are thin. In fact, one could say Billy too looked as though he might have had rickets as a child." Mavis sighed.

"I know what you mean, they were both bandy-legged. I never knew Billy but Ben was almost deformed. Like Tweedledum because his legs were thin sticks supporting his body. He had a terrible time at school, poor little soul."

"And Billy died when he was how old? A teenager, in his early twenties?"

"Yes but *Ben* hasn't died," Mavis protested. "He's had one or two accidents, that's all." Mr Pringle frowned.

"There are similarities, nevertheless."

Lenny leaned across from the driving seat. "You weren't planning on climbing the rock, were you Mavis?"

"No, dear. I shall sit at the bottom and admire Mr Pringle." She squeezed his hand. "He's going right to the top!"

"Do you consider I am attempting too much?" Mr Pringle was nervous. This morning Ayers looked twice as big as it had before. Lenny glanced at his shoes.

"Those got good soles?"

"Oh, yes. Very sturdy. And I have my pack." He was proud of his haversack; it had weathered the five decades since his scouting days pretty well. "Water bottle, first aid pack, signalling flare. . ." Lenny raised his eyebrows.

"Have you a sweater?" he asked. "It may be ninety out there now but when we get to the top, it gets real windy." Mrs Bignell made him open the haversack and show her his woolly.

"I knew I could rely on you, dear, but I just wanted to be sure."

"Funny thing about the rock," Lenny mused. "It gets to people. They find it strange . . . outside their experience. Some of 'em get dizzy up there. It's the view. There you are, on top of the world, and there's nuthin' whichever way you look, 'cept the Olgas . . . and Mount Connors. Miles and miles of empty space. That's what does it. People fall off."

"Oh, my Lord!" Now he'd really upset Mavis.

"I shall take great care," Mr Pringle assured her. "I shan't venture near the edge on any account."

"They put brass plaques up." Lenny wanted to comfort them with authority's concern. "Everyone that fell off, there's a plaque with his name and the date on it . . . five of 'em, so far. I tell people, make sure the next one isn't yours."

He flicked on the mike and spoke to the other passengers. "We're makin' a detour, folks, round the old holiday village. This is where tourists used to stay but they stopped usin' it after that business with the dingo and the baby, right?"

Heads nodded up and down the coach.

"The black fellas live here now . . . and one of the rangers—they look after the religious sites and whatnot—he's a mate of mine. Thought you wouldn't mind if I stopped to say hello. Won't take five minutes."

They turned on to a dirt-track in the shadow of the rock. Here, scrub and thorn were already clawing back the shacks. As they approached, Mrs Bignell got her first real sight of the Aborigines. Black faces, some with incongruously fair hair above the jet skin. Faces with *retroussé* noses that would have been pert but for the hopelessness in their eyes.

Women sat with their backs to the trees, in the shade; lassitude emanated from them. Children played in the dust. Men stood and waited to see what this day would bring. There was a feeling of resignation as well as inevitability that was disturbing. This ghost of a white man's holiday village was now inhabited by the dispossessed. "What do they do?" asked Mavis. "Living here?"

"Not a lot," Lenny replied. "They don't have to work. Most of 'em don't particularly want to. This is their bit of territory, the rock. Much of it belongs to them now. They like it here. Right, here we go . . ."

166

He pulled up beside a thatched hut, in better repair than most, and called "Anyone home?"

In the coach, Mrs Bignell was unnerved by the silence of the watching blacks. Lenny had left the coach door open. Like one or two of the party, she descended and walked towards a group of children, uncertain for once how to greet them. "Hallo . . ." None of them answered. Lenny ducked his head and went into the hut. He came out smartly.

"My word, he's got problems."

"Oh?" Mr Pringle was casual as he descended from the coach.

"White ants . . . place is swarming with them. Guess that's why my mate's decided to move out for a while . . . He's taken his things. Hang on a minute. I want to find out where he's gone." Lenny walked over to the watching black men. One of them recognized him. Immediately the atmosphere relaxed and greetings became friendly.

"Have you got a bit of string in your haversack?" Mavis asked Mr Pringle.

"Yes, of course." He handed it to her. She put down bag and parasol and began a cat's cradle. The children watched, silent, impassive. After a few minutes, one indicated Mrs Bignell should give the string to him. He tied it to a stick as a whip and began flailing the others.

"Oh well . . . you can't win them all, can you dear?"

One of the girls disappeared inside a hut and brought out a home-made toy, two rusty cans linked with string, knotted at either end to make a primitive telephone.

Mrs Bignell accepted a can with delight, checked it for ants and held it to her ear, pulling the string taut. "Come on then, send me a message . . ." There was a bout of giggling among the children. None had the courage to begin. Mr Pringle took the can and spoke into it.

"Burr . . . burr . . . burr . . . burr . . ." he said solemnly. "Hello? Can anyone hear me?" More giggles but another child made as if to listen. "Burr . . . burr . . . burr!" he cried, much encouraged. On the other side of the dusty square, a man had joined the group round Lenny. The movement attracted her attention and Mrs Bignell glanced across. The next minute she began to wave

167

vigorously. "Look, dear, look—it's him! Ooh-hoo!" She lifted her parasol and twirled it high. "Gary! It's me . . . Mavis, from The Bricklayers."

Dust rose in flurries as, both hands outstretched, Mrs Bignell hurried across, full of the pleasure of finding him. FONEs and Aborigines alike saw first Gary's disbelief then his astonished laughter.

On his side of the square, Mr Pringle realized what had happened. "Lines to the rest of the world are engaged," he announced hurriedly, "please try later," and handed back his receiver.

He walked more slowly, not wanting to interrupt the first precious moments, but very conscious of the heat through his straw hat. Mrs Bignell was bursting with happiness and as he arrived, turned to introduce him. "This is Mr Pringle who's come with me to Australia. Gary's living here, dear, above the garage. He's working as a mechanic with the Aborigines." She turned back, full of happy anticipation. "Now, Gary, tell me, how's Ben?"

It was as though she'd extinguished a vital spark. Gary stuttered but couldn't speak. Mr Pringle murmured a politeness to fill the embarrassed pause. It was a shock to see how much older Gary looked than the photographs.

Gary unfroze as though aware of the awkward situation. Lenny came to his rescue. "Look . . . it's too hot, folks. How about sittin' in the coach? I've got the fan on in there." Under her parasol, Mavis dabbed at her forehead.

"What a good idea . . . A few minutes and I've had enough. Can you spare the time to come with us, Gary? Some of our party are going to climb the rock but you and I can stay in the coach and chat."

After a brief word with the Aborigines, Gary followed as though compelled to by the presence of so many strangers. Mr Pringle sensed his complete reluctance. He stood back courteously for him to board the vehicle. Gary's expression was that of a man entering a trap. He made one effort to save himself.

"Look . . . my overalls are covered in grease . . . don't want to dirty the seats in here."

"That's all right, mate—" Lenny was amiable "—Got a toilet on board with soap and water. You can use that."

Gary stood motionless as though they'd taken away his last chance of escape. Mr Pringle waited. When he spoke, it was to mutter, "OK, I'll come."

The rest took their seats and Lenny started the engine. As the cool air built up, Mrs Bignell's energy returned and she began an animated account of Bricklayers' news. She made occasional references to Mrs Hardie and Gary's apprehension appeared to grow. He answered questions about work; it had been hard to find any on his return. When the money ran out, he'd had to turn his hand to anything, anywhere. He'd hitched lifts, away from towns where there were plenty of locals for every vacancy. He'd been employed as a janitor at the holiday complex when he'd heard of the need for a motor mechanic.

"Not many are willing to work alongside the black fellows. I don't mind." Gary hesitated as if seeking the right words. "They don't—interfere." Mrs Bignell didn't understand.

"About Ben, dear—" Gary stood abruptly.

"Guess I will go and clean up . . ." He hurried to the back of the coach. He looks ill, thought Mr Pringle. He cut through Mavis's surprise.

"May I suggest you avoid all mention of Ben, for the present."

"What an extraordinary thing to say!"

He knew it wouldn't satisfy her but he didn't understand himself, not yet. Finally he said, "I think we should go carefully. It might be to do with Billy," which annoyed her even more.

"Look dear, I'm not one for riddles."

"Would you say Gary looked pleased to see you?"

"At first, yes, of course he did. Why shouldn't he?"

"But when you asked about Ben?" Annoyance changed to alarm. "You don't think—something's wrong?"

"I'm not sure. Will you let me talk to Gary? In private?"

In the car-park at the base of the rock, the three of them sweated in the Toyota. "Lenny's takin' a bloody long time back at the village."

169

"He's catchin' up with an old mate," said Charlie. "Relax. There're all of them FONEs aboard. Vincent wouldn't attack in a place like that. Too public."

"It can't be worse than this," said Anthony Pelham-Walker irritably. "This is like Piccadilly on a bank holiday."

Tourists of every nationality walked past, some laden with climbing equipment, most in shorts and trainers. Beyond where their coaches were parked, an old pick-up truck pulled in and stopped.

"Here they come," said Kev suddenly. "Here's Lenny . . ." The Wallaby Tours coach swung past in a slow arc to park alongside the rest. "Hey, just a minute . . ." He focused his glasses. "Isn't that an extra passenger getting out?" He handed them to Charlie. "Quick, take a look; blue T-shirt and overalls. I haven't seen that one before."

"Nor me." Charlie stared at Kev. "Reckon we could've been wrong about Vincent?"

"Gary has very kindly agreed to accompany me on my climb," Mr Pringle told her. "You don't mind, do you, Mavis? Now that we're here, it's a little larger than I anticipated. I might require assistance to reach the top. You and he can have your chat when we return."

Privately, out of Gary's hearing, he whispered, "You gave him a shock, appearing out of the blue like that. I think it'll be all right once he's recovered."

"Yes of course. Thoughtless of me." Then, brightly, "Lenny's been telling me about the caves at the foot of the rock, where the Aborigines have their fertility rites. He's offered to show the rest of us."

"They don't go in for that sort of stuff nowadays," Lenny put in hastily. "It's all in the past. But there are wall paintings datin' back thousands of years. You need to know where it's OK to go. Some's forbidden because it's sacred ground. It offends the black fellas if you pry too close to those."

"Look after Mr Pringle for me, won't you Gary? See that he doesn't get blown over the edge."

The two followed the rest of their party across the soft sand, ochre colour in the harsh light, a deeper, richer red under the sparse tufts of porcupine grass. Sand flowed over their feet and burned through the soles of their shoes.

They reached the low outlying boulders that marked the beginning of the climb, letting the scientists go on ahead.

Lenny waited to see them all go then backed his coach out of the parking lot, turning right along the road at the base of the rock. Seconds later, the old truck did the same. In the Toyota there was a rapid debate.

"The seed-packet lady's stayin' on the coach!"

"Yeah, but look, Kev . . ." Charlie pointed excitedly at the haversack on the inoffensive back. "See what Pringle's carrying? There's more than two kilos of weight in that—and why's he actin' so friendly with a complete stranger?

"I've been tryin' to tell you 'bout how he behaved at Yunta—dashing across the road as soon as a stranger talks to the seed packet—he knows about the stuff all right, he must do. Either *she* told him or he's been in on the deal from the start, who knows? What the hell! Pringle's carrying more than two kilos on his back and he's with a contact!"

"Yeah but it's not Vincent!" Kev was adjusting his binoculars frantically. "He's too skinny, he's got dark hair—"

"He could've dyed it for Chrissake!"

"But what about the seed packet!"

"What about her? She's on the coach with no one but the FONEs and Lenny? We saw her get on this morning—she wasn't carrying more'n a purse and that brolly thing," Charlie insisted urgently. "But up there, disappearing by the minute, is Pringle with a fella we haven't seen before."

"OK, we don't know for sure that it should be Vincent. And where the two of 'em are goin', there's loads of places you can be private."

"Right! C'm on, Kev, it's got to be the contact. Couldn't be anyone else."

"OK." Kev made his decision. "Let's go."

Charlie leapt out and flung open the boot, throwing a camera at the astonished Pelham-Walker. "But why go up the goddam rock?" Kev asked obstinately. "When there's millions of square miles of nuthin', why go to all that trouble?"

171

"I dunno!" Charlie answered sharply. "All I do know is I can see them with my own eyes, going up, up, up—and if we want to get a shot of the exchange, we'd better decide pretty damn soon. Quick, Pelham, on your feet."

"I? You're surely not suggesting—"

"*We* is goin' up there, all three of us. Me and Kev to take care of the contact—you to photograph the exchange, now *c'm on*!"

Gary had paused so that Mr Pringle could read the notice at the foot of the rocks. "'Prepared mentally and physically?'" He was brought up short by the implication.

"Yes," Gary nodded. "That's the way to describe it. You'll find out. Go in front, I'll follow. Rest whenever you feel you have to, especially on the chain. And don't look down until there's room to sit and rest."

"You don't mind accompanying me?" Mr Pringle asked, a little shyly. "It was partly a ruse, I'm afraid, to escape Mrs Bignell's eagerness. Now that we're here, I don't mind admitting I welcome your companionship."

Gary smiled, the first untroubled smile since they'd met. "I'd guessed the reason. But I don't mind, honestly. At the top, it's the most peaceful place I know." He was about to add something but changed his mind, and they began the climb.

It was smooth where Mr Pringle rested his hand, weathered by sun and wind since before the Dreamtime, and by the ocean on which the rock had once floated. Sun had dried up any lichen. Ridges banded the surface in parallel curves that looked as if they continued for ever, down through the red sand to where the rest of the rock lay hidden; uninterrupted ridges, seven kilometres long.

How vast was the unknown portion? It was another of the mysteries and swamped Mr Pringle's imagination. That there should be more than this immensity was unnerving. A tiny human ant, he concentrated on putting one foot in front of the other. Already it was becoming steep. He could see the first of the iron posts ahead and beyond it, the chain that was the handhold over the steepest part; if he could only reach that, he would allow himself the luxury of a rest.

*

172

Between the road and the entrance to the caves there were bushes and scrub. The rest of the passengers came to a decision. "We'll wait," they told Lenny. "We'll be quite comfortable here until you two get back."

He and Mavis had to push their way through bushes and he grew concerned about her dress. "There's always been water here, that's why there's so much growth. See the marks where it gushes out of the rock? After there's been a wet, of course. They call it Maggie Springs here." Mrs Bignell took a few deep breaths and dabbed on eau-de-Cologne.

"I've never had a spring named after me but they do call it Mavis's bar in The Bricklayers."

"You know, I think I may pay a visit one day. Your pub sounds real nice."

"You'd be most welcome," said Mavis hospitably, "but try not to make it a Thursday: We sometimes get a rude class of person on Thursday nights. I always discourage Mr Pringle from coming round then because it upsets him."

"I'll remember," said Lenny. "Now, in here—mind your head—this is what they call the Hunters' Cave. There's some paintings of animals right behind this stone."

He crouched down and so did she, intent on the bright, primitive outlines, protected by the boulder from the sun. Behind them, someone slipped unnoticed into the cave.

"See the shape of the bird?"

"Oh, yes . . . like an emu. And what's that, a crocodile?"

"Move!"

"I beg your pardon?" Mavis, startled, looked at Lenny. He reacted slowly, too slowly for the vicious kick that thrust him into the dirt. Even as Mavis opened her mouth to scream, the butt of the pistol thudded down on his unprotected neck. Ray Vincent continued the swing, hitting Mavis hard with the edge of his hand.

"Where is it, where's the stuff?"

She closed her mouth and jaw, dizzy with pain.

"It's not in the tent—what've you done with it!"

"If you want my handbag, take it." Her voice was muffled but she managed to cry out as she saw him about to strike again. "Take it, I'm not stopping you!"

173

He thrust something cold into her face. "Those two bags? You got five seconds." Genuine bewilderment mixed with terror slowed Mrs Bignell's life to a standstill. It was ridiculous, a man with a gun? You only saw those on the television.

"Talk!"

"D'you mean the powder that Evan—?"

"Where is it!" His whisper hissed round the cave. Without thinking, in agony from the barrel pressed into her eye, she whimpered, "I gave them to Mr Pringle—"

He should've fired but he didn't, he hit her instead, slamming the pistol against her skull.

As he drove away, the image of her—red hair, red blood—merged with Amy's face, Amy with a knife at her throat and behind Amy, Parker. Laughing.

A cloud of dust covered his car, fine, powdery and deepest red. The sand under his feet as he ran was the colour of blood. He pushed his way past groups of Dutch and Japanese tourists and began the ascent. The sun burned down out of an empty sky and the rock burned red with the heat.

They'd taken frequent rests for which Mr Pringle was extremely grateful. Gary was a kind young man, very considerate. A face so much thinner than the photographs. Hair no longer dark but mixed with grey and with bleak, sad eyes.

They'd avoided discussion but each of them knew it couldn't be postponed indefinitely.

About half-way up, for no apparent reason, Mr Pringle said, "I was talking to Mrs Bignell about Billy. She wasn't able to tell me much." Gary looked at him.

"You know?"

"No. I made the connection. More than that . . . a lack of necessary medical knowledge." He shrugged.

"I knew Billy, you know," said Gary. "When we were kids we used to play together. But I never guessed. And they never let on, Linda nor her mother." Gary was trying to make him understand, he realized that. He caught various phrases above the wind and began to put the whole together.

It took an hour to reach the top and when they'd got there it was so tremendous he could think of nothing else. It was impossible to be anything but exhilarated. This was the summit of the world, God's not man's; with a bird's-eye view of a continent. He and Gary stood on a plateau. Mr Pringle wanted to whoop and shout but the wind tore the sounds away. He staggered like a crazy man until Gary stopped him. In the end, exhausted, he sank into a hollow in the rock.

"Oh good gracious . . . I never expected it would be so marvellous. Oh, I must take another look . . . I can't just sit here!" He was wobbling about, drunk with the view, the sun and the wind. His legs gave way a second time and Gary hauled him back into the hollow.

"Take it easy . . . it's been there for billions of years, you can risk another half-hour."

"Yes, I'm so sorry . . . how foolish."

It was strange; being on top of the world had taken away fear and brought him to an Olympian realm detached from everyday reality. He couldn't put it off any longer.

"I have to tell you, Gary, at first I thought Ben was ill. I thought you'd brought him here because of the climate . . . then I remembered the pictures of Billy. Ben's uncle. The same features, the same—illness?" He felt rather than saw the nod.

"I decided it must be hereditary. Lack of knowledge made me wonder about haemophilia but there the joints are swollen. Ben's limbs were emaciated." There were tears in Gary's eyes and they weren't caused by the wind.

"I do not pass judgement," Mr Pringle said softly, "I've never had a child—but is Ben dead?"

"Yes . . ." It wasn't loud but Mr Pringle heard it.

"You never brought him to Australia?"

Gary shook his head. Inside Mr Pringle a coldness began that he knew the sun couldn't warm. He forced himself to ask, "If you didn't bring him. . . ?"

"We did it together, me and Linda."

"Ah." He didn't want to move, he was too old and cold. Instead he let Gary talk.

"There wasn't a cure, even out here. I sent a couple of letters and a postcard so Linda's mum would think I'd got Ben."

"Yes." And two people had recognized that a child hadn't written it.

"Ben was like Billy. Worse. Linda knew—before she had him, she knew." Livid anger, controlled until now, burst out of Gary. "She kidded me about it but she knew. Because of her brother. Her mother was a carrier, it ran in the family; Linda wouldn't have tests because of that."

"What was it, that Billy and Ben had?"

"Osteogenesis imperfecta." Gary managed a sad smile. "They're the only big words I know . . . Got the doctor to write them down so I could learn them."

"They're beyond me, I fear. What do they mean?"

Gary reached inside his jacket, taking care that the gusts didn't whip the contents out of his hand.

"I think this could be it . . ." Kev had the binoculars now. He was on a lower ledge, braced against the wind and in danger of losing his balance. He took no notice of the scruffy, stocky figure scrambling up below. "The contact is taking something out of his pocket . . . handing it to Pringle—could be the cash—Pringle's looking at it closely! Get a shot of it, Pelham!"

"I'm in an extremely dangerous position because of the overhang—there's no possible way I can take a photograph—"

"Get the other side, Charlie, quick! Hold on to Pelham while he gets those pictures!"

Below, Ray Vincent caught sight of them. He veered away, on a route that would bring him round the edge of the plateau, to the opposite side from the two sheltering in the hollow in the centre.

"Pringle's taken it. He doesn't seem surprised." Astonished, then angry, Kev said, "Whatever it is, the bloody fool's looking at it closely."

"Give me the glasses, let me see!" Pelham-Walker's sudden desire to participate nearly sent Kev off his perch.

"Watch it!"

Charlie began inching forward on his belly, to a higher rock,

176

slightly above and over twenty metres distant from Pringle and his contact, but if either man stood up they would see him.

On the opposite side, Ray Vincent moved forward, hand over hand clinging to the rock below the edge. Beneath him the void was so deep it made him sweat. His hands were wet. As his grip slipped, the strap of the binoculars case ran down his arm to his wrist and swung to and fro in space. He could feel the gun banging about inside. Closing his eyes he pressed his body against the rock, lifted the strap over his head and eased the case round to lie in the small of his back.

Over three hundred metres below, a dot that was an ambulance moved away from the caves and began the return journey to Yulara.

177

Chapter Nineteen

The two men, sheltered from sun and wind, sat with the few pathetic mementoes of a life. "They remind me why I did it," Gary said simply.

The photographs had been handled so often, wept over so many times, the stains were a part of them, but sorrow wasn't enough. "I thought I'd get over it. You never do. I know that now."

"No." Mr Pringle had meant what he said earlier, he was neither judge nor jury, but he needed to understand. He picked up the first photograph. "One woman suggested Ben had rickets."

"No, it was the disease. Those words mean imperfect bone development. Ben was born with fractured legs. By the time he'd begun to crawl, they looked like that."

These weren't bland snapshots, they'd been taken deliberately to show the nature of the illness. "See this one? Ben's first day at school, on calipers. He was back home by dinner-time. He'd dislocated his arm." Gary relived the bitterness. "We lost count of the number of fractures in the end: arms, legs, ribs—his bones were too soft and they'd never be anything else. There was no way he could grow up to be normal. And there was pain every time he broke a bone. Ben wasn't spared that."

"No." Mr Pringle had another picture. "I can see it in his face." Ben's stunted puny body in a hospital cot with traction applied to both limbs. The eyes with their blue-white fringing, dark with apprehension. "What were they trying to do here?"

"Insert nails into his bones. They'd broken his legs on purpose that time, to try and straighten them. It didn't work. He was such a brave kid . . ." Tears were falling now. "I used to sit beside him in that hospital, willing him to take my strength, holding his hand through the worst of it . . ." Gary turned away to recover and Mr

178

Pringle waited. Up here they weren't god-like after all, they couldn't shed their burdens.

"I knew by then we shouldn't have had children." Gary's voice was rougher now. "I got one of the doctors to explain. She wrote down the words for me, admitted there wasn't a cure . . . 'Some day,' she said. 'Just hang on, for Ben's sake.' Only I couldn't.

"When I got home that night I shouted the words over and over again at Linda. She knew all right. She'd always known. I should've killed her, not Ben, to stop her having any more."

"Nevertheless, what happened . . . what you did to Ben was murder."

Tired eyes acknowledged it to be true, but Gary didn't speak. "What do you intend to do now?" Mr Pringle asked sadly. "You can't run away from it for ever."

"Stay here." Gary was defiant. "The black fellas know. I told them. They see it differently. They don't think I did wrong, they understand. I loved Ben!" he shouted. "He'd got nothing to live for. He'd got it so bad all they could do was keep breaking his little bones, hoping they'd grow straight next time. Every day he was in pain! It was going to take years for him to die, years of pain! I did it the kindest way, you've got to believe that, while he was asleep. He didn't wake up, that's all. That night, Ben stayed asleep."

Gary rocked to and fro. "We buried him . . . We had to do it that night. Linda's mother was away, the neighbours were on holiday—"

"You don't mean Ben's still there!" Mr Pringle was horrified.

"What else could we do? Linda told everyone the rockery was her idea. I left her to get on with it. Never went back. I couldn't stand any more of it."

"Oh, Lord . . ." Mr Pringle felt old again. "Ben deserves a Christian burial, Gary—"

"What good will that do?" Gary was on his feet. "Will it bring him back? Stop the pain? It might make *you* feel better if they lock me up. No, I'm staying. They accept me here."

"Somethin's happening," Kev called quietly. "They're on the move."

Spread-eagled on the red-hot slab Charlie murmured, "About bloody time."

Anthony Pelham-Walker had the binoculars but could no longer make things out. Shimmering heat distorted the outlines. He was light-headed from the sun on the back of his neck. The wind elated him; he knew if he cast himself off it could bear him up like an eagle. He swept the glasses over the plateau—and saw the face!

Ray Vincent was impatient. He couldn't manoeuvre in this confined niche. He'd waited long enough.

He hated looking down but there in the distance was the head of the climb and below, the stanchions supporting the safety chain. There was no other way down. He couldn't see the three on the opposite side but it didn't make sense for them to be there still, not in the heat, so where they hell were they?

There were blisters on the backs of both his hands, his skin was almost too hot to touch. Much more of this and he'd pass out! He checked the descent one last time; not a soul, either climbing up or going down. The three men must've gone down while he was clinging on for dear life, making his way round the rock face; he hadn't dared look down then!

He heaved himself up. Pringle and his companion were still in their hollow. Pringle was on his knees, unfastening his old-fashioned haversack. Christ, was he about to hand over the stuff? Who the hell was the other chap? He'd have to go, too. There couldn't be any witnesses.

There was the flash of sun on glass. Vincent instantly dropped back into his niche—careful! Pringle's spectacles must have caught the light. Give it a few more seconds, to make sure neither of them were looking in this direction. The second hand crawled round the dial, twenty-nine . . . thirty . . . a last check of the other two then placing both hands flat, he levered himself up on to the edge of the plateau.

"At least have a drink," Mr Pringle was saying. "We're both tired after that climb and there's no need to go down until we're feeling calmer. I took the precaution of bringing a bottle of water."

He was reaching for it when Pelham-Walker made his move. This was the opportunity he'd been waiting for; his life would have a meaning after all! He had to get there first, to haul Ray Vincent from his hiding place, before Macillvenny did. He flung the binoculars aside, leapt on to the plateau and was off.

Mr Pringle and Gary turned to see a stranger hurtling towards them as though his life depended on it. Behind him, a much larger man appeared and lumbered in pursuit.

It was most extraordinary.

From farther back, behind the first two, a third, tough-looking younger chap jumped down from a slab, pulling at something tucked in his belt.

Gary cried, "Look out! That one's got a gun!"

"Pardon?"

And Gary fell on him, pushing him flat.

Anthony Pelham-Walker was running too fast to stop. As Pringle and the stranger dived, he saw Ray Vincent face to face for the first time, crouched above the edge, arms fully extended: in his hands he, too, had a gun.

Ray Vincent couldn't retreat, behind and beneath him was the void. He screamed and shouted but the wild-eyed fool kept on coming, blocking his view of the two in the hollow. Anthony Pelham-Walker was less than two metres from him when Vincent fired twice, at the target beyond.

Closing the gap and with his gun in his hand, Charlie tripped and fired simultaneously.

The corpse, one hollow-point bullet mushrooming to maximum devastation inside, changed its trajectory. There was sufficient impetus to carry it forward as gravity took over. Ray Vincent ducked but one of the outspread arms caught in the strap of his binoculars case. The jerk halted the downward flight and the body hung there momentarily, spiralling in space. For several seconds, Vincent tried to rid himself of the dead-weight, clinging to the rock with terrified, sweaty hands, but the nylon webbing was strong, and Anthony Pelham-Walker completed his mission.

Chapter Twenty

In the Yulara medical unit, the sister said caustically, "Oh, she'll live. First thing she asked when she regained consciousness was 'Do they have male nurses in Australia?' "

"She's out of immediate danger, I take it?"

"You can see her for five minutes, that's all. At her age, whatever lies she tells about it, nature has to take its course. She's still suffering from shock and it's too soon for her to have visitors."

Mr Pringle crept into the cool room. The face on the pillow was so badly swollen, he wanted to weep. Only the familiar titian strands escaping from the bandages confirmed it was Mavis. He touched her hands and she opened her one good eye. "Hello, dear . . . are you all right?"

"Yes."

"I thought he was a mugger at first . . . but he wasn't. Did you tell him you'd got rid of the stuff?"

"There was no need."

"Poor Evan. Fancy being mixed up with people like that."

"Don't worry about that now."

"How's Lenny? He kicked him so hard, then he hit him—"

"Lenny is recovering. He'll be all right."

"What's going to happen tomorrow? Will they leave us behind?"

Mr Pringle pulled his weary senses together and put the terrible events from his mind. "Another driver is taking Lenny and the FONEs back to Sydney. We're to stay on here and return with Pete when he's well enough. He'll travel down from Alice Springs and collect us. You'll be here about four or five days, according to Sister."

"Lenny suggested we might like to visit Darwin. He says there's a very nice pub there, the Vic."

182

"It's nearly two thousand kilometres to Darwin!"

"How about the barrier reef? Can we pop over there instead? I could wear my costume."

"That would be even further." Mavis shrugged then winced.

"It is a big place, isn't it, Australia? That article didn't give you any idea . . . Never mind, we found Gary. Has he said yet how Ben is?"

"Try and sleep. Sister said you were to rest as much as possible—" but Mavis had seen the parcel.

"What have you got there?"

"Oh—yes." He was reluctant. "The ladies in the party, Mrs Protheroe and, er, Mrs Piggybum—her name is Wilkinson, by the way—when they heard of the attack, they thought, in view of the shock, you might need a warmer nightgown."

He shook out the folded garment and Mavis inspected it with the bloodshot eye.

"My God, I wouldn't wear that as a shroud!"

"No. I thought as much." He shook his head over the hideous colour. Large buttons restricted access at every aperture. "I believe Mrs Wilkinson donated it herself . . ."

"I've often wondered who wore things like that." Mavis's croak was strong suddenly. "Now I know." The eye swivelled round. "You can tell them from me, it's the thought that counts, all right?"

"Yes." There must be a polite way of expressing it but he was blessed if he could think of one.

They had lifted Gary and Charlie off the rock by helicopter and taken them to Alice Springs. Mr Pringle had watched until it was out of sight. For several minutes, he stared at the edge where one man had toppled on top of the other and dragged him over. The second had screamed and screamed and then disappeared, the wind mercifully bearing all other sounds away.

Someone had led him back down, taking all the time in the world. Mr Pringle thought it kind but Kev Macillvenny knew there was no need to hurry. At the foot of the rock, Kev sat him in the Toyota and tried to explain what had happened.

One word made sense. "Oh, the drugs! The packets that Evan Jones. . . ?"

"Exactly," said Kev. "All you got to do is tell us what you've done with them."

And Mr Pringle admitted to the manslaughter of Sydney harbour seagulls. As Kev and Charlie agreed afterwards, with that old-fashioned sort of a Pom, it couldn't have happened any other way.

In Men's Surgical in Alice Springs, Pete was feeling better. He began to take an interest in his neighbours, especially as one of them, surprisingly, was Charlie. With a heavily bandaged foot. Pete was sympathetic. "Hope you fixed the bloke that did that?" The sister overheard.

"Go on. Tell him what happened."

"Go to hell!"

"He did it himself," she told Pete. "Just climbed to the top of Ayers Rock and shot himself through the foot. Comes from New South Wales, which might explain it."

It had taken all her strength. First the coach journey, then the difficulty of finding the address in London, but Mrs Jones had made up her mind she would do it. She stood outside the block of flats with the card in her hand. Number four. It was the right name beside the bellpush. She rang and waited. Crispin Sinclair's voice crackled through the answerphone, "Yes?"

"It's about . . . Evan Jones." She spoke so quietly he told her to repeat it.

"I need to—see you," she said urgently. When the buzzer went it took a moment before she realized the front door had been unlocked. She pushed it open and went upstairs, taking the kitchen knife from her bag.

He overpowered her but not before she'd stabbed him badly. As she explained first to the police, then the court, she wanted to hurt at least one of those responsible, because of what had happened to Evan.

On this occasion, press and television couldn't be muted by the department. Every savage detail was described. Torture and murder had resulted from a lack of concern on the part of the authorities, declared the magistrates. Crispin Sinclair considered it grossly unjust. Sacked, attacked, and now held solely responsible for a Welsh peasant's death.

The ultimate insult was that Batman should end up a hero!

Kev Macillvenny broke the small item of news himself.

"'Fraid Gary passed away last night."

"Oh, no!" Mr Pringle cried out in distress. "I thought—they'd found the bullet and operated?" Kev shook his head.

"That bullet was vicious; it was designed to explode inside the body—the bastard who fired it knew that. It smashed Gary's spine and paralysed him. No future for a bloke like him, you know."

But he did it to save me, Mr Pringle wanted to shout; it was my fault that he died. Kev guessed his thoughts exactly.

"Look, mate, try and see it from another point of view. They let me talk to Gary yesterday. He knew by then he wasn't going to make it. I explained how that bullet and the one that killed Pelham were intended for you 'cause Vincent must've assumed you'd got the drugs.

"Gary didn't bear you any grudge. Can't speak for Pelham but he did what he did off his own bat. Must've recognized Vincent through the binoculars and decided to go for him. He knew Vincent was armed." Kev sighed over the stupidity. "Anyways, Gary told me all about that business with his kid. Said you were to tell Linda it was his fault. He reckoned if he took the blame, she'd be off the hook.

"I'll be sending a copy of his confession to the UK authorities, but Gary definitely wanted you to be the one to tell his ex-wife, OK?"

Mr Pringle nodded. It wasn't much in return for what Gary had done for him. Perhaps, when she was well enough, he could share the burden with Mrs Bignell. She would find words to help him bear it.

Kev sat, smug with pleasure, beside Charlie's bed. "Written your report yet?"

"No!"

"Keep your voice down or Sister'll get upset. Got to write it sooner or later, you know."

185

"OK, OK. What 'bout Pelham? What's happened 'bout him?"

Sun poured down on the mottled skin beneath the sparse hair. After a few days in the desert, Kev was beefy red. Talk of Whitehall made him clench his fists.

"Like you and me could've guessed. They were embarrassed by what Pelham did, right? They already sacked him—but what do they do now? They make him out to be a hero! It was on the TV last night." Kev attempted the sugary-solemn tones: "'Regrettable mishap to British public servant attempting a civilian arrest on Ayers Rock.'"

Charlie said reluctantly, "Aw, c'mon Kev, Pelham was brave, you gotta admit that."

"He was bloody dumb! He was a gunny idiot to jump a man with a pistol pointing at his belly! Pelham got between Vincent and the target—"

"OK, OK . . . so what 'bout Mrs Pelham? Did you talk to her? Was she upset?"

"Nope." Kev's voice was neutral as he helped himself from the six-pack in the locker.

"What?" Charlie was shocked. "Not even a little bit?"

"What she said was—" Kev ripped the tab off a can "—when I told her Pelham fell off of Ayers Rock while tryin' to apprehend this dangerous British criminal . . . She said, '*Where* did you say all this took place?'" Kev imitated a supercilious voice this time. "'Where on earth's that?' Then she said, 'Do you mean to tell me he's been in Awstraliah?'"

"You mean, she never knew Pelham was out here?" Charlie was incredulous. "He'd been gone over a week, an' she hadn't even noticed?"

"Maybe the butler forgot to tell her."

"Poor old bugger!"

"Yeah . . ." Kev paused to finish his beer before pronouncing the epitaph. "I never liked Pelham. He was the worst Pom I ever met but he ain't half saved the tax-payers some money . . ."

"An' Vincent?"

"They bin workin' hard in Macquarie Street," Kev admitted. "Traced the bullets—bought by a Chinese woman, would you believe?"

186

"Not another missionary!"

"They're checking it out. That telephone number Pelham recognized. Belongs to Mrs Vincent. The daughter was kidnapped a week ago."

"Christ! She's a goner, considerin' how he blew it," Charlie said flatly.

"Yep."

"So what about you and me, Kev? We collectin' a vote of thanks, or what?"

"Nope." Kev enumerated the reasons: "We ain't got evidence 'cause Pringle fed it to the birds, we lost our link with the organization 'cause he got yanked off the rock, and we lost a Pom who'd just bin sacked because Vincent shot him by mistake. But they ain't grateful in Whitehall. They sent a telex with two big words in it, Charlie." Kev rolled them round his tongue, "'Considerable ineptitude.' So . . ." He tossed the beer-can into the basket. "Comin' back to that report of yours, why not tell 'em the truth? Just say you was on Ayers Rock, and fell arse over tit and blew this great big hole in your foot?" He shrugged sadly. "It's what the Poms expect. It's what I bin warnin' you 'bout for years. Anyone who's dumb enough to wear them tight jeans—"

"Aw, shut up!"

On their last night in Sydney, Mavis insisted they watch the news, "To see what's been happening while we've been away." Mr Pringle could have wished that the first close-up hadn't been of Protheroe.

"A highly successful visit!" Mavis was outraged. "They practically threw those FONEs out of Australia!"

With his years of experience in the Revenue, Mr Pringle was able to present a different point of view.

"Protheroe has obviously been schooled by one of those failed television directors on how to handle the media. I came across quite a few in my last district."

"But the FONEs weren't successful!" Mrs Bignell insisted angrily.

"Ah, but that's part of the current work ethic: never admit to failure. What Protheroe is doing is an illustration of creative thinking. He is being economical with the Truth."

187

"Twaddle! It's a complete fabrication from start to finish."

"Alas . . . I fear falsehood isn't a word included in current vocabularies. It would be considered counterproductive, especially if it interfered with the facts." Mavis snorted.

"Talking of fibs, I've still got to phone Mrs Hardie. I can't put it off any longer."

"Wait until we're back in England," he begged.

"I'm sorry, dear, I've got to do it while I still have the courage."

But when she put down the receiver, she said quietly, "They've found Ben. Linda confessed. She didn't know about Gary admitting to it first. She's told the police it was all her idea."

Chapter Twenty-one

Mrs Bignell said she would go alone. Mrs Hardie would prefer it. He could come with her when she visited Carmarthen because that would be far more gruelling but not this time.

She and Mrs Hardie took a taxi to the cemetery. Her friend chattered throughout the short journey and led the way, apparently undisturbed, stopping occasionally to point out the features.

"They call this part the Children's Corner. It's better kept than some of it. See the way they've trained that rose across the arch? That's the entrance." Birdlike and trim she bobbed across wet earth. "You should have worn flat shoes," she called; then, "This is the place . . . this is where they've buried Ben."

It was a small mound among many, grassed over and featureless apart from the tablet:

BEN COLES, AGED 7 YEARS
"SUFFER THE LITTLE CHILDREN"

"They let Linda choose the words."

Mrs Bignell stooped and laid the small posy beside the stone. "I'm glad for your sake Linda admitted it in the end." Mrs Hardie nodded, head tilted in the familiar way.

"She thought I'd guessed, you know . . . We never talked about Billy, about him being . . . about the illness. It may sound stupid that I couldn't, Mavis, even after he'd died. When someone's like that because of what he got from you—you can't begin to describe what that's like.

"Anyway, when Linda told me she was pregnant, I kept hoping Ben would be—normal. It was unfair to Gary, wicked. But there was still a chance, you see. At least, Linda and me hoped there was."

Mrs Bignell took her friend's arm. Together they stood in silence at the foot of the grave.

"What happened to Gary? He didn't kill himself did he?" Mrs Hardie asked timidly.

"Oh no, dear, nothing like that." Mavis considered for a moment how to describe what Mr Pringle had told her, to avoid more upset for her friend.

How could you explain about men appearing from nowhere on top of that great rock and firing at one another, and Gary being shot instead of Mr Pringle, or so he claimed?

All because a misguided Welsh boy with nice manners had asked her to do a favour . . .

A dreadful thought began to take shape in Mrs Bignell's mind and swell to frightening proportions: it wasn't all *her* fault was it? She hadn't started it all those weeks ago when she'd first smiled at Evan on board the aircraft?

"It was an accident," she replied firmly. "Gary saved Mr Pringle's life but everything that happened, including Gary being shot, was accidental. Take my word for it."